RESPONSIBLE AND EFFECTIVE COMMUNICATION

RESPONSIBLE AND EFFECTIVE COMMUNICATION

Wayne N. Thompson
University of Houston

Houghton Mifflin Company   Boston
Dallas   Geneva, Illinois   Hopewell, New Jersey   Palo Alto   London

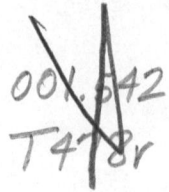

Copyright © 1978 by Houghton Mifflin Company. All rights reserved. No part of this work may be reproduced or transmitted in any form or by any means, electronic or mechanical, including photocopying and recording, or by any information storage or retrieval system, without permission in writing from the publisher.

Printed in the U.S.A.

Library of Congress Catalog Card Number: 77-77006

ISBN: 0-395-25075-7

CONTENTS

PREFACE   xi

1 BETTER COMMUNICATING: PRINCIPLES, PRACTICE, AND RESPONSIBILITIES   1

Principles of Communication   2
   The Content / The Communicator-Receiver Transaction / Rhetorical Techniques / Conclusion

Steps in Preparation and Presentation   10
The Ethics of Communication   15
Conclusion   18
Problems and Exercises   18
References   19

I CONTENT: THE BASIS OF RESPONSIBLE COMMUNICATION   21

2 RESEARCH AREAS AND METHODS   22

Content and Communication   23
Research Areas for Student Speeches   24

> Problems of Campus and Community / Social Issues / Economic Problems / Problems in International Relations / Summary

Research Areas in Business and the Professions   33

> Internal and External Sources of Information / Student Research for Speeches

Research Resources and Methods   37

> The Location of Materials / General and Specific Materials / Note Taking

Conclusion   43
Problems and Exercises   43
References   43

3 INVENTIVE THOUGHT   45

Levels of Creativity   46
The Bases of Inventive Thought   48

> The Full Mind / The Open Mind; Brainstorming / The Inquisitive Mind

Opportunities for Originality   51

> Possible Causes / Solutions and Programs / Predicted Outcomes / Summary

Ancient and Modern *Topoi*   56

> Ancient *Topoi* / Modern *Topoi*

Conclusion   62
Problems and Exercises   62
References   63

4 MATERIALS: THE SUBSTANCE OF COMMUNICATION   64

Kinds of Material   65

> Examples as a Type of Material / Statistics / Quotations / Other Kinds of Material

Selection of Materials   71

> Purposes of Material / Desirable Qualities in Material / Listener Analysis and Adaptation as Factors in Selecting Material / Interest

Conclusion   87
Problems and Exercises   88
References   89

II THE TRANSACTION: PROCESSES AND DYNAMIC FACTORS AFFECTING COMMUNICATION 91

5 THE TRANSACTION: PROCESSES 92

Decoding 94

    External Cues / Internal Cues / Third-Party Cues / Circular Cues

Feedback 103

    Feedback in Interpersonal and Small-Group Situations / Feedback in Platform Address

Conclusion 109
Problems and Exercises 109
References 110

6 THE TRANSACTION: DYNAMIC FACTORS 111

Personality Traits 113

    Trust / Involvement / Role, Status, and Self-Esteem / Authoritarianism, Dogmatism, and Closed-Mindedness

Motivation 122

    The Basic Theory / Fear / The Desire for Consistency

Beliefs, Values, Attitudes, Opinions, and Stereotypes 127

    Beliefs / Values / Attitudes and Opinions / Stereotypes / Persuasion Through Beliefs and Values

Conclusion 134
Problems and Exercises 135
References 137

7 THE TRANSACTION: IMPROVEMENT IN EACH ROLE 139

The Role of Interactant 140

    First Impressions / Social Conversation: A General View / Social Conversation: Specific Factors / Touch and Interpersonal Communication / Transactional Levels / Defensive and Supportive Communication / Summary

The Role of Speaker 153

    Adaptation to Three Types of Cues / Responsiveness to Feedback / The Development of Identification / The Utilization of Credibility / The Utilization of Similarity / Summary

The Role of Listener 161

    Constructive Feedback / Increased Comprehension in an Audience / Increased Comprehension During Group Participation / Critical, Responsible Listening

Conclusion   165
Problems and Exercises   166
References   167

8 COMMON INTERPERSONAL AND SMALL-GROUP SITUATIONS   169

Introduction: Objectives and Materials   170
Information-Seeking Interviews   172
Job Interviews   173

    Preparation and Conduct / The Résumé / Conclusion

Information-Sharing Discussion   179

    Organization of a Discussion / Leadership / Participation / Conclusion

Problem-Solving Conferences   187

    Techniques / Practice Sessions

Conclusion   192
Problems and Exercises   192
References   193

III RHETORICAL FACTORS: CHOICES FOR GREATER CLARITY AND EFFECTIVENESS   195

9 ARRANGEMENT: ORGANIZING, BEGINNING, AND CONCLUDING   196

The Bases for Choices   197

    Choices for Exposition / Choices for Persuasion

Outlines and Rhetorical Plans   203

    The Outline / Rhetorical Plans for Persuasion / Rhetorical Plans for Exposition

Beginning the Speech   214

    Purposes of the Introduction / Types of Introductions / Conclusion

Concluding the Speech   225

    Purposes / Types / Concluding Observations

A Practice Session in Exposition   233

    Topic and Purpose / Further Steps in Preparation and Presentation / Criticism and Response to Criticism

A Practice Session in Persuasion   235

    Topic and Purpose / Further Steps

Conclusion 236
Problems and Exercises 237
References 238

10 DELIVERY: ORAL AND VISUAL ELEMENTS 239

Methods of Delivery 241
Talents and Options 242
Apprehension 243
Oral Elements 244

    Desirable Oral Qualities / Specific Suggestions for Improvement

Visual Elements 250

    Desirable Visual Qualities / Specific Suggestions for Improvement

Delivery in Small Groups 254
Conclusion 255
Problems and Exercises 255
References 257

11 THE MEDIUM: USING LANGUAGE 258

Language Choices: Their Purposes 259

    Attaining Clarity / Increasing Emotional Power / Enhancing Credibility and Improving the Sender-Receiver Relationship / Summary

Stylistic Devices 276

    Figurative Language / Special Kinds of Sentences / Other Stylistic and Rhetorical Devices

Conclusion 285
Problems and Exercises 286
References 288

12 THE MEDIUM: COMMUNICATING NONVERBALLY 290

Nonverbal Cues: Research Findings, Principles, and Practices 291

    Kinesics and Paralinguistics / Proxemics / Habits and Choices / Nonverbal Cues as Suggestion / Improvements in the Use of Nonverbal Cues / Conclusion

Multimedia Presentations 299

    Simple Media of Transmission / Projectors / Materials / Factors Determining Choices / Practical Hints

Conclusion 310
Problems and Exercises 310
References 311

APPENDIX A: DEVELOPING COMMUNICATION SKILLS THROUGH MODELS: TWO EXAMPLES OF STUDENT SPEECHES 313

APPENDIX B: DEVELOPING COMMUNICATION SKILLS THROUGH PRACTICE: SPEECHES FOR SPECIAL OCCASIONS 323

INDEX 331

PREFACE

A fresh text for the beginning speech communication course requires a fresh approach. The author must not ask "What are today's educational fashions?" "What have others written?" or "What will sell?" Instead, he must go to his own experiences, and he must put into print his own priorities as educator, rhetorician, behavioralist, and communication philosopher. More than thirty years of teaching and research, both behavioral and rhetorical, are the background for the present volume. During these many years the writer has evolved a set of guiding beliefs that now constitute the philosophic foundation for *Responsible and Effective Communication*.

Content the Basis   The first requirement for meaningful communication on any serious topic is a sound, thoughtful message. Not only are thorough research and creative thought a practical means of exerting influence and building respect, but also they are an ethical responsibility. Respecting both the college student as a mature human being and speech communication as a worthy academic field, the writer believes that neither a textbook nor a college class should be a series of entertaining exercises, immature projects, and trivial, simplistic ideas.

Rapport and Techniques   Besides informed, inventive content, the two essential elements in clear, effective communication are the maintenance of a trusting, respecting relation among participants and the skillful use of rhetorical techniques. A distinctive feature of this text is the organization of the many specifics of communication as subpoints of three imperatives: Have sound content; maintain a good transactional relation; use techniques effectively.

Choices The essence of message preparation and presentation is the making of choices. Students should know the options that commonly are available and the factors to consider in decision making.

Knowledge Plus Skill Since the student needs both to learn about the principles of communication and to develop specific skills, the author has written this textbook at two levels, one to meet each need. In Parts I and III the chapters include sections that are expositions of broad principles, often with references to research findings, and other sections, sometimes in the form of lists, that are plain statements giving specific, detailed advice. In Part II, Chapters 5 and 6 are mainly on principles, and Chapters 7 and 8 are largely applications.

Integration of Sources Both classical rhetoric and modern behavioral sciences provide insights of value to the student of communication. The writer respects both sources, draws on both, and tries to blend the two into a coherent body of instructional material.

Integration in Application Although emphases and specifics differ, the principles of communication apply to all of its forms. Enlightened, inventive content is the basis for responsible, effective discourse in all settings—platform address, conference, discussion, and serious conversation. Transactional influences, although the most readily observable in dyadic and small-group situations, bear significantly on the reception of messages during platform addresses and on eventual speaker behavior. Similarly, the instruction in Part III on arrangement, delivery, and the verbal and the nonverbal media is of value to conferees and discussants as well as to the public speaker.

The development of a textbook based on the six preceding precepts has resulted in a number of features that are to differing degrees unique: A full chapter on research areas and methods; a chapter on creative thought with original materials on levels of creativity, the bases of inventiveness, and opportunities for originality; a modern section on *topoi;* an analysis of the individual as playing three roles in communication—interactant, speaker, and listener; an original and detailed section on conversation; a careful analysis of the major factors affecting the dynamics of the sender-receiver relation—trust; involvement; role, status, and self-esteem; authoritarianism, dogmatism, and closed-mindedness; motivation; and beliefs, values, attitudes, opinions, and stereotypes; practical advice on four common interpersonal and small-group situations; a stimulating and informative analysis of the levels of language usage; a chapter on nonverbal communication; and a thorough treatment of the multimedia presentation, which is commonplace in business and professional communication.

Responsible and Effective Communication, thus, is an attempt to be both thorough and discriminating, to present both broad principles and specific advice. Objectives at the beginning of each chapter and closing exercises and lists of references at the end should help both student and teacher in shaping meaningful learning experiences. The opening chapter includes a section that should assist the student in preparing and presenting a speech early in the semester; and in later chapters other sections provide clear, step-by-step assignments on the problem-solving discussion or conference, the expository speech, and the persuasive speech. Since the text is written at two levels—broad principles of communication and specific advice—it is adaptable to beginning courses with varied philosophic foundations and teaching methods in community colleges, four-year colleges, and universities. Moreover, because of the moderate length and the freedom from pedantry, the book also should be well adapted to courses that run for only a quarter and to courses for adult groups or for students in schools of business, education, or engineering.

This flexibility of the present textbook extends to the variety of syllabi to which it is adaptable. Every instructor will make his or her own decisions on the emphases given to the different parts and on the number and kinds of communication activities. In the writer's own courses, oral assignments are of two kinds: (1) "workouts" whose aim is to teach specific techniques and to build sound habits; and (2) a limited number of thoroughly prepared speeches whose content warrants the respect of any listener. For each major assignment the student chooses a topic consistent with his or her own interests but intellectually challenging and amenable to library research. He or she gives progress reports and engages in discussions while moving toward a mastery of the topic that culminates in an address combining research with original thought. Two major speeches in a semester, along with "workouts" and subsidiary reports, have resulted in a substantial degree of success in attaining the major objectives of *Responsible and Effective Communication*—a respect for content, skill and sensitivity in utilizing the dynamics of the behavioral transaction, and competence in using rhetorical techniques for clarity and emphasis. A reasonable level of mastery of these three objectives should be a solid foundation for worthy and satisfying achievements in communication as a student, as a citizen, and as a participant in business and professional life.

The author acknowledges the critiques of the following reviewers that the publisher chose: Paul Burkhart, Shippensburg State College; K. C. Kennedy, University of Arizona; Gayle Levison, Herbert H. Lehman College; N. Lamar Reinsch, Western Illinois University; Voncile Smith, Florida Atlantic University; Harry Strine, III, Bloomsburg State College; and Al R. Weitzel, San Diego State University.

W.N.T.

1
BETTER COMMUNICATING: PRINCIPLES, PRACTICE, AND RESPONSIBILITIES

After studying this chapter the reader should be able to do the following:

Phrase a speech purpose when given a topic

Revise a brief passage from written style to oral style

Deliver an expository five-minute speech of two to five main points with such clarity that 75 percent or more of the class members can take notes identifying the main points

A popular movie in the 1970s indicted contemporary society by contrasting the loyalty, candor, and trust of two dolphins with the selfishness, treachery, and cruelty of human beings. Significantly, the emergence of the dolphins, Alpha and Beta, as lovable beings coincided with the development of their powers of communication. In the first part of the movie, to the fascination of audiences, the two mammals learned slowly and painstakingly to speak, to listen, and to understand.

All that was new about the movie was the use of dolphins as main characters, for people, or at least the philosophers, have long understood that the ability to communicate is the power that enables society to form governments, to conduct trade, to pass on scientific discoveries, and to attain humaneness. Today, improved communication skills are the means for better interpersonal relations, for greater success in business and the professions, and for increased influence in clubs and other social and community groups. Thoughtful, successful men and women each year spend large sums voluntarily for adult courses and seminars in communication, and hardheaded corporations subsidize training programs for promising employees.

How does one become a more capable conversationalist, discussant, conferee, or platform speaker? Although not the only possibilities, the two major means of improvement are the study of communication principles and practice through a series of group situations and speeches. Through a knowledge of principles, one develops resources for responding intelligently and self-reliantly to varied and complex circumstances throughout life. Through practice followed by criticism, one develops skills and forms habits. Trying to improve as a communicator without practice would be as senseless as attempting to learn to play tennis without hitting a ball.

The purpose of the three sections forming this chapter is to help the student get started. The first section is a brief statement of certain principles that underlie clear, effective communication; the second is a step-by-step description of a sound method for preparing and delivering a short speech; the third is a brief essay on ethics for the communicator.

PRINCIPLES OF COMMUNICATION

The basis of this text is the belief that the essentials of communication are reducible to three encompassing ideas:

Worthwhile content is the basis of responsible, effective communication.

The dynamics of the relations between or among participants largely determine whether communication is effective and responsible.

Rhetorical skills, such as those used in organizing, wording, and delivering ideas, are of value in enhancing clarity and effectiveness.

This introductory chapter obviously cannot include all of the principles of communication or treat in detail those selected; the purposes are to introduce the student to the field and to provide a sound basis for fulfilling the initial assignments of the semester.

THE CONTENT

The recognition of the importance of content to communication is as old as Classical Greece. Isocrates believed that a sound education was a combination of rhetoric with broad knowledge. Aristotle's *Rhetoric* (c. 330 B.C.), the most influential work on speechmaking ever written, gives twice as much space to the development of the message as it does to arrangement, style, and delivery combined. Three centuries later Cicero, in describing the perfect orator, continued the emphasis on knowledge: "No man has ever succeeded in achieving splendour and excellence in oratory . . . without taking all knowledge for his province."[1] Applied to present-day education, the philosophy that content is central to communication means that student and instructor alike should stress the importance of the message and that textbooks should include substantial instruction on research, inventive thought, and materials.

Purpose, inventive thought, and materials are the three subtopics chosen for inclusion in this introductory treatment of content.

Purpose

Is the objective to feel better by venting one's anger or to work out a fairer division of labor with spouse or roommate? Is the goal to gain acceptance of a plan during a conference or to impress others as being fair-minded and cooperative? Is the aim to stimulate one's political friends to greater efforts or to change the views of voters who are undecided? Without answers to such questions the communicator is like the marksman who fires without using the gunsight. Only by knowing the purpose can the communicator avoid aimlessness in research and lay a foundation for organizing ideas, selecting materials, and making strategic choices of language and type of delivery.

The step-by-step process described below serves to pinpoint the purpose. First, one decides what one wishes to accomplish. Traditionally—at least since Cicero—all purposes are grouped under the general headings *to inform, to entertain,* and *to persuade.* Second, one considers what one would like to attain under ideal circumstances. The highest aspiration of a campaigner, for example, is to arouse such great enthusiasm that every person at the rally will contribute money liberally and become a vigorous volunteer worker. Third, one decides what goal is realistic. What is the present attitude of the audience toward the speaker's topic, thesis, or proposal? How great a shift in the desired direction is a reasonable expectation? The student who has cut class and missed assignments can scarcely convince the professor in a single conversation that he or she is serious and responsible, but the professor may be persuaded to grant permission to do make-up assignments.

Examples of useful purposes are the following:

---

[1] Cicero *De Oratore* ii.1.5.

To inform my audience on the principles of the catalytic converter

To explain the rights of a citizen who is picked up by the police

To give a humorous account of my first trip to Paris

To persuade my listeners that they should sign a petition calling for the preservation of an historic landmark

To produce the belief that the space program is not worth what it costs the taxpayers

To persuade my listeners that visual aids are of value in oral presentations

To move my audience from a position of skepticism about student government to a position of willingness to participate in some of its activities

To move my audience from a position of naiveness about television newscasts to a position of skepticism

To move my audience from a position of support for the Salvation Army to a position of willingness to make a donation

Inventive Thought

As a member of society, the conferee or the speaker has the responsibilities to be well informed, to think through problems carefully, and to take positions that are likely to be beneficial to society. To generate sound, insightful analyses or solutions requires time, effort, and talent.

Effectiveness depends largely on creativeness. Many options are open when one organizes ideas, chooses examples, and decides which arguments to use. The first thoughts on how to present a proposal in a meeting or from the platform are rarely the most strategic. One should give oneself time for inventing several possibilities and then should choose astutely. Martin Luther King, Jr., made an address memorable when he decided to begin each paragraph in a series with "I had a dream." Thomas Henry Huxley, a distinguished British scientist, found a way to explain a complex concept when he thought of a piece of chalk as the basis for an extended comparison.

Materials

To attain the purpose, whatever it is, one must develop arguments, collect evidence, devise or locate examples and comparisons, and find a diversity of materials to give substance to the basic ideas. This advice, although seemingly simple, often is hard to apply. An ample amount of such content is a necessity, and items should be interesting, relevant, and authoritative. In addition, variety is desirable. Warm, specific, personal items, preferably from the communicator's own knowledge and experiences, are important for holding attention, humanizing the message, and building rapport; but examples, historic facts, statistics, and quotations from authorities are necessary if one is to give a broad and convincing presentation.

THE COMMUNICATOR-RECEIVER TRANSACTION

The importance of knowing the audience and adapting to it was clear to Aristotle, but modern behavioral scientists have provided new insights into the part that human relations play whenever anyone attempts to discuss with others or to inform or to persuade through a speech. The word *transaction* includes two major concepts that are relevant at this point: (1) Much that occurs during communication is an outcome of intentional choices (the behavioralist uses *interaction* when describing unintended influences); (2) every communication event, to some degree, involves stimuli coming from all participants. The old idea that one person speaks and another listens is simplistic, the behavioral scientist says; the receiver interprets what is heard in the light of past experiences, personal beliefs and values, and perceptions of the responses of others who are present. In all groups most members are interacting and/or transacting with their fellows, and the outcome is dependent on all of these complex forces and relations.

Listener Analysis and Adaptation

Certain special opportunities, nevertheless, are available to the individual who is the primary communicator. Whether the number of listeners is two, three, or a multitude, the prudent course is to learn as much as one can about their attitudes toward the topic and toward the sender, about their beliefs and prejudices, and about their needs, desires, and motivations. The principal means of persuasion, according to Aristotle, is the *enthymeme*, which consists of (a) an attitude or a belief already held by the listener, (b) an idea that the sender supplies, and (c) a conclusion that follows when (a) and (b) are combined.

Adaptation can take many forms. Intellectual honesty requires that the communicator take certain positions in particular circumstances, but options still exist—for including one argument and omitting another; for using a humorous story in place of straightforward expression; for dramatizing a statistic instead of citing the original; for making one section of the presentation long and another short; for quoting a local professor and leaving out a passage written by an eminent philosopher. In all of these choices, the more effective item will be the one that listeners find most pleasing and understandable.

Credibility

Through many kinds of cues listeners decide, often in the first thirty seconds, whether they like, trust, and/or respect the newcomer to the group or the speaker on the platform. Rightly or wrongly, they judge the sender to be well informed, prudent, sincere, and well intentioned or the opposites. Not to be overlooked as a factor influencing these perceptions is personal grooming, as exemplified by Emmeline Pankhurst, a nineteenth-century British women's liberationist who toured the United States:

Habitually well-dressed, she shocked the public, commented the *Cleveland Plain Dealer,* because she did not "Bear the Faintest Resemblance to the Expected Amazon." Nor was she "the nervous or hysterical person one might expect to see," wrote the *Minneapolis Morning Tribune.*[2]

Besides being attentive to appearance, what else can one do to bring about positive responses? Much depends, of course, on the observers, for their ages, sex, cultural backgrounds, and beliefs and values determine the ideas they approve and the qualities they admire. Certain advice, nevertheless, is broadly applicable:

Show that you are well prepared on your topic. Avoid immodest claims, but through the content of the speech indicate that your background is extensive and that your specific preparation is thorough. References to the speaker's own observations and experiences related to the topic, according to one experiment, increased ratings for competence and trustworthiness.[3]

Be vigorous and forthright in expressing your views, but be reasonable and fair toward those who disagree.

Use language that is simple, direct, and correct. With some listeners use technical terms, but with others use language that is colloquial and unpretentious.

Be composed while waiting to speak. Be courteous, but speak firmly, fluently, and with good eye contact.

Without being insincere, show that you like and respect your listener(s). Be friendly, and be sensitive to their needs and interests. Secure information in advance about them, their affiliations, and their community. When campaigning by train in the Midwest, Harry Truman carried a notebook with information on each of the small towns where stops were scheduled. He began his speeches with facts and historic references showing his awareness of each locality.[4]

---

[2] John C. Zacharis, "Emmeline Pankhurst: An English Suffragette Influences America," *Speech Monographs,* 38 (August 1971), 200.
[3] Terry H. Ostermeier, "Effects of Type and Frequency of Reference upon Perceived Source Credibility and Attitude Change," *Speech Monographs,* 34 (June 1967), 137–144.
[4] Eugene E. White and Clair R. Henderlider, "What Harry S Truman Told Us about His Speaking," *Quarterly Journal of Speech,* 40 (February 1954), 40.

Bring out similarities between yourself and your listeners. Establish common ground by capitalizing on likenesses in age, sex, religion, race, occupation, political party, fraternal memberships, and beliefs and attitudes toward current problems.

Express attitudes and beliefs that listeners will like. Falsehood and shallowness, when detected, can be ruinous, but the sender usually can find honest points of agreement. "People confer more credibility on those with whom they agree compared to those with whom they disagree."[5]

Manifest and praise values that listeners admire. These vary with the group; but moderately to well-educated Americans as a rule admire courage, patriotism, self-reliance, generosity, friendliness, "a good try," scientific achievement, and similar qualities and concepts.

In summary, to increase credibility the communicator should prepare thoroughly, seem sincere, and show concern for the welfare of his listeners. "It is the character of a speaker, not his speech, which persuades us"[6] is an exaggeration, but the importance of understanding and applying principles of credibility is beyond question.

RHETORICAL TECHNIQUES

Rhetoric is the art of devising, organizing, expressing, and delivering ideas clearly and effectively; rhetorical techniques are the strategies, devices, and procedures that the communicator uses to attain clarity and effectiveness.

Arrangement

One set of techniques pertains to the organization of points and materials. Which argument should come first? Which pattern of organization is likely to be effective? Should the example precede the quotation or vice versa? If the speaker has two sets of statistics, which should he or she present initially? Rhetoricians, through their analyses of observations of good speakers, have developed a body of useful advice. The following items are a practical introduction to the fuller treatment of arrangement in Chapter 9:

1. Organize the presentation around a limited number of points—often three, sometimes two or four, occasionally five, and almost never six or more.

---

[5] Blaine Goss and Lee Williams, "The Effects of Equivocation on Perceived Source Credibility," *Central States Speech Journal*, 24 (Fall 1973), 166.
[6] Menander as cited in Frank B. Jevons, *A History of Greek Literature* (London: Charles Griffin, 1889), p. 385.

2. Clarify the structure by listing the main points at the beginning, by numbering each point as it appears in the body, and by summarizing.

3. Commence each part of the presentation with a clear, concise topic sentence.

4. Clarify the structure of each section that is more than a paragraph long. In some talks the main points are plain, but the development of each is a tangled jungle.

5. Use transitional words and phrases to connect each new idea or piece of material with either the preceding item or the overall structure. Besides using *first, second,* and *third,* employ such connectives as *for example, in proof of this,* and *on the other hand.*

6. Decide on the distribution of time among the points. Different circumstances call for different decisions, but the best strategy in many instances is to begin with one or two lengthy sections and then to move rapidly through the remaining points. The reason that this strategy may be desirable is that listeners find it easier to remain attentive to detailed arguments when they are fresh than when they are fatigued.

Research evidence neither supports nor refutes the preceding advice, nor does it provide consistent results on most of the other issues pertaining to organization. On the value of good arrangement, however, conclusions are becoming increasingly impressive. McCroskey and Mehrley in a study involving 352 students at Michigan State University found that "The presence of either serious disorganization or extensive nonfluencies was sufficient to significantly reduce the amount of attitude change produced by the speaker."[7] They also found that both faults substantially reduced the communicator's credibility.[8] Jones and Serlovsky also found that organization was related to persuasiveness and credibility.[9] In 1974 Baird reported that good organization was beneficial likewise when the measure was the amount of learning.[10]

Verbal Language

The sender may use a style that is technical or simple, formal or colloquial, neutral or emotional, oral or written. The possible choices are many, and

---

[7] James C. McCroskey and R. Samuel Mehrley, "The Effects of Disorganization and Nonfluency on Attitude Change and Source Credibility," *Speech Monographs,* 36 (March 1969), 21.
[8] *Ibid.*
[9] John A. Jones and George R. Serlovsky, "An Investigation of Listener Perception of Degrees of Speech Disorganization and the Effects on Attitude Change and Source Credibility," *SCA Abstracts: 1971,* p. 54.
[10] John E. Baird, Jr., "The Effects of Speech Summaries upon Audience Comprehension of Expository Speeches of Varying Quality and Complexity," *Central States Speech Journal,* 25 (Summer 1974), 119–127. See also Christopher Spicer and Ronald E. Bassett, "The Effect of Organization on Learning from an Informative Message," *Southern Speech Communication Journal,* 41 (Spring 1976), 290–299.

one needs guidelines to apply to each specific set of circumstances. A number of speakers, such as Stokely Carmichael,[11] vary their language to adapt to different audiences; and experienced communicators during speech revision often decide that their first drafts are drab, jargon-ridden, overly technical, or so strongly worded that they will antagonize listeners. Improvements require effort, but the time is well spent.

For the beginning student the most immediate concern is the use of oral style, which is best described as language that is spontaneous, personal, natural, and in many ways conversational. According to research studies, a presentation that "sounds like speech" uses the following freely: (1) personal pronouns, especially *I, we, us, our,* and *you;* (2) questions to introduce new points; (3) concrete and specific words (*murder* is more definite than *a crime; a sleek, tiger-striped kitten* is more vivid than *a pet*); (4) contractions, such as *we're, I'll, don't,* and *can't;* (5) examples; (6) real or invented dialogue and direct address ("Fellow dorm residents, think about what this change would mean to you!"); (7) varied sentences, including the use of imperative, interrogative, and exclamatory forms ("Grip the racquet firmly"; "What can we do about the problem?"; "What a surprise for all of us!"); (8) active voice rather than passive; (9) simple sentences and sentence fragments; (10) short, familiar words; (11) repetition of words or patterns of words; and (12) references to oneself and to listeners.[12]

The Nonverbal Medium

Posture and movement, clothing and grooming, facial expression, muscular tensions, and still other sources provide cues that lead observers to decide that the communicator is untruthful, insincere, shy, hostile, hesitant, or their opposites. Indeed, one respected modern scholar estimates that in the normal two-person conversation the verbal signs carry less than 35 percent of the meaning.[13] A finger on the lips, a hand cupped behind the ear, a beckoning of the hand, a silent clapping motion, a clenched fist, and a spontaneous hug are examples of nonverbal cues whose eloquence may surpass that of words.

A second type of visual stimulus is the map, picture, or diagram that reinforces spoken language. These materials, when properly used, clarify ideas and add interest and variety. A further advantage is that visual materials assist some speakers in handling the nervousness that is natural to an unfamiliar activity. These aids give the communicator something to do with his or her hands, they provide a natural reason for walking on the platform, and they include cues that jog the memory.

[11] Pat Jefferson, " 'Stokeley's Cool': Style," *Today's Speech,* 16 (September 1968), 19–24.
[12] For a summary of research studies see Wayne N. Thompson, *Quantitative Research in Public Address and Communication* (New York: Random House, 1967), pp. 73–75.
[13] Ray L. Birdwhistell, *Kinesics and Context: Essays on Body Motion Communication* (Philadelphia: University of Pennsylvania Press, 1970), pp. 157–158.

The principal reasons for not using diagrams, tables, maps, pictures, slides, scale models, and objects are trouble and expense. Locating or making visuals requires time, effort, and sometimes money; and in many instances the gains do not offset these costs. Negative effects may even occur when drawings are of poor quality or when the materials distract attention. Nevertheless, if one were to look at one hundred speeches critically, the number needing more visual aids would exceed the number harmed by poor devices. Even so, benefits depend on following three simple suggestions for intelligent, skillful management:

1. Be sure that the visual aid is large enough and plain enough for all members of the audience to be able to see it readily.

2. Be sure that you can handle the aid efficiently. Check to see that models and objects are in working order, and ascertain whether thumbtacks, chalk, and other necessities will be on hand.

3. Plan so that the visual and the verbal parts of the speech will be coordinated. Display the map or the picture only during the time that it reinforces the verbal message.

CONCLUSION

Suppose that a typical student has read this far. What is he or she to conclude? First, principles of communication do exist: there are broad guidelines that the individual can apply in solving the problems that arise during preparation and participation. Second, these principles generate numerous items of specific advice, a sampling of which appears in the preceding pages. Third, the foregoing information covers aspects of communication that individuals should apply even in early assignments. Fourth, detailed instruction on content, on the sender-receiver transaction, and on rhetorical techniques is to be found in the eleven succeeding chapters.

STEPS IN PREPARATION AND PRESENTATION

Besides studying about communication, the learner needs to participate in interpersonal, group, and platform situations. Since the least familiar of these to most students is the public address, the advice that follows is focused on the speech; but to a considerable extent the steps in preparation for a serious discussion or conference are the same. Effectiveness in all types of discourse is most likely to occur when the speaker follows an orderly process. The ensuing pages are a step-by-step guide.

1. Select the topic, and phrase the purposes. Outside the classroom circumstances frequently dictate the topic. One speaks out either favoring or

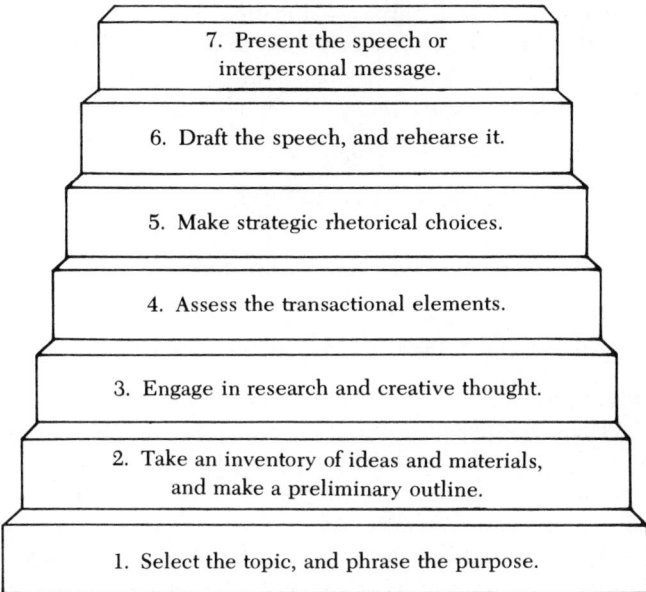

Figure 1.1 The steps in preparation and presentation.

opposing the school bond issue, the reelection of the school board, the proposed new stop-and-go light, higher academic standards for admission, the appropriation to send officers to a convention, or the legalization of mixed drinks on campus. The classroom is one of the few places where the speaker has a choice of topic—a feature that is both burden and opportunity.

What should one talk about? Much of Chapter 2 is on possible topics for major speeches; here the advice pertains to four critical tests:

Significance. A topic should be worthy of the time of both speaker and listener.

Interest. A topic should be relevant to the vital concerns of both communicator and hearer. It should satisfy a need or evoke curiosity and suspense.

Authoritativeness. No one has the right to take the time of an audience unless he or she is already well informed on the topic or is willing to do thorough research.

Originality. A topic should permit the sender to draw on personal experiences and/or to convey ideas that come from individual analysis. The deadliest speeches are those in which materials move from the printed page to the speaker's lips without any intervening mental activity.

Besides a topic, one must have a purpose—a matter discussed earlier in the chapter. As pointed out there, speakers move from a general idea of what they wish to accomplish to a precise statement of what is attainable. Further examples of satisfactory purposes are the following:

To show that a federal tax cut will help the economy

To establish the belief that the United States should withdraw from the United Nations

To prove that a new form of welfare would be advantageous

To prove that listeners should actively support Common Cause

To show that the listeners should support _____ for public office

Besides the content purpose, which serves as the basis for almost all of the subsequent decisions in speech preparation, speakers often have personal or strategic goals. Sometimes the topic of the speech is not especially important, for the long-range outcome depends on the contribution of the presentation to the speaker's image. As an example, Jim Bowen, a freshman member of the Young Democrats, is eager to move rapidly into a position of leadership. His purpose in volunteering to speak at the next meeting of the club is to impress his colleagues with his knowledge, his incisiveness, and his speaking ability. At least in the back of his mind he has a self-image that he wishes to portray—an image that affects the decisions that he makes throughout the period of preparation.

"What topic will give me the best opportunity to present myself favorably?" Jim asks himself. After some searching about, he decides on "The Republican Legislative Record Last Year." "What kinds of material will be impressive?" he asks. "Much of it must be factual," he concludes. "I must go to the newspapers and to state documents. I must know what I'm talking about. I should include at least some factual items that my listeners will not have known about before—that is, my knowledge must appear to go deep." "What tone should my speech have?" Jim next questions. "This is a partisan group," he reasons. "I must be aggressive and hit hard at the Republicans; but on the other hand, these listeners are intelligent and can distinguish between well-founded and irrational attacks." And so Jim sets the guidelines for his presentation.

2. *Take an inventory of ideas and materials, and make a preliminary outline.* What are possible subtopics or arguments? What stories or examples are relevant, and do any comparisons or contrasts come readily to mind? Are there striking statistics that are usable if verified? If the speech were given now, what would be the sequence of points? Some communicators can make an inventory and a rough outline in their heads, but most persons profit from setting down preliminary ideas on paper. Besides clarifying certain thoughts, a written inventory helps to identify further materials that are needed.

Putting the tentative outline into written form, likewise, is advantageous. Doing so gives the communicator something to revise; and as time goes by, he or she can rework the outline. With each attempt, if all goes well, the draft will become better ordered and more shrewdly adapted. The speaker, however, should remain flexible. As Richard Whately advises, "[The outline] should serve merely as a *track* to mark out a path for him, not as a *groove* to confine him."[14]

3. Engage in research and creative thought. Whether these improvements occur in successive speech drafts depends on the quality of research and creative thought, processes so important that Chapters 2 and 3 are devoted to them. Speeches do not write themselves, and significant thoughts do not come from empty minds. Successful preparation normally requires a substantial period of time, a certain amount of trial and error, and the ability to attack a problem from more than one direction. The history of oratory contains many examples of people who at times secluded themselves in order to give their full creative powers to important speeches. Franklin D. Roosevelt, Winston Churchill, and John F. Kennedy were among these.

The prerequisite for success in this third stage is the realization that both library research and creative thought are necessary. Speakers must broaden their backgrounds, search for specific information, turn over ideas in their minds, and seek solutions to problems and causes of known difficulties. Without research a speech is likely to be thin and superficial, but without original thought it often is dull, impersonal, and trite.

4. Assess the transactional elements. What will be the mood of listeners? What comments or speeches will they have heard previously? What are their prejudices toward the topic? How much do they already know? How do they regard the speaker? Are they trusting, anxious, and high or low in self-esteem? Will they provide feedback? Whether a joke will fall flat, a fear appeal seem exaggerated, or a personal opinion appear credible are only samples of possible strategies whose outcome depends on the particular audience and situation.

Chapters 5–8 are on the speaker-listener transaction, which is even more important in two-person or small-group situations than it is in public address. As time goes on, students should become increasingly skillful in handling the dynamic elements of their human relations. Until they have time to study theories and research findings, they should exercise fully their powers of observation, common sense, and natural astuteness. Visualizing the listeners and questioning oneself about moods, prejudices, and personality traits are good ways to begin.

---

[14] Richard Whately, *Elements of Rhetoric* (Carbondale: Southern Illinois University Press, 1963), p. 25.

5. *Make strategic rhetorical choices.* With a clear view of the audience situation, a preliminary outline, a purpose, and a supply of ideas and research materials, the speaker is ready to make the rhetorical choices essential to final preparation. "Which rhetorical plan or pattern of organization am I going to use?" "How will I begin?" and "How will I conclude?" are critical questions. Experienced speakers also weigh the probable effects of such devices as strong fear appeals, irony or satire, strong language, reliance on personal credibility, indirection, and common ground. Seasoned performers even make conscious choices on movement and position on the platform, decorations for the auditorium, and preliminary parts of the program. Most preachers, for example, have the sermon in mind when they select the hymns.

6. *Draft the speech, and rehearse it.* The outline is never the speech. Of the available ideas and materials, some are indispensable points and subpoints, but others are supporting or illustrative materials that the communicator may either include or omit. One must not only state an argument or a viewpoint, but also must talk about it for a certain period of time. How long—how much amplification—is a matter of choice. In general, one gives more time to ideas that he or she wishes to emphasize than to lesser contentions.

One way to turn an outline into an address is to write out the speech word for word. For some persons on some occasions this is the best procedure, but the wording often is stiff, formal, and inflexible. A better method for most people is that of drafting the speech in the mind and going over it, silently or orally, until the presentation is fluent and confident.

No matter what the method of drafting, rehearsal is desirable. For the written-out speech, the objective is a degree of familiarity that frees the individual from the manuscript so that he or she can maintain eye contact with the audience much of the time. If the delivery is extempore (prepared but neither written nor memorized), the series of rehearsals should result in greater communicativeness and in lessened reliance on notes. One procedure is to prepare a new set of notes for each rehearsal, to use them as sparingly as possible, and to make each new set briefer than the one before. Eventually a speaker may find that the only written materials that he or she needs at the lectern are quotations and statistics.

7. *Present the speech or interpersonal message.* All now should be ready. A feeling of nervousness is natural; and unless excessive, it provides an extra energy, alertness, and vitality that adds liveliness and force to the performance. Advice to the beginner goes like this:

Keep your mind off yourself and on whatever else is happening in the room. If you must think about your presentation, go over the opening words. During delivery, look at individuals in all parts of the room, be in earnest about your message, and realize that you are addressing real, live people whose minds you wish to influence.

Other aspects of presentation are also important. The speaker should stand erect, move occasionally, gesture for a purpose, and refrain from constant, repetitive, nervous mannerisms. He or she should move the speech along fluently, but should use pauses to clarify meaning and to add emphasis.

During a performance a speaker receives feedback that may suggest needed adjustments. For beginners on-the-spot changes are difficult, but learning to respond constructively to feedback is part of the overall process of developing proficiency. Among the more common listeners' reactions and the appropriate responses to them are the following:

The audience looks puzzled. Add an example, or explain the idea in a different way and in altered language.

The audience seems to be losing interest. Change your position on the stage, change your tempo, or insert a blackboard diagram. Move toward the audience, and give a personal example or translate your point into a situation relevant to them. Use a story.

The audience seems to disbelieve or disagree. Cite an authority, put the argument into an analogy that is personal to the listeners, or dramatize the statistics. Reword your position so that it seems less drastic than it did originally.

The audience looks tired or uncomfortable. Shorten your remarks; or if that is impossible, have everyone stand and stretch. Open a door or a window to relieve stuffiness.

THE ETHICS OF COMMUNICATION

The inclusion of the word *responsible* in the title of this book is a deliberate choice, for the writer believes that interpersonal, small-group, and public communicators have ethical obligations. No two persons probably would ever agree on all of the details of a code of conduct, but four propositions are a starting point for further thought on this complex topic.

First, the communicator has a responsibility to know the topic and to think carefully about it. "You must know the truth about the subject that you speak or write about," Plato recorded.[15] The most distinctive feature of this book, as compared with other texts, may be the emphasis on the importance of content.

---

[15] Plato *Phaedrus* 277B.

16　BETTER COMMUNICATING

Communication occurs in many settings. (Credits: *opposite top*, Charles Harbutt/Magnum; *others*, Jonathan Rawle)

Second, the communicator should serve the welfare of the immediate listeners and of society generally. Knowing what is best can be very difficult, for many topics worthy of discussion are complex and inherently controversial; but as with the first proposition, a reasonable minimum test for ethical behavior is that of taking the soundest positions that judgment permits. No one can always be right, but everyone can advise to the best of his or her capability.

Third, the communicator has an ethical obligation to bring out the best in fellow participants. Whereas the other three propositions are equally significant for interpersonal, group, and public address situations, the third imperative is especially important when the number involved is small. Every individual should develop his or her potentialities for independent thought, self-expression, growth, and self-respect as fully as possible; and the ethical communicator through manner and word is supportive of others.

Fourth, both senders and listeners have the obligation to be active even though noninvolvement may be easier. Activity, in Aristotle's ethical system, was a necessary partner of virtue, and Quintilian's conception of the *vir bonus* (good man) centered in the theme that the ideal orator was an active participant in Roman life. The need to speak out is no less today, for in every place and time there are the evil, the selfish, or the stupid who, if unchecked, debase and corrupt society.

Activity also should characterize the listener, who should neither reject all nor accept all, be neither cynic nor naive fool. The person who follows a bad leader uncritically is neglecting responsibility as surely as is the individual who remains silent when the circumstances call for the exposure of poor advice.

Ethical imperatives for discussants, conferees, conversationalists, and platform speakers are variables and not absolutes, personal viewpoints and not authoritarian pronouncements. The four preceding propositions are starting points, whose applications to specific situations provoke controversy among individuals who are equally intelligent and responsible. The student, the business tycoon, and the citizen, through thought, experience, and discussion, should gradually build their personal ethical codes. That the communicator should be responsible is beyond dispute.

CONCLUSION

Conferences, interviews, conversations, and discussion groups differ from speaker-to-audience situations significantly, but much of the advice on step-by-step preparation is applicable. A successful conferee or discussant, like an effective platform speaker, learns in advance the purpose of the gathering, researches the topic, engages in creative thought, assesses the transactional elements, makes rhetorical choices, outlines and prepares the message, and meets ethical responsibilities. In interpersonal situations the transactional elements are especially important, and the frequent switching of roles from speaker to listener and back makes flexibility a great asset. Instead of composing a set speech, the well-prepared participant plans several lines of development, chooses according to circumstances, and modifies the initial choice as may become necessary.

All communicators—one-to-one, one-to-few, and one-to-many—have options to exercise in the development of the message, the maintenance of favorable sender-receiver relations, and the application of rhetorical techniques. The eight topics included in the first section are an introduction to some major aspects of the art of communication. These topics are purpose, inventive thought, materials, listener analysis and adaptation, credibility, arrangement, verbal language, and the nonverbal medium.

PROBLEMS AND EXERCISES

1. Write a brief paper of self-analysis. Include an appraisal of both your present assets as a communicator and your liabilities.

2. Along with four or five of your classmates, discuss the question, "What should the student learn in a course in speech communication?" Appoint one member of the group to report your conclusions to the class.

3. Prepare a three-minute talk on a topic appropriate to this chapter. Possible topics include the following:

    The Most Credible Speaker That I Have Ever Heard
    How *Not* to Give a Speech
    Some Qualities That Contribute to High Credibility
    My Pet Peeves about Public Speakers
    Materials for a Speech
    Advice on Using Visual Aids
    An Ethical Code for the Communicator

4. Assume that you are going to address a senior English class in the high school from which you graduated. (1) Select a topic. (2) Phrase a purpose. (3) List some ideas and materials that you might use. Meet with four or five of your classmates for reactions to your tentative plans and for suggested additions and alterations.

5. Find at least three items of evidence (statistics, examples, or quotations) on any one of the following topics:

    Crime in the Streets
    Teen-Age Drug Abuse
    World Hunger
    The Dangers of Smoking
    Corruption in Government

6. Draft an outline for the topic chosen for "5." Include two to five main points and at least two subitems for one or more of the main points.

7. Rewrite the following passage so that it is in oral style:

For an example of glittering generalities the critic can look at almost any political campaign. To avoid offending any element within the electorate, candidates state that they are for law and order, good schools, high wages, ethics in government, protection of personal freedoms, reduction of pollution, and lower taxes. Whether they are for or against capital punishment, legalized abortion, police review boards, or any other specific proposition often remains in doubt. Not only is no one offended, but also through wishful thinking voters may conclude that any candidate's true view is the same as theirs.

8. Through gestures or some other type of nonverbal cue, present five simple messages such as "It's OK" or "We've won." To test for clarity, have your classmates write down the messages as they perceive them.

9. Deliver a five-minute expository speech with two to five main ideas. Test for clarity by having your classmates write down the principal points.

10. Present an oral report on one of the references. Include both a summary of the content and your own ideas and criticisms.

REFERENCES

Applbaum, Ronald L., Owen O. Jenson, and Richard Carroll, eds. *Speech Communication: A Basic Anthology.* New York: Macmillan, 1975.

Barnlund, Dean C., ed. *Interpersonal Communication: Survey and Studies.* Boston: Houghton Mifflin Co., 1968.

DeVito, Joseph A., ed. *Communication: Concepts and Processes.* Englewood Cliffs, N.J.: Prentice-Hall, 1971.

Giffin, Kim, and Bobby R. Patton, eds. *Basic Readings in Interpersonal Communication.* New York: Harper & Row, 1971.

Goldhaber, Gerald M. *Organizational Communication.* Dubuque, Ia.: Wm. C. Brown Co., 1974.

Greenwald, Anthony G., Timothy C. Brock, and Thomas M. Ostrom, eds. *Psychological Foundations of Attitudes.* New York: Academic Press, 1968.

Insko, Chester A. *Theories of Attitude Change.* New York: Appleton-Century-Crofts, 1967.

Mortensen, C. David. *Communication: The Study of Human Interaction.* New York: McGraw-Hill, 1972.

Mortensen, C. David, ed. *Basic Readings in Communication Theory.* New York: Harper & Row, 1973.

Rokeach, Milton. *Beliefs, Attitudes, and Values.* San Francisco: Jossey-Bass, 1968.

Sereno, Kenneth K., and C. David Mortensen, eds. *Foundations of Communication Research.* New York: Harper & Row, 1970.

I
CONTENT: THE BASIS OF RESPONSIBLE COMMUNICATION

The objective of this textbook is to help the student to be an effective, responsible communicator in interpersonal, small-group, and platform-address situations. To attain this objective, the speaker or discussant must have something to say that is worth saying. Worthwhile content, in turn, depends on understanding and practicing three related arts or skills:

Productive research on well-chosen topics

Inventive thought

The utilization of sound, purposeful materials

2
RESEARCH AREAS AND METHODS

After studying this chapter the reader should be able to do the following:

Phrase in one sentence a speech topic suitable for a responsible, informative ten-minute address to the class or to some other designated audience

List at least five authoritative and accessible sources of information on the topic chosen for an address

Converse readily for five minutes on such aspects of his or her topic as its significance, its history, and its relevance to campus or community

Stand before the class and answer questions on the topic

State an informed judgment on the suitability of a possible speech topic that a classmate is considering

Discuss informally the problems of adapting his or her topic to a particular audience—relevance to their probable interests, possible special approaches, and desirable limitations and emphases

List at least three stories, examples, or comparisons that are likely to add interest and pointedness to the next major presentation

Explain orally how to find a government document in the local library, how to find a journal article on a topic, and where to find such reference resources as biographical works

"What shall I talk about?" is the first question of many prospective speakers. "Whatever is on the agenda for the conference or the business meeting" is one answer; "Whatever will interest my audience and give a favorable impression" is a second; "Whatever my professor expects of me" is a third. Such pragmatic statements are appropriate, for speeches—both within and outside the classroom—vary widely in purpose, length, informativeness, and intellectual maturity. The professor, who has his or her own educational objectives, may assign a personal-experience speech, a talk using visual aids, an interview, a discussion, a conference, or a platform address that is informative, entertaining, or persuasive.

All such assignments serve worthwhile ends, and the final section of this chapter should be useful in completing many of them. The focus of the principal parts of the chapter, however, is on intellectually mature discourse in which the speaker or the conferee has something worth saying and in which the principal benefit to the listener is a better grasp of some significant topic. The assumptions are that university students are competent to handle meaningful issues and that a consideration of worthwhile topics and of ways to approach such topics should be helpful to them. These kinds of information also should be valuable to those who participate in communication situations in business, the professions, and the community.

CONTENT AND COMMUNICATION

What is the role of content in communication, and how important is it? Its least important setting, seemingly, is light conversation, whose principal features are showing concern and building a warm, trusting relationship. Even here, however, a sustained transaction profits from at least the beginnings of intellectual maturity.

In other circumstances content ordinarily is the most significant single factor in determining informativeness, persuasiveness, and the degree of respect accorded to the speaker. How much the conferee or the discussant knows determines how much he or she can contribute, and the social value of the platform speech depends on the quality and the amount of information and on the accuracy and the originality of the reasoning. These truisms go back to classical times, when Cicero, among others, set a course for rhetoric that even today is the basis for responsible, effective discourse:

To begin with, a knowledge of very many matters must be grasped, without which oratory is but an empty and ridiculous swirl of verbiage. . . . no man can be an orator complete in all points of merit, who has not attained a knowledge of all important subjects and arts. For it is from knowledge that oratory must derive its beauty and fullness, and unless there is such knowledge, well-grasped and comprehended by the speaker, there must be something empty and almost childish in the utterance. . . . For excellence in speaking cannot be made manifest unless the speaker fully comprehends the matter he speaks about.[1]

The preceding paragraph, of course, does not say that friendliness, sincerity, wit, and good humor are not assets. These and other personal qualities, as Aristotle recognized with his emphasis on the persuasive power of *ethos* or credibility, are valuable to the individual both when conversing and when speaking formally. Dwight Eisenhower was a success in politics primarily because people liked him, and Gerald Ford's strongest asset in the opening months of his presidency was his apparent honesty and candor. For the long pull, however, a winning personality is not enough; communicators must have facts, examples, opinions, and analyses that are new, challenging, and/or perceptive. As Woodrow Wilson said, "Eloquence is never begotten of empty pates."[2]

RESEARCH AREAS FOR STUDENT SPEECHES

Whether a speech is substance or froth is sometimes hard to judge, and listeners sometimes feel dissatisfaction without knowing the reason. An example of this was a talk on "Vacation Travel" given in a freshman class. The young man's organization was faultless, and the subtopics could have been the basis for an interesting, informative presentation. In regard to travel by air he said that service is now available to almost any city in the United States and that planes provide quick service. On railroads he said that the government, through Amtrak, had brought about a slight revival of passenger service; and on buses he reported that they go almost everywhere and are relatively economical but slow. The weakness in this dull effort was that the speaker had nothing to say that was not already common knowledge. He had given his topic only superficial thought, and he had done no research. He had no precise facts and figures, no actual examples, no self-created illustrations, and no pictures or other visual aids. The fault was not the choice of topic but the quality of preparation. And behind that

---

[1] Cicero *De Oratore* i.5 and i.11.
[2] As cited in A. Craig Baird, ed., *American Public Addresses, 1740–1952* (New York: McGraw-Hill, 1956), p. 10.

poor preparation was a failure to understand communication principles and the speaker's responsibilities.

The best speeches usually are a combination of personal materials with facts, statistics, examples, and authoritative quotations derived through research. Without library work the speech is likely to be vague and general; without the individual's own ideas and experiences, it is likely to be dull and impersonal.

PROBLEMS OF CAMPUS AND COMMUNITY

Selecting a topic and generating worthwhile ideas and materials, thus, are the beginnings of responsible communication. The most obvious areas for interesting choices are campus and community problems; and for timely ideas one needs only to look at a local newspaper, to listen to conversations, and to observe firsthand outward signs of situations that can be improved.

If either the professor's assignment or the circumstances for a talk outside the classroom require serious treatment of an important contemporary issue, what are the possibilities? Some of the best choices are those that pertain to the quality of education that the student is receiving:

Evaluation of teachers

Admission policies: possible changes; how the suggested changes have worked where tried, and how they would work here

Graduation requirements

What do prospective employers expect of college graduates, and how well satisfied are they with the persons they are hiring?

What is the open university, and how well is it working?

Honors courses

Alumni evaluations of the education that they received, and particularly their responses to such requirements as physical education and foreign language

The value of special programs, such as Black Studies

The preceding and similar topics can result either in uninteresting, trite rehashes or in informative, provocative presentations. Materials for such speeches can come from interviews with students, faculty members, administrators, alumni, and community leaders and from college catalogs and reports; but the speaker also should refer to educational journals and recent books.

A second area for student speechmaking is extracurricular activities:

Are intercollegiate sports worth what they cost? (How much do they cost, how many benefit directly and how many indirectly, and what are the arguments for the programs?)

Women's intercollegiate athletics: Should these programs exist, and how should they differ from men's?

Recruiting practices and athletic scholarships

Nonathletic programs, such as debate, band, yearbook, and the school paper: competition for student support; costs, objectives, abuses, and justifications. On most campuses activities compete with one another for money collected through fees assessed on the individual student. Facts and informed opinions are the bases for developing a thoughtful personal viewpoint.

Student government: How well does it operate? What reforms, if any, are needed? Are certain expenditures questionable?

Still other kinds of services call for investigation and responsible speechmaking. Most universities provide parking, health centers, child-care centers, grants and loans, tutorial services for the disadvantaged, special facilities for the physically handicapped, recreational areas and equipment, intramural programs, food services, police protection, and dormitories. If an institution does not provide some of these, perhaps it should; if it does, the student speaker can appraise the services by obtaining relevant facts and weighing opinions from both students and administrators.

To a considerable extent students as a group are responsible for their own well-being. Living together involves both working with college authorities and self-regulation. Thievery, personal safety, vandalism, the mutilation of library books and journals, and good study conditions are some of the problems that cry out for solutions. Closely related are problems arising from the interplay of rights and responsibilities. Smoking marijuana, alcohol on campus, and the visitation of men and women to each other's rooms may be viewed as personal rights, but they affect third parties and the group collectively. Which policies are best? What should be the role of student government in solving these problems? What are the arguments on each side, and how good are they? What have been the effects on other campuses of a proposal now under consideration? In conclusion, meaningful discourse is possible on a great variety of campus issues.

Community problems, likewise, are a rich source of topics worthy of research and thought:

The quality of local education

Drug pushers in or near the schools

Traffic safety in the neighborhood

Local recreational facilities

Crime in the streets

Protection against home burglaries

Improvement of the environment

Research on topics such as the preceding should include both materials on local conditions and information from publications giving the national picture. The speaker's opinions can be significant contributions to an address, but they must have a solid foundation.

Carelessness and superficiality are incompatible with responsible communication, and the familiarity of some topics traps the lazy and the unwary into the false belief that they already know all that is necessary. Such mastery is rare, and in most instances speakers need to engage in the same careful research on campus and community topics that they do on issues of international consequence. On most subjects opportunities exist both for library research and for interviews and personal investigations. No speech—including those on the campus or the community—should be a bland restatement of ideas already well known.

SOCIAL ISSUES

A similar sense of responsibility should characterize the preparation of speeches on those social issues whose scope is larger than campus and community. Many of these problems, such as prison reform and slum housing, are well known, but materials on them in the news columns of daily papers are meager. Front-page stories often report the consequences of social sores, such as prison riots, disastrous fires, and hideous crimes; but for detailed information on the basic problems the student must go to editorials, feature stories, magazine articles, and reports of investigative committees.

Social problems are visible almost everywhere, and the apparent simplicity of them, as with campus issues, is deceptive. The student may claim to understand drug addiction, alcoholism, racial prejudice, and poverty, but the probability is that he or she possesses few facts and only superficial ideas. Such problems involve an intricate combination of psychological, economic, political, technological, and ecological forces. For an example of the gap between what the average individual already knows and a true understanding, readers should judge themselves in relation to one of the best-known of all social problems, drug abuse. Typical readers have in mind some miscellaneous facts, a few personal observations, and some unoriginal ideas and opinions that are much like those of their friends. The most valuable of these resources are likely to be the firsthand experiences, but these are scattered examples that prove little until research and thought establish a framework into which they can be fitted.

The social issue chosen as a speech topic thus poses an exciting challenge. Typically it is a topic in which the individual has a strong interest but limited knowledge—the ideal setting for a stimulating period of research. The practical question is "Where does one go for the needed information?" For printed material the first answer is that one begins with

Social issues are of many types. In this picture a trained social worker is interviewing an Indian woman. (Office of Information, University of Houston, and Gloria Shatto)

feature stories in newspapers and with articles in readily accessible magazines. Then, for deeper and more scholarly materials, one goes to professional and learned journals, to government documents, to research pamphlets, and to books. To find these resources, one uses the card catalog, periodical guides, and the help of the reference librarian (see pp. 38–40). Next, one follows up on footnotes and bibliographies, which often lead to original sources, and locates specialized trade and professional magazines that pertain to the topic, whether it be social work, nursing, medicine, prisons and correctional facilities, or urban planning. For nonprint materials the speaker can go to counselors at halfway houses, members of city commissions, heads of law enforcement agencies, directors of family-planning centers, and a variety of other persons whose jobs pertain to some aspect of the chosen topic. The resourceful student also may find opportunities to interview some of those who are victims of poverty, broken families, alcoholism, or other sources of social pressure.

Possible social issues for speeches are many, and the preceding examples are only a few of the most promising. Besides prison conditions, housing, drug addiction, alcoholism, racial discrimination, sexism, poverty, and broken homes, there are such additional problems as the plight of senior citizens, migrant workers, newly arrived immigrants, refugees, unwed mothers, the unemployed, and residents of rural slums. Many of these situations are also community problems, and many have economic, political, and even international ramifications; but precise classification is less important to the speaker than are intelligent analysis, careful research, and thorough understanding.

Limiting the Scope of Discussion

Since almost all of the preceding issues are too broad for thorough research, some limitation is advisable; and, fortunately, narrowing the scope often transforms a tired, much-discussed topic, such as drug abuse, into a presentation with a viewpoint that is new and fresh. The types of limitation are several, and combinations of them are possible:

Geographic Restriction Local conditions are of special interest to most audiences. What are the problems of senior citizens in *this* community? What are the statistics that describe local conditions? What are some human-interest examples? How do the immediate circumstances compare with those elsewhere? What, if anything, here at home is unique? Similarly, one's research may center on a local immigrant colony, on the health dangers created by a nearby industrial plant, on the implications of a neighborhood drug bust, on the work of a local agency for runaway children, or on home-town prison conditions.

Narrower Classification Rather than speaking on problem pregnancy, one may discuss its special consequences for the early teen-ager, the black, the Chicano, the socialite, the public school teacher, the mentally retarded, or the rape victim. To concentrate research and later the speech itself on a single aspect of a problem permits greater thoroughness and often increases originality. For example, whereas speech-weary auditors may dread yet another talk on drug addiction, they may react favorably when they learn through the title or the introduction that the presentation will be on a drug that they have heard little about, on a new method of treatment, or on some other novel aspect of the topic.

Concentration on Causes Another means of arousing interest is to probe deeply. It is tiresome to listen to yet another description of the hazards of smoking, but a probing analysis of the deep-down reasons for the habit can be enlightening. "Why?" is a challenging question. Why do teenagers turn to dope? Why has crime in the streets increased? Why do many parolees commit burglaries or assaults? Answers to such questions can come from original thought or from interviews with authorities on the topic, but the more common sources are special reports that go beyond superficialities to backgrounds, analyses, and detailed investigations. For such materials the speaker must locate documents, books, scholarly journals, and other sources that the average person does not ordinarily read.

Emphasis on Solutions Also unfamiliar to many listeners are specific plans or proposals. Is there a promising solution that no one else has advanced? Is there one in print that has attracted but little attention? Is there a lightly regarded or unpopular plan for which the thoughtful speaker can make a solid case? Proposed remedies can make informative and interesting speeches, but they must go beyond the obvious and the trite.

Summary

Original, thoughtful, well-researched, relevant, interesting speeches, in summary, are possible for a vast number of topics and subtopics within the field of social issues. "Is there anything to talk about?" is not the question; rather the questions are "Which problem?" "Which limitation of the problem?" and "Which special aspect or viewpoint?" And as with any type of topic, "Where do I get material?" and "Is my material accurate, informed, and responsible?" also are necessary inquiries.

ECONOMIC PROBLEMS

The conclusion to the preceding section is a suitable introduction to the present one. Indeed, many problems are both social and economic; the two are closely intertwined—the second a cause of the first, the first a cause of the second. Poverty, for example, is both economic and social. Its sources are such economic causes as unemployment, low wages, and poor budgeting; its immediate consequences are such social problems as slums, prostitution, and violent crime; and its ultimate results are such economic effects on the community as a shrinking tax base and reduced purchasing power.

Some problems, nevertheless, are predominantly economic and financial. Under such headings as "The Economic Outlook" and "The State of the Economy," newspapers and magazines carry articles on such potential speech topics as these:

The international balance of payments	Housing and construction
	New sources of energy
Unemployment	Inflation
Farm income	Recession
The cost of medical care	Strikes

Control of monopolies	Exploration for minerals
Productivity	Strip mining and land reclamation
Interest rates	Drought and crop failures
Taxes	Technological changes
Wage settlements	Pending legislation
Consumer credit	

For still other ideas the student can refer to specialized publications, including the *Wall Street Journal, Barron's, Forbes,* government pamphlets, trade journals, and the house organs of major corporations. Finally, economics textbooks are readily available for basic theory.

One division of economic problems is into theoretical and practical. Many topics, such as unemployment, can be treated in either category, and the speaker may limit discussion to one or the other. Textbooks, special papers, and scholarly journal articles are the best sources for theoretical material. In them the research worker can find definitions of unemployment, analyses of causes, and ideas on how to manage the problem. For one's own understanding an overview of a topic is desirable, but thoroughness comes with specialization. In dealing with unemployment, for example, a speaker might elect to find material and to develop ideas on any of the following subtopics:

Causes

Comparisons of the present problem with conditions during other recessions

Local pockets of severe joblessness

How worldwide conditions affect unemployment in the United States

Some proposed fiscal and monetary solutions

Relief and make-work programs

The social consequences of unemployment

The relation of unions to the problem

The effects of buying power

The best speeches on economic issues, as on other topics, are those that combine scholarly materials with personal information and analyses. For most topics statistics are essential to provide a broad view and a solid base for both description and prediction. Such sources as the *Wall Street Journal* and the news magazines reprint figures first published elsewhere; these secondary publications generally are accurate, but if possible the research worker should go to the original documents, many of which come from the Bureau of the United States Census, the Bureau of Labor Statistics, the Department of Commerce, the Department of Agriculture, and other governmental agencies. Still other documents originate with divisions of the United Nations and with foundations and private research organizations. The Brookings Institute is especially well known.

Such statistical materials, along with authoritative statements and authenticated facts, are the foundation for the responsible speech, but skillful speakers increase interest and pointedness with stories, examples, and vivid descriptions. Whereas the statistic shows how serious the situation is in the state or the nation, the single instance demonstrates just what the problem means to human lives. Such materials sometimes appear in print, but they also come through interviews and personal investigations. At times they are fabricated, with the speaker presenting in specific (though imagined) detail a typical case. This final strategy calls for an acknowledgment that the instance, although based on fact, is invented.

PROBLEMS IN INTERNATIONAL RELATIONS

London, Paris, Moscow, Rome, Tel Aviv, Tokyo, Buenos Aires—news stories with datelines in Europe, Asia, Africa, South America, and elsewhere report events that often have consequences for the government of the United States and its people. "No man is an island," wrote John Donne,[3] a statement whose truth not even the staunchest isolationist can deny and whose significance the passing decades enhance.

What kinds of problems, more specifically, originate in foreign countries and affect the United States? Some pertain to world peace, others to economic conditions and political stability, and still others to crops, food, poverty, political freedoms, and other humanitarian considerations. Other issues of global importance are the following:

The development of new armaments in the Soviet Union

The increasing number of countries with nuclear weapons

The relative military strengths of nations in the Middle East

The provisions of recent treaties

Overpopulation in India

Starvation in Africa

Racial disorders in Johannesburg

Price fixing by the oil-producing nations

The Palestinian refugees

Strife in Ireland

The faltering economy of Britain

The effectiveness of the Common Market

---

[3] John Donne, *Devotions*, xvii, as cited in John Bartlett, comp., *Familiar Quotations*, ed. Emily M. Beck (Boston: Little, Brown and Co., 1968), p. 308b.

The present status of NATO

Threatening national bankruptcy in Italy

The communist threat in Western Europe

A change in leadership in any major nation

The predicted policies of communist China

The economy of Japan

Opportunities for resettlement in Australia

Economic progress in Cuba

New Candian laws on imports and exports with the United States

Recent actions of the United Nations

The preceding list contains only a small portion of the total number of international topics that in any given year are significant. For other ideas the student should refer to newspapers, news magazines, and television and radio news reports and commentaries.

As with domestic subjects, the original choice of an international topic almost always is too broad. In narrowing it the first question to ask is "Why is this situation important to the United States generally and to my prospective audience specifically?" Britain may be considering withdrawing from the Common Market or the government in Spain may be tottering, but how may this affect the member of the audience who owns a butcher shop or the parent who has a son or a daughter in high school? Knowledge for its own sake is not without its values; and whatever the topic the responsible speaker investigates it fully—its background, its causes, its present status, and the possible consequences for the United States. Of these four facets, although the narrowed topic may emphasize any one, the last is likely to have the greatest appeal for an American audience.

SUMMARY

Throughout the preceding sections on four groups of issues—campus and community, social, economic, and international—the emphasis is on responsibility. Taking the speaker's platform, although an opportunity, poses obligations. Meaningful communication requires full and accurate information, careful thought, a search for implications significant to listeners, and the composition of a well-organized, interest-holding address.

RESEARCH AREAS IN BUSINESS AND THE PROFESSIONS

Still another field that affords excellent opportunities for selecting worthwhile topics and for devising challenging classroom assignments is that of business and the professions. Students preparing for careers in these areas should be especially interested in communication, for the importance of oral skills is well recognized. Interviews lead to jobs, conferences result in decisions, and presentations secure contracts, sometimes worth millions of dollars. Large corporations hire communication specialists to improve the flow of information among their divisions and to supervise in-service training. Regional sales conferences rely on talented speakers for inspiration as well as information, and speakers' bureaus to build good will are common. The Philadelphia Electric Company, for example, between 1959 and 1975 sent employees out three thousand times to give speeches before an estimated total audience of 220,000.[4] Another American corporation, so it was reported, had "trained a battalion of 500 executives to spread the gospel of company views of public issues."[5]

INTERNAL AND EXTERNAL SOURCES OF INFORMATION

Annual corporate reports, updated by brief quarterly statements, are the basic resource for many business speakers. Ordinarily these documents cover all aspects of the business, including new products, labor relations, sales, new financing, future prospects, and the present and predicted effects of the economy on the company. Their content is a combination of what the law requires and what the officers consider it advantageous to reveal. Selective reporting and tricky writing sometimes conceal unfavorable information.

Additional internal sources are open to officers and members of their staffs. In briefing other members of the organization on problems and developments and in presenting proposed changes, speakers clearly should secure all relevant facts. Doing so inevitably requires effort, but insiders usually know the materials they need and the appropriate sources. If not, they should seek advice from those who are more experienced.

As a supplement to these company materials, external sources such as government reports, surveys by private research groups, and essays written by scholars or persons of practical experience are likewise necessary. Wise decision making on most topics requires broadly based data on inventories, changes in interest rates, new legislation, international developments, research on new products, revisions of the tax structure, and cultural changes that may affect buying habits. A company library may be available to help in obtaining such information, but in many instances business executives, like most other people, must rely on their own efforts.

---

[4] "Report to Shareholders," June, 1975, n.p.
[5] Randall M. Fisher, "Modern Business Speaking," *Southern Speech Journal*, 30 (Summer 1965), 327.

STUDENT RESEARCH FOR SPEECHES

To a considerable extent the student preparing for a classroom audience uses the same resources as those described for the company executive or representative, but what is convenient through the campus library is somewhat different from what is handy to the corporate employee. To obtain printed annual reports, for example, the student must either send a request to company headquarters or ask for help from a local branch office or a brokerage firm. Unpublished material, confidential data, and advance projections almost always are unavailable.

Offsetting these losses are the abundant holdings of a university library on business management, finance, and economics. Subject headings in the card catalog lead the student to books with their in-depth analyses, and lists of periodical holdings contain the names of journals with up-to-date articles. The documents collection often contains reports of special studies by government agencies and research foundations.

What kinds of topics are well adapted to the probable resources? For college students addressing their own classes, such topics as the following are possibilities:

The nuclear reactor as a source of electric power

The prospects for new sources of petroleum and natural gas

Extracting petroleum from coal shale

The environmental problems of strip mining

The effects of anti-pollution devices on automobile engines

America's problem with the balance of trade

"Fair-trade" laws

Are foreign interests taking over American industries?

Franchising

Stronger laws for consumer protection

The outlook for the American auto industry

How inflation affects different segments of our population

Possible tax reforms

The economic outlook for Great Britain (or any other country)

The economy of the Indian reservation

How well is the American farmer doing?

Helping small businesses

Paying for the high costs of health care

Improving communication within the corporation

Problems in enforcing antitrust laws

How better business bureaus work

Problems in starting a law practice

Do utilities charge too much?

Speech of Presentation

Still other topics are workable if a classroom assignment calls for a speech of presentation, a significant communication event in business and industry. Outside the classroom, contracts involving large sums of money sometimes depend on the quality of a presentation, usually including extensive visual aids, showing the advantages of a product or a service. In a speech course through simulation a student can portray an architect showing a city council a proposal to remodel the municipal building, or a sales manager can explain to automobile executives why a new carburetor component would lead to better performance and higher sales. Some other possibilities are these:

New office furniture for the headquarters of the company

A plan for remodeling a hotel kitchen

Automated equipment for the hotel front desk

A new floor plan for a restaurant

Adding a deodorizer to every new car

A proposal for urban renewal

A revision of the company's incentive program

An automation plan for a supermarket

A revised procedure for handling incoming mail

A request for a loan for a new restaurant

A proposal for a neighborhood newspaper

Good Will Speech

A second situation that is uniquely important in business and the professions is the meeting calling for the "good will" speech. How many of these addresses occur each year is unknown, but even a city of moderate size has a dozen or more service clubs, church organizations, and garden societies, each with an enormous capacity for using up program resources. Planning for fifty-two meetings a year, or even for twenty-six, strains a program committee to the point that an available "good will" speaker of even modest accomplishments is welcome. Since the prime rule for these situations is that the speaker should avoid direct sales attempts, addresses are more often informative than persuasive. With interestingness essential, topics that are nostalgic or historic are excellent—how the hotel industry began; colonial hostelries; the earliest automobiles; ancient forms of currency.

Also of interest are reports on the latest developments and dramatic descriptions of the future. As examples, speakers may talk about the newest telephone equipment, the fully automated bank, or the supermarket of tomorrow. Still other kinds of topics that are suitable are the biographical sketch of an important figure in the speaker's industry or an autobiographical recounting of bizarre or unusual happenings. Thus, an insurance agent might give an entertaining speech on the most unusual claims ever handled or the oddest requests for insurance ever received. Every student or corporate representative, of course, has his or her own background, interests, and talents. From these come the most fitting topics.

RESEARCH RESOURCES AND METHODS

Whatever the topic, certain procedures and reference tools are likely to be helpful. This final major section of the chapter is on the location of information, general and specific materials, and note taking.

THE LOCATION OF MATERIALS

Where does one go for facts, figures, quotations, and examples? The two broad divisions of resources are personal investigations and library holdings.

Personal Investigations

In developing the topic "Minority Attitudes Toward the Police," one student interviewed black classmates and through them contacted social workers, patrolmen, teachers, black ministers, and alleged victims of brutality. The individual also talked with attorneys and with representatives of the local police administration. On many issues the material that one uncovers through field studies enriches understanding and provides examples and descriptive materials that add interest and authoritativeness. Seeing for oneself and interviewing experts are major sources of nonlibrary information.

Other nonprint sources include radio and television programs, especially commentaries and documentaries. The items on newscasts are so brief that they have little value except as leads for the fuller accounts in newspapers the same or the following day. Two other limitations on the electronic media as research resources are the rarity with which a substantial program occurs on a previously chosen topic and the impossibility of "rereading" to check accuracy in note taking. Because of these limitations, radio and television are useful to speakers primarily for stories and examples and for background information.

Planning and *persistence* are the key words for locating materials through personal investigations. One must list places to visit, persons to interview, and areas for research. Next, one must make appointments, list items to observe, and prepare a set of questions to ask. Since city officials, agency administrators, and college professors are likely to be busy men and women, finding ones willing to answer questions may require time and effort. Nevertheless, for many topics personal materials add so much to persuasiveness and interest that they are well worth any difficulties that may arise.

Library Holdings

For many topics, however, printed materials are the only means for obtaining a full, rounded view. The following answers to common questions should be timesavers:

How do I find a book on my topic? If you already know the name of the author or the title, use the card catalog, which is an alphabetized list of all books that a library holds. If you do not know the name of a book, you may use the subject section of the catalog by looking under one or more subject headings relevant to your topic.

Other ways to find promising titles are to look for references in journal articles on the topic and to use bibliographies in textbooks, magazines, and specialized publications. The *Bibliographic Index* lists bibliographies printed during the time covered by that particular volume.

How do I find a journal article on my topic? Bibliographies often include the titles of articles, but one may also use a periodical index. These appear by time periods, and one uses the volumes for the months and years deemed appropriate. Three indexes that cover a variety of topics are *Readers' Guide to Periodical Literature*, which covers more than one hundred well-known, general publications, and the *Social Sciences Index* and the *Humanities Index*, each of which is a guide to more than two hundred and sixty specialized, scholarly journals in its own area. A number of other works, such as the *Education Index* and the *Business Periodicals Index*, cover the areas indicated by their names. *Ulrich's International Periodicals Directory* tells where each magazine is indexed.

How do I find pamphlets and documents? The individual library has a catalog of its holdings; anyone who is unfamiliar with it should consult the documents librarian. The more general guides are the *Vertical File Index*, which is a monthly annotated list of pamphlets, and the *Monthly Catalog of United States Government Publications*, the most complete guide to federal materials. Less comprehensive but biweekly is *Selected United States Government Publications*. The *Public Affairs Information Service* is a classified list of books, articles, and documents in the fields of sociology,

The card catalog is a sensible starting point for research on a number of topics for speeches and discussions. (Owen Franken/Stock Boston)

political science, economics, and finance. Each volume is for a designated period. For publications of the United Nations, the principal guide is the *United Nations Documents Index*.

How do I find news stories? *The New York Times Index* is a partial guide to all daily papers, for stories of an event appear on the same day in most cities. Subject headings, alphabetically arranged, bring together the titles of articles appearing within the time period covered by a particular volume. The numbers at the ends of the entries (IV, 6:5) refer respectively to the section of the paper, the number of the page, and the column.

Where do I obtain statistical information? The most usable sources of data for the United States are the *Statistical Abstract of the United States* and *The World Almanac*. For the British Commonwealth the most comprehensive source is *Whitaker's Almanack*. Especially authoritative and detailed for the United States are the numerous special volumes issued by the Bureau of the Census and the Office of the Census.

Where do I obtain general background information, such as material on the geography, history, resources, and government of a country? Encyclopedias often are the most convenient source for general information, and in many instances the information that they give is sufficiently detailed and recent to meet the speaker's needs. The *Britannica* and the *Americana* publish annual supplements, and for some topics this updating is critical. Other good sources are the *Information Please Almanac*, the *News Dictionary, The Europa Year Book*, and *The Statesman's Year-Book*, which is organized by countries and includes both historic and current material. *Facts on File* is the best guide to very recent happenings.

What are the sources for biographic information? Besides *Who's Who* (for living Englishmen) and *Who's Who in America* (for living Americans), there are several dozen specialized volumes of *Who's Who* that cover designated states, regions, countries, and special groups. Among the many other sources the best known are the following: *Contemporary Authors, Current Biography* (monthly with annual cumulation), *Webster's Biographical Dictionary*, the *Biography Index* (appears quarterly and is cumulated), *The National Cyclopaedia of American Biography* (both living and dead), the *Dictionary of American Biography* (most authoritative source for deceased Americans), *The Dictionary of National Biography* (deceased Englishmen), and the *Directory of American Scholars*.

In the long run the person who does frequent research saves time by learning how to use the local library and how to solve most ordinary problems. For unusual requirements, however, the help of a trained librarian saves time and frustration. At most hours of the day, specialists in government documents and in reference resources are on duty; the wise student goes to them for assistance.

GENERAL AND SPECIFIC MATERIALS

How Shirley, a typical college speaker, helped herself illustrates the two types of research tasks, which are roughly sequential. First, she sought to obtain an overview of her topic, which was "Have Women Gained Equal Rights?" In this early stage she looked for laws and court decisions, for descriptions of different areas where equal rights are significant, for conflicting viewpoints, and for fact-finding studies. Fortunately, Shirley found a book and a detailed article that were comprehensive surveys of her topic. Such convenient materials are valuable, for they provide a framework for organizing the ideas and the bits of information that come from diverse sources. Such surveys, however, endanger originality: no one source should dominate a speaker's thinking to the extent that it becomes the outline for the presentation. Not all knowledge or wisdom rests with any one book or author, and students such as Shirley should weigh carefully what they read and then create viewpoints and organizational structures that are largely their own.

After the individual gains an overview of the topic and prepares a first draft of the speech outline, he or she begins to identify specific needs—a copy or an authoritative digest of a law, statistics on past and present productivity, figures on repeaters among criminals, precise knowledge of the terms of an international treaty, or a careful assessment of the potentialities of solar energy. Sometimes the soundness of an argument depends on the outcome of specific effort, and in other instances the special investigation reveals facts that add interest and substance. The reference resources described in the preceding section are especially important in carrying forward specific research.

NOTE TAKING

"I don't need to take notes; I can remember what I read" is wishful thinking. Note taking, true enough, requires time and effort, but so does a second trip to the library when the communicator finds that memory is uncertain. And how much better it is to go to the trouble of recording data than it is to be inaccurate—whether one does or does not get caught!

Techniques

Systematic note taking, if habitual, is as easy as writing down haphazard words and phrases. The following simple rules increase efficiency:

1. Take all notes on file cards of a uniform size, such as four inches by six inches.

2. Write legibly, and record enough information so that the entry will be intelligible a month later. Words and phrases sometimes are satisfactory substitutes for sentences, and improvised abbreviations may be clear at a later date, but be wary of short cuts. Be sure, for example, that the antecedents are unmistakable for such indefinites as "he," "the man," and "the report."

3. On the top line of the card, place a heading that indicates the principal topic covered in the note. These headings can serve as the bases for filing, and they save time when one is retrieving information.

4. Just below the heading cite in full the name of the author, the title, and the place of publication (see the sample card in Figure 2.1).

5. Use quotation marks for passages that are copied exactly. If the passage is clear and pointed, record the exact language in preference to writing the idea in your own words.

6. At the end of the entry, record the number of the page on which it appears.

7. If you have twenty or more cards, file them in a box or a case. Arrange them by headings, which may be alphabetized. Another possibility is to

> Research, Importance of
>
> Edward Teller, "The Energy Disease," *Harper's*, CCL (Feb. 1975), 16–22
>
> "Coal seams perhaps 50 feet thick can be broken up by the use of conventional explosives. As the coal is converted into rubble it becomes accessible to oxygen pumped down in measured amounts to maintain a controlled fire underground. If we mix high-pressure steam with this fire, we produce a gas quite similar to natural gas. The dirt will be left below the surface, and the surface itself will be hardly perturbed. The *in situ* conversion of coal into gas may well provide us with a substitute for natural gas for centuries to come. Unfortunately, the process described is not yet practicable; research is needed to turn hope into fact" (pp. 18, 22).

Figure 2.1 A sample note card.

organize the cards according to the successive subtopics of the speech outline.

8. If words are omitted when copying a quotation, indicate the omission by using three dots (. . .). If the omission follows a period, the three dots follow the period (. . . .).

9. If you must add words in order to clarify a quotation, enclose the addition in brackets. Example: "He [Governor Brown] replied with the following statement . . ."

Content

"Record any fact, statement, or idea that you think you may be able to use in the speech" is the basic advice for the note taker. Specifically, the body of the note card may contain any of four types of material:

1. Quoted passages whose authority or color can add impressiveness and variety to the fully worded speech

2. Examples, statistics, and facts that transform generalities into specifics and whose inclusion increases the substance of an address

3. Paraphrases of ideas whose thought is of value but whose original wording is clumsy or long-winded

4. Statements summarizing the content and suggesting possible future uses. This fourth type of entry is a sensible compromise between taking no notes and recording material in detail that may be useless. In many instances at the time that one reads a book or an article it is too early to foresee accurately whether its materials eventually will be of value. As a broad generalization, the beginner is more likely to take too few notes than too many.

CONCLUSION

The value of sensible, orderly research is indisputable, but the critical message of this chapter pertains to the soundness of the content that goes into the speech. The basis for responsible speaking is knowledge that goes beyond the superficialities of the topic to a true understanding. A speech is worthwhile only if the communicator knows more than do the members of the audience. Likewise, a participant in a conference, a discussion, or even a serious conversation, is a meaningful contributor only if his or her ideas have a sound basis. Without knowledge, contributions are of limited value, reflect discredit on the speaker, and at times mislead rather than enlighten.

PROBLEMS AND EXERCISES

1. Divide a page into columns, each of which is headed with one of the research areas for student speeches listed in this chapter. Select three or more topics from each of the following sources, and place each topic in the appropriate column: (a) the campus newspaper; (b) a metropolitan newspaper; (c) other courses in which you are enrolled; (d) conversations with friends; (e) self-analysis of present interests.

2. Meet with four or five of your classmates for a discussion of the advantages and the disadvantages of the potential speech topics that each of you is considering.

3. After choosing a topic, prepare an inventory of your resources. On the first page make a list of facts, opinions, examples, arguments, and ideas that you already have. On the second page list kinds of information that you need.

4. Prepare a bibliography for your topic that includes both general, popular sources and materials that are detailed, scholarly, and analytical.

5. After about one week of research on your topic, give a five-minute speech to your class on the progress that you are making, problems that you are encountering, interesting items of information that you have found, and some tentative ideas that you have developed.

6. Prepare a rough outline for the final speech on your topic. Meet with four or five of your classmates to talk about your outline. Make a copy available to each one.

7. Analyze the two student speeches forming the Appendix for choice of topic and for research problems and methods. Were the topics likely to lead to responsible speechmaking? What must have been the most serious problems of each student in preparing the speech? What kinds of research did each student do, and how effective were the research attempts?

REFERENCES

American Statistic Index: A Comprehensive Guide and Index to the Statistical Publications of the U. S. Government. Washington, D. C.: Congressional Information Service, 1973.

Hooker, Zebulon V. *An Index of Ideas for Writers and Speakers.* Chicago: Scott, Foresman and Co., 1965.

Pinson, William M., Jr. *Resource Guide to Current Social Issues.* Waco, Texas: World Books, 1968.

Sheehy, Eugene P. *Guide to Reference Books.* Chicago: American Library Association, 1976.

Shores, Louis. *Basic Reference Sources.* Chicago: American Library Association, 1967.

White, Carl, *et al.*, eds. *Sources of Information in the Social Sciences.* Chicago: American Library Association, 1973.

3
INVENTIVE THOUGHT

After studying this chapter the reader should be able to do the following:

Phrase at least two sentences praising or criticizing the originality of a talk that he or she hears

Assign a speech that he or she hears to one of the four classifications discussed in the chapter: plagiarized, one-source, "scissors-and-paste," or original

Identify at least one cause for the problem that he or she is studying for the next speech

Cite one prior attempt to solve the problem he or she is studying, and discuss informally the likelihood that a similar solution would be successful

Apply one of the ancient *topoi* to the topic of his or her next speech

Give one example of an application, a correlation, or an analogy that is creative

Four students this Friday morning have just finished giving ten-minute addresses in Speech Communication 101. Each has chosen a topic in the area of educational issues, and each for four weeks has been doing research, narrowing the topic, adapting, outlining, and revising. Ted has just heard the presentations, and he is trying to explain to Sally why some were better than others.

"I thought that all of them were pretty good," he began. "All of them were easy to follow, and everybody seemed to have worked hard on the research. Harry's, though, was dull and seemed—well, *mechanical* might be the word for it. I don't mean that he cheated and stole the speech from a magazine, but he seemed to be unwinding a series of ideas without having given them much real thought himself. I had the feeling that anybody in class might have given the same speech."

"I know what you mean," Sally agreed. "The ideas seemed sound enough, but there just wasn't anything there that sounded like Harry—as if he really had thought about the topic himself. But, then, what did you think of Debby's speech? It seemed to lack something, too."

"Right," responded Ted. "I give her credit, though, for bringing in some of her own ideas. When she listed the three causes of the problem, I felt that it was her own list and what she really believed. Her trouble was that her speech became so tiresome to listen to, and I'm not sure why."

"Remember what the professor said about variety in material?" asked Sally. "That was Debby's problem. She had plenty of quotations and statistics taken from books, but she hadn't looked around for real-life examples."

Inventiveness, originality, creativity—these and similar terms describe a quality of speech composition that is closely related to knowledgeability. Without substance a speech of consequence is impossible, but diligence in research is no guarantee of a speaking performance of the highest order. Through the years the writer has heard tens of thousands of speeches, many on the same topic; but likeness of topic, of content, and of outline did not mean talks of equal quality.

LEVELS OF CREATIVITY

What is meant by creativity? Is speechmaking a creative art? How does one improve one's talks through greater originality? Tough questions, all three. Perhaps the best approach to answering them is to describe several levels of inventiveness.

Lowest of all—so low as to be intolerable—is the speech that is plagiarized. In this instance the lazy, unimaginative student—possibly the hard-pressed, desperate student—finds a magazine article on the topic, copies it with a few deletions here and there, partly memorizes the ideas, and reads the manuscript as if it were original. Such a dishonest performance cannot be condoned; and although the true origin of the speech may be hard to prove, telltale signs quickly arouse suspicion; and the basic differences between an article written for a multitude and a speech designed for a specific audience are so noticeable that the attempted deception rarely succeeds. The vocabulary of the professional writer is usually not that of the college student; and even though the written paper may be a witty, brilliant, delightful essay, it rarely sounds like the John Jones or the Susan Smith that teacher and classmates think they know. Popular writers, also, have a trick of sliding from one idea to the next that is not characteristic of speakers, who normally label each new idea as they introduce it. Even more obvious as a shortcoming of the plagiarized speech, however, is its lack of adaptation to both speaker and audience—to the personality of the former, to the needs and interests of the latter, and to the situational factors of time and place.

Second lowest in inventiveness is the one-source address. In this type speakers find one pamphlet, article, or chapter that they like, and they pass on to the listeners this particular set of ideas. The ensuing presentations differ widely in their degrees of originality. At one extreme is the speaker who digests the materials and who gives listeners a series of subpoints that are a thoughtful reorganization of the original and whose selection shows careful adaptation to the specific purpose and audience. Such a speech, although wider research would have provided a stronger background, is in many ways commendable. At the other extreme is the talk that uses the same outline as the article and whose originality does not go beyond the rewording of ideas and the choice of sections to omit. This type of report, especially if the speaker fails to credit the source, is scarcely better than the plagiarized paper.

Third from the bottom is the undigested "scissors-and-paste" speech, so-called because the speaker chooses a series of sources, slices them into segments, and reassembles these particles in a new sequence. This type of address requires effort and a degree of intelligence, for finding relevant materials and selecting and arranging blocks of ideas are time-demanding tasks. To be realistic, some speakers on some topics may be unable to do much better, for inventiveness is a gift that most people achieve only at exceptional times. The "scissors-and-paste" speech, nevertheless, is less than satisfactory. The personality of the speaker is missing; the globs of material go through the mind without anything happening to them—or to the communicator. The individual reads and understands, but does not think and remold.

Shaping ideas, as the introductory dialogue between Ted and Sally indicated, is the most critical aspect of creativeness—combining thoughts, modifying received viewpoints, finding analogies, perceiving relations, locating causes, inventing solutions, and tracing through the probable consequences if a proposed solution became operational. Second, and also mentioned in the dialogue, are the rhetorical skills of devising an interesting introduction, finding an original organizational framework, preparing an effective conclusion, and filling out the outline with examples, stories, comparisons, and other materials that will give the finished address polish and listening appeal.

THE BASES OF INVENTIVE THOUGHT

How can a person improve his or her speech composition through greater inventiveness? No "one . . . two . . . three" answer is possible, but conditions favorable to creativity are identifiable.

THE FULL MIND

"What solutions do you have to prevent the destruction of coral reefs near Australia?" is a request that would draw blank responses from most Americans. The reason is clear: The individual has no starting points for generating ideas. From this extreme one can hypothesize a continuum (see Figure 3.1) that illustrates a plausible assumption: The more information that a person has, the more likely he or she is to have original ideas. Such a correlation is imperfect, and exceptions abound; nevertheless, the basic idea is reasonable.

At least two arguments support the idea that a full mind is conducive to originality. The first of these is that creativity, which is not well understood, often takes the form of combining two "old" ideas into something new. Thus, a business investor who reads that (a) there are vast coal reserves in Wyoming and Montana and (b) industrial plants are likely to convert from oil and gas to coal may conclude that (c) stock in railroads serving the Northwest will probably increase in value. In this example the first item of information without the second is useless, and in other situations a second item may have no perceivable connecting link to a first. But with still further bits of knowledge—third, fourth, fifth, and sixth items—the possibilities for meaningful connecting links increase. In theory, since these increases are geometrical, adding items of information increases the opportunities for creative thought immensely. Not only do six items provide five possible links with Fact #1, but also they may be combined with one another; for six items the potential connections are fifteen, whereas for three items the number is only three.

Second, the process of "filling" the mind increases the number of times that inventiveness may occur. New ideas most often arise in an instant, but they do so only when attention is on the topic. When such a "flash of inspiration" may occur is unpredictable—and on some topics it never happens—but the likelihood of such an event increases proportionately the longer the mind is active in respect to the particular problem. So, as the

```
0                              4                              8
```

The empty mind   The full mind

Figure 3.1 A generalized continuum suggesting that the amount of knowledge
that a communicator has on a topic may be great, slight, or between the extremes.

student does the research from hour to hour to enlarge his or her knowledge of a subject, the number of opportunities for original thought increases.

Ideally, student speakers continue their research until they become so thoroughly acquainted with their topics that they can move as readily through the subfeatures as they can through those areas of life with which they have long been familiar. With such a close acquaintanceship they do not rely unquestioningly on what they read, but they challenge, compare, and form independent judgments.

THE OPEN MIND; BRAINSTORMING

A second basis for original thought, open-mindedness, is a concept that Milton Rokeach popularized.[1] A somewhat elusive idea when examined fully, it has as a core meaning "receptiveness to diverse viewpoints and to new arguments." Not only does this mean a freedom from prejudice and a willingness to consider new ideas whatever their source, but also it means a capacity for suspending judgment. Since the first article that one reads on a topic is not necessarily the most reliable and authoritative, one should be willing to weigh diverse and even contradictory views on their merits before combining them with previous ideas to form one's own conclusions.

The closed mind, in contrast, often is overdependent on persons perceived as authorities. The qualifications of sources, true enough, should influence the degree to which one accepts what one reads and hears, but even the most learned expert makes mistakes and even the best-intentioned person sometimes gives bad advice. The expert, moreover, often is looking at the problem in a different context from that of the specific topic being examined by the student. Whereas these distinctions pose difficulties for persons with closed minds, open-minded individuals can remain flexible as they evaluate and apply whatever they read. "I do not have all the answers," says the open-minded communicator while reading further and putting his or her powers of originality to work. "This new information deserves consideration; and perhaps if I think about this problem myself, I'll see something that so far others have missed."

A process designed to promote open-mindedness is brainstorming, the

[1] Milton Rokeach, *The Open and Closed Mind* (New York: Basic Books, 1960).

most publicized technique [2] that appears in the rather limited literature on creativity. In writing about this device, past authors have had in mind group situations; but the mental attitudes necessary for group participation also can help the individual to achieve greater flexibility. In the original form the brainstormers were responding to a problem by generating as many solutions as they could. For the time being they were not to criticize; in fact, they were to value "far out" ideas because of their potential for breaking the bonds of traditional approaches. Among the approved practices was "hitch-hiking," or the adding of one idea to another. A. Conrad Posz gives this summary of advice for brainstorming:

1. Quantity is desired.
2. Let yourself go; wild ideas are welcome.
3. Don't hold back an idea because you think someone may laugh at it.
4. Don't evaluate . . . don't judge.
5. In addition to contributing new ideas, try to improve on ideas presented by others.
6. Try to get into the spirit of [the] "free-wheeling," almost free association, type of creative activity in the session.[3]

Although interacting with others stimulates thought processes, the individual can apply the basic tenets of brainstorming when preparing alone for a speech or a conference. One possibility is to avoid structuring or outlining in the initial stages of consideration and to let one's mind roam freely. A practice that some individuals find helpful is that of jotting down on paper as many ideas as they can generate prior to evaluating or organizing.

THE INQUISITIVE MIND

Also conducive to inventive thought is inquisitiveness, a quality that abounds in some persons but must be developed in others. The one preschool child takes a toy apart to see how it works; another accepts the toy for what it is and uses it. The one child brushes his or her teeth without question; a second needs to know why this time-consuming act serves a valuable purpose. The one schoolchild can look at pictures of the Roman Forum without excitement; a second is eager to read about the civilization that produced such strange and magnificent structures. "Why did it happen?" "What are the causes?" "What is the theory behind this?" "How did the problem arise?" "What does someone else have to say?" "What is the solution?"

---

[2] See especially Alex F. Osborn, *Applied Imagination* (New York: Charles Scribner's Sons, 1957).
[3] A. Conrad Posz, "Brainstorming in an Educational Crisis," *Journal of Communication*, 8 (Autumn 1958), 129.

For some persons raising such questions seems to be natural; for them a challenging issue is a delight. Those who are less inquisitive, however, must motivate themselves to do research, to raise questions, and to think inventively. From one viewpoint their problem is one of arrested development; having slid through a number of years of school attendance without exercising their minds, they are ill equipped for dealing with any larger problems than those of eating, dating, and going to rock concerts.

For those persons whose natural processes of curiosity have been retarded, the closing sections of this chapter are of special importance. "Opportunities for Originality" is an examination of the aspects of a topic that offer opportunities for inventiveness and an exposition of the possibilities for creativeness in each. *"Topoi,"* whether ancient or modern, are lines of thought that the communicator can apply no matter what the topic.

OPPORTUNITIES FOR ORIGINALITY

The opportunities for inventive thought vary with the topic, and the speaker should exercise his or her mind in all promising directions. Three areas, however, are of special importance: possible causes, solutions and programs, and predicted outcomes.

POSSIBLE CAUSES

"Nothing happens without a cause," a maxim at least as old as Aristotle, suggests the potential fruitfulness of this first area for analytic thought. Nor is a search for causes a mere intellectual game; instead, finding the reason often is the best course for ascertaining a solution or at least a partial remedy. Traffic engineers some years ago, for example, were puzzled by the large number of serious auto accidents at an approach to a tunnel. As soon as they discovered that the sun at a particular hour created a deceptive mirage, they were well on their way to devising remedial measures.

Aspects of Causation

The cause in the preceding example was the mirage, and the effect was the accident. In many instances causation is not so simple and straightforward. In fact, further analysis of even this seemingly obvious example reveals counteracting factors and contributory causes. Since many drivers approached the tunnel without having fatal accidents, the initial explanation was incomplete. To uncover the related elements and to create a fully accurate analysis would have required the accumulation and the scrutiny of a large body of data.

Causes often are *multiple*. A tennis player whose serves go into the net may be swinging the racket too fast or tossing the ball too low or too far forward. Any one of these errors or any combination of them can produce the observed result. In more complex areas, such as juvenile crime, the possible causes again are many—poverty, boredom, revolt against authority, watching violent shows on television, broken homes, sibling rivalry, need for money to support a dope habit, and still others. Hardly any two sociology books give the same lists. A practical inference to draw from multiplicity as a quality of causation is that the investigator never should assume that a list of causes is complete. Thus, the student speaker, no matter how impressive a printed list, should not be satisfied but should use his or her own mind in the search for reasons previously overlooked.

Other opportunities for inventive thought arise because in a given situation causes may be *independent, joint, contributory,* and/or *sequential.* In the first of these four possibilities, most clearly evident in physical events, each factor is sufficient by itself to produce the effect. In other circumstances, as in certain chemical reactions, causation must be *joint,* for the result occurs only if two or more forces appear together. In still other instances causes are *contributory*—that is, the event can occur without them, but their presence either increases the probability or intensifies the result. Finally, causes may be *sequential* or in a chain relationship with the one triggering an effect that in turn produces a further happening: ". . . for want of a nail the shoe was lost; for want of a shoe the horse was lost; and for want of a horse the rider was lost." [4]

Further adding to the richness of opportunity is the great variation in simplicity and directness. At one extreme are the *immediate* or *precipitating* causes, such as the desire for equipment to go fishing, the urgings of a friend, and the sight of a seemingly unwatched rod and reel. These causes, however, do not result in attempted theft when most children walk by an open garage door. Essential also to the result are the *underlying* causes, such as poor parental supervision and inadequate educational guidance.

Since both precipitating and underlying causes are important to understanding events as diverse as unwanted pregnancy and an unfavorable balance of trade, the analyst needs to search for both. The immediate cause of the march on City Hall in one municipality was a rumor that a white policeman had beaten up a black prisoner, but for a real understanding of the confrontation the analyst needed to study the recent history of that particular ghetto community and even the effects of nationwide television coverage of similar protests elsewhere.

Finally, *counteracting* forces sometimes invalidate predictions of cause/effect sequences. Both immediate and underlying causes, for example, may make it likely that one pupil will throw an eraser at a class-

---

[4] Benjamin Franklin, *Maxims Prefixed to Poor Richard's Almanac,* as cited in John Bartlett, comp., *Familiar Quotations,* ed. Emily M. Beck (Boston: Little, Brown and Co., 1968), p. 422. The statement also is credited to George Herbert.

mate, but the appearance of the principal may lead to outwardly peaceful behavior. Similarly in law enforcement, where the presence of a police officer is a deterrent, and in medicine, where the right drug prevents the progression of disease, counteracting factors play significant roles in causation.

Thus, many aspects are important if the student is to understand published analyses and make his or her own assessment intelligent and thorough. The list that follows concludes this section by noting still further considerations:

Is the alleged cause sufficient to produce the observed effect?

Did the alleged cause precede the event?

Were there any factors—perhaps matters of time and place—that made a connection between the alleged cause and the effect impossible?

If the alleged cause is absent, does the effect ever occur?

If the alleged cause is present, does the effect invariably happen?

If the alleged cause is strengthened or intensified, does the effect vary accordingly?

Further materials on causation are available in philosophy and in logic. These analyses are complex and voluminous, but rewarding to the communicator who studies them. Even the present simplified treatment, however, should be helpful to the beginner in finding areas for critical thought.

The Student and Research Materials

In preparation for a speech, a discussion, or a conference, the materials that the student reads largely determine how he or she analyzes the topic or problem. The following are possible relationships between one's own position on causes and those that one finds through research.

1. The communicator may accept without revision the analysis given in a source. Doing so has the advantage of adding authoritativeness to the ideas that one presents, and at times this full acceptance of another's views is the best course to follow. Such an unaltered adoption, however, should occur only after a stringent examination of the situation and only from the conviction that no improvement on the published set of causes is possible.

2. One may take a single written analysis of causes as the basis for one's own list, but make modifications. This practice largely preserves the authoritativeness of citing a respected source, and it has the further advantage of letting the audience know that one has made one's own examination. The most common modifications are the additions of further causes, the deletions of items deemed erroneous or unimportant, and the revisions of certain details. This second course is preferable to the first for several

reasons; the most important of these is the desirability of adapting to the audience and to time limitations.

3. One may combine analyses from two or more sources either with or without further revisions of one's own. In this instance the speaker should cite all sources, and it may be advantageous to explain the reasons for relying on several. Perhaps a single work is essentially sound, but is incomplete; possibly one reference deals with immediate causes and the other with those in the background.

4. One may cite a printed analysis, but go beyond it to deeper considerations. This stance says in effect, "Author So-and-So's book is correct as far as it goes, but it does not go beyond the obvious to the really basic problem." One cause for crime, for example, is the need for money to support a drug habit, but the further question is "Why did this individual take up drugs?"

5. One may utilize the written material, but adapt its general view of the topic to one's own special purpose. The source, for example, may give an analysis of the causes of poverty nationwide, whereas the speaker's topic may be "The Causes for Poverty in the Fifth Ward of Houston." Although some items on the general list are likely to be applicable to the speech, local circumstances often suggest needed modifications, deletions, and additions.

6. One may develop one's own set of causes. Research materials sometimes do not include sections on causation, and in other instances the speaker may decide that he or she can construct a clear, concise list that is superior to anything in the sources. Such a highly original section of a speech can be impressive, but the outcome of this sixth approach, as is true of the other five, depends both on the astuteness of the list of causes and on the cogency of the explanation.

Summary

In summary, strong work in causal analysis includes applications of these guidelines: (1) an intelligent adaptation to the circumstances of such aspects of causation as multiplicity, independence, jointness, contributiveness, sequence, immediacy, inwardness, and even counteraction; (2) a careful citing of all sources used; (3) a clear explanation of the reasons for any doubtful elements and especially for omissions, additions, and modifications of authoritative lists; (4) an adjustment in the final speech to time limits and to the audience's interests and needs. These four items of advice are applicable regardless of whether the entire speech is on causes—one means of limiting a topic—or whether causation is only a section of the whole.

SOLUTIONS AND PROGRAMS

Similarly, a speech may either include solutions as a section of the whole or deal exclusively with proposed remedial measures. Whichever the selection, the communicator has a number of options that present opportunities for inventiveness. What course should one recommend? Should one suggest a single possibility or several; and if several, should one weigh the advantages and the disadvantages of each? Should one formulate a program consisting of a series of proposals? Should one give solutions a large or a small amount of time? In respect to this final question, the best answer depends on the circumstances, including the probable attitude of the audience toward the plan to be advanced. The natural reaction of a communicator, according to one study, is to reduce the time given to the solution if he or she senses opposition to it.[5] Proposals are more likely to be controversial than are descriptions of a bad situation; nevertheless, messages that offer nothing constructive are dissatisfying, and responsible discourse strikes a balance between spineless acquiescence in the view of an audience and unadapted advocacy of a position so extreme that persuasion is unlikely. The proper course, this writer believes, is to support measures that the speaker thinks will be beneficial but to limit requests for change to degrees that seem attainable (see Chapter 6).

In inventing solutions and programs, the speaker can apply much of the advice given earlier in the chapter. As with causes, he or she may (1) accept without revision the solutions printed in a single place, (2) rely on one list but make modifications, (3) combine proposals from two or more sources, (4) cite an authority but analyze further, (5) adapt a program to the specific topic or situation, or (6) develop original solutions.

PREDICTED OUTCOMES

One step beyond the offering of a program is the prediction of effects, a particularly fruitful area for originality because so few sources attempt to visualize the outcome. Moreover, working out the probable results is not necessarily an exercise in make-believe; rather, as one speaker said, "Let's be hardheaded and practical about what would happen if this solution were put into operation. Theories can suggest results, but our interest now is not in theories but in operational outcomes." After such a beginning the speaker should develop the predictions step by step, taking time in each instance to show the plausibility of the conjecture. Such a section during speech preparation or in the speech itself is most often an exercise in cause-to-effect reasoning, either a single step or a chain. "If the United States withdrew its troops from South Korea," said one speaker, "the first

---

[5] Michael D. Hazen and Sara B. Kiesler, "Communication Strategies Affected by Audience Opposition, Feedback, and Persuasibility," *Speech Monographs*, 42 (March 1975), 56–68.

consequence would be . . .."; and he proceeded to explain why the result would be probable. "Then, given this change," he continued, "the communist Chinese . . ."

Challenging to the speaker and refreshing to the audience, predictions often are the most inventive and the most attention-holding parts of a presentation. The quality of the material depends on the speaker's grasp of the topic and on the ability to develop cogent explanations.

SUMMARY

The opportunities for originality in speech preparation, therefore, are numerous. Possible causes, solutions and programs, and predicted outcomes are three especially fruitful areas for the exercise of originality. The full, the open, and the inquisitive mind, however, should overlook no possibility.

ANCIENT AND MODERN *TOPOI*

Susanne K. Langer in one of the most famous books of this century made this observation on creativity: "The limits of thought are not so much set from outside by the fullness or poverty of experiences that meet the mind, as from within, by the power of conception, the wealth of formulative notions with which the mind meets experience."[6] If she is correct, this final section of the chapter, which is on patterns of thought or lines of reasoning, is even more important than are the preceding pages.

ANCIENT *TOPOI*

The best-known and fullest analysis of *Topoi*, which are possible lines of thought, is that of Aristotle, who regarded them as important tools for the person who was preparing a speech. In the *Rhetoric*, book ii, chapter 23, he describes and illustrates twenty-eight argumentative lines, eighteen of which are still useful:

1. Consider the opposite of the point in question. If the proposal is greater leniency for juvenile criminals, develop an argument by examining what would happen if punishment was more severe.

2. Argue *a fortiori* that if an event occurred under unfavorable circumstances, it would be even more likely to happen if the situation were advantageous. If Big City has been successful with a new mass transit authority in a terrain that made construction costs expensive, then Hometown

---

[6] Susanne K. Langer, *Philosophy in a New Key* (New York: The New American Library, 1951), p. 19.

with its favorable geography is even more likely to do well if it installs a comparable system.

3. Apply against the other speaker the line of argument that he or she has used against you. Thus, if your opponent says that your experience as an insurance agent does not qualify you for the city council, allege that his or her background, whatever it is, is poor training to be an alderman.

4. Develop your topic by defining relevant terms and by then expanding on the definitions. If the purpose, for example, is to support "national health insurance," define each of the three words and show how the features related to each would be advantageous.

5. Divide the topic into its logical divisions, and consider each separately. In the *residue argument,* which is a special form of this *topos,* the progression is (a) to identify each possible solution and (b) to show that all are undesirable except the one that you favor.

6. Use induction. Collect and examine all possible instances, and then develop the appropriate generalization.

7. Utilize a widely held opinion that is on the precise topic or on one like it. Such an opinion is especially forceful, Aristotle points out, if everyone has agreed; or if the wisest and best have agreed; or if the actual judges of the present question have expressed the view.[7]

8. Pose a dilemma. Analyze the situation so that there are only two possibilities, both of which are bad. Aristotle gives this example to show that in many instances dilemmas can be reversed. The priestess, he says, enjoined her son not to take to public speaking because if he were to say what was right men would hate him and if he were to say what was wrong the gods would hate him. The reply, states Aristotle, is that the son should take up oratory because if he says what is right the gods will love him and if he says what is wrong men will be pleased.[8]

9. Look beneath the surface for the true views of a person or a group; these may differ from those expressed. "I, too, heard Matthews say that our president has done a fine job, but is that the true opinion? Let us look at the details of some of Matthews' speeches, and let us read between the lines."

10. Test a line of thought or a principle by applying it to diverse or expanded circumstances. In many situations this test will show an allegation to be ridiculous. "It has been argued," said one speaker, "that we should

---

[7] Aristotle *Rhetoric* ii.23.1398^{b}20–23.
[8] *Ibid.,* 1399^{a}21–25.

eliminate our tariff on wine because doing so would build good will with France and other wine exporters. If this argument is sound, then why not eliminate all tariffs and make ourselves popular with everybody?"

11. Examine the possibility that an authority has not always taken the same position on an issue.

12. Look for real motives that may differ from those that are apparent. Sometimes an analysis that shows the plausibility of previously unsuspected motives will reduce the credibility of an opponent or will place an event in a new light.

13. Consider inducements and deterrents, the motives people have for doing or avoiding the actions in question.

14. Note any contrasts or contradictions in the materials that you obtain through research.

15. Show that alleged "facts" are less certain than they appear to be. A magazine article reported in 1975 that all evidence of the Santa Barbara oil spill had disappeared, but letters to the editor disputed the claim and stated that pollution remained. Just because something is in print is no guarantee of its accuracy. The individual should consider the possibility that the first information that he or she receives may be incomplete, misleading, and even deliberately biased.

16. Argue that an effect regularly accompanies a cause. Citing examples often convinces people that the introduction of a causal factor into a new situation will produce the same effect as in previous analogous situations. "Alpha City cut bus fares by ten cents, and ridership increased 15 percent. Betatown reduced fares in non-rush hours, and revenues increased. Gamma Village lowered fares last summer, and the transit company now is making a profit. The conclusion must be that decreased charges result in greater patronage."

17. Consider the possibility that a participant in an event could have taken a wiser course than the one that he or she did follow. Speculation on what would have happened if the choice had been different may suggest ideas applicable to the present topic.

18. Examine a contemplated action for its consistency with a past event. Analyze the differences, and develop an argument based on the probable effects of these discrepancies.

The usefulness of the preceding list, despite the condensation and modernization, is much the same today as in Aristotle's time. No matter what the topic, certain lines of argument are possibilities. Some will work well on one occasion; others at another time. Some speakers find that certain *topoi* fit their own particular habits of thought, whereas others find different *topoi* more to their liking. Whatever these specific differences, the objective is to increase the inventional resources—the number of possible ways of approaching the problem of composing a set of arguments.

MODERN *TOPOI*

Through the twenty-two centuries since Aristotle, the prominence of *topoi* in treatments of invention has varied. Even though the word itself has not appeared in many books on speechmaking, the topical approach has always been to some degree inescapable. When a debate textbook advises students to think about inherency, significance, and whether the affirmative plan will produce the alleged advantage, it is suggesting general lines of thought.

Recent years have brought a renewed interest in *topoi*, and several authors have set forth their own systems.[9] Support for the use of *topoi* includes quantitative studies showing that questions or cues to "start" the mind increase productivity. Nelson found this increase to occur in recalling items of information,[10] and Infante obtained similar results in a study of the discovery of arguments.[11]

These benefits from using *topoi* do not mean, however, that they are a substitute for other approaches to invention. They become useful only when communicators know their subjects well and when their minds are flexible and inquisitive. General *topoi*, moreover, are not in conflict with the possible approaches presented to creativity on causes, solutions, and outcomes; rather they are means for increasing the richness of thought in respect to each. The parts of this chapter, in short, are complementary—the qualities of the mind, the places for exercising originality, and the lines of thought are diverse approaches to the single goal of increasing inventiveness.

Three lines of reasoning have been especially prominent in discussions of creativity—the application of the results of one situation to a second set of circumstances, the drawing of correlations among facts or events, and the forming of imaginative analogies.

---

[9] Among the more prominent of these are the following: John F. Wilson and Carroll C. Arnold, *Public Speaking as a Liberal Art* (Boston: Allyn & Bacon, 1974), pp. 78–81; Chaim Perelman and L. Olbrechts-Tyteca, *The New Rhetoric*, trans. John Wilkinson and Purcell Weaver (Notre Dame, Ind.: University of Notre Dame Press, 1969), pp. 85–95; and Karl R. Wallace, "*Topoi* and the Problem of Invention," *Quarterly Journal of Speech*, 38 (December 1972), 393–394.
[10] William F. Nelson, "Topoi: Functional in Human Recall," *Speech Monographs*, 37 (June 1970), 121–126.
[11] Dominic A. Infante, "The Influence of a Topical System on the Discovery of Arguments," *Speech Monographs*, 38 (June 1971), 125–128.

Applications

Of these three related opportunities for creativity, the least demanding intellectually, but not necessarily the least useful, is the application of historical knowledge to present conditions. A drug problem among young people is worrisome here in Arbor City; a "Youth-Faces-Youth" program in Rapidstown has had good results, so perhaps it would be beneficial here. A decrease in the Federal Reserve interest rate stimulated the economy when tried in the past; a similar step might have the same effects if tried again. A policy of appeasement did not stop Hitler; today's diplomats should not make the same mistake. Such reasoning is not always sound, and events do not always repeat themselves; but carrying over a former solution to the present difficulty is always a possibility worth considering.

Problems nevertheless arise in the use of applications as an approach to creativity. The first of these is the location of the relevant example. If the drug program in Rapidstown, for example, is new and little publicized, finding out about it requires both good luck and diligent research. The more that one reads, of course, the more likely one is to come across useful instances; but one can increase the likelihood of finding a useful example through such questions as "Has this problem ever arisen before?" and "If so, what was done about it, and how successful were the attempted solutions?"

The second problem, next to finding a relevant item, is determining the extent to which a solution somewhere else seems likely to fit the present circumstances. How much alike are Rapidstown and Arbor City, and to what extent is the present recession like the one that was responsive to the reduction in interest rates? Perhaps the success in Rapidstown was largely because of the charismatic personality of a talented young priest who was the moving force behind the program. If so, the likelihood of similar success in another city is questionable.

Correlations

Similar pitfalls arise in drawing correlations; this type of creative thought, nevertheless, is worth attempting. A familiar example of this type of reasoning is the detective story. Whereas the assistant in the story, as well as the reader or the listener, finds the montage of clues bewildering, the detective perceives the relationships correctly—the missing file folder, the man who had access to the locker, the bullets of a different caliber, the lost valise, and the midnight telephone call.

Less spectacular but equally challenging is the perception of previously unnoticed correlations among the available facts on world trade, inflation, academic dropouts, street fighting, or almost any other social or economic problem. *Unnoticed* is the key word in the preceding sentence, for in most instances certain relationships—though perhaps they should be challenged—are generally assumed; creativity is the act of going beyond these correlations that are common currency to new perceptions about the items. As a minimum advantage, these new judgments stimulate interest; and if correct, they lead to solutions previously unformulated. The foundation of many discoveries in astronomy, for example, has been the hypothesizing of a force never before suspected; similarly, advances in some fields of medicine await the genius who can relate correctly certain groups of facts.

"Do any of these facts or events fit together?" is the self-question that the student-researcher-creative thinker-speaker must ask.

Analogies

"What new idea does that fact or relationship suggest?" becomes the question as the communicator changes his or her focus to the creation of analogies—to the striking of the intellectual spark that leaps from an established fact or firm concept to something new.

Unlike the form of inventiveness described as "applications," the characteristic leap in analogy, as the term is used here, is from one field to another. An observer discovers an efficient method of toasting three slices of bread in a two-slot toaster and soon after devises a comparable laborsaving change in office routine. A second person watches squirrels playing in a tree, and the idea for a new children's game with dice and counters follows. A clinical psychologist watches the metering device that controls access to an expressway and begins to formulate a new technique for treating the hyperactive. How one responds to a fiercely slicing serve in tennis may suggest the best way to handle a problem in business, and the value of the relief pitcher in baseball may lead to revisions in assigning personnel to clients in a counseling agency. The sight of a leaf blowing in the air, according to one story, led to the idea of attaching a sail to a boat, and "Men first learned to create shelters for themselves," the ancient Vitruvius believed, "in imitation of the nests and building of swallows out of mud and wattle."[12]

As speakers work through their speech topics, they should keep their minds open to possible insights from every source. At least in theory every course that they are taking, every hobby that they have, and every human happening that they observe has the potential for inspiring ideas on their topics that never occurred to anyone previously. No prescriptive rules for creating through analogies are possible; the individual can only have a willingness to think imaginatively, a high sensitivity to the surroundings, and a great persistence in following through if fortunate enough to have the beginning of a new idea. One other thought is worth expressing: The right kind of coworker can be helpful—one who also is flexible and willing to extend a line of thinking, no matter how improbable it may at first seem.

---

[12] As cited in Nelson W. Aldrich, "Nostalgia and Shelter," *Harper's*, 250 (April 1975), 112.

Together, two or more persons can be mutually stimulating, and each can add details as the original idea evolves into a form that is worthy of sober testing.

CONCLUSION

Chapter 3 is part of a unit. Together with Chapters 2 and 4 it provides instruction for meeting the first test of responsible speaking—having something to say that is worth hearing. Passing this test requires research on almost every topic significant enough to warrant discussion, and only those who know their subjects should presume to take the time of listeners. Beyond knowledge are two other essential elements in discussion, public address, and all other forms of communication—the dynamics of the relations between or among participants and rhetorical techniques that increase clarity and effectiveness.

PROBLEMS AND EXERCISES

1. Form a circle with four or five of your classmates. Begin by having one member make a statement on "Inventive Thought: Its Nature and Its Encouragement." The next person to the left then should make a statement that is related to the first but adds something to it. The individuals should continue until someone is unable to make an addition. That person then should start a new line of thought by making an assertion on some other aspect of the topic.

2. Repeat the first exercise, but with a different group. Use "Causation" as the subject.

3. Using the references or other sources, read further on "brain-storming." Form a discussion group in class to make a list of its main principles and to appraise its values and weaknesses.

4. With a group of five or six classmates, hold a brainstorming session on a topic that is well known to all of you. Possibilities are "Better Parking on Campus" or "Solutions to the Traffic Problems in the City."

5. Review the six points under "The Student and Research Materials." Perhaps remaining seated, talk informally on which of these six seems the best one for you to use in developing a causal analysis for your own topic.

6. Repeat Exercise 5 but talk about the six points in reference to how you plan to handle solutions and programs.

7. Using the topic for your next major speech as the basis, deliver a three- to five-minute talk on one or more of the following subjects:

    Causes of the Problem
    Solutions to the Problem

Predictions on the Outcome If the Solution Were Tried
Applications, Correlations, and Analogies
Possibilities for Using *Topoi*

REFERENCES

Guilford, J. P. "Creativity: Yesterday, Today, Tomorrow," *Journal of Creative Behavior*, 1 (Winter 1967), 3–14.

Haefele, John W. *Creativity and Innovation*. New York: Reinhold, 1962.

Infante, Dominic A. "The Influence of a Topical System on the Discovery of Arguments," *Speech Monographs*, 38 (June 1971), 125–128.

Mooney, Ross L., and Taher A. Razik, eds. *Explorations in Creativity*. New York: Harper & Row, 1967.

Nelson, William F. "Topoi: Functional in Human Recall," *Speech Monographs*, 37 (June 1970), 121–126.

Osborn, Alex F. *Applied Imagination*. New York: Charles Scribner's Sons, 1957.

Parnes, Sidney J., and Harold F. Harding, eds. *A Source Book for Creative Thinking*. New York: Charles Scribner's Sons, 1962.

Petelle, John L., and Richard Maybee. "Items of Information Retrieved as a Function of Cue System and Topical Area," *Central States Speech Journal*, 25 (Fall 1974), 190–197.

Wallace, Karl R. "*Topoi* and the Problem of Invention," *Quarterly Journal of Speech*, 58 (December 1972), 387–395.

4
MATERIALS: THE SUBSTANCE OF COMMUNICATION

After studying this chapter the reader should be able to do the following:

List eight kinds of material

Cite briefly two examples, two statistics, and two quotations suitable for his or her next major speech

Give an example of a dramatized statistic

Give examples for each of the qualities that enhance interest

Cite three items that might heighten interest in a speech that he or she is preparing

Make three statements, favorable or critical, about the attention-holding materials in a speech that he or she hears

"Very well," Debra said, partly to herself and partly to her classmate, "I've found a topic, I've gone to the library, and I've done some hard thinking. What's next?" She paused and then continued, "And I guess that I've come to agree with our professor that in communication having something worth saying is more important than anything else."

"Yes, the message, he called it," Sandy added. "The message is the beginning of meaningful communication. But the message isn't just one big something. It's a lot of things, all put together. It's like a house, which is built of bricks and wood panels and shingles and the like."

And both Sandy and Debra are right. The content of any conversation, discussion, or speech consists of materials; its worth depends on their quality—their significance, pertinence, and interest. For competence in communication, therefore, the student needs (1) to understand the attributes and the limitations of the major kinds of material and (2) to know what to consider in deciding which items to use.

KINDS OF MATERIAL

Debra and Sandy now are in class. "What is meant by *speech material*, and what kinds are there?" the professor asks.

"Examples," one student volunteers. "Statistics," calls out someone else. And after a pause a third conscientious participant suggests, "Funny stories." This start is not especially promising, but the professor persists. By asking some leading questions and volunteering some entries of his own, he finally assembled on the blackboard the following list:

Examples	Personal experiences
Statistics	Humorous incidents
Dramatizations of statistics	Historic events
Quotations from authorities	Happenings in literature
Comparisons	Biblical stories and parables
Contrasts	Fables, myths, and folk tales
Figurative analogies	References to characters in comic strips or on television programs
Hypothetical examples	
Examples from campus life	References to personalities in athletics, entertainment, or politics
Invented dialogue	
Human interest stories	References to popular songs or movies
Familiar sayings	Lines from poetry

What is the point of the preceding story? Foremost, many kinds of material are available to the communicator. Although some types—three of which deserve detailed description—are more common than others, all are resources that the inventive person sometimes uses. A single speech, for example, may begin with a relevant personal story, develop the first main point through statistics and a summarizing quotation, continue with examples and analogies supporting the second main point, relate the thesis to the audience through a human-interest story and a hypothetical example, and close by showing that an old saying applies to the present situation.

EXAMPLES AS A TYPE OF MATERIAL

The puzzled request, "Give me a 'for instance,' " is one type of evidence for the importance of the example as a means of clarification. Probably no other device is as common; the demands on the teller are relatively simple. Natural, straightforward, unadorned exposition is suitable. The most serious problems are finding an illustration that fits the content and that falls within the realm of the listeners' prior experiences. Although farmers, to use an example, can understand many kinds of illustrations, they find those pertaining to agriculture especially interesting and illuminating.

As formal proof, examples rarely are numerous enough to meet the requirements of the logician, but they often are sufficient to persuade listeners. The more examples, in theory, the stronger the effect; but after three or four, still others add but little. Besides the number of examples, typicality, believability, and relevance to the point under consideration are major factors that determine the degree of influence. In instances speakers can assume that listeners will accept their offerings, but at times they need to cite sources for greater authoritativeness or believability and to explain why the chosen illustrations are fair or typical representatives of all possible illustrations.

Contrary examples are a special problem. If they are as numerous and as strong as those favoring the argument, then both ethics and good sense dictate that the speaker abandon the contention. If they are few, then the speaker should reduce possible damage to the case by acknowledging their existence and arguing that they are exceptions.

But where does one find examples? Research is a possibility, and sometimes the communicator hunts for a report on a city that has a publicly owned electric utility or on a citizen review board that is monitoring police. More commonly, however, examples come from the memories of what one has read, observed, and done. Thus, in one round of classroom speeches the students used examples drawn from these sources: a recent movie; the story in a popular ballad; a well-known cartoon strip; the Olympics; a television news report; a column on advice to the lovelorn; the Bible; the most recent production of the drama department; a biography of Lincoln; a trip to Alaska; a tour of a state hospital; the speaker's childhood; and experiences while working. Ordinarily, useful instances come to mind spontaneously; but if they do not, the communicator can jog his or her memory by asking such questions as these: Did I ever have such an experience? Have I seen such an event? Has any character in literature faced such a problem? Has anything of this sort happened in history?

The outcome of this self-questioning may be a short reference—"An example of this is the Democratic convention of 1924"—or it may be a full narrative. If the latter, the communicator should employ the arts of the storyteller. He or she should capitalize on elements of suspense and conflict, establish characters with whom listeners can identify, arouse curiosity and concern over the outcome, and employ vivid language and dialogue.

STATISTICS

Unlike examples, statistics rarely come from memory. At best one may recall having seen certain figures in a particular book, pamphlet, or magazine; but usually one must go to such sources as the *Statistical Abstract of the United States, The World Almanac, Whitaker's Almanack,* and the annual supplements of the major encyclopedias.

Not all statistical data are equally respected, and both speakers and listeners should be discriminating. In general, people believe statistics from governmental agencies, university research groups, and major nonprofit foundations. Data from organizations with known biases, such as the American Petroleum Institute, call for caution, but the questionable part of a pamphlet or an article is likely to be the interpretation of data rather than the figures themselves. Statistics rarely are outright lies, but biased writers can give them deceptive but plausible twists.

In judging statistics, besides taking a hard look at the source, one should apply the following tests:

1. Are the statistics recent? Speakers and listeners should be on guard if the date is omitted.

2. Do the statistics cover enough time and territory to be reliable? Crime figures for one week compared with those for a like period a year earlier are less meaningful than those for a month or an entire year. Similarly, a study of the drug habits of thirty freshmen at Stillwater College has less significance than one covering students nationwide. Both senders and receivers should discount data unless the source gives the date of the study, the area covered, and the number of subjects.

3. Is the statistic an accurate indicator of what it supposedly measures? The number of points that a basketball player scores does not necessarily indicate the player's value to the team, nor does a grade point average always measure aptitude for graduate study or for performing well in a particular position. In less familiar areas than sports and grades, misinterpretations are even more likely. Does the number of planes indicate the strength of an air force, and is the size of a corporation related to the quality of its product?

4. If the statistics are a report on a sample, how justifiable is a generalization about the population? Subquestions to ask are "How large was the sample?" "How was it drawn?" and "To what extent was it representative of the whole?" Well-managed organizations, including the major institutes of public opinion research, use refined sampling techniques that produce useful data, but reports from little-known sources warrant skepticism.

5. *If the figures make comparisons, are the reporting procedures and the definitions of units always the same?* Figures on crime, by general agreement, are difficult to compare. *Felony* and *misdemeanor* differ in definition from state to state, and diligence in reporting varies from city to city and from year to year. If the statistics show more cases of armed robbery in Big City than in Metropolis, one cannot be sure whether crime is more prevalent in Big City or whether its police are more efficient in investigating offenses and keeping records.

6. *Are the reported differences significant?* Since minor variations often are attributable to chance, a person should be suspicious when a prejudiced source draws a conclusion based on a small difference. One cigarette manufacturer, for example, used the results of laboratory tests to claim that its product was the lowest in tars and nicotine when the figures for several brands were almost equal. One cigarette, of course, was certain to be lowest; but a rerun of the test probably would have changed the rank order.

7. *If an average, is the figure a meaningful estimate for the group?* One extreme case—one millionaire, for example, in a group of alumni—can make an average a misleading measure of the condition of most members.

8. *If a percentage, is the base a source of distortion?* Whereas an increase in annual income from five hundred dollars to one thousand dollars is 100 percent, a change from five thousand dollars to six thousand dollars is only 20 percent. Despite the impression given by the percentages, the extremely poor persons have lost ground in relation to those just above the poverty line.

The preceding tests, which are important to both sender and receiver, suggest that the communicator should view any statistic thoughtfully, even cautiously. This type of material, nevertheless, is valuable in giving an overall picture of a situation and in adding persuasiveness to a message from the platform or to a contribution in a discussion or a conference.

Several devices increase the interest and the impact of statistics. The sender should know about these in order to strengthen the message, and the receiver should be aware of them to guard against being overly impressed. First, the speaker can *personalize* or *dramatize*. "If this class has average luck, only two of the twenty of you will be mugged on a public street in the next year." "If the silt deposited at the bottom of this lake each year were put into boxcars, the train would reach from Texarkana to Little Rock." Second, the speaker can *minimize* through simple arithmetic. "A four-hundred-thousand-dollar bond issue sounds like a lot of money, but over a ten-year period it's only one dollar per resident per year or two cents per week." Third, the speaker can *maximize*. "The senator has said that the sum for defense is only 30 percent of the budget, but we must realize that the total is $110 billion." Fourth, the speaker can increase impressiveness by *cumulating* data. The following is an attempt to show the efficiency of the Bell system in responding to a major fire: "In three weeks 6,000 tons of debris were cleared, 66 miles of cable replaced, nearly 3,000 tons of equipment and material shipped in and installed—and most important—170,000 telephones were restored to service."[1] Fifth, the speaker can *compare* a place or an object that is remote from the audience with something that is close to them:

Exxon's U.S. tankers reduced fuel consumption by 5.5 million gallons last year, or enough to fuel 5700 average-sized farm tractors for one year; . . . Exxon's Houston office has reduced its annual electric consumption by 7.3 million kilowatt-hours, or enough to provide electricity for 575 average-sized homes for one year; . . . [and] by the end of this year, Exxon expects to cut the energy its U.S. refineries use by 15%. This will save about 252 million gallons of oil, or enough to produce electricity to run New York City for one month.[2]

QUOTATIONS

Either long or short, sometimes embellishing and at other times serving as proof, quotations vary enormously in character and in function. Those that embellish, of course, should be worded with a distinctiveness that makes them pointed, pleasing, and easy to remember.

Those whose intended function is proof, such as examples and statistics, need to meet numerous tests. The most important are these:

1. Is the quotation consistent with other opinions and other types of information?

2. Is the statement consistent with the facts that it reports or interprets?

3. Is the author in a position to know the facts, and is he or she an expert on the topic?

4. Is the source biased?

5. Is the source reluctant—that is, is the statement the opposite of the position that seemingly would promote the author's interests?

6. Is the statement consistent with the entire book or article from which it is taken?

---

[1] Pacific Northwest Bell, "June 1975 Dividend Statement to Shareholders," n.p.
[2] "Saving Energy," *Harper's*, 250 (May 1975), 29. "Saving Energy" is a paid advertisement.

7. Is the author highly regarded? Especially, will the listeners regard the source as credible?

8. Does the opinion appear in a respected book, periodical, or document?

9. Is the citation accurate? If words have been deleted (customarily indicated by a series of three or four dots), has the meaning been distorted?

In introducing quotations speakers have two tasks. First, they must point out the relation between the quotation and the contention that it supports. Next, they need to state the qualifications of the authority: "Mr. Russell Hodgin, who is Research Professor of History at Harvard University"; "Dr. Louise Blake, who is reporting as executive secretary of the federal commission that investigated the problem of crime in the streets."

OTHER KINDS OF MATERIAL

No detailed discussion of the other types of material seems necessary, but illustrations may stimulate thought.

Comparisons "When we examine what inflation has done to Great Britain, we can predict its probable effects in this country." "A side effect of the drug is that you feel as if you were catching a cold."

Figurative Analogies (A literal analogy compares two instances of the same class and is a means of logical proof, but a figurative analogy involves two members of different classes and serves only as a device for clarity and emphasis.) "Just as a hammer is only as useful as the carpenter who wields it, so too is a training session only as useful as the trainer who conducts it."[3]

Historic Events "War can serve useful purposes. When Alexander of Macedonia made his expedition through the Middle East, he collected botanic samples that he sent back to Aristotle for study."

Happenings in Literature "Resourcefulness can provide a solution to almost any problem. In Mark Twain's novel *A Connecticut Yankee in King Arthur's Court* the central character was to be executed unless he could convince his captors that he was a wizard with supernatural powers. By utilizing his knowledge of a noonday eclipse, the Yankee gained freedom and safety."

---

[3] Lyle Sussman, "Communication Training for Ad-hocracy," *Speech Teacher*, 24 (November 1975), 335–342.

Invented Dialogue "Let's imagine that you, Mr. Average Citizen, were conversing with the President about the state of the economy. It might go something like this:

"*Mr. Average Citizen:* 'You say that everything is just fine. But what about unemployment?'

"*President:* 'Well, it's around 8 percent, which some people say is the highest in twenty years. But, then, we have to expect a little unemployment if we're going to fight inflation.'

"*Mr. Average Citizen:* 'Well, what about inflation?'

"*President:* 'We're just fine there, too. It's about 12 percent per year, which some people think is high, but we need to realize that it's higher than that in some countries.'

"*Mr. Average Citizen:* 'And what about construction?'

"*President:* 'Housing starts, I understand, are about 50 percent of what they were two years ago. But everything is just fine.'

"And that's about the way the conversation would go. We are in the worst mess in forty years, but our president keeps saying, 'Everything is just fine.' "

Familiar Sayings "One of the great truths that most parents ignore in rearing today's children is the saying, 'All play and no work makes Jack a dull jerk.' "

Lines from Poetry "In concluding I turn to the poetry of Henry Wadsworth Longfellow, whose observations are as true for today's graduating class as they were in his own time:

'The heights by great men reached and kept
   Were not attained by sudden flight,
But they, while their companions slept,
   Were toiling upward in the night.' "[4]

SELECTION OF MATERIALS

"I have got plenty of facts but do not know how to use them," a nineteenth-century British statesman and orator confided in a letter to his wife.[5] In the intervening century almost every communicator, whether a famous person or an ordinary citizen, has had similar feelings. Sadly, the accumulation of

---

[4] Henry Wadsworth Longfellow, "The Ladder of St. Augustine," as cited in John Bartlett, comp., *Familiar Quotations*, ed. Emily M. Beck (Boston: Little, Brown and Co., 1968), p. 623.
[5] John Bright, June 26, 1867, Bright MS, University College of London Library.

materials is not the speech; the communicator still must choose, distribute, and apportion according to purpose and taste.

The process of selection plays a role in communication too significant for a quick, simplistic treatment. Just as one can learn more about an engine, an automobile, a suit of clothes, or a piece of statuary by examining it from several viewpoints, so can one gain competence in choosing material by a many-sided approach. In deciding between or among available items, the communicator can consider with profit these questions:

What purpose(s) should my material serve?

To what extent do the respective items possess qualities that generally are desirable?

How well adapted are the items to the listeners?

How strong are the materials in gaining and holding interest?

PURPOSES OF MATERIAL

Whatever the situation—a rap session, an interview, a business conference, a public address—a message has a purpose, and essential to attaining the overall objective are the materials, each making its own distinctive contribution. One useful approach in deciding which items to use and where to put them is through a consideration of seven purposes.

1. To clarify. Generalities and abstractions mean little to most listeners unless the speaker amplifies through comparisons, examples, and other devices. Amplification, also, is important as a means of giving the receiver time to dwell on the point that he or she is hearing. The following is an example. The speaker says, "One effect of the new law is to make the prosecution of environmental polluters easier." "What's that?" "Why?" and "Say it again" are the probable puzzled reactions. But the speaker, using amplification, proceeds. "For example, consider what would happen if . . . ." The audience is relieved; an example is something that the mind can hold on to; the speaker, moreover, is giving them time to think. Or the communicator may say, "In comparison with the former law, what this new legislation provides is . . . ," and again the audience has the needed time for grasping the idea and a second means for doing so. Examples and comparisons, although not the only useful materials for clarifying, probably are the easiest to use and the most common.

2. To prove. Receivers should not and usually do not accept assertions without proof. An example tells the respondent that some event happened; statistics provide a single, general picture of scores of events or persons; a quotation states that someone other than the sender shares the latter's position. In using all types of material, the communicator needs to show the relevance of the item of proof to the contention. Claim . . . connecting link . . . evidence, as illustrated below, is the sequence:

The range of the bald eagle is great [claim]. For example [connecting link], a nestling banded near Grand Rapids, Minn., was found dead exactly four months later near Llano, Texas, 1,185 miles away [evidence].

Facilities on the island are extensive [claim]. Consider the most recent statistics [connecting link]. At last count the island had 53 tennis courts, four 18-hole golf courses, six marinas, a dozen restaurants with nightly entertainment, and more than 1,000 first-class hotel rooms [evidence].

3. *To intensify.* Communication is in many ways a psychological event, and one function of materials is to create fear, bring dormant motives to the foreground, and strengthen the intensity of desires. Human interest stories, vivid descriptions, and examples that relate the speech to the receivers' immediate and vital interests are excellent means of increasing impact.

4. *To increase credibility.* Persuasive strength also depends on the extent to which the respondent perceives the sender as credible—a generalization that suggests still another purpose that materials serve. Recently a student in a simulated job interview illustrated both the wrong and the right ways to build credibility. "I always was very popular" is an unprovable self-appraisal that listeners may construe as conceit; "I was elected president of my dormitory council" is a factual, verifiable statement. Other good ways to enhance *ethos* are through examples reporting personal experiences, references to associations with respected authorities, and evidence showing knowledge, objectivity, and fairness.

5. *To create rapport between speaker and listener.* Closely related to the fourth purpose, yet significantly different, is the use of materials to create rapport or a feeling of closeness. References to common beliefs, values, aspirations, needs, personal qualities, and backgrounds are effective means for developing perceptions of similarity and for creating a sense of closeness between receiver and sender. Especially useful are examples and other materials that come from a background shared by communicator and listener. As an illustration, a labor leader who has risen through the ranks might find it advantageous to report a personal experience that occurred on an assembly line similar to those on which the listeners work.

6. *To add interest.* Material that builds rapport probably also heightens attention. Indeed, one piece of material may serve several of these seven purposes. At times, nevertheless, the primary reason for including a story, a striking example, an unexpected historic or literary allusion, or a humor-

ous remark may be that of heightening interest. So important is this aspect of the message that this chapter includes a separate section on attention.

Foreseeing during preparation when interest may lag is so difficult that speakers often need to make impromptu adjustments during delivery. For beginners such changes are difficult, but even they should try to develop an awareness of the need for inserting a story, for changing the pace in delivery, or making direct appeals or references. In time, skillful communicators build a reserve of interest-restoring devices, such as interrupting the prepared text, pausing, and saying, "Let's stop for a moment and see what these principles mean in the daily lives of each and every one of you."

7. *To amplify.* Finally, materials add substance or body to a set of ideas, length to the amount of time listeners spend with each contention, and added paragraphs to the manuscript. Like an artist who senses that a little more blue in the sky is too much and a little less is not enough, so does the speaker "feel" that each part of an address needs greater development, should be condensed, or is just right. Humor here, one decides, is out of place, but somewhere else an anecdote to mellow and relax would be helpful. A bit more is needed in the second section to round out the point, but the story about the crippled dog is 20 percent too long. In general, the most important points should receive the fullest treatment.

DESIRABLE QUALITIES OF MATERIAL

A second way to approach the selection of material is through an evaluation of the available items against a list of desirable qualities. Perhaps no piece of material ever will satisfy all of the tests, and which criteria are significant in a particular situation depends on the purposes of the speaker and other circumstances. The following list, nevertheless, should be helpful in answering such questions as "Should I use this story or omit it?" and "Is this quotation or that one the more impressive?"

Authoritativeness Statistics, for example, should come from a reliable source, which the communicator should identify with a simple statement such as "These figures come from the National Bureau of Labor Statistics and were published in the *Wall Street Journal,* June 24, 1976." Similarly, a quotation expressing an opinion can gain in impressiveness through its author's position or background. Once more the speaker should cite the source and point out qualifications: "This statement is from Milton Friedman, a distinguished economist at the University of Chicago. The source is *Forbes,* Feb. 1, 1976."

The preceding advice also applies to materials other than statistics and quotations, but less often. In many instances the communicator should tell the source of an example, and in still others he or she should give credit for a set of causes, for a suggested solution, or for an analysis pointing out a historic parallel. Not only does intellectual honesty demand that a speaker credit the sources, but also adding this information sometimes increases impressiveness.

If the speaker is the source, persuasiveness may be especially strong. In one experiment Ostermeier inserted three, six, and nine items of personal observations into three versions of a speech, and he found that the greater the number of self-references, the higher the effectiveness.[6] Such a finding obviously occurs only when the audience has no reason to suspect the speaker of bias or falsehood. To protect against distrust, according to a second study, the communicator can stress the verifiability of the report.[7] In other words, if receivers know that it is possible to check the accuracy of a statement, then they are likely to believe it.

Germaneness The example must fit the point it supposedly illustrates, and the statistics or quotations must stand as proof of the contention under consideration. In this area the problems are the materials that *almost* belong and those that the desperate speaker uses for lack of the evidence that logic requires. The deliberate violation of germaneness, of course, is unethical, but at times only a highly alert listener can detect faulty choices.

Clarity Quotations and statistics vary in intelligibility, and for both types of material honest manipulations can be helpful. "Three out of every five" is more meaningful than "three million" or even "60 percent," and "one thousand dollars for every man, woman, and child" is more comprehensible than "$210 billion." By simple arithmetic the communicator can calculate what any large figure means in terms of "dollars per day" or "amounts per person."

"In other words" is a useful phrase when it follows a statistic, a quotation, or an example. In even a well-written quotation, the total verbiage may partially conceal the group of words that is exactly relevant to the speaker's message.

Appropriate Length A speech consists of points and subpoints, and in theory a certain time division among them is ideal. Too much time spent in one place causes the presentation to drag and leaves too little time for somewhere else. The speaker, as a result, must condense some stories, prune certain examples, and even discard some materials. Quoted passages, which are especially likely to be long-winded, often take up too much time and lack focus and emphasis. Rejecting such a passage may be

---

[6] Terry H. Ostermeier, "Effects of Type and Frequency of Reference upon Perceived Source Credibility and Attitude Change," *Speech Monographs*, 34 (June 1967), 137–144.
[7] Paul I. Rosenthal, "Specificity, Verifiability, and Message Credibility," *Quarterly Journal of Speech*, 57 (December 1971), 393–401.

the only practical course, but sometimes the communicator can condense the lines without distorting the thought. The possibilities are omitting opening explanations that are unnecessary, deleting closing sentences that are anticlimactic, and removing superfluous sentences or dependent elements within the body. The omissions can add clarity and pointedness, but again, let it be emphasized, they must not distort the original meaning.

Variety An example and a quotation, as a rule, are better than two quotations, and citations from three sources are preferable to three taken from the same authority. Not only should amplifying materials be of different types, such as stories, comparisons, examples, and statistics; but also they should be varied in length, in source, and in tenor. Some should be personal and add human interest; others should be universal and authoritative. A statistic can give the overall picture, but a single case shows in human terms what muscular dystrophy or multiple sclerosis really is.

Interest Specific cases, thus, hold attention better than statistics, and variety in itself is a means of adding interest. So important is this final quality of material that a separate section on it follows.

LISTENER ANALYSIS AND ADAPTATION AS
FACTORS IN SELECTING MATERIAL

The following dialogue is imaginary but not improbable:

DEBRA: "All right, selecting materials is important to communication, and I should pick the ones to use according to my purposes and their qualities. But that still leaves me uncertain."

SANDY: "I know how you feel; and one thing that I remember from a former speech class comes to mind. When you are planning a talk, think about your audience."

DEBRA: "That's right. Adapt to your audience when you choose your topic, when you work out your purpose, and also when you decide which materials to use."

Debra and Sandy, of course, are right. The closely related processes of listener analysis and adaptation are as critical to the successful choice of materials as they are to other aspects of speech preparation.

Listener Analysis

Who will the listeners be, and what characteristics will they have? For their next speech situations Debra and Sandy have different problems in answering these questions. Debra, who spent the preceding summer as a religious worker in the inner city, has received an invitation to talk about her experiences before "The Good Fellowship Club" in a nearby community. Since the invitation went little beyond specifying time and place, Debra knows nothing about the group except that it is related to a congregation of her own denomination. As she begins thinking about what she is going to say, she realizes that she cannot make sensible decisions without securing more information. Not having a personal friend in the nearby city, Debra decides to write or telephone the program chairman. She prepares the following list of questions:

How long should my speech be?

How large an audience do you expect?

Will the group consist entirely of young adults, or will there be a number who are middle-aged, elderly, or very young?

Am I right in assuming that the group will be about evenly divided between men and women and that almost everyone present will be a member of the church?

Will I deliver my speech from a banquet table or from a lectern at the front of an auditorium?

What events will precede my speech? How long will they take?

How much formality is customary in the programs?

If I wish to bring slides, will there be equipment for projecting them?

If the situation were different, Debra, of course would vary the questions.

Sandy's problem in listener analysis is unlike Debra's in that she is going for a job interview and thus needs information on only one person. For Debra with a sizable audience in prospect, individual analysis is impossible, and the only practical course is to secure information on age, sex, type of work, income level, and other factors and then to make intelligent guesses about probable motives, interests, beliefs, and values. Sandy, nevertheless, needs to learn as much as she can about the likes and the dislikes of the personnel officer with whom she has an appointment. Sometimes securing advance information is impossible, but in this instance Sandy has a girl friend who already works for the company. "What can I expect?" Sandy asks. "What does the interviewer think are the most important qualities for an applicant to have?" In the conversation Sandy discovers that the prospective interviewer regards activities as more important than grade point average, prefers people who are willing to learn to those that may have been mistrained on previous jobs, and considers family background important. With this information Sandy can make judicious decisions on what to stress when she meets with the personnel officer.

Listener Adaptation

"About this speech tomorrow—what was that funny story? What are the best arguments I've heard?" These may sound like good questions to ask oneself, but they indicate a serious and common error. Instead of looking for stories that are funny to themselves, communicators should be searching for narratives that will be entertaining to listeners; and instead of

78 CONTENT: THE BASIS OF RESPONSIBLE COMMUNICATION

Visualizing the audience situation in advance is important to speech preparation. (Credits: *above,* Charles Gatewood/Magnum; *opposite top,* Richard Kalvar/Magnum; *opposite bottom,* René Burri/Magnum)

choosing arguments that they rate highly, they should be devising contentions that listeners will find compelling. "The audience is just like me" is the mindless and unannounced assumption that too often governs preparation.

Adaptation to listeners in some respects is much the same for small groups as for audiences, but differences are noteworthy. In dealing with an individual, the application can be obvious. If Mr. B does not like people who smoke in his office and if he dislikes jovial, forward young persons, a prudent job applicant refrains from smoking and curbs any action that might seem familiar. If the personnel officer thinks that activities are important, the applicant spends more time telling of extra-curricular affiliations and offices than he or she would otherwise.

When the audience is large, the speaker can do no more than adapt to the majority. If a story will seem tasteless and be offensive to a church group, one omits it. If the situation demands brevity, one leaves out some materials and condenses others. If the group is well educated, one stresses facts and careful reasoning. If many of those present are Republicans, one quotes Dwight Eisenhower and Gerald Ford. If the occasion is a meeting of the English Club, one chooses examples from Shakespeare and other literary figures rather than from history.

Such statements and examples as the preceding are deceptive, because they make adaptation to listeners seem simpler than it really is. Success in choosing tactful, effective materials requires accurate information, sound judgment, a willingness to select what will please others rather than what will please oneself, and a large enough stock of materials so that selectivity is possible.

INTEREST

Interest also depends on analysis and adaptation, but the topic of attention is so important that it deserves detailed analysis. Not only is it a factor for consideration in choosing materials, but also it is basic to the very existence of sustained communication.

Nature and Importance of Attention

"Pay attention," says the beleaguered teacher to a squirming roomful of youngsters; "Keep your eye on the swinging pendant," intones the hypnotist. Total control of attention produces hypnotism; no attention means no learning; most situations are somewhere between. As a result average listeners grasp some ideas, but not others; they know vaguely that the speaker said something on the topic, but they are not sure what it was. The person who wishes to be a more effective listener in the classroom or elsewhere must acquire the self-discipline to be more attentive; the person who desires to be a better communicator must understand the nature of attention and become skillful in choosing materials that will gain and hold interest.

Since certain myths about attention mislead the young speaker or discussant, it is important to identify and to dispel several false notions.

Myth One: When I speak, people listen "That seems reasonable, doesn't it? I know that what I'm saying is important. People are polite, and it's polite to listen. Most of them are looking at me. They look as if they're listening." Not necessarily. Some people can look straight at the speaker, but their minds are far away. Distractions are numerous, and some persons hardly listen at all and others respond halfheartedly and part-time. John is thinking about the test in economics; Helen is wondering whether her boy friend is angry or only pretending; Ralph is watching the dogs frolicking outdoors; Sam wants to listen, but the whispered words of two nearby students are bothersome; Mary starts out with the speaker, but a remark sets her thinking her own thoughts. Each person has worries that he or she brings along, and a procession of noises, sights, and even smells creates distractions. The stimuli competing for attention are numerous; people listen to the speaker only if he or she makes it easy and gives them strong reasons for doing so.

Myth Two: Starting with a joke is all that is necessary A magazine article told of a restaurant owner to whom Pete Rose, a baseball star, turned for advice when given his first offer to speak at a banquet. "I kept telling him we'd think of something," the owner recalled. "Finally I said, 'Well, one thing I can tell you is [that] people who make speeches always start out with a joke.' "[8] The story illustrates the pervasiveness, if not the stupidity, of the myth about using a joke for a beginning; but more significant is the implication that the speaker who gains initial attention has done all that he or she needs to do. Nothing could be much further from the truth, for psychologists have found that attention fluctuates about every twenty or twenty-five seconds and that even conscientious listeners must work at the task of bringing their minds back to the speaker repeatedly. Attention-holding efforts, thus, must occur throughout a presentation; indeed, as fatigue builds, self-discipline may become increasingly necessary. The writer, to inject a personal note, often puts his long points at the beginning of an address and then moves quickly in the closing part.

Myth Three: My listeners and I have the same interests Perhaps, but not always. If you and your respondents are the same age and have similar majors, hobbies, and backgrounds, common interests are likely, and you may not do a bad job even if you think only of yourself during preparation. Under any other circumstance the myth can be disastrous. The principle is simple: Use materials that will be of interest to your listeners rather than those that to you are funny, charming, or striking.

Myth Four: Listeners may miss details, but they'll get the general drift Again, not so; certainly, not inevitable. Frequently listeners remember the jokes or one or two striking details, but have little grasp of the main points. If the situation described in the myth comes true, it is because the speaker has been skillful. Since attention fluctuates frequently and since no listener is going to hear every sentence, the speaker must try to manage the situation so that the receiver is attentive at the right times. A rather small number of sentences, usually the topic sentences of paragraphs, carry forward the sequence of major ideas. By numbering points, by pausing, by varying the voice, by moving on the platform, and by using still other devices of wording and delivery, the speaker needs to draw attention to that limited number of sentences. If one does this and then summarizes effectively, one may succeed in actualizing this fourth myth.

---

[8] Willard Bailey, "Coffee, Dessert and A Little Sneaky Pete," *Signature*, 10 (May 1975), 32.

Myth Five: Good ideas are all that are necessary This myth is the refuge of the intellectual snob who knows nothing about speechmaking and is disdainful of it as an academic field of study. Such a person drones through classroom lectures for years; and if the reputation of a scholar is sufficient, he or she even receives offers for public appearances. The pity is that such an individual knows so much about a topic, but communicates so little.

Myth Six: A person can be attentive to only one stimulus at a time Technically this statement is true; but in a practical sense it is false. By shifting attention back and forth rapidly, most people attend during a given time period to more than one source. The importance of this common practice is that receivers form significant impressions from nonverbal cues during the time that they are responding to the sequence of sentences and paragraphs. The way the speaker stands, facial expression, control over the hands, and the inflections in the voice provide stimuli that lead listeners to make judgments as "she is earnest," "he doesn't know what he is talking about," and "she is untrustworthy." Some of the signs that produce these conclusions are beyond the speaker's control, but others are not. Personal grooming, for example, is an element that a speaker can manage.

Qualities That Enhance Interest

In selecting materials, what qualities should one look for if one's purpose is gaining attention or heightening interest? No two authors would produce the same list, but the following items are among the most useful: animation and progress; conflict and suspense; concreteness and specificity; humor; immediacy and vitalness; intrinsic importance; familiarity and novelty; and change and variety.

Animation and Progress The flashing sign attracts more attention than the unchanging set of neon lights; the vivacious person is noticed more than the one who remains quiet at the cocktail party; the lively, enthusiastic speaker carries listeners along, whereas the lethargic, monotonous person engenders apathy. Gestures, if coordinated with the thought and if not overdone, also can be desirable as a means of increasing the level of animation. "Be alive! Be enthusiastic!" is good advice.

Speeches that seem to be moving along tend to maintain attention. Stories, examples, and other materials should be pointed and at least reasonably concise. Summaries, previews, and the numbering of points are devices that give listeners a sense of progress—a feeling that they and the communicator are accomplishing something and are moving forward to new ideas. The opposite effect results from the formless presentation that after fifteen minutes or even thirty appears to have gone about in a circle and to be back at its starting point.

Conflict and Suspense Likewise conducive to holding interest are the qualities of conflict and suspense. The essence of any story is conflict—the good guys against the bad, man and woman against the hurricane, those trapped inside an overturned luxury liner against the natural elements, the potential victims in a skyscraper against fire, the one lover in competition with the second, the life styles of one generation against those of another, the sheriff versus the outlaws, the settlers against the Indians. A typical night's offering on television illustrates the importance of conflict to drama, and the ratings bear out the judgment that this element is what people want. Even the news story, according to one network executive, should be cast into the form of a conflict.[9]

Suspense usually accompanies conflict. One keeps watching the dramatic program in order to find out which suspect committed the crime, whether Leslie or Terry will marry Robin, or who is going to receive the inheritance. Sports events, which involve conflict between the Steelers and the Cowboys or the Celtics and the Lakers, illustrate with unusual clarity the importance of suspense. If the outcome of a one-sided game becomes clear, many fans leave early; and if the teams are so unevenly matched that the result is predictable, attendance is poor.

Applied to speech preparation, the foregoing principles mean, first, that in the selection of a story one should try to choose a narration in which suspense is sustained and in which the conflict is strong and clear-cut. Second, in reworking a story for presentation, one should highlight the competitive element and keep the outcome in doubt. Third, in the inventive processes one should try to utilize conflict and suspense. One speaker charmingly explained his tardiness with an incident-by-incident account of his combat with the combined forces of nature and bumbling bureaucracy. One writer produced a delightful essay with herself as the protagonist and a large department store as the antagonist; she reprinted her letters, which were attempts to straighten out an error in billing, and the succession of computer-produced, inappropriate replies. One public performer, the manager of a lecture bureau, delighted audiences with a series of stories about his experiences in trying to get eccentric personalities to the right city at the right time. Jacques Cousteau's documentaries include the conflict between human beings and the sea.

Suspense is a factor in speech composition in yet another way. Although introductions usually should include a preview of the structure of the speech, they should not give away the details. What plan will the president propose? Whom is the senator going to endorse? What really happened during the recent trip? Individuals attend or tune in speeches in part because of curiosity; and when the answers emerge, they lose a part of

---

[9] Edward Jay Epstein, *News from Nowhere* (New York: Random House, 1973), p. 241.

their interest. A particularly striking use of suspense was a sermon on "Three Sure Ways of Going to Hell." Since the introduction gave no hint of the three points, the church-goers had to listen until near the end before finding out the third way.

Concreteness and Specificity   One small, crippled child is of greater interest than a set of statistics or scientific facts about the disease from which he or she suffers. Effective speakers talk about individual cases, real or hypothetical, and they often give their main characters names. They talk about crime on the streets by reporting the beating of an elderly man, and they discuss the need for assistance to earthquake victims by spelling out what is happening to a particular family. Listeners can understand and identify with other individuals; they find it difficult to do so with a generalization or a statistic.

Sometimes specificity can underlie an entire presentation. In telling about a predicted shortage of energy, one speaker created a fictional character and followed him through a day's activities under the hypothesized conditions; and instead of giving a straightforward scientific lecture on the moon, one scholar conveyed the basic information by describing an astronaut on an imaginary journey. With comparable inventiveness student speakers can use specificity in analyzing almost any past event or present problem. Many successful novels are a retelling of history through the experiences of a fictitious character who plays the role of a participant.

Tending to accompany specificity is concreteness, but two accounts of an event can vary greatly in vividness. Concrete language appeals to the senses; it reconstructs a happening so that listeners can see and hear. Word choice and the use of details both contribute to concreteness, which in turn is a major source of descriptive and narrative power. Such devices sometimes are overdone, but in general the more vivid a speaker makes the scenery of a resort area, the plight of the grape picker, or the pleasures of a good wine, the more successful will be the persuasive appeal.

Humor   Adding to the pleasantness of most occasions, according to almost everyone's experience, is humor. "That reminds me of a funny story" or "Let me illustrate the point with a humorous experience" are sentences that usually perk up tired listeners. Also helpful in maintaining interest is the brief witticism or the spontaneous, cheerful aside.

Dangers, however, attend the use of humor, which must be in good taste as judged by the audience. Stories about one's own foibles and misadventures usually are safe, but at times such materials cast doubt on the teller's intelligence and judgment. Such tales, nevertheless, have the advantage of freshness, whereas stories or jokes taken out of reference works may be familiar to some members of the audience and at best seem contrived and uninventive.

Some of America's most respected presidents were effective in the use of humor. Abraham Lincoln was famous for his ability to use a homely story to reduce tension. Franklin D. Roosevelt delighted friends and observers with a sarcasm that somehow did not seem petty or nasty. John F. Kennedy's wit in fielding questions at press conferences, many thought, made him more likable and respected. The results of quantitative research on the values of humor have been mixed, but according to at least one study, it does relieve dullness[10]—the exact point under consideration in this section.

Immediacy and Vitalness Material that directly affects the listeners or those close to them also prevents dullness. A burglary in a neighbor's home creates more concern than the robbery of an armored truck on the other side of the continent. The achievements of a local professor receive more attention than do those of a scholar somewhere else. In the recent crash of an airliner the first question that arose in the writer's own city was "Was anyone from Houston aboard?" For the next few hours television stations included in each news report a statement that the local office of the airline was refusing to give them information on Houston residents.

Closely related to the immediate is the vital. "Is this a matter that affects my own safety, health, or financial welfare?" is an unspoken question that listeners use in deciding whether a speech is worthy of their time. The speaker, as a result, does well when planning a presentation to ask, "Why should the audience listen to me?"

Some applications of the principle of immediacy and vitalness include the following: The speaker on the nuclear power plant tells how much money it will save each individual customer and how much it will mean to the local citizen by eliminating blackouts and brownouts. The lecturer on pending tariff legislation explains what will happen to the prices of coffee, bananas, and cocoa in the local grocery store. The discussant of crime in the streets cites figures for the city where the meeting is occurring. The environmentalist talks about what may happen in the local community. "One out of every three persons in this room someday will have cancer" arouses more interest than a national statistic, no matter how large.

The use of immediacy and vitalness sometimes requires research on conditions in the community, but more often the sender's task is that of applying general information to the local situation. Effort and ingenuity are requirements, but potentially the principles explained in the preceding paragraphs are applicable to almost any topic.

---

[10] Charles Gruner, "The Effect of Humor in Dull and Interesting Informative Speeches," *Central States Speech Journal*, 21 (Fall 1970), 160–166.

Intrinsic Importance Psychologist H. L. Hollingworth states, "Intrinsic interest of the subject matter is the most effective factor in sustaining attention."[11] The opinion is a valuable corrective to the tendency to underestimate listeners and to rely too much on the clever and the spectacular. Most audiences that college students or college graduates face consist of persons with sufficient intelligence to distinguish between the important and the trivial. Usually they go to speeches or discussions with the expectation of being informed, and the advance announcement of the title or the question means that those in attendance, with some exceptions, are present because they have an interest in the topic. The speaker, therefore, profits by saying something that is sufficiently worthwhile to fulfill their desires.

This principle, moreover, is not inconsistent with the other generalizations that constitute this section. Solid and informative content, for example, is compatible with adaptations to immediate concerns and vital interests. Similarly, animation and progress, conflict and suspense, concreteness and specificity, and humor can characterize materials that *in toto* develop meaningful ideas.

Familiarity and Novelty Likewise valuable in conveying worthwhile ideas is the familiar, whose power to heighten interest is readily observable. Returned travelers enjoy seeing film segments showing Piccadilly Circus, the Eiffel Tower, and other places where they have been. Golf enthusiasts listen attentively when the speaker refers to their favorite sport, whereas a comparable reference to tennis has little effect. Those who play chess find accounts of its masters or its great matches unusually interesting, whereas bridge players respond better to what is familiar to them. Close to the familiar, but harmful to attention, is the commonplace. Few persons wish to have repeated what they have already heard many times.

Rather strangely, novelty, if not too extreme, also tends to hold attention. The critical factor probably is whether the listener has *some* point of contact that makes the material comprehensible and relevant. Thus, since most communicatees know something of marriage customs, they find the novelties in other cultures interesting.

Especially strong in holding attention is a combination of the familiar with the unusual. Initial credit for this observation goes to the famous psychologist, William James, who wrote as follows:

And the maximum of attention may then be said to be found wherever we have a systematic harmony or unification between the novel and the old. It is an odd circumstance that neither the old nor the new, by itself, is interesting: the absolutely old is insipid; the absolutely new makes no ap-

[11] H. L. Hollingworth, *The Psychology of the Audience* (New York: American Book Company, 1935), p. 61.

peal at all. The old in the new is what claims attention—the old with slightly new form.[12]

Change and Variety   Finally, change and variety are sources of attention. In choosing materials, the speaker should avoid the overuse of a single source or of a particular type of material. If one uses numerous quotations, they should come from several sources; and if one employs a number of stories, they should be from different fields and varied in type and length.

Conclusions on Holding Attention

Not all advice on maintaining interest pertains to speech materials, but much of one's success in this vital aspect of the communication process does depend on skill in research and in selection. Without attention, both learning and persuasion are impossible; with it, whether they occur depends on a variety of factors, one of which again is effectiveness in amplification. As a minimum, during preparation one should consider problems in retaining attention, and during the presentation one should attempt to make appropriate adjustments if one senses that listeners are slipping away. Since attention fluctuates, no speaker can hope for perfection, but controlling the situation so that the listeners are fully aware of the main ideas is a realistic goal.

This control over which words, sentences, and ideas listeners receive out of the total presentation involves a combination of materials and other rhetorical factors. The following brief list highlights major strategies of practical value. (1) One can say that the next words will be important. "Be sure that you get this *next* step." "Now we come to my *main* contention." (2) One can tell the audience that a new point is coming. "Let's go on to the third reason." "So much for the causes; now let's look at some solutions." (3) One can associate the message with rewards or punishments. "A test on this lecture will occur at the end of the hour." "Those scoring more than ninety will be excused from the next unit." (4) One can make the message strong, striking, and intense through vivid language and such practices in delivery as pauses, changes in pitch and tempo, stress on key words, and heightened eye contact and intensity.

CONCLUSION

Materials are the substance of all forms of serious communication, but their functions in public address and in interpersonal or small-group discourse

---

[12] William James, *Talks to Teachers on Psychology* (New York: Holt, Rinehart and Winston, 1939), p. 108.

differ in some respects. In public address, speakers of necessity weave together a continuous message, and the choice of a particular item in one part of the message affects decisions about selections in adjacent sections of the address. The final advice to the speaker is reducible to these injunctions: Have enough material. Include both items of personal knowledge and those secured through library research. Order and apportion skillfully. Use variety. Adapt to the audience. Hold interest at a high level.

In discontinuous discourse, materials serve both as elements in preplanned remarks and as resources for unexpected situations. If one has a definite objective for a meeting, one may choose to prepare strategies in advance and to decide tentatively on materials to include for clarification and support; but since much that happens in a conversation, interview, discussion, or conference depends on the contributions of the other participants, one also must have a storehouse of information to draw on as different points arise. If one is to be an effective, responsible communicator and is to earn the respect of fellow members, nothing less than careful preparation will suffice.

Except for the differences just mentioned, the uses of materials are similar in situations ranging from the small group discussion to the auditorium lecture. The instruction in the body of this chapter on kinds of materials and tests for them, on purposes that materials serve, on desirable qualities, on listener analysis and adaptation, and on interest is generally applicable.

PROBLEMS AND EXERCISES

1. In reference to a major speech that you are preparing, write a paper that contains many of the points in the following outline:

    I. Introduction to the paper: topic, purpose, and scheduled time and place for the speech
   II. Description of the audience
      A. Probable size and composition (e.g., a college class; members of a union local; a fraternity gathering; a teen-age church group)
      B. Distinctive features, if any (all senior citizens; all of the same religious group; all men or all women)
  III. An inventory of the materials that you have
  IV. An analysis of materials to be used
      A. The purposes that materials should serve in the speech
      B. The most important qualities for materials in this speech
      C. The materials that will be best adapted to this audience
      D. The materials that are likely to be the most interesting
   V. Conclusion
      A. Problems that still are troublesome
      B. An estimate of the probable outcome of the speech

2. Prepare and deliver an expository speech on a topic with which you are familiar, such as a hobby, a sport that you play, or a device or mechanism. As you speak, have members of the class take notes on your materials. After your speech, answer questions about your choices.

3. Secure a copy of a speech delivered within the last five years. One possibility is to photocopy an address reprinted in *Vital Speeches of the Day*. Make the following observations on the use of materials: the kinds; the purposes that the items serve; their quality as tested against the principles discussed in this chapter; the adaptation of materials to the audience; the probable value of the materials in holding attention. Give examples that clarify and/or support your judgments.

4. Form a discussion group with four or five of your classmates, and analyze the use of materials in one of the speeches in the Appendix.

5. Recall the most interesting speech you ever heard. Try to analyze the reasons that you responded so favorably. Participate in a class discussion in which the members share their recollections.

6. Of the qualities that enhance interest, which ones do you think are the most important? Participate in a class discussion on this topic. Are any of your conclusions different from those in this chapter?

7. If possible, attend a speech with a group from your class. Take notes on the logical adequacy of the examples, statistics, and quotations. Form a discussion group with the others who attended, and compare your observations.

REFERENCES

Ayres, Joe. "Observers' Judgements of Audience Members' Attitudes," *Western Speech*, 39 (Winter 1975), 40–50.

Egeth, Howard. "Selective Attention," *Psychological Bulletin*, 47 (January 1967), 41–57.

Gruner, Charles R. "The Effect of Humor in Dull and Interesting Informative Speeches," *Central States Speech Journal*, 21 (Fall 1970), 160–166.

Holtzman, Paul D. *The Psychology of the Speakers' Audiences*. Glenview, Ill.: Scott, Foresman, 1970.

McCroskey, James. "A Summary of Experimental Research on the Effects of Evidence in Persuasive Communication," *Quarterly Journal of Speech*, 55 (April 1969), 169–176.

McCroskey, James C., and Walter H. Combs. "The Effects of the Use of Analogy on Attitude Change and Source Credibility," *Journal of Communication*, 19 (December 1969), 333–339.

McCroskey, James C., and David W. Wright. "A Comparison of the Effects of Punishment-oriented and Reward-oriented Messages in Persuasive Communication," *Journal of Communication*, 21 (March 1971), 83–93.

McGhee, Paul E. "Development of the Humor Response: A Review of the Literature," *Psychological Bulletin*, 76 (November 1971), 328–348.

Mettee, David R., Edward S. Hrelec, and Paul C. Wilkens. "Humor as an Interpersonal Asset and Liability," *Journal of Social Psychology*, 85 (October 1971), 51–64.

Moray, Neville. *Attention*. London: Hutchinson Educational, 1969.

Murray, Frank S. "Judgment of Evidence," *American Journal of Psychology*, 81 (September 1968), 319–333.

Newman, Robert P., and Dale R. Newman. *Evidence*. Boston: Houghton Mifflin Co., 1969.

Ostermeier, Terry H. "Effects of Type and Frequency of Reference upon Perceived Source Credibility and Attitude Change," *Speech Monographs*, 34 (June 1967), 137–144.

Posner, Michael I., and Stephen J. Boies. "Components of Attention," *Psychological Review*, 78 (September 1971), 391–408.

Rosenthal, Paul I. "Specificity, Verifiability, and Message Credibility," *Quarterly Journal of Speech*, 57 (December 1971), 393–401.

Sears, D. O., and J. L. Freedman. "Selective Exposure to Information: A Critical Review," *Public Opinion Quarterly*, 31 (Summer 1967), 194–213.

Taylor, Pat M. "An Experimental Study of Humor and Ethos," *Southern Speech Communication Journal*, 39 (Summer 1974), 359–366.

Whitehead, Jack L., Jr. "Effects of Authority-Based Assertion on Attitude and Credibility," *Speech Monographs*, 38 (November 1971), 311–315.

II
THE TRANSACTION: PROCESSES AND DYNAMIC FACTORS AFFECTING COMMUNICATION

Part II of this textbook builds on Part I. What one says is the substantive base of responsible communication, but the eventual message—the message as received and interpreted—is an outcome, also, of interactional and transactional forces. When human beings come together in interpersonal, small-group, and platform situations, they affect one another in many different ways, and the total of all these influences has much to do with their eventual attitudes, beliefs, and actions. These forces even affect the messages that individuals produce as a communication event continues.

Students need to understand transactional processes and the dynamic factors affecting perceptions and interactions. They need also to know how to play transactional roles and how to apply knowledge of dynamic factors advantageously in interviews, discussions, and conferences.

5
THE TRANSACTION: PROCESSES

After studying this chapter the reader should be able to do the following:

List elements other than the overt message that probably affected the decoding in a live or video-taped conversation

Convey three responses through feedback that at least 75 percent of the participants in a small group can identify

Describe at the end of a presentation at least one point at which the audience provided feedback indicative of agreement, doubt, or perplexity

Department stores at one time included a system of tubes or parallel wires that conveyed capsules back and forth between clerks and a central cashier. The slips that the salesmen and saleswomen prepared moved from stations on the floor to the office, and these slips arrived unaltered and unmistakable. For many years the prevailing model of communication was analogous to this conveyor system; the assumption was that "A" invented and verbalized a message, that sight or sound waves carried this message to "B," and that the content eventually reached "B's" brain unaltered and unmistakable.

The oversimplification in this old model should be apparent to anyone who observes a day's communication events. Participants commonly receive messages from several sources, an individual sometimes sends and at other times responds, and the communicatee's interpretations of a set of sentences may differ from the meanings intended. These dynamic factors are strongest and most evident in two-person and small-group situations, but they affect public speeches as well. Anger, mistrust, boredom, enthusiastic approval, and still other reactions, for example, can spread from one or more focal points to other parts of an audience; and the speaker's perceptions of listener response can affect delivery and even the further ideas that he or she verbalizes.

This strong emphasis on the significance of interpersonal forces is not a denial of the position in the preceding chapters that sound content is the basis of responsible communication. The two factors—content and the dynamics of human relations—interact with each other, and each is important in its own way. Content is information and argument; with its potential for evoking anger, producing trust, or arousing other attitudes or emotions, it can affect the dynamics of a gathering. Interacting forces, for their part, affect the receiver's interpretations of what he or she hears and the perceptions of the sender's competence and trustworthiness. Basic to an understanding of the transactional nature of communication are certain assumptions: (1) Every perceivable stimulus, no matter how slight, is a part of the matrix comprising the total event. Not every person, however, notes every cue. (2) Meanings exist in the mind, not in words. The receiver re-creates the sender's intended message on the basis of the entire field of stimuli as he or she perceives the whole. (3) Usually communication is a joint and circular process with both the original sender and the original receiver contributing cues so that the re-created message comes from both. (4) No communication situation is repeatable. For example, the second time that someone says, "Listen carefully," the context for evaluating the command is not the same as it was the first time that the receiver heard the same words.

The pages that follow, it should be evident, are significant for both receiver and sender. For the former an appreciation of the totality of a communication event is the first step toward understanding his or her own reactions and toward guarding against irrationality. The irritability that one feels when a roommate says, "I used the last cube of butter," is attributable only in part to the statement and to the action that it reports. The impetuosity that leads one to purchase an expensive bracelet or wrist watch is a result only in part of the claims that the clerk has presented. The feeling of unfairness that one experiences when the professor gives a longer assignment than expected, likewise, is not entirely a response to the immediate stimulus. Anger, envy, suspicion, doubt, hurt feelings, and their opposites are both common consequents of the reception of messages and mediators affecting what one thinks one is hearing and seeing. The receiver's interpretations, thus, are joint products of the sender's intended message and of contextual, situational, and affective or emotional forces. That "one hears what one wants to hear" often is true.

To listen objectively and to behave sensibly are goals whose significance for healthy, happy living is as great as their attainability is difficult. Research on human rationality is discouraging; most men and women permit their emotions and their biases to intrude when they supposedly are making objective judgments. To claim that this book or the course based on it will revolutionize behavior during communication would be to exaggerate. Improvement, nevertheless, is possible for those who are willing to learn about themselves through the following pages and who will then make the effort to sort out the factors that are affecting them. Self-analysis, self-criticism, and the suspension of judgment—"sleeping on it" or "taking a second look"—are wholesome correctives. How unfair, for example, is the new assignment? How valid are its objectives? Is it actually as long as I first thought it was? Did it seem unjust because of its provisions, or did the adverse reaction occur because of the new due date on a term paper in another class, because of a pending attack of influenza, or because of the realization last night that getting a part-time job is necessary?

The sections that follow, therefore, are important to receivers so that they can better understand themselves and make more rational judgments; but these sections also have significant implications for the sender. The interpretations given to the words that one speaks or writes will depend on scores of interrelating factors, and to ignore this truth is to risk being both misunderstood and ineffective. A message to a neurotically anxious person, for example, is likely to elicit no response beyond superficial politeness. Statements to someone who lacks trust are almost certain to evoke suspicion. A girl's friendly word and smile to a young man who has just been jilted may produce either cautious skepticism or eager response, depending on whether he is on the rebound or "through with women for good."

DECODING[1]

Communication events often take unexpected turns. When Marijane walks into the office (five minutes late, it's true; but bright, cheerful, perky, and good-humored), she hardly expects her routine "Good morning and what a beau-beautiful morning it is" to produce a gruff, "What's good about it?

---

[1] Decoding occurs in the mind of the listener or observer. It is the process of creating meanings from the sounds that one hears and the sights that one sees.

And you're late again." And Sonny Boy on his third plea for a stop at a service station, a strategy that has become habitual and that evokes good-natured refusals and occasional successes, finds the world suddenly confusing and unpredictable when Daddy Dear responds, "Sit down and shut up." And, of course, results can be surprisingly positive, too. Joe Nobody has admired Belle Sweetheart timidly and respectfully, with never an encouraging sign, until one particular morning when she smiles glowingly at an invitation to a coffee date after class.

Why the unexpected turns? Anyone who is reading this chapter can produce some hypotheses. Gruff Boss had a frustrating battle with traffic driving to work, the water cooler was empty, an early telephone call was about a canceled contract, and in going over Marijane's most recent letters he found two misspelled words and one omitted line. No need exists to carry forward this kind of analysis for Daddy Dear and Belle Sweetheart, but in each instance the stimuli affecting their responses were numerous and varied, both external and internal. Sometimes, but not always, these cues are observable, in which case Sonny Boy or Marijane with a little sharper attentiveness and a little additional tact and self-control could have forestalled the outbursts. At other times, however, important influences on participants are internal, private, and unobservable—but sometimes guessable.

EXTERNAL CUES

Barney Borwinkel is trying to persuade Lucy Miller to meet him in the library the following evening to help him with a term paper. The two are standing in a corridor outside a classroom; and although at times Lucy will speak and Barney will listen, the example is one in which Barney is primarily the communicator and Lucy the receiver. Complications, however, are almost certain, for the influences on Lucy are so numerous and so potent that the message as she re-creates it will inevitably differ to some degree from the message that Barney intended. "What are these forces?" and "Why won't the message-as-conceived and the message-as-re-created be the same?" are the central questions for the present and succeeding subsections.

First, and not to be overlooked, is Barney's *overt message*. As important as Lucy's prejudices, pains, and immediate past experiences may be, the fact remains that Barney does transmit a stream of words, sentences, ideas, and appeals that he has organized in a certain way and that he has encoded or verbalized more or less artfully. Unless external noise makes it impossible to hear or unless anxiety or self-centered concerns are overpowering, Lucy receives enough of what Barney is saying to comprehend the essence of his proposal and its supporting arguments. How she interprets these ideas and what value judgments she makes, however, may or may not be in accord with Barney's desires.

Many factors determine whether the message-as-received is the message-as-presented.

Second, a *covert message* is likely to accompany the outward line of argument. Sometimes the covert message is deliberate, as in a conversation between two parents when the language conveys meanings at two levels, only one of which their children supposedly understand. In the present extended example Barney may or may not wish to include cues that his invitation is also an expression of admiration. To add this dimension, he can use various nonverbal indicators, such as tone of voice or a touch on the shoulder; or he can include a verbal sign such as, "Several in the class could help me, but I thought of you first." More often, however, the covert message is unintentional. For instance, if Barney is bashful, he would prefer not to acknowledge that his reason for the invitation is anything other than scholastic.

Third, the *cognitive context* will affect Lucy's re-creation of the message. Perhaps the professor in one of her other classes has lectured his students sternly on the importance of doing their own work. Self-reliance is a goal of education, he said, and the line between receiving help and turning in dishonest work is indistinct. With these ideas in mind, Lucy gives Barney's message a distinctive coloration: His request, although perhaps innocent, is improper.

The context, on the other hand, may be favorable, and Barney himself may be the source. Prior to suggesting the library meeting, Barney could converse about some of the other students in the class, about seeing them working together, and about hearing them talk about how valuable these experiences had been.

Fourth, the *affective context* is likely to influence decoding. In the present example the primary emotional factor is whether Barney seems admirable and likeable. Human beings, according to psychological theorists, strive for consistency. If Lucy thinks well of Barney, she probably will approve of his ideas. If he seems like a pleasant, interesting fellow, the suggestion that she meet him in the library will receive a positive interpretation.

Fifth, *noise*, which in communication theory includes all factors that disrupt the transmission of a message, may influence Lucy. Loud conversations may prevent her from hearing all that Barney says, and passersby who call out greetings may interrupt the flow of ideas. Worse yet, the constant stream of students and the occasional loud voice may be distractions that reduce attentiveness.

Sixth, *situational factors*, particularly those of time and place, produce cues that influence decoding. Interacting with other stimuli, they strengthen some, weaken others, and change some valences from positive to negative or vice versa. Parts of the preceding paragraphs suggest that Barney may have been unwise to talk with Lucy about help in the library as they came out of class into a busy corridor. On the other hand, the situation may be advantageous in that the context is more academic than personal. The "boy-likes-girl" overtone is less strong than it would be if Barney phoned Lucy at her apartment and made the same request. In that situation the girl would interpret the message as saying "I want to date you," and her answer would depend on whether she wished to begin any kind of emotional involvement.

How one perceives a message often depends on the time and the place. Barnlund, in a transactional analysis of a conversation, refers to a doctor who asks, "How are you today?"[2] On a street corner or at a bar, the communicatee would construe the question as nothing more than an expression of politeness and friendliness, but in a medical office one might interpret the same words as a request for a recitation of symptoms. Another example is the professor who greets a student entering the office with "I'm glad you came in." If the teacher does not invite the visitor to be seated, the situation evokes the judgment, "This conference is going to be brief and not very friendly." If the man or the woman invites the student to be seated but remains behind the desk, the reaction is likely to be, "You are the professor, and this conference is going to be formal and strictly business."

---

[2] Dean Barnlund, "A Transactional Model of Communication," in Larry L. Barker and Robert J. Kibler, eds., *Speech Communication Behavior* (Englewood Cliffs, N.J.: Prentice-Hall, 1971), pp. 71–80. Also in Johnnye Akin *et al.*, eds., *Language Behavior* (The Hague: Mouton, 1970), pp. 43–61.

Finally, if the visitor is seated and the teacher comes from behind the desk and sits in an easy chair, the perception probably becomes, "True enough, I am the student, but we are going to talk as two human beings. This professor is concerned about me as a person."

A complete catalogue of the cues that form the total "mix" as the receiver responds to the overt message is impossible and probably unnecessary. The point must be clear by now that how the communicatee mentally recreates a message is the product of numerous forces that operate both independently and jointly. Making the communication transaction even more complex are the many internal cues.

INTERNAL CUES

As Lucy hears and observes Barney make his plea for help with his term paper and as she notes and responds to many of the other external cues, she also is incorporating into the decoding process a number of internal stimuli. How she feels, whether she slept well, the comment on the paper the professor returned, the value system that she has been developing since infancy, her own self-image, what she has read recently, and her opinion of Barney—in a sense, all that she has ever done, felt, read, heard, or thought—have the potential to color her perceptions.

Among the most important of these internal cues that affect decoding are the *private cognitive factors*. This class includes all knowledge relevant to the topic under consideration—knowledge that has come from reading, observing, and talking to others. In the present example if Lucy knows that Barney is almost a straight "A" student, she is likely to perceive the library request as a stratagem for obtaining a date and not as a genuine appeal for help. If she knows that last semester the professor flunked two students for collaborating on a paper, then she views the proposed project with alarm.

In other types of communication events, private cognitive factors may loom larger than in the present example. One interprets the statements of a car salesman in the light of what one already knows about a particular make and model. One evaluates predictions on the economy against one's own knowledge of economic history, the information one has on business indicators, and the expert opinions previously read or heard. One responds to a movie critic's conclusions in accord with one's estimate of the reliability of past critiques and one's accumulation of appraisals obtained from friends who have already attended. Every individual has his or her own store of private cognitions, and differences in them largely explain why two persons may respond in opposite ways to the same sales pitch or the same political speech. In the language of the psychologists, each individual applies his or her own frame of reference to each new message. Much of the time one fits the item into an existing framework, perhaps distorting the former or modifying slightly the latter, but in some situations one rejects the fresh claim as untrue or irrelevant. Only in rare instances, when the new information is highly dramatic and of unquestionable authenticity, does an individual change a frame of reference markedly.

Closely related to the forces just described are *private affective factors,* whose importance is implied by the old saying, "We believe what we wish to believe." An old but interesting study on this point is the one by Hans Sebald on the Nixon-Kennedy debates in 1960. Sebald had 152 college students indicate whether they agreed or disagreed with statements taken from the debates and whether they thought that Nixon or Kennedy was the author. In about three fourths of the instances, the answers showed prejudices to be more powerful than reality.[3] In the example of Barney, Lucy almost certainly has feelings that affect her perceptions of the message and her reactions to it. Negative ideas about going to the library at night would tend to create an unfavorable response; and critical attitudes toward students who don't do their own work, likewise, would move her toward rejection. Her feelings toward Barney, on the other hand, may lead her in the opposite direction. Perhaps she likes boys with curly hair, or maybe she finds a boy who is a bit shy "rather cute."

Affective influences, besides the relatively stable, long-range ones mentioned in the preceding paragraph, also may be transitory. A person feels better on some days than on others—more cheerful, more cooperative, healthier, and more energetic. At times the reasons for being "up" or "down" are identifiable—a bit of bad luck, a compliment from an unexpected source, a check from home, a low grade, a job offer, or a good win in a competitive sport. At other times the whole world looks rosy or dark for no particular reason; to greater or lesser degrees, every human being experiences alternating upward and downward movements of an emotional cycle. Rational or irrational, these short-range influences affect a respondent, who in one mood perceives a message as offering promising opportunities but in another sees in it only dangers calling for caution. If Lucy is feeling lonely, bored, and sorry for herself, she may perceive Barney's message as an opportunity for escape; but if she is tired out and has a headache, an evening in the library will be a tiresome prospect.

Fully as important as generalized feelings are the receiver's *private perceptions of the sender.* A speech attributed to a person of high credibility, according to numerous research studies, produces more attitude change than does the same address when credited to someone of low credibility. One example of such a study is the experiment by Zagona and Harter on smoking. In each of three presentations the content was the same, but introductory material attributed the messages respectively to the *Surgeon General's Report on Smoking and Health, Life Magazine,* and an advertisement from the American Tobacco Company. The summary reads in part:

---

[3] Hans Sebald, "Limitations of Communication: Mechanisms of Image Maintenance in Form of Selective Perception, Selective Memory and Selective Distortion," *Journal of Communication,* 12 (September 1962), 142–149.

Statistically significant results indicated that: (1) Ss [subjects] receiving the information attributed to sources of high and low credibility retained more information than those receiving the information attributed to a source of medium credibility; (2) Ss who perceived the information as unbiased retained more than those who perceived it as biased; and (3) as credibility of the source increased, the percentage of Ss who agreed with the information and perceived it as trustworthy also increased.[4]

Not all experiments show a relation between credibility and learning, but almost all, beginning with Franklyn Haiman's research in 1949,[5] show a connection between credibility and attitude change.

In plain language, people tend to believe a person that they like, respect, or find attractive. Closely related to all three of these perceptions are apparent similarities—i.e., if the respondents see the communicator as being like themselves in age, sex, race, interests, or attitudes, then they tend to find the latter to be likeable, attractive, and worthy of respect. Similar problems and faults also tend to unify; and as Hitler illustrated with his scapegoating technique, perceptions of a common enemy or danger are especially potent forces for bringing people together.

Of the research studies that support the preceding statements, one of the most interesting is an experiment on attractiveness that involved a systematic variation of slides as the observers played the roles of jurors. The following is a summary:

During the playing of the trial, slides were shown . . . depicting each of the trial participants as they were testifying or otherwise speaking. The slides representing the plaintiff and defendant were systematically varied according to previously rated physical attractiveness.

Significant differences were found in verdicts and amount of damages between the attractive and unattractive litigants [sic].[6]

A very different experiment that confirmed a relation between liking and believing dealt with the reactions of children to TV commercials: "The investigation revealed that children generally tended to believe in those commercials they liked, and liked the commercials they believed."[7]

---

[4] Salvatore Zagona and M. Russell Harter, "Credibility of Source and Recipient's Attitude," *Perceptual and Motor Skills*, 23 (August 1966), 155.
[5] Franklyn Haiman, "An Experimental Study of the Effects of Ethos in Public Speaking," *Speech Monographs*, 16 (September 1949), 190–202.
[6] Joan B. Kessler and Richard A. Kulka, "The Influence of Physical Attractiveness on Jury Decision," a paper presented in New York at the convention of the Speech Communication Association, November 10, 1973, as summarized in *SCA Abstracts*, 1973, p. 43.
[7] Myles P. Breen and Jon T. Powell, "The Relationship Between Attractiveness and Credibility of Television Commercials as Perceived by Children," *Central States Speech Journal*, 24 (Summer 1973), 101.

The application of the preceding information to the example of Barney and Lucy should be plain. If Lucy likes Barney, sees relevant similarities between the two of them, and/or finds him attractive, she is likely to respond favorably to his message. Through prior conversations with him, her observations of his behavior, and statements she has heard from others, she has made tentative judgments about his competence and trustworthiness. As a result, she regards his plea for help as believable or otherwise, and she evaluates his proposed evening in the library as likely to be either dull or interesting. As in many other communication events, these private perceptions that the receiver has of the sender may weigh more heavily on the decoding of the message than all other forces combined.

Finally, among the internal factors affecting Lucy's re-creation of the message are her *needs, motives,* and *individual traits.* Is she trusting or suspicious, desirous of helping others or self-centered, cautious or impetuous, open-minded or closed, submissive or domineering, high in self-esteem or low, confident or anxious, optimistic or pessimistic? Is she more strongly motivated by a desire for admiration or a desire for good grades? Does helping someone else give her a good feeling, or does she regret the time lost from serving her own interests? Chapter 6 contains material on motivation and on personality traits that are important to group processes as well as to dyadic (two-person) conversations. Application of this knowledge of needs, motives, and individual qualities should include the realization that they have both long-range and short-range dimensions. Anxiety, trust, and self-esteem, for example, have a degree of constancy from day to day, but they also change with the circumstances in the degree of influence that they exercise on the handling of incoming information and on the making of judgments and decisions.

What Lucy thinks that Barney is saying when he talks about meeting her in the library, in summary, depends upon how she processes a vast number of stimuli at about the same time that she is receiving the overt message. Of all the stimuli, both external and internal, that are potentially influential, only a few will be decisive in a given situation; and which these will be is a complex matter involving personal traits, recent happenings, and the words and actions of the speaker, discussant, or conversationalist. Precise analysis is impossible, and the interpretations given to messages often surprise the sender. In a rough way, however, the responses of those whom one knows well are predictable, and to a degree the outcome of the verbal and the nonverbal signs that the communicator sends is foreseeable. The more that the sender knows about influences other than the overt message, the greater the accuracy in prediction and the better the chances of making strategic adjustments. As for receivers, the better they understand the stimuli that lead to a particular judgment, the more likely they are to appraise their own rationality and to "take a second look" before speaking or acting.

THIRD-PARTY CUES

Although the two preceding subsections on decoding are important, they are incomplete; for they consider only the forces that Barney creates as sender and that Lucy draws forth as receiver. A further possibility is the participation in the conversation of additional persons. Lucy, of course, hears what they say, sees their facial expressions, and receives various other signals; these cues become as much a part of the matrix for decoding as those that Barney originates or those that she generates from her internal store of knowledge, feelings, and needs. The contributions of the third party may clarify what the sender says, they may distract from the message by introducing irrelevancies, and they may either support or weaken the argument. In all instances they alter the context and affect the receiver's perceptions of the sender.

The mere presence of a third person has implications for *role, group norms,* and *commitment*. With the involvement of more than two individuals, the pressure on the receiver to fulfill role expectations increases. If Lucy sees herself as a student leader with responsibilities for helping others, she now has added incentives for agreeing to assist Barney. If she sees herself, on the other hand, as one of the social elite, she may now see a library date with a nonentity as a violation of her role. Acceptance of the invitation may be contrary to group norms, whose influence on behavior is likely to be stronger when other members are present. Campuses probably are more democratic now, but some years ago sorority women did not date independents; and if a woman was tempted to ignore the norm, the presence of a sorority sister was a strong reminder. Finally, the presence of a third party increases the power of commitment to affect behavior. In other words, any position that Lucy enunciates will be hard for her to change.

The presence of the third person thus changes Barney's invitation from a private matter between two people into a public happening. Lucy now must perceive the request as requiring her to take a public stand on liking or not liking Barney and on willingness or unwillingness to help a fellow student. With a third party present, any individual loses some of the freedom to act according to his or her own inclinations.

Sometimes, also, the third or the fourth party may become an active participant in the conversation. Sheila may, for example, bring in an additional element by reminding Lucy that the dormitory council has a meeting at eight o'clock or by mentioning that the two young women had planned to wash their hair and then review for an examination in French. Sheila may also express disapproval nonverbally by raised eyebrows, a frown, or tone of voice. "Catching someone alone," in conclusion, can be as sound a tactic as "catching someone in a good humor."

CIRCULAR CUES

The final set of cues for the receiver are those arising through the circularity that occurs in many situations. Although the possibility exists that the present extended example consists of a single speech by Barney, Lucy's answer, and nothing more, a series of efforts, either with or without remarks by additional conversationalists, is more likely:

BARNEY: "I'm sure having a hard time with my term paper."

LUCY: "Is that so? Well, they're always rough to do."

BARNEY: "I was wondering. If you don't have something else planned, maybe you could meet me in the library tonight and help me out."

LUCY: "Oh! I hadn't ever thought about anything like that."

BARNEY: "Yeh. I really need the help. And I've been thinking about it. I think you could be more help than anyone else in the class."

LUCY: "Really? What kind of help?"

BARNEY: "Oh, getting things organized. I've got a bunch of notes, but I don't seem to know what to do with them."

LUCY: "I see. How much time were you thinking about?"

BARNEY: "That would depend a lot on you. I thought we might meet about 7:30 and work a couple of hours."

LUCY: "I don't think I have that much time, but an hour maybe."

And so the conversation may continue, but even this excerpt shows how the give-and-take helps Lucy clarify the nature of the request and gain an increasingly sound basis for perceptions of the sender as a person. With further questions she can probe both topics in any direction she chooses. As for Barney, in the continuing exchange he has opportunities to revise his overt message and, if he is keen enough, the covert cues as well.

FEEDBACK

Norbert Wiener, who is credited with originating the term *feedback*, defines it as "a method of controlling a system by reinserting into it the results of its past performance."[8] Among mechanical feedback devices, the most familiar is the thermostat, which notes and sends information that in turn controls the furnace or the air conditioner. The parallel of this system to human behavior is clear, as the following passage from a famous book on communication indicates:

---

[8] Norbert Wiener, *The Human Use of Human Beings* (Boston: Houghton Mifflin Co., 1954), p. 61.

104   THE TRANSACTION: PROCESSES AND DYNAMIC FACTORS

Feedback is an important part of the communicating process. How would you describe the responses that these groups are feeding back to the respective speakers? What adjustments, if any, do you think that he or she should make? (Credits: *above,* National Education Association Communications Services/Joe Di Dio; *opposite top,* Olive Pierce; *opposite bottom,* Bob Fitch/Black Star)

When a person has expressed an idea in words to another, a reaction is necessarily expected. And this reaction contributes to clarify, extend, or alter the original idea. Feedback, therefore, refers to the process of correction through incorporation of information about effects received. When a person perceives the results produced by his own actions, the information so derived will influence subsequent actions. Feedback of information thus becomes a steering device upon which learning and the correction of errors and misunderstandings are based.[9]

---

[9] Jurgen Ruesch and Weldon Kees, *Nonverbal Communication* (Berkeley: University of California Press, 1956), p. 4.

What kind of nonverbal feedback is the woman giving to the message that the man is presenting? What effects do you think this feedback will have on his continuing attempts to communicate? (Charles Gatewood)

Important as the preceding functions are, still more significant is the danger of breakdown. As Thompson and Insalata observe, "Feedback may be the most vital phase in the communication process, for failure in this phase renders misunderstandings permanent."[10]

FEEDBACK IN INTERPERSONAL AND SMALL-GROUP SITUATIONS

The near universality of feedback is one of its most impressive qualities. A sender gives directions, and the receiver asks a question for clarification.

[10] Wayne N. Thompson and S. John Insalata, "Communication from Attorney to Client," *Journal of Communication*, 14 (March 1964), 33.

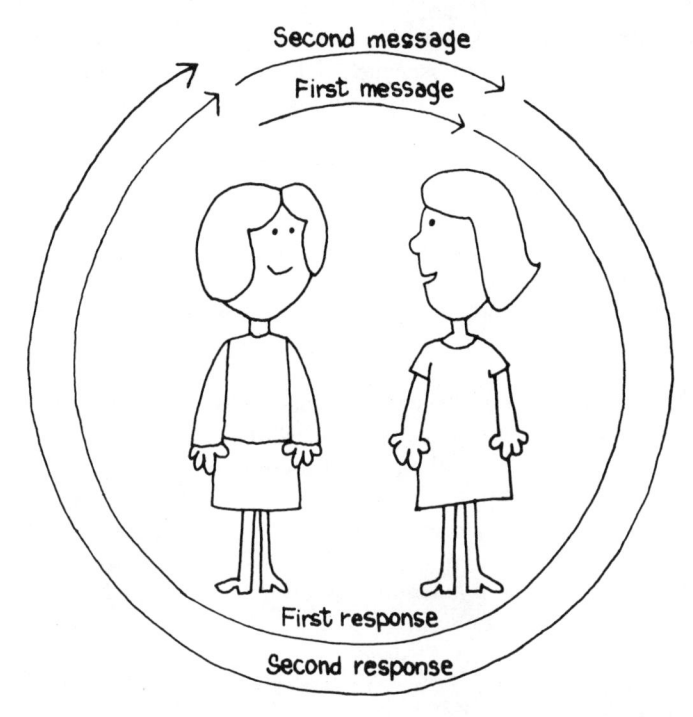

Circularity is a characteristic of communication.

An interviewee summarizes his experience, and the interviewer by manner, if not word, indicates that she is unimpressed. A discussant suggests a solution to a problem, and a colleague shows both agreement and dissent by offering a modification. The automobile dealer tells how many miles a car gets to the gallon, and the prospective buyer conveys skepticism by both comment and manner. A student in a conference tells of his or her research attempts, and the professor expresses either approval or doubts. Forthright comments, innuendo, raised eyebrows, frowns, silent clapping, and many other cues let the sender know how a small group or a second person is responding.

The message-response sequence, which is the format of the preceding examples, however, is in most situations only the beginning. Still more important is the circularity that feedback commonly institutes. The student responds to the professor's reservations by asking about additional sources, and the latter readjusts the original advice by inquiring further about the exact nature of the research project. The usual situation in dyadic communication is that the two persons alternate in the roles of sender and receiver. Each speaks a number of times, and together they work through the topic until no misunderstanding exists or until they shape each other's thoughts into agreement on a solution to the problem.

Similarly, in a discussion feedback is critical to the process of modifying views in any movement toward consensus. Scheidel and Crowell, two respected authorities on group thought, give this description:

In summary, we can report that the feedback process, as defined here, occupies a major portion of the total effort in group interaction. It is a sub-process which occurs within the usual sequence of discussion interaction. It is characterized by increased attempts at clarification and agreement and by decreased efforts in questioning. It is a circular process which probably serves an anchoring function in the group communication process.[11]

Why so much stress on the importance of feedback and circularity? Is it not evident that most communication events consist of a series of contributions with individuals alternating in the roles of sender and receiver? One reason for the emphasis here is the neglect by traditional speech textbooks of the transactional nature of discourse. A second and better reason is that many persons when preparing for conferences, interviews, and discussions give too little thought to the possible feedback messages and to the best adjustments that they might make to each.

FEEDBACK IN PLATFORM ADDRESS

In contrast with group situations, circularity occurs during public communication to a limited degree, if at all; even the customary question period after a speech rarely goes beyond a single inquiry followed by a response. Since simple verbal feedback is uncommon, the speaker must depend primarily on observing and interpreting such nonverbal cues as restlessness, smiles of approval, and puzzled looks. A darkened auditorium and glaring lights make even these signs hard to perceive.

How well a speech is going is of such importance that speakers should cultivate the art of receiving feedback and adjusting to it. Only in this way can they know whether to add an example, shorten the address, eliminate the now needless plea, or change from one line of argument to another. Among the talented speakers who have been sensitive to their audiences is Stokely Carmichael: "In this respect he was acutely aware of the feedback gained from his audience's faces, making use of repetitive and reiterative devices to complement or redefine his extended illustrations and examples."[12]

---

[11] Thomas M. Scheidel and Laura Crowell, "Feedback in Small Group Communication," *Quarterly Journal of Speech*, 52 (October 1966), 278.

[12] Art Pollock, "Stokeley Carmichael's New Black Rhetoric," *Southern Speech Communication Journal*, 37 (Fall 1971), 93.

CONCLUSION

Communication usually is a transaction. Although each situation has its own special set of characteristics, in many instances two important attributes are circularity and jointness. In other words, the total message created in many communication events is the joint product of the participants, and its creation occurs through a circular process. In interpersonal and small-group situations jointness and circularity are paramount, but even in platform speaking their influence is greater than most persons realize.

To understand communication and to be an effective participant, students need to appreciate the nature of the transaction. They need to recognize that the message created by the receiver in his or her mind is a product of many influences other than the stimuli encoded and transmitted by the sender. External, internal, third-party, and circular cues are all influential.

Of major importance to the communication process is feedback, whose precise nature varies from the small-group to the platform situation. Decoding and feedback are processes that affect the outcome of conversations, discussions, and platform speeches. The basis of meaningful discourse, according to Part I of this text, is the invention of worthwhile, responsible content; but success with the message depends on understanding the dynamics of interpersonal relations and on applying those insights intelligently.

PROBLEMS AND EXERCISES

1. Observe communication situations for one day. In one column list those in which the intended message and the re-created message probably were similar, and in a second column those in which the two seemingly differed either in substance or in emotional connotations.

2. From the log prepared for the preceding exercise, select one instance of breakdown for analysis. Record your wordings of the essences of the two messages (the intended and the re-created), and identify the cues that probably were responsible for the misunderstanding or misinterpretation. (One example of a misinterpretation would be an intended compliment that the receiver perceived as an insult.)

3. Deliver a brief speech to the class with the prior knowledge that at some point they will appear to be puzzled and that at a second point they will indicate that they disagree. Watch for these signs, and adjust the content to meet the problems.

4. Form a group of five or six students with one as sender and the others as receivers. The sender should make a brief descriptive statement about a dog, a cat, or some other pet. The receivers should record phrases expressing ideas that come to mind as they listen to the statement, and at the close they should take five minutes to try to identify the influences that affected their decoding. Among the possible reactions are ideas on the size, the color, and the actions of the pet and emotional responses such as fear, distrust, or affection. The group should discuss their decoding experiences before repeating the exercise with a different student as sender. Other possible topics besides pets for descriptive statements are vacation spots, concerts, movies, and sports events.

REFERENCES

Adams, W. Clifton. "The Effect of Various Channels of Feedback on the Communication of Information," *Speech Monographs*, 40 (June 1973), 147–150.

Blubaugh, J. A. "Effects of Positive and Negative Audience Feedback on Selected Variables of Speech Behavior," *Speech Monographs*, 36 (June 1969), 131–137.

Borgatta, Edgar F., and William W. Lambert, eds. *Handbook of Personality Theory and Research*. Skokie, Ill.: Rand McNally & Co., 1969.

Giffin, Kim, and Bobby R. Patton, eds. *Basic Readings in Interpersonal Communication*. New York: Harper & Row, 1971.

Johannesen, Richard L. "The Emerging Concept of Communication as Dialogue," *Quarterly Journal of Speech*, 57 (December 1971), 373–382.

Rhodes, Steven C. "A Unit in Feedback Utilization for Basic College Speech Courses," *Speech Teacher*, 24 (September 1975), 282–286.

Rossiter, Charles M., Jr., and W. Barnett Pearce. *Communicating Personally*. New York: The Bobbs-Merrill Co., 1975.

Saulnier, Leda, and Teresa Simard. *Personal Growth and Interpersonal Relations*. Englewood Cliffs, N.J.: Prentice-Hall, 1973.

Stewart, John R. *Bridges Not Walls*. Reading, Mass.: Addison-Wesley Publishing Co., 1973.

Swenson, Clifford H., Jr. *Introduction to Interpersonal Relations*. Glenview, Ill.: Scott, Foresman and Co., 1973.

Vick, Charles F., and Roy V. Wood. "Similarity of Past Experience and the Communication of Meaning," *Speech Monographs*, 36 (June 1969), 159–162.

Wilmot, William W. *Dyadic Communication: A Transactional Perspective*. Reading, Mass.: Addison-Wesley Publishing Co., 1975.

6
THE TRANSACTION: DYNAMIC FACTORS

After studying this chapter the reader should be able to do the following:

Make at least one statement in a brief conversation that at least 75 percent of the observers will recognize as trust-building

Distinguish between high and low ego-involving situations when given examples

Give two or more examples of persons of high status

List at least three roles that he or she plays during a typical week

Analyze a personal experience in which behavior was closed minded

Identify the primary motive appeals after hearing an advertisement or a persuasive speech

Invent two original examples that illustrate consistency theory

State at least three values that are prevalent among today's college students

Give one or more original examples of beliefs, attitudes, and stereotypes

Understanding the processes of decoding and feedback is important to students of communication, but they need also to comprehend the dynamic factors that affect interactions whenever two or more human beings assemble. An instructive example is a meeting of the executive officers of the Humburger Toy Company, which manufactures and sells games, puzzles, and similar products nationwide. At this meeting Horace Lowman, the assistant sales manager and a newcomer, made a presentation calling for setting up three regional offices with a sales supervisor in each. Using an overhead projector, he presented a series of graphs contrasting the flat sales totals for the Humburger Company with the rising figures for its principal rival. Lowman then explained his proposal by displaying a map and by enumerating in detail the duties of the three regional heads. Finally, he named a publishing house and a producer of novelties and notions that were using a plan similar to his, and he presented statistics indicating that their sales had increased.

So commendable were Lowman's research, reasoning, and methods of presentation that the failure of his proposal invites analysis. The first opposition came from an unexpected source—Ray Fowler, the sales manager. Fowler had worried about keeping his top position ever since the night that "Hi" Humburger, the founder and president, had phoned him in Kansas City and offered him the promotion. The flat sales figures had increased Fowler's sense of insecurity, and he fearfully sensed that "Hi" in recent weeks had been less cordial in his morning greeting than in the past. Feeling that failure for his assistant's plan would be more strategic than its success, Fowler pointed out that the three regional supervisors would command large salaries without being directly productive, and he bolstered his slender ego by drawing on his own experiences as support for his comments.

Joining in the opposition was Lucille Blaha, a vice president and the company treasurer. Like Fowler, she was low in self-esteem; but in addition she distrusted all of her colleagues and bright, new ones like Lowman especially. She, too, wondered about his motivations and ambitions, but in addition she questioned in her own mind the accuracy of some of his data. Her comments were neither numerous nor sharply critical, but she showed her approval of Fowler's objections and her questions disrupted the continuity of Lowman's presentation and suggested her doubts about his materials.

The critical force, however, was "Hi" Humburger, the company president. Despite his outward joviality and his pride in his vigorous health, though in the sixties, he was inwardly a closed-minded authoritarian. It was his company; and although he conducted meetings with a show of democracy, in reality he resented any idea that came from a source other than himself. The old ways of doing business, he thought without appreciating his own generalized inflexibility, had worked for thirty-three years, and they should be sufficient for another twelve months. As was his custom, "Hi" did not say much; but his failure to express approval encouraged Fowler and Blaha to continue their opposition.

As time went on, tension built. The lack of enthusiasm puzzled Lowman, and his confidence diminished. Eventually, to the relief of almost everyone, "Hi" commended Lowman for his presentation, mentioned the lateness of the hour, and said that the proposal was too important for hasty action. Shortly thereafter the meeting adjourned.

Is the preceding case typical? In a broad sense it is, for dynamic factors, including self-esteem, trust, and closed-mindedness, often are decisive when a group weighs a possible change. Involvement, motives, beliefs, values, attitudes, and the desire for consistency also affect outcomes. These factors, singly or in combination, often produce within the individual a *hidden agenda*. Often knowingly, but sometimes unconsciously and unintentionally, conferees go into meetings with purposes that they would never announce. To discredit another individual, to strengthen one's self-image, to enhance one's credibility, and to indulge in the pleasure of having one's own way are among the personal objectives that are irrelevant to the merits of a proposal.

PERSONALITY TRAITS

Irrational and *unpredictable* are words that puzzled participants often use when describing the behavior of their companions in two-person and small-group situations. *Uninformed* and *unanalyzed*, however, are more appropriate terms, for the failure to foresee what will happen is a result of knowing too little about human nature and of giving too little thought to the dynamic forces that will influence the conversation, interview, or conference. Human behavior, true enough, is complex, but scholars have found out much about the dynamic forces that are common in meetings; and the individual participant over a period of time should be able to learn which qualities are peculiar to each friend or coworker. The purpose of this first section is to describe the most important of the personality traits that affect cooperativeness, persuasibility, and other dimensions of the communication event.

TRUST

Two familiar truths form a good starting point for a study of trust: (1) If Lucy trusts Barney, to continue the example from Chapter 5, she is more likely to respond favorably to his requests and arguments than if she does not; and (2) if mutual trust prevails in a group, its members are more likely to be cooperative and productive than if there is suspicion. But the student of communication must go beyond these obvious generalizations if he or she is to improve in interpersonal skills. Two practical questions are "What are the conditions conducive to trust?" and "How does one conduct oneself so that others will be trusting?"

For answers to these questions, the student can turn to the work of Morton Deutsch, who for about twenty years has been the foremost authority on trust. He makes the following generalizations:

We trust a person whose internalized values are likely to give him or her a sense of responsibility.

We are more likely to engage in trusting behavior ourselves if we think that the other person is trustworthy.

We predict the probable behavior of the other person according to our perceptions of his or her intentions.

We trust the other person if we think that he or she has the power and the ability to do what he or she promises.

We are likely to be trusting if it appears that the other person has nothing to gain through untrustworthy behavior.

We trust others if we have the power to exert control over them.

We trust those who treat us well.

Our trust increases toward a second person when a mutually disliked third party is present.

Mutual trust is likely when participants are concerned about one another's welfare or when all seem to be in the same situation.

Communication among the participants can increase mutual trust. Specifically, individuals should (1) state their intentions, (2) express their expectations of others, (3) indicate what they will do if others violate expectations, and (4) point out a means of restoring cooperation after a violation of expectations occurs.[1]

Research since 1958 has not refuted any of Deutsch's recommendations, all of which seem sensible. Be frank and open about intentions and expectations. Communicate freely with your companions and coworkers. Emphasize ways in which decisions and actions that are in their best interests are also in yours. Try to display qualities of sincerity, honesty, and truthfulness, but also give practical reasons that others should think you trustworthy. Be trusting if you wish others to have confidence in you.

A scene in a movie exemplifies the preceding point. The principal character was a young woman who was a member of the Big Sisters society of her city, and the plot dealt with the attempted rehabilitation of a Little Sister, who had been a teen-age shoplifter. In one scene Big Sister showed her trust by running an errand and leaving Little Sister alone in the apartment. The latter, in turn, contributed to the slow building of a trusting relationship between the two by resisting the temptation to take advantage

---

[1] Morton Deutsch, "Trust and Suspicion," *Journal of Conflict Resolution*, 2 (December 1958), 265–279.

of the opportunity to commit petty thievery. The two steps in this episode—A's putting herself in jeopardy and B's refusing to profit from the opportunity—according to an experiment by Swinth are effective in building trust. ". . . in summary, . . . it was necessary that *both* participants give something to the relationship before trust was established."[2] Later Swinth observes, "Whether it be in interpersonal relations or international relations, the participants cannot be expected ever to trust each other in critical moments if these constitute their only opportunity to interact."[3]

A continuing relationship is indeed necessary for the creation of mutual confidence between two persons or among the members of a group, but other factors also are important. Even the physical furnishings of the room can make a person feel secure and comfortable or the reverse, and the manner in which an individual enters and begins a discussion sets a tone that affects the eventual outcome. Gesture, the look in the eyes, muscular tensions, a quaver in the voice, and a mistimed hesitation are further examples of cues that affect judgments.

Finally, to what extent should the student who is reading this book trust others? As an ethical man or woman, one has a responsibility to be trustworthy; as a member of a group, one will be more productive in an atmosphere of mutual trust than in one of suspicion. But can the individual expect others to adhere to the same high standard? Unfortunately, not always. Every situation requires a separate evaluation. One should neither suspect everyone, nor should one trust everyone. The preceding paragraphs are double-edged: They suggest ways to build trust, but they also identify factors useful in judging others.

INVOLVEMENT

Also tending to determine the responses of listeners to an address and the course of a discussion or a conference is the degree of involvement, or intensity of emotion, that people feel about the topic and its subissues. Barney, whose brother died when struck by a drunken driver, becomes aroused whenever anyone discusses greater leniency for traffic offenders. Lucy, as president of her sorority, regards adverse comments on Greek houses as seriously as she does personal criticism. In contrast, neither Barney nor Lucy is ego-involved when someone says that the electoral college should be abolished or that the prime interest rate is too high.

Relation of Involvement to Attention

For information on how ego-involvement affects communication, today's scholar still relies heavily on the research findings and the theories of the

[2] R. L. Swinth, "The Establishment of the Trust Relationship," *Journal of Conflict Resolution*, 11 (September 1967), 343.
[3] *Ibid.*

Sherifs.[4] Three statements, the third following from the first two, summarize their work on attention:

1. Low involvement is likely to cause disinterest in the message and loss of attention.

2. Extremely high involvement often interferes with the clear, objective reception of the message. Through selectivity the involved person hears what he or she wants to hear.

3. The relation of involvement to persuasibility, as Sherif and Hovland were the first to theorize, is curvilinear. Those of low involvement are too inattentive to receive the message fully, and those of high involvement resist change.[5]

Of what practical value to the persuader are the preceding insights? Briefly, they suggest the adaptations that one should make—the kind of audience that is especially hard to motivate and the kind that one must approach with patience, moderation, and a considerable amount of restatement. Knowing the potential cause of a breakdown in communication is the first step toward devising effective countermeasures.

Relation of Involvement to Persuasibility

High involvement, according to one research study, makes it difficult to agree. The objective of the experiment was to study the frequency of consensus when two persons started with opposing views. By manipulating the placement of individuals according to whether their involvement was high or low, the experimenters confirmed the prediction that those who were highly involved reached consensus less often than did those who were not.[6] In other words, when people really care about an issue, they are reluctant to relinquish their positions.

The principal significance of the findings on high involvement and persuasibility is that they provide a guide to the speaker in deciding how much attitude change it is strategic to request. Not only is partial success preferable to failure but also limited progress can be the beginning of a step-by-step movement toward the eventual attainment of the full goal. The teen-ager who has wrecked the family car is unlikely to have full driving privileges restored immediately, but in a single conversation he or she

---

[4] Their works include the following: Carolyn W. Sherif and Muzafer Sherif, *Attitude, Ego-Involvement, and Change* (New York: Wiley, 1967); Muzafer Sherif and Hadley Cantril, *The Psychology of Ego-Involvement* (New York: Wiley, 1947); Muzafer Sherif and Carl I. Hovland, *Social Judgment* (New Haven, Conn.: Yale University Press, 1961); Carolyn Sherif, Muzafer Sherif, and Roger E. Nebergall, *Attitude and Attitude Change* (Philadelphia: Saunders, 1965).
[5] Sherif and Hovland, *Social Judgment*, p. 197.
[6] Kenneth K. Sereno and C. David Mortensen, "The Effects of Ego-Involved Attitudes on Conflict Negotiation in Dyads," *Speech Monographs*, 26 (March 1969), 8–12.

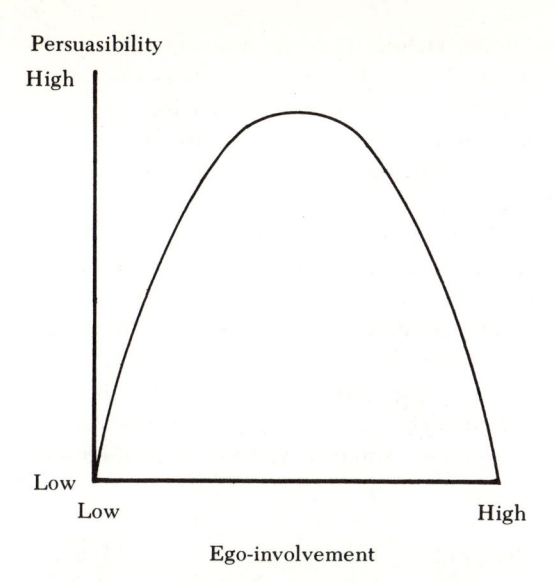

Figure 6.1 The relation of persuasibility to ego-involvement. Poor attention may reduce persuasibility when involvement is low; preoccupation may reduce it when involvement is high.

may secure permission to drive a short distance to church or to drive when adults are present.

The tolerable degree of discrepancy between the listener's attitude and the position that the speaker advocates has been the topic for a considerable body of sophisticated theorizing and experimenting. The foremost scholars again have been Carolyn and Muzafer Sherif, who developed the theory that every individual has a range of positions that he or she can accept in reference to an issue. They go on to say that if the advocated position is within this "latitude of approval" or only slightly beyond, then persuasive success is probable.[7] An excessive request directed to a highly involved receiver, on the other hand, may create such severe antagonism that the communicator's effort boomerangs.[8]

The outcome, of course, depends on a number of factors besides the size of the discrepancy and the degree of involvement. Whether the teen-ager's message evokes a favorable response, for example, depends also on the kind of day the parent has had at the office, how responsible the youngster

---

[7] The Sherifs have written on this topic in more than one place. See, for example, *Attitude, Ego-Involvement, and Change*, pp. 115–116, 129–136.

[8] Kenneth K. Sereno, "Ego Involvement: A Neglected Variable in Speech-Communication Research," *Quarterly Journal of Speech*, 55 (February 1969), 71.

has been recently, and many other factors. Among these additional influences are credibility and liking. Prospective persuadees, as one would predict, will tolerate more extreme statements when they like and/or respect someone than they will when these conditions are absent.

Often, in conclusion, the only realistic way to attain an objective is through a campaign involving a series of small demands. In this way Shakespeare's Iago undermined Othello's confidence in Desdemona; and in this way, if at all, a young person can influence a brother or a sister to give up an undesirable friend.

The coin, however, has its other side. When the receiver feels low involvement for the topic, according to research, the larger the change in attitude that the sender requests the greater the probable effect.[9] Rare instances may call for a totally different strategy—making an extreme demand with the hope of securing a compromise somewhere near the desired position.

The Estimation of Ego-Involvement

The wise communicator, therefore, adjusts purposes and appeals to the estimate of the listener's degree of involvement. Obvious signs at times make an appraisal easy. Strongly worded outbursts, noncommittal responses, apathetic bodily reactions, a flushed face, clenched fists, trembling, tense muscles, strained voice, and nervous movements are well-known indicators of whether emotion is high or low. As a rule, the stronger the involvement, the easier its detection; and according to one experiment, the observers judged females more accurately than they did males.[10]

In some situations, however, the communicator may wish to estimate the level of involvement beforehand. Such a prediction is possible if one knows the prospective receiver, for certain factors are related to ego-involvement:

The closeness of the issue to personal needs and interests An interesting research study illustrating this generalization used as materials one experimental message calling for stricter rules for boys' dress and a second arguing for stricter control over girls' dress. The outcome, as anticipated, was that the first was more ego-involving for male subjects and the second for female. For each sex, moreover, the more involving message resulted in stronger reactions toward both content and speaker.[11]

---

[9] Jonathan L. Freedman, "Involvement, Discrepancy, and Change," *Journal of Abnormal and Social Psychology*, 69 (September 1964), 290–295.

[10] Joe Ayres, "Observers' Judgements of Audience Members' Attitudes," *Western Speech*, 39 (Winter 1975), 40–50. Ayres also reports that his subjects were more accurate in judging those of high involvement than those of low.

[11] Alice H. Eagly and Melvin Manis, "Evaluation of Message and Communicator as a Function of Involvement," *Journal of Personality and Social Psychology*, 3 (April 1966), 483–485.

The closeness of the issue to self-image Every person pictures himself or herself in a particular way—as scholar, athlete, jovial companion, or model of propriety. Whatever the self-image is, its preservation is so important to the individual that any threatening event or information creates intense ego-involvement.

The closeness of the issue to central values Again, individuals vary, each having personal priorities and his or her own unique way of joining separate values together to form a system. If the center for one's world is religion, any challenge to this faith—perhaps a slurring attack or reported misconduct by a clergyman—is ego-involving.

Commitment on the issue A public stand deepens involvement, for it makes adjustments in attitudes and beliefs difficult.

Conclusion

Even this brief discussion indicates the importance of ego-involvement to human behavior in conversations, interviews, discussions, conferences, and audiences for platform speeches. This factor is a major force in determining not only the general atmosphere of a meeting but also the responses of individual observers or participants.

ROLE, STATUS, AND SELF-ESTEEM

Other determinants of how individuals respond in communication situations are self-esteem and perceptions of status and role. They are likely to act and speak in ways that they think meet expectations. The juvenile troublemaker, for example, upon assuming the role of school safety guard sometimes becomes conscientious and responsible; and the college graduate upon becoming teacher rather than student ordinarily makes the necessary modifications in dress and behavior to fit the new position. To a degree, therefore, the communicator can predict responses by thinking about the roles of listeners and fellow participants.

Status, like role, has been the topic for a considerable body of research and theorizing of significance to the sender. First, messages that threaten status are almost sure to provoke resistance. One example of this situation is the need that sometimes arises for a responsible citizen to take a stand that arouses opposition because the change would curb someone's power. If possible, the communicator should include face-saving elements that permit the receiver to continue to see himself or herself favorably. As a minimum, the sender should recognize the powerful effect of self-perceived status when developing the details of the message and verbalizing the ideas. Second, a proposal by a group, rather than one by an individual, increases support for the plan because with skillful management no one

Each individual has several roles, such as teacher, parent, scout leader, and member of the choir. These roles affect responses to communicated messages.

loses status. Artfully handled, the conference has no losers. Each member contributes and receives respect; the outcome belongs to all. Third, when several persons are available to present a proposal, choosing an individual of high status is strategic. This advantage of the person of high status over one of lesser position is increased, according to one experiment, if the communicator also can exercise coercive power.[12] Fourth, situations in which status is ill defined are troublesome, for participants feel insecure and see themselves as competitors. Newcomers in particular are likely to have no clear-cut and recognized priorities among themselves and to be less concerned with the topic under discussion than they are with self-advancement. Under these circumstances meetings rarely are productive. Rivals for status are not inclined to accept one another's ideas.

Related to role and status is self-esteem, which also affects persuasibility. The person of high self-esteem, according to most research, is harder to persuade than is a colleague whose self-esteem is low. Those who think well of themselves tend to regard their own ideas as superior to the contributions of others. Persons of low self-esteem, on the other hand, take their own views lightly and are eager to please others by agreeing with them. Partly offsetting these influences, however, is the relative freedom of the high-esteem person to change positions. Unlike the colleague of low self-regard, confident individuals can acknowledge that they were wrong without feeling a severe threat to their security.

---

[12] Barry R. Schlenker and James T. Tedeschi, "Interpersonal Attraction and the Exercise of Coercive and Reward Power," *Human Relations*, 25 (November 1972), 427–440.

This speaker is in costume. What effects do you think his dress will have on the attentiveness of his audience and on the effectiveness of his presentation? (Norman Hurst/Stock Boston)

Students who have seen as a late, late movie *Moulin Rouge* have observed in Toulouse-Lautrec a dramatic example of low self-esteem behavior that an experimenter found to be true. The study offers support for "the assumption that low-self-esteem individuals are unusually receptive to affection when they realize that it is being offered, but that it is most difficult for them to recognize affectionate overtures."[13]

Other research has produced still other interesting findings. The degree to which the individual influenced the group, according to Roland L. Frye, affected self-esteem.[14] Men and women, Charles R. Berger reports, differ in the importance of being liked: ". . . part of females' self-evaluation is contingent on their certainty about others liking them. This relationship does not appear for males."[15] "Members of the high self-esteem groups," Kwal and Fleshler write, "expressed more satisfaction with the results of

---

[13] A. Rodney Wellens and Donald L. Thistlethwaite, "Comparison of Three Theories of Cognitive Balance," *Journal of Personality and Social Psychology*, 20 (October 1971), 84.
[14] Roland L. Frye, "The Effect of Orientation and Feedback of Success and Effectiveness on the Attractiveness and Esteem of the Group," *Journal of Social Psychology*, 70 (December 1966), 205–211.
[15] Charles R. Berger, "Sex Differences Related to Self-Esteem Factor Structure," *Journal of Consulting and Clinical Psychology*, 32 (August 1968), 442.

the discussion, believed their groups to be more cooperative, and evaluated the atmosphere as being more pleasant."[16] Finally, those of high self-esteem were more likely to see the leadership of the group as being shared than were those low in self-concept.[17]

AUTHORITARIANISM, DOGMATISM, AND CLOSED-MINDEDNESS

Also among the personal qualities that may affect the communication transaction are the related traits of authoritarianism, dogmatism, and closed-mindedness. Since these attributes have little to do with status or any other factor that one can observe readily, a newcomer to a group rarely can predict which associates have these characteristics. In time, though, words and actions reveal the presence or the absence of these traits. Predictions, then, become possible, for these qualities are fairly consistent from topic to topic and from one situation to another.

The most significant research finding in this area is the conclusion that the most effective way to influence an authoritarian is to cite experts or to capitalize on one's own expertness. Other interesting findings are these: (1) The closed-minded person has difficulty in judging the message and the source independently, each for its own merit.[18] (2) The closed-minded individual, especially if male, is slow to recognize humor.[19] (3) Dogmatic persons resist new information and tend to regard compromise as a defeat.[20]

MOTIVATION

A second, but related, set of dynamic factors affecting the communication transaction comes under the heading of motivation. The basic theory is simple: Every human being has certain needs and desires; if a message seems to fulfill one of these, the receiver responds favorably. A father desires the safety of his family; he buys one set of automobile tires in preference to another. A high school girl wishes to be attractive; she wears braces so that eventually her teeth will be straight. A young man hopes to

---

[16] Teri Kwal and Helen Fleshler, "The Influence of Self-Esteem on Emergent Leadership Patterns," *Speech Teacher*, 22 (March 1973), 105.
[17] *Ibid.*
[18] Milton Rokeach, *The Open and Closed Mind* (New York: Basic Books, 1960), pp. 58–60.
[19] Gerald R. Miller and Paula Bacon, "Open- and Closed-Mindedness and Recognition of Visual Humor," *Journal of Communication*, 21 (June 1971), 150–159.
[20] An article that reports original research and that summarizes earlier studies is Timothy G. Plax and Lawrence B. Rosenfeld, "Dogmatism and Decisions Involving Risk," *Southern Speech Communication Journal*, 41 (Spring 1976), 266–277.

Self-actualization needs
Esteem needs
Belongingness and love needs
Safety needs
Physiological needs

Figure 6.2 Maslow's hierarchy of motives. Each lower need must be at least largely satisfied before a higher need becomes a significant motivating force.

be respected; he tries hard to make the basketball team or the debate squad. A politician craves power; he supports the candidate who promises him an important position. A college student wants money; she answers a job advertisement and goes for an interview.

Not all persons have the same motivations, or at least they respond in varying degrees to the different inner forces. Motives change as people grow older, and at all ages they reflect sociocultural influences. One cannot assume that the priorities of one's listeners are the same as one's own. The strength of motives and the means of fulfillment, moreover, change as the situation varies. In church a person seeks social approval by refraining from clapping and whistling, but at a rock concert the same individual shouts and applauds to show oneness with others in attendance.

THE BASIC THEORY

An especially respected work on motivation is that of Abraham H. Maslow, who presents a hierarchical theory.[21] The basic needs, he says, are fivefold: (1) physiological, such as the need for food, water, and sex; (2) safety, including the need for security, stability, and structure; (3) belongingness and love, including the need for contact and association; (4) esteem, including the desires for a sense of adequacy or competence and for recognition, appreciation, and prestige; and (5) self-actualization, including the urge for self-fulfillment as musician, painter, or some other sort of artist or craftsman. These five groups, Maslow continues, function as a hierarchy, with the physiological forces dominating behavior until they are fulfilled. If a human being has enough food, water, and the like, then the principal concern is for safety; and so the order continues until the time comes that the

[21] Abraham H. Maslow, *Motivation and Personality* (New York: Harper & Row, 1970), esp. pp. 35–47, 51–57.

four lower needs have been met and the engrossing desire is for self-actualization. This step-by-step sequence, Maslow adds, is not rigidly compartmentalized; the near fulfillment of the physiological need permits safety to become a factor. In other words, some overlapping is normal, and both special circumstances and individual differences produce exceptions.

Maslow's work, although it provides valuable insights for the analysis of human behavior, is perhaps of less immediate value to the beginning communicator than is a simple program for utilizing motivation in a speech, conference, or conversation. The following is a four-step program that is applicable to any topic and any persuasive purpose:

Step One: Choose the motive or the motives that seem likely to accomplish your objective. What are the desires of this particular person or of the majority of those in the audience? When dealing with members of one's family and other close associates, this question is easy; but when addressing a large gathering, one can only make informed guesses based on the age, sex, religious preferences, political affiliations, occupations, and socioeconomic levels of most of those who are present. One prospective persuadee wants more money; a second wants popularity; and others are concerned about reputation, health, financial security, physical attractiveness, or power. Some are vulnerable to motivational appeals pertaining to loved ones or cherished institutions—to the desire for opportunities for their children or to the belief that one's church deserves greater financial support. Thus, if half of the commission on a magazine subscription goes to a church or a charity that the buyer designates, he or she may be moved to place an order.

Step Two: Connect your objective with a motive that is important to the listener. "Ordering the magazine [your objective] provides money for the church [the listener's motive]" is an illustration of the process of clarifying the connection between the proposed act and the motivational satisfaction. In this instance the relation is simple, but with some topics clarification is necessary. "A vote for Candiate Whatzis [your objective] means higher prices for wheat and corn and soya beans [the motive of listeners in a farm audience]. Why is this so? In the last session of Congress, he voted for higher agricultural price supports, and he also voted to approve the export of foodstuffs to the Soviet Union."

Step Three: Energize the relevant motive. The level of desire is subject to manipulation, but in what ways? Effective persuaders choose ideas and materials that show the consequences of nonaction or that help the listener to visualize himself or herself in improved circumstances. They use pictures and other visual aids that concentrate attention on how things will be. They create vivid descriptions by choosing language that is specific and concrete and that has rich associations. They are energetic and earnest in delivery. They sell popcorn to the movie patron by filling the lobby with an attention-catching aroma, and they sell a piece of home exercise equipment by leading the prospective buyer to visualize himself or herself as trim and fit.

Step Four: Make the appeal explicit; call for an immediate response. Finally, to succeed with a motivational appeal—and, in fact, to succeed with any kind of attempted persuasion—one must make the desired action clear and make it possible for the receiver to respond immediately and easily. Knowing that enthusiasms die quickly, the evangelist closes the sermon with a request that all who wish to be saved come forward immediately. Applying the same truism, the advertiser places deadlines on special offers. "You have won the grand prize," the letter from the real-estate developer says, "but to collect it you must come to Tall-Pines-by-the-Sea this coming weekend." "Of course, you can think it over," agrees the salesman, "but I can't promise that this dress will be here tomorrow." Act now! Here's what to do! It's easy!

FEAR

Fear, a special means of motivating, has been the topic for its own body of research. These studies go back to the famous experiment on the effects of strong and moderate fear appeals on the willingness of children to brush their teeth. In this instance the moderate were the more effective, for boys and girls apparently found the strong appeals unbelievable.[22] More recent research, although far from consistent, generally, has continued to show that overly vivid and frightening materials can produce rejection. The reason for the frequent ineffectiveness of parental pleas to their children about the dangers of marijuana, sociologists speculate, is that the consequences depicted are too terrible to be credible.

The practical question for the speaker is "How strong a fear appeal should I use?" and research provides little guidance.[23] The speaker of high credibility probably can use stronger materials than the one with less prestige, but the outcome depends also on how much the listeners already know about the topic, on the firmness of their existing attitudes, and on various personal and situational factors. "People with high self-esteem," according to K. L. Higbee, "are more persuaded by a high-threat appeal than are people with low self-esteem."[24] Ultimately, the communicator must rely on personal judgment in using threat appeals. If an early draft seems too tame, one may wish to increase vividness; but on the other hand

---

[22] Irving L. Janis and Seymour Feshbach, "Effects of Fear-Arousing Communications," *Journal of Abnormal and Social Psychology,* 48 (January 1953), 78–92.
[23] Gerald R. Miller and Murray A. Hewgill, "Some Recent Research on Fear-Arousing Message Appeals," *Speech Monographs,* 33 (November 1966), 377–391.
[24] K. L. Higbee, "Fifteen Years of Fear Arousal: Research on Threat Appeals, 1953–1968," *Psychological Bulletin,* 72 (December 1969), 426–444.

if the preliminary version contains elements that listeners will find hard to accept, the speaker may wish to revise in the direction of moderation. *Ethics requires the speaker to say what is true; strategy dictates that the statements also be believable.*

THE DESIRE FOR CONSISTENCY

Still another factor affecting the sender-receiver transaction is the desire for consistency among one's attitudes, beliefs, and values. For this reason a mother finds it difficult to accept a bad report on her son, and a belief that a certain politician is dishonest is likely to lead a voter to interpret a news event as further proof of wrongdoing. "With how much ease believe we what we wish!" John Dryden wrote more than three hundred years ago.[25]

Distortion of new information, however, is only one way of producing consistency. The important point is that when dissonance arises, the individual tries to find some means of removing it. The following is an analysis of an example:

LUCY'S PRIOR ATTITUDE: Barney is a fine young man.
NEW INFORMATION: Sally says that Barney cheated on an examination.
LUCY'S POSSIBLE RESPONSES:
• Sally is lying [rejection of the source].
• Not everyone defines cheating in the same way, and I need more information [evasion and postponement[26]].
• There must have been reasons that justified cheating [readjustment of prior values].
• If I consider Barney in the light of everything that I know about him, he is a fine person [transcendence].
• I was wrong about Barney [unlikely, but a change in the prior attitude is a possible means of gaining consistency].

Consistency theory suggests several items of advice that the communicator may find helpful under certain circumstances.

1. Reinforce the method of dissonance resolution that will further your purpose. As the preceding example shows, the possible methods are numerous.

2. Do not attack an existing attitude or belief head-on, for doing so almost always results in failure and often causes the receiver to dislike the sender.

---

[25] *Oedipus,* act III, sc. 1.
[26] The scholarly word for this process is *differentiation;* one sometimes can achieve consonance by dividing a general concept into two or more specifics and then responding separately to each.

3. Attack a weak or unstable attitude or belief that is related to the one that is the ultimate target. As one attitude or belief changes, those connected with it become vulnerable.

4. Associate the desired objective with something or someone that the receiver already values. For example, point out that someone whom the communicatee respects already favors your proposal.

5. Heighten the discomfort caused by inconsistency by making the receivers feel that the situation is their responsibility. In an experiment in which the participants had to work with disagreeable partners, they felt discomfort if they had made the choice but not if someone else had assigned them the partners and they felt no personal responsibility for the unpleasantness.[27]

6. Manipulate the situation so that the receiver must generate the attitude that the persuader desires in order to justify a previous action. An example of this mechanism was the requirement in Hitler's Germany that Nazis pay admission to attend a party meeting.[28] Since people like to see themselves as prudent and since paying to attend a meeting is senseless unless the meeting is worthwhile, charging admission promoted a favorable attitude toward the party. Similarly, in a campus study fraternity hazing heightened loyalty, for a good attitude toward the organization was the only way the student could justify to himself the undergoing of pain and humiliation.[29]

Much about consistency theory remains puzzling and even controversial; but it provides a reasonable explanation for many human actions that otherwise would be bewildering, and it gives the participants in a transaction a useful approach for predicting responses and for understanding reactions after they occur.

BELIEFS, VALUES, ATTITUDES, OPINIONS, AND STEREOTYPES

The preceding section indicated that the interaction of prior thoughts with messages as received strongly affects whether a person perceives the sender as trustworthy, feels involved, sees a threat to self-esteem, reacts

---

[27] Joel Cooper, "Personal Responsibility and Dissonance: The Role of Foreseen Consequences," *Journal of Personality and Social Psychology*, 18 (June 1971), 354–363.
[28] Randall L. Bytwerk, "Rhetorical Aspects of the Nazi Meeting," *Quarterly Journal of Speech*, 61 (October 1975), 307–318.
[29] Elliot Aronson and Judson Mills, "The Effect of Severity of Initiation on Liking for a Group," *Journal of Abnormal and Social Psychology*, 59 (September 1959), 177–181.

closed-mindedly, is motivated, or suffers the discomforts of inconsistency. The present section is an analysis of the types of mental constructs, or "thoughts," and of their roles in two-person, group, and public communication.

A *belief*, as psychologists usually employ the term, is a judgment that a claim is either true or false, whereas an *attitude* is an evaluation that something is good or bad. An *opinion* is a verbalized public expression of an attitude, and a *value* is a systematized and organized set of related attitudes. A *stereotype* is a generalized, partial, and usually biased picture of reality. Examples of these terms are as follows:

BELIEF: Senator Whiffle accepted the illegal campaign contribution.

ATTITUDE and *OPINION:* Accepting an illegal contribution is wrong.

VALUE: Honesty is a desirable quality.

STEREOTYPE: A Hollywood starlet is pretty but empty-headed.

How these mental constructs function in determining the response to new information depends on *salience* and *connective choices*. The first of these terms refers to the closeness of the new item to the individual's central needs, goals, and self-concepts. Without consciously doing so, every person orders his or her beliefs, as well as his or her attitudes and values, according to their importance to himself or herself, and those that are central are the ones that most resist change. Since everyone tries to form a consistent pattern of beliefs and attitudes, the tendency is to adjust peripheral constructs to fit the central rather than the converse.

Connective choice is a term that pertains to the selection that the respondent makes out of his or her existing beliefs, attitudes, and values when processing new material. The following example shows the importance of the chosen connection:

NEW INFORMATION: A campus professor is doing marijuana research on dogs secured from the pound.
PRIOR VALUE THAT IS A POSSIBLE CONTEXT: Human life is sacred.
JUDGMENT: Since the research may increase medical knowledge, it is commendable.

A SECOND POSSIBLE VALUE: People should be kind to dumb animals.
JUDGMENT: The research is despicable and should be stopped.

A BELIEF THAT IS A POSSIBLE CONTEXT: Scientific research makes a university strong.
JUDGMENT: The report on marijuana research reinforces my attitude that this is a great university.

What determines which prior attitude, belief, or value comes to the fore when the receiver obtains new information? The time of day, the surroundings, and even chance are sometimes decisive, but the message itself usually is the principal influence. One means of persuasion, thus, is the manipulation of the content so that the receiver makes the association that is favorable to the sender's purpose.

BELIEFS

The desire for consistency, to apply a general principle, causes the receiver to tend to develop new beliefs that fit the old ones. If one thinks, for example, that a particular professor is a fine scholar, then one is inclined to give credence to the rumor that the man or the woman is about to resign to accept a new appointment at an outstanding university.

The significance of this tendency to form clusters is that the persuader needs to find a prior belief with which to associate the desired conclusion. One example of this process was a written argument in the *New York Times* on the justification for higher steel prices. Since this stand was unpopular, the author's first task was difficult. What position that most readers already held could be connected with the case for higher prices? The choice was the generalization that the United States should produce its own steel and avoid dependence on foreign countries. But how would higher steel prices prevent dependence on imports? Connecting the prior belief with the proposition that price increases were beneficial was the task that consumed the most space in the presentation, which was a combination of facts, figures, and specific arguments.[30]

VALUES

Functioning in much the same way as beliefs, values are especially influential because they are broad, long held, and closely related to one's cultural and social heritage. Many values go back to preschool training. "Education is desirable," "those who work are admirable," "a person should try hard," "everyone deserves an equal opportunity," "church and clergy are to be respected," and "freedom of speech is a basic right," therefore, are powerful forces when the individual receives a message or confronts a new situation. When one forms an attitude about a newcomer, for example, one decides whether the latter does or does not work hard, whether he or she really tries, and whether noticeable actions and attitudes generally are in accord with the prevailing values or in violation of them.

Since values are standards used in forming new judgments, the persuader can profit by choosing appeals that are consistent with them. The argument for the Head Start program, thus, has been that every child deserves an equal opportunity; the objection to abortion, that human life is

---

[30] William Verity, "How Armco Justifies Higher Steel Prices," *New York Times*, August 24, 1975, sec. 3, p. 12. Mr. Verity was the chairman and chief executive officer of the Armco Steel Corporation.

sacred; the argument for abortion, that the individual has the right to determine her own destiny. During the Vietnam War those who favored escalation claimed that bombing raids on Hanoi and mining harbors would save American lives; those who opposed any extension of the war appealed to the same value.

Other examples of appeals to values are numerous, but those appearing in two articles on presidential speechmaking are of special interest. The first of these, an analysis of an address by Richard Nixon, records his use of the following basic assumptions about American thought:

Betraying allies and letting down friends is an evil.

Loyalty to friends and allies is the virtue of a great nation.

Policies that come from representative government are good, whereas those made on the streets are bad.

The right thing to do is the opposite of what is easy.[31]

The second analysis, on speeches by Truman, Eisenhower, Kennedy, Johnson, and Nixon, shows that all of them appealed to the following values:

We should preserve the peace and advance the cause of freedom.

We should make sure that the American way of life survives.

We should protect human life and strive for international stability.

Communist dishonesty and aggression are bad.

To be the leader of the free world is good.[32]

ATTITUDES AND OPINIONS

Attitudes, dealing with relatively specific matters, are like beliefs and values in that they predispose an individual to view new information in ways that are consistent with constructs already held. Especially influential in its power to affect ideas and behavior, according to almost all research studies in the area,[33] is the verbalized attitude, or opinion. Whereas uncommitted persons can reverse themselves without embarrassment, doing so when the opinion is on record is an admission that the first judgment was wrong. Even so, reversals sometimes occur, but more often a committed person persists in the original stand and adjusts the new information so as to maintain consistency. The more public the commitment, moreover, the greater

---

[31] Forbes Hill, "Conventional Wisdom—Traditional Form—The President's Message of November 3, 1969," *Quarterly Journal of Speech*, 58 (December 1972), 382.

[32] Karen Rasmussen, "An Interaction Analysis of Justificatory Rhetoric," *Western Speech*, 37 (Spring 1973), 115.

[33] The first major publication on this topic was a section in Carl I. Hovland, Irving L. Janis, and Harold H. Kelley, *Communication and Persuasion* (New Haven, Conn.: Yale University Press, 1953), pp. 215–228.

its force. A statement before a group, for example, has greater influence than does the same declaration written in a diary.

Forestalling an unfavorable commitment, therefore, should be a part of a communicator's strategy. Asking someone what he or she thinks about an issue is risky, because the response may be a public declaration that is the opposite of the view that the communicator hopes to produce. Thus, expressing one's own position before the other person has had a chance to state his or hers, has advantages.

A second strategy that research in this area supports is the use of external commitment, which occurs when the communicator tells the prospective persuadee that the latter holds a particular belief, attitude, or value. "I know that you take a firm position against cheating," says the supervisor to the young teacher; the latter then finds it difficult to be lenient. "You're always so good to your kitty" and "I know that you will do the right thing" are further examples of attempted control through external commitment.

STEREOTYPES

Also controlling behavior are stereotypes, which are constructs that ordinarily include both beliefs and attitudes. Stereotypes are generalized, partial pictures of reality that one group and individuals within it hold for all or almost all members of some other racial or social group. Thus, many persons think that all professors are impractical, all Baptist ministers conservative, and all members of certain minorities greedy, lazy, or stupid. These generalities function in communication by serving as reference points for making individual judgments. Thus, the prevailing belief among middle-aged, middle-class people, including policemen, that all bearded young men are irresponsible sometimes leads to harsh, unfair treatment for a particular young man. Likewise, the stereotype of an ethnic group as shiftless and undependable may cause an employer to refuse to hire an individual who applies for a job.

Some of the more interesting studies on stereotypes are those in which human subjects evaluate speakers on the basis of their recorded voices. Speech by itself, according to many experiments, elicits judgments because of the stereotypes that are widespread for certain voice qualities, types of delivery, and ethnic accents. In one study in which thirty-three teachers, both black and white, heard the recordings of forty children, judgments of the child's social status largely coincided with whether he or she sounded black. When rating a child as having high status, the white teachers tended to identify the individual as being white, even if actually black.[34] A second study showed that the initial rating of intelligence was higher for

---

[34] Frederick Williams, "Psychological Correlates of Speech Characteristics: On Sounding 'Disadvantaged,'" *Journal of Speech and Hearing Research*, 13 (September 1970), 472–488.

persons when they wore glasses than when they did not;[35] and a third experiment resulted in the following as one of its conclusions: "Females emulating increased breathiness were perceived as being more feminine, prettier, more petite, more effervescent, and more highly strung, while at the same time they were perceived as being shallower."[36]

Individuals differ in the stereotypes that they hold and in the extent to which these prejudgments influence them. Both the group being characterized and the person doing the judging contribute to the final generalized picture. Once formed, stereotypes change slowly, if at all. According to one summary of research findings, ". . . considerable experience with members of the stereotyped group or very specific information concerning an individual's beliefs and characteristics is necessary before the stereotype will yield."[37]

Properly condemned for their unfairness to individuals, stereotypes are helpful in adjusting to the complexities of the real world. ". . . without them," one author writes, "it would be necessary for us to interpret each new situation as if we had never met anything of the kind before. Stereotypes have the virtue of efficiency, not accuracy."[38] Trial lawyers, as Joseph Jenkins describes, use these general judgments in jury selection:

The Pole and Italian and Jew are supposed to be emotional and softhearted and liberal with other people's money. The Swede and German are characterized as cold and aloof, very intolerant, and therefore not prone to sympathy. This categorizing extends with equal facility into trades, occupations and professions. Even the ladies are stamped with certain personality features which I lack the courage to detail.[39]

PERSUASION THROUGH BELIEFS AND VALUES

The observation that shared beliefs and values are powerful forces in communication goes back to Aristotle. "Connect your purpose with a belief or a value that the receiver already holds," he advised in essence. He gave the name *enthymeme* to a unit of thought consisting of (1) a previously held idea, (2) a newly transmitted idea, and (3) the conclusion formed by joining

---

[35] Michael Argyle and Robert McHenry, "Do Spectacles Really Affect Judgements of Intelligence?" *British Journal of Social and Clinical Psychology*, 10 (February 1971), 27–29. The difference, however, did not occur in later ratings.

[36] David W. Addington, "The Relationship of Selected Vocal Characteristics to Personality Perception," *Speech Monographs*, 35 (November 1968), 502.

[37] Jesse G. Delia, "Dialects and the Effects of Stereotypes on Interpersonal Attraction and Cognitive Processes in Impression Formation," *Quarterly Journal of Speech*, 58 (October 1972), 287.

[38] Sri Chandra, "Stereotypes of University Students Toward Different Ethnic Groups," *Journal of Social Psychology*, 71 (February 1967), 93.

[39] Joseph P. Jenkins, "Communications and the Law," *Colorado Journal of Educational Research*, 2 (Winter 1972), 39.

| A communicated idea | + | A prior belief or value | = | The conclusion |

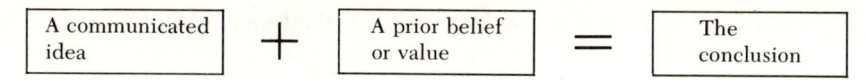

Figure 6.3 An explanation of how persuasion occurs. Persuasion occurs through the enthymeme when the receiver combines the specific communicated idea with a previously held belief or value in such a way that he or she formulates the conclusion that the sender intended.

the two. "Enthymemes," he said, ". . . are the substance of rhetorical persuasion,"[40] and much of the *Rhetoric* is an expansion of this view. The process, although often difficult to carry out, in theory is simple: (1) Find a belief or a value that the listener holds; and (2) supply a second idea that connects with the prior belief or value and that leads the receiver to the conclusion that the communicator desires. For example, knowing that the prospective persuadee believes strongly in safeguarding the First Amendment suggests the argument that a proposed law on wire-tapping threatens free speech and, hence, is objectionable.

As a matter of deliberate strategy, the public speaker or discussant often should search for the ideas that will have great appeal to the prospective receiver(s). Does the communicatee believe strongly that women deserve equal rights, that all persons over thirty are "out of it," that the best government is the least government, that charity begins at home, that policemen are "pigs," that citizens should support law enforcement agencies, or that work is desirable? Having received answers to these and similar questions, the speaker invents arguments for a change in welfare legislation, a modification in foreign policy, the defeat of a pending tax bill, or the adoption of a proposal for a civilian police review board. Some further examples are the following:

PREVIOUSLY HELD IDEA: This famous athlete is a cool person.
IDEA PRESENTED BY THE PERSUADER: This famous athlete supports registration in the special playground program.
DESIRED CONCLUSION: I should register in the program.

PREVIOUSLY HELD IDEA: Every child deserves an equal opportunity.
IDEA PRESENTED BY THE PERSUADER: Bilingual education will give Chicano children an equal opportunity.
DESIRED CONCLUSION: The bill providing for bilingual education deserves support.

PREVIOUSLY HELD IDEA: Those who live permanently in the United States should be Americans.

[40] *Rhetoric* i.1.1354^{a}15.

IDEA PRESENTED BY THE PERSUADER: Bilingual education perpetuates differences within the United States.
DESIRED CONCLUSION: The bill for bilingual education should be defeated.

A final and especially important point to remember in using attitudes, values, and beliefs for persuasive purposes is this: "It is the receiver's mental construct, not yours, that determines response." The communicator, hence, should realize that time, nationality, and social background all affect the ideas that individuals hold. To try to settle a dispute by talking about it is not considered manly in a "rough" neighborhood, according to one research study.[41] In 1865 ministers attributed Lincoln's assassination to God, but in 1963 they rejected divine intervention as the cause of John F. Kennedy's death.[42] In Japan, unlike the United States, ". . . it is taboo for a salesman to boast about himself or his company,"[43] talking business over the telephone is considered an insult,[44] and precision and ceremoniousness are preferable to novelty.[45]

CONCLUSION

Why is it useful to understand the factors that affect the dynamics of communication? If Horace Lowman, the main character in the example that began the chapter, had known about trust, self-esteem, and authoritarianism, could he have handled his problems any more successfully than he did? Probably. First, if aware of the importance of dynamic factors, Lowman could have planned his presentation more astutely. Realizing that an orderly, logical message would be insufficient, he would have found out as much as possible about his fellow executives as one part of his preparation. Then, knowledgeable about them, he would have tried to predict the probable responses to the various potential appeals. Second, an understanding of dynamic factors would have enabled Lowman to understand what happened during the meeting. Although on-the-spot analyses are difficult unless one has previously thought through the possibilities, post-session appraisals are practical; and even though too late to alter the

---

[41] Gerry Philipsen, "Speaking 'Like a Man' in Teamsterville," *Quarterly Journal of Speech*, 61 (February 1975), 13–22.
[42] Charles J. Stewart, "The Pulpit in Time of Crisis: 1865 and 1963," *Speech Monographs*, 32 (November 1965), 427–434.
[43] Kazuo Nishiyama, "Speech Training for Japanese Businessmen," *Speech Teacher*, 24 (September 1975), 255.
[44] *Ibid.*, p. 254.
[45] John L. Morrison, "The Absence of a Rhetorical Tradition in Japanese Culture," *Western Speech*, 36 (Spring 1972), 89–102.

initial meeting, they may lead to strategic adjustments in subsequent conferences.

The nature of these adjustments has been of concern throughout this chapter. Knowledge of trust, involvement, self-esteem, authoritarianism, motivation, beliefs, values, attitudes, and the other factors discussed earlier can be the basis for sensible adjustments on the platform, at the conference table, and in the living room. Prescriptive advice, however, is unwarranted, for the dynamics of communication is much too complex for recommendations to be anything more than suggestions or guidelines. "Be frank and open about intentions and expectations" is desirable most of the time, but not always. "Avoid threatening anyone's status when presenting a proposal" is kind as well as strategic, but sometimes doing so is unavoidable. Persuasion through external commitment often is an effective technique, but at times circumstances do not permit its use and at other times the listener sees the maneuver as a tricky attempt at manipulation. "Avoid attacking an attitude or belief head-on," as a final example, also is good advice, but only on some occasions. Meaningful communication is not a bag of tricks, an art for Machiavellians, or an activity for spineless intellectuals. The communication transaction involves whole human beings, whose many dimensions include trust, involvement, motives, and many other factors. By necessity a textbook includes separate sections on the different dynamic elements, but in actual situations at any given moment all, most, or scarcely any are functioning. The application of the content of this chapter, finally, should be thoughtful, discriminating, well-intentioned, intellectually honest, and respectful of others.

PROBLEMS AND EXERCISES

1. Prepare a five-minute speech on any one of the dynamic factors. Consider theories, reports on experiments, and indicate implications for the communicator of the theories and findings. Use the references at the end of the chapter, but draw also on other books and journal articles in psychology, social psychology, and communication.

2. Meeting with four or five classmates, discuss one of the following topics:

    What are the prevailing values among college students?
    Have values changed in the last twenty years?
    How do values differ among the subcultures within my community?
    How strong are the stereotypes that are common among my own group of friends?

3. Recall as carefully as you can the details of a conversation or a meeting that was noteworthy for either the presence or the absence of trust. Prepare notes on your recollections, and tell the class informally about the experience.

4. Who is the most trustworthy individual that you know? Analyze the reasons for your confidence and report informally.

5. How much ego-involvement is likely in each of the following situations? Explain the reasoning for your answer.

> a. Someone tells Barney that the star center on the university's basketball team has been suspended for accepting a new car during recruitment.
>
> b. Barney receives a notice from the university telling him that he is on probation and will be dismissed if he makes any grade lower than "C" in the current semester.
>
> c. Lucy reads a notice on the bulletin board stating that the choice of her best friend as student president has been invalidated and that another election will be held.
>
> d. The auditor tells "Hi" Humburger that it appears that the company treasurer, who helped "Hi" start the company, has embezzled about $100,000 over a period of several years.

6. List the roles that you play during a normal week, and make notes on how changes in role affect your self-esteem, your status, and your behavior. Examples of roles are those of student, practice teacher, intramural referee, big sister, fraternity president, Sunday-school teacher, grandchild at a family gathering, and safety warden.

7. Examine yourself for issues or situations that evoke some degree of dogmatism or closed-mindedness. In one column list topics on which you consider yourself open-minded, and in the other list those on which you probably are closed-minded. In which column do you put yourself on the following situations and on others that you find interesting and significant: an unmarried brother or sister who is living with a member of the opposite sex; a clergyman who is having an affair; a politician who has accepted a bribe; a woman who has had an abortion; a drunken driver who has killed someone; an individual who dresses immodestly; a classmate who is homosexual; and a black and a white who are dating?

8. Applying consistency theory, estimate the changes in attitude that are likely in each of the following situations:

> a. You see a friend shaking hands with someone that you do not like.
>
> b. You see someone that you consider mature and dignified, such as a favorite professor, entering a low-class bar.
>
> c. The candidate that you favor for governor receives the endorsement of an organization that you strongly oppose.
>
> d. The candidate that you favor makes a statement with which you disagree.
>
> e. You have paid more money than you can afford for a composite tennis racquet or for some other piece of sports equipment.

9. For one day keep a log of communication events. Include both ones in which you participate and ones that you observe. All lists will include conversations, and some will include interviews, discussions, and even speeches. For each event record as much of the following information as is pertinent: participants; time, place, and situation; persuasive purpose; the size of the appeal; motivational factors; the use of fear appeals; the importance of beliefs, values, attitudes, opinions, and/or stereotypes.

10. Select the most interesting event from your log, and report on it to the class.

11. In reference to a major speech that you are preparing, write a paper based on the following outline:

I. The extent of the request that you should make
II. Motives in the audience that you hope to connect with your objective (Explain your choices and how you hope to be effective.)
III. The strength of the fear appeals, if any, that you plan to use (Explain your decisions.)
IV. Values and beliefs that are relevant to your thesis

REFERENCES

Abelson, Robert P., *et al.*, eds. *Theories of Cognitive Consistency: A Sourcebook.* Chicago: Rand McNally & Co., 1968.

Adams, R. C. "Persuasibility as a Correlate of Certain Personality Factors," *Western Speech*, 36 (Summer 1972), 187–197.

Adorno, T. W., *et al. The Authoritarian Personality.* New York: John Wiley & Sons, 1967.

Baird, John E., Jr. "Sex Differences in Group Communication: A Review of Relevant Research," *Quarterly Journal of Speech*, 62 (April 1976), 179–192.

Bersheid, Ellen, and Elaine H. Walster. *Interpersonal Attraction.* Reading, Mass.: Addison-Wesley Publishing Co., 1969.

Borgatta, Edgar F., and William W. Lambert, eds. *Handbook of Personality Theory and Research.* Chicago: Rand McNally & Co., 1968.

Broverman, Inge K., *et al.* "Sex-Role Stereotypes: A Current Appraisal," *Journal of Social Issues*, 28, no. 2 (1972), 59–78.

Cauthen, Nelson R., Ira E. Robinson, and Herbert H. Krauss. "Stereotypes: A Review of the Literature 1926–1968," *Journal of Social Psychology*, 84 (June 1971), 103–125.

Coopersmith, Stanley. *The Antecedents of Self-Esteem.* San Francisco: W. H. Freeman and Co., 1967.

Deutsch, Morton. "Trust and Suspicion," *Journal of Conflict Resolution*, 2 (December 1958), 265–279.

Ehrlich, Howard J., and G. Norman Van Tubergen. "Exploring the Structure and Salience of Stereotypes," *Journal of Social Psychology*, 82 (February 1971), 113–127.

Festinger, Leon. *A Theory of Cognitive Dissonance.* New York: Harper & Row, 1957.

Fishbein, Martin, ed. *Readings in Attitude Theory & Measurement.* New York: John Wiley & Sons, 1967.

Fulton, R. Barry. "Motivation: Foundation of Persuasion," *Quarterly Journal of Speech*, 49 (October 1963), 295–307.

Giffin, Kim. "Interpersonal Trust in Small-Group Communication," *Quarterly Journal of Speech*, 53 (October 1967), 224–234.

Higbee, K. L. "Fifteen Years of Fear Arousal: Research on Threat Appeals, 1953–1968," *Psychological Bulletin*, 72 (December 1969), 426–444.

Hill, Timothy A. "An Experimental Study of the Relationship Between Opinionated Leadership and Small Group Consensus," *Communication Monographs*, 43 (August 1976), 246-257.

Johnson, David W. "Communication and the Inducement of Cooperative Behavior in Conflicts: A Critical Review," *Speech Monographs*, 41 (March 1974), 64-78.

Karlins, Marvin, and Herbert I. Abelson. *Persuasion: How Opinions and Attitudes Are Changed.* New York: Springer-Verlag, 1970.

King, George W. "An Analysis of Attitudinal and Normative Variables as Predictors of Intentions and Behavior," *Speech Monographs*, 42 (August 1975), 237-244.

Mansfield, Dorothy M. "A Blessitt Event: Reverend Arthur Blessitt Invites Youth to 'Tune In, Turn On, Drop Out,' " *Southern Speech Communication Journal*, 37 (Winter 1971), 163-173.

Maslow, A. H. *Motivation and Personality.* New York: Harper & Row, 1970.

Mortensen, C. D., and Kenneth K. Sereno. "The Influence of Ego-Involvement and Discrepancy on Perceptions of Communication," *Speech Monographs*, 37 (June 1970), 127-134.

Plax, Timothy G., and Lawrence B. Rosenfeld. "Dogmatism and Decisions Involving Risk," *Southern Speech Communication Journal*, 41 (Spring 1976), 266-277.

Rokeach, Milton. *Beliefs, Attitudes, and Values.* San Francisco: Jossey-Bass, 1968.

Rokeach, Milton. *The Open and Closed Mind.* New York: Basic Books, 1960.

Scheibe, Karl E. *Beliefs and Values.* New York: Holt, Rinehart and Winston, 1970.

Sherif, Carolyn, and Muzafer Sherif, eds. *Attitude, Ego-Involvement, and Change.* New York: John Wiley & Sons, 1967.

Triandis, Harry C. *Attitude and Attitude Change.* New York: John Wiley & Sons, 1971.

7
THE TRANSACTION: IMPROVEMENT IN EACH ROLE

After studying this chapter the reader should be able to do the following:

Play the role of an arriving guest in such a way that his or her classmates give ratings of above average for friendliness, warmth, and apparent wholeheartedness

Use either defensive or supportive techniques in a conversation before the class with enough clarity so that the observers identify the role correctly.

Judge accurately the audience response to a brief speech as attentive or inattentive, friendly or hostile, understanding or confused, and believing or skeptical. The speaker's written choices for one or the other of each of these four pairs of terms should coincide with those recorded by the majority of the listeners

Give three examples of statements whose objectives are to enhance credibility

Give three examples of statements designed to show similarity between sender and receiver

Take sufficiently accurate notes on a classroom lecture for the central idea and the main points to be the same as those in the speaker's outline

How can a person become a clearer and more effective communicator? If the purpose is to influence attitudes, beliefs, and actions, how can one increase the power to do so? If the objective is to be liked and respected, to relate closely to others, and/or to increase one's circle of friends, how should one alter present habits of communication? The two preceding chapters, which are on the processes and the dynamic factors most vital to transactions, are the foundation for a practical look at the means of improvement.

As used here, *improvement* means a heightened likelihood of attaining goals, some of which relate to the content of the message and others of which pertain to human relations and satisfactions. During interpersonal communication people repeatedly play three roles—interactant, sender or initiator of messages, and listener. They play these in no particular sequence; and being whole persons, how well they perform in one capacity affects both their self-concepts and the perceptions that their colleagues have of them as they change from one to another. The focus of the following pages, although much of the advice is important to group communication and to platform address, is on situations in which the number of participants is so few that each one plays all roles frequently.

THE ROLE OF INTERACTANT

Success in interpersonal communication depends primarily on what one says and does as a whole person and on the perceptions that others have of one. What does one do as an interactant? What determines effectiveness in performing this communicative role? How can one improve in interpersonal relations? Subtopics answering these questions pertain to first impressions, the art of social conversation, touch, transactional levels, and defensive and supportive communication.

FIRST IMPRESSIONS

Lasting judgments of speakers, according to some research studies, occur in the first thirty seconds of an address; and job seekers, the writer included, have been dismissed in interviews that lasted scarcely more than one minute. Thus, a person's looks—grooming, posture and bearing, facial expression—are crucial, for others usually see a person even before he or she speaks. Although something distinctive in hair styling, apparel, or costume jewelry can create a bad impression, the probability is that the added interest generated by the unusual will be advantageous. Actors, actresses, and models become highly skilled in the details of appearance—indeed, their professional survival depends on whether they can continue to sell themselves—and a course in New York for executives on grooming themselves to get ahead costs five hundred dollars per night. A flower in the buttonhole sometimes is the right touch for the occasion; but at other times, as a look in the mirror may show, a tentative choice is too large, the wrong color, or otherwise inappropriate. A particular style of glasses will be just right for a person with a certain coloring, hair line, and facial shape, but wrong for everyone else. Carrying a book with an impressive binding can draw attention favorably; and other properties, such as minicalculators, unusually large notebooks, and distinctive neckties or handbags, offer interesting possibilities.

Soon after this initial visual impression, speech ordinarily begins; and both what one says and how one sounds and looks contribute to continuing judgments, either favorable or unfavorable. Warmth and sincerity should characterize greetings; trite sayings, supposedly cute, can be damaging. The life that one puts into the voice, the light that shines in the eyes, and the feeling in the handshake can make "Jim, it's so good to see you again" either a tired, routine salutation or a heartening experience that makes Jim feel treasured. Shaking hands, a common and important element in interpersonal interaction, can give a "dead fish" feeling, seem neutral and noncommital, or convey delight and togetherness.

SOCIAL CONVERSATION: A GENERAL VIEW

After the exchange of greetings, one or the other of the participants must say something else (to do otherwise is to seem dull, antisocial, and peculiar). By custom, human beings abhor silence, which they commonly interpret as unfriendliness. Such inanities as "It's a nice day, isn't it?" are preferable to muteness, even though they communicate no substantive information. They say in effect, "I'm friendly; I see you there; you're important, and I want to talk to you." The second communicator, who knows through experience what the outwardly vacuous words really are saying, then has the burden of reply. To say nothing, as one may do when one wishes to demonstrate displeasure with one's spouse, creates silence and usually tension; to say, "Yes, isn't it?" is to maintain contact without furthering the conversation; and to say, "Yes, I noticed that, and I wondered whether you would be going to the beach," is to respond constructively.

Moving the conversation on is more than politeness; it is essential if one is to build a relaxed, cordial relation with the other party. At a dinner, according to one story, the hostess tried hard to converse with a man famous for his scholarship:

These students conversing in a bar are demonstrating the give and take necessary for communication. (Jim Scherer)

HOSTESS: "Mr. Admirable, I suppose that you have read Norman Mailer?"
SCHOLAR: "No."
HOSTESS: "And what about James Michener?"
SCHOLAR: "I haven't read him."
HOSTESS (*discouraged but too polite to give up*): "I'm fascinated with Hemingway and Steinbeck. I'm sure that you are familiar with them."
SCHOLAR: No.
HOSTESS (*desperately*): "What about Fitzgerald and Wolfe?"
SCHOLAR: "Madame, I do not read anything that was written after 1500."

Social conversation, like a Ping-Pong ball, goes back and forth; and essential to the art is the addition of a detail that will permit the partner to keep the ball in play. Such laconic responses as "yes," "no," "I agree," and "isn't that the truth" put the burden back on the other person; no follow-up remark flows naturally from such statements, and the other conversationalist must search his or her mind for something that will be more

Foundations of Conversation
1. Friendliness
2. "Returning the ball"
3. Interest in the other person
4. Wholeheartedness
5. Interesting content

productive. In the example given above, the scholar could have avoided rudeness by commenting in this fashion:

HOSTESS: "Mr. Admirable, I suppose that you have read Norman Mailer?"

SCHOLAR: "No, but I do have a hobby that I find interesting. I collect chess sets that are historic or unique."

HOSTESS: "How fascinating! How far back do they go—what is the oldest one that you have?"

"Returning the ball" to the other fellow is quite different from "picking up the ball and running with it," usually the act of a tiresome, inconsiderate, self-centered person. Such boors present lengthy monologues about themselves, their illnesses, their talented nieces, their gardens, or their dogs. In the beginning others have scant interest in these topics, and as the monologue continues this initial slight concern diminishes steadily. The temptation to be the life of the party afflicts many persons at times, and the effort occasionally is successful; but the safer course is that of collaborating with others. The probability is that they, too, like to hear themselves talk.

The observation that the principal interest of the typical person is himself or herself led years ago to perhaps the oldest advice commonly given to the conversationalist: "Ask your companions about themselves, their families, their work, their hobbies, and their other interests; talk about the things that they care about." Some authors, pointing to the absurd deadlock that would ensue if two speakers used this device simultaneously, have ridiculed the rule. Nevertheless, employed with discretion, it works well. During the closing days of the Great Depression the writer did his job-hunting by hitchhiking, and he recalls his application of the rule to a series of farmers, truck drivers, and salesmen. Not only did they appear to enjoy talking about their work, but also he benefited by receiving information on a variety of topics.

Whatever special ploys one may use, successful social conversation depends on two ingredients: wholeheartedness and interesting content. Of the two, the first may be the more important, for the individual whose voice, face, and body convey vivacity, warmth, enthusiasm, and undivided attention is a delight to companions. One Christmas evening a woman in her early eighties, violating the admonition against monologues, charmed the gathering at dinner with a succession of hilarious accounts of her experiences. She also broke the rule about concentrating on the other person, but her high spirits, her total absorption, and her lively, infectious humor produced an enjoyable and memorable experience. Many of the "do's" of conversational manner she brilliantly illustrated; but the "don't's" that she avoided also are noteworthy. Don't show disrespect for your audience by being halfhearted; don't look away at some passing person or stray dog; don't lose track of the idea and ask to have something repeated; don't be lethargic in posture and manner; don't dwell on unpleasant matters; don't change the topic before others are ready to do so; and don't be a dogmatic, contentious know-it-all. Underlying these specific items is the principle of empathy: The receiver's muscles tend to imitate those of the person providing stimuli. Lethargy begets boredom; vivacity engenders energy; high humor produces good spirits. The manner of the communicator, in short, is contagious.

But conversation must be about some topic. If brief, true enough, it may not go beyond the weather, the day's assignment, and inquiries about the other's health; and for conversations at cocktail parties, where the custom calls for guests to circulate, a store of nonsubstantive remarks is almost a necessity. Even here, however, one can add a bit of originality by making individualized remarks complimenting the momentary companion on a gown, a jacket, a piece of jewelry, or a recent accomplishment.

When the period of contact is longer, substance becomes important. The writer has known two men—one a college dean and one a project engineer—who could talk intelligently and enthusiastically, so it seemed, on any topic that arose. Both had read widely, not only in their professional fields but also on topics as varied as the endangered species of East Africa and the most recent research findings on cancer. Their own experiences also had been varied, and through the years they had used the expertise of their many conversational partners as a means of adding to their own stores of knowledge. The man or the woman who hopes to be a stimulating talker, as these two men illustrate, must read as much as possible, live an interesting life, and associate with alert, informed companions. In addition, he or she must have the knack of pulling from memory facts and anecdotes that relate to the topic at hand.

An experiment that tends to support the preceding emphasis on wholeheartedness and worthwhile content is a study by Powell and Kitchens on the extent to which communicators were satisfied with their earlier dyadic (two-person) conversations. The principal conclusion is that the individual's perception of the contributions of the partner was a significant factor in determining the degree of satisfaction felt about the dialogue. A second finding was that the contributions of the other person were even more important for males than for females.[1]

SOCIAL CONVERSATION: SPECIFIC FACTORS

In general, then, good social conversation requires interesting content, wholeheartedness, and a willingness to "keep the ball in play." Specifically, warm and satisfying interpersonal communication depends on praise and rewards, common qualities and interests, other-orientation, and self-disclosure.

The first of these, *praise and rewards*, is among the surest devices for winning friends, but some safeguards are necessary. One of these is the use of deserved praise in preference to unfounded flattery. With effort the communicator can usually find at least one quality or achievement worthy of commendation even for a generally inept nonentity. Joe may be struggling as a student, but his new shirt is striking. Harry may be clumsy in sports, but he plays a guitar well. Susan may have braces on her teeth, but her new hair style is attractive.

Two strategies make praise especially effective. First, a compliment in the presence of a third party is particularly meaningful. "Mr. B, meet Miss C. And I want you to know that Miss C has given the best talk of any student in my section of Speech Communication." Second, as Aristotle observed, "And we also feel friendly towards those who praise such good qualities as we possess, and especially if they praise the good qualities *that we are not too sure we do possess.*"[2] Astute as he so often is, Aristotle is saying that a novelist, for example, will be less responsive to praise for his writing, which he knows he does well, than to favorable comments about his tennis, an activity which he pursues with more enthusiasm than talent.

Second, *common qualities and interests* are sources of material that a

---

[1] James L. Powell and James T. Kitchens, "Elements of Participant Satisfaction in Dyads," *Southern Speech Communication Journal*, 41 (Fall 1975), 59–68.
[2] Aristotle *Rhetoric* ii.4.1381^{a}36–1381^{b}1. Italics added.

conversationalist can utilize in building close interpersonal relationships. How often has almost everyone had an experience like the following?

JOE (*meeting Moe for the first time*): "Nice meeting you, Moe; I appreciate the introduction."
MOE: "Same to you. And isn't that a Dodgers' insignia on your breast pocket?"
JOE: "It sure is. The Dodgers are a passion with me."
MOE (*brightening*): "Me, too. I go to as many home games as I can."

Any shared enthusiasm would do as well as baseball—golf, opera, theater, chess, or coin collecting; commonness not only leads to a friendly, animated exchange, but also to a feeling of togetherness. "This person is like me. We both like double chocolate cake, and we both hate phoniness in TV commercials." The binding element may be important, such as a strong opinion on politics, or it may be trivial, such as bow ties that look alike. All Volvo owners feel a common bond; at a party where almost everyone is a stranger to everyone else, the hunters gravitate to one corner and the stockbrokers to another.

Even stronger than enthusiasms in tying people together are shared attitudes, beliefs, problems, fears, and—unfortunately—hatreds. Examples of these include the outlook on organized religion, modern poetry, or equal opportunity hiring; problems in learning a foreign language or in dieting; the fear of unemployment or of increased pollution; and dislike for the office supervisor or for the police. In short, almost anything that is common to two people has the potential to bring them together; the power to do so depends on the depth of emotion attached to the shared element.

Whether the commonality serves a binding function, of course, depends on its emergence, and usually this happens spontaneously as two persons converse. In some instances, however, the shared interest is less obvious than an insignia sewn to a shirt, and only deliberate probing reveals the opportunities.

Third, *other-orientation or concern*, is still another possibility for improving interpersonal relations. Ideally, this quality is reciprocal, and in a truly beautiful relation all persons sincerely desire happiness for one another. Already mentioned is the tactic of steering the conversation toward topics that are of special interest to the other person, but the present advice goes beyond this to a concern for the other's welfare. This practice includes expressing sympathy, listening when the other individual needs a hearer, giving constructive advice, and offering to help. Sincerity should be the basis for these conversational elements, but even sincere persons can be careless in choosing the topics for a particular meeting. A good habit is that of asking oneself prior to a phone call or an anticipated get-together, "What problems have been bothering Miss C? What should I ask about?"

At times, of course, one should refrain from introducing certain topics directly. If Mr. and Mrs. D are on the verge of separating, the situation may be painful to discuss; or they may simply prefer to maintain their privacy. Much depends on how well Mrs. D knows the other conversationalist, on the exact nature of the problem, and on her emotional state at the moment. By indirection a person can make himself or herself available as a listener without appearing to be overly curious.

The plight of Mr. and Mrs. D is hardly the occasion for *cheeriness and good humor*, but *friendliness* would be in good taste. An interpersonal relationship depends on the tone of the conversation as well as on the content. An illustrative incident occurred some years ago when a college debate coach took four students for a presentation before a young men's group in a synagogue, and the father of one of the students attended and afterwards entertained the professor and his debaters at a nearby ice-cream parlor. The father, whose son had the same quality, throughout the evening exuded happiness, good cheer, and a zest and appreciation of the world about him. His buoyancy made the evening a pleasure for everyone concerned, and any one of his guests would have welcomed an opportunity to repeat the experience.

The preceding example is exceptional, but the person whose outlook on life is average can control the balance in his or her conversation between cheerful, optimistic statements and those that are depressing. All is never right with the world, and serious thought about its many real problems at times is appropriate. A willingness to face reality and a harping on bad news and dire predictions, however, are not the same. The person who makes others feel good has more friends than the prophet of doom, whose interpersonal circle is likely to extend no further than his or her family, associates by necessity, and others who share in the constant expectation of disaster.

Even worse than the preceding group of characteristics is the syndrome of pettiness, viciousness, and character assassination. A person with this set of attributes, unfortunately, does appeal to a limited number of colleagues whose minds are as sick as his or her own. Like this individual, they bolster their fragile self-images through both giving and receiving snide remarks degrading others. For those with healthier personalities and more astute perceptions, the purveyor of criticism, sarcasm, vicious rumor, and unfavorable innuendo, along with the constant harbinger of bad news and doomsday prophecy, is a man or a woman to avoid. After all, the individual who makes bad reports about others is likely to include today's conversational partner in criticisms whenever that person is absent.

Finally, *self-disclosure* is a means of improving interpersonal communication. For most persons Will Rogers's famous statement, "I never met a man I didn't like," is extreme; "I never *knew* a man I didn't like" comes closer to the truth. At one level self-disclosure is nothing more than occasional remarks that reveal one's hobbies, vacation plans, minor honors, and reading habits. Even this kind of information is helpful in humanizing the boss to the secretary—or vice versa—and the professor to the class. Individuals of different status often prefer to maintain distance, but this objective does not require silence on many items that serve to fill out a characterization and to build a relationship with the desired degree of cordiality and closeness.

In general, though, self-concealment retards or prevents the development of rapport. Although everyone keeps some thoughts and actions private, the principal sustenance of a maturing, ever-closer relationship, whether with a person of the same or the opposite sex, is a sharing of one's ambitions, successes, plans, and innermost thoughts. A little later perhaps comes the disclosing of disappointments, problems, worries, and failures. As this kind of sharing progresses, the two persons may begin making joint plans for doing things together.

Individuals differ in many ways, and the capacity for self-disclosure is one point of difference. Those who lament that they have acquaintances but no friends or that they don't feel "really close" to anybody need to examine their habitual conversational behavior. For some, happiness may lie in continuing to be essentially private persons, but such individuals should stop complaining about the coldness of others.

In conclusion, most scholars, according to Richard L. Johannesen, agree on the following list of major components essential for "dialogic communication": (1) genuineness; (2) accurate empathic understanding; (3) unconditional positive regard; (4) presentness (full attention to the dialogue); (5) spirit of mutual equality; and (6) supportive psychological climate (encouragement of the other to communicate).[3]

TOUCH AND INTERPERSONAL COMMUNICATION

A well-known television preacher precedes his Sunday-morning prayer by asking those in his studio congregation to reach out and join hands with those seated on either side. The act of touching another person, he realizes, has a magic in it that defies psychological analysis. Perhaps the comfort and security go back to infancy, when the baby finds safety and reassurance in being held against the mother's body. Among adults an arm around the shoulder is a comfort in time of grief, and a hearty handshake or a firm embrace shows warmth when two persons, especially if long separated, greet one another.

[3] Richard L. Johannesen, "The Emerging Concept of Communication as Dialogue," *Quarterly Journal of Speech,* 57 (December 1971), 376.

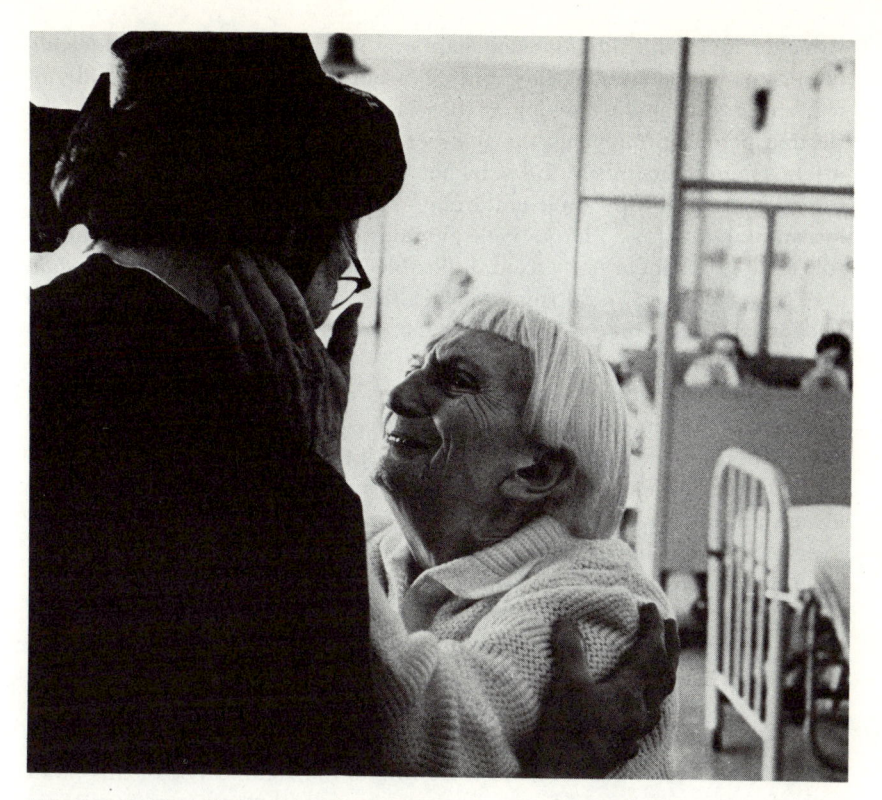

How many kinds of supportive behavior are shown in this picture? What are the elements that make this a moment of affection, warmth, and reassurance? (Phil Mezey/DPI)

Touch, of course, can have sexual overtones, and casual acquaintances may resent a hug or any other act that they consider overly familiar. One problem for a convention delegate is deciding which of those that he or she meets will respond favorably to an affectionate greeting and which will not. As in all aspects of interpersonal relations, tact, or a consideration of others, is important.

TRANSACTIONAL LEVELS

Whether touch is or is not an element in the transaction, the levels in a relationship may be either *complementary* or *crossed*. These terms come from Eric Berne's book on transactional analysis,[4] which is a stimulating and

[4] Eric Berne, *Games People Play* (New York: Grove Press, 1964), pp. 23ff.

valuable tool for studying what happens when two people try to communicate. Three ego states, according to Berne, exist inside every individual, and understanding which of these is in control at the moment is the starting point for analyzing the transactional process. The *Parental State* originates in memories of the behavior of one's father or mother (or substitutes for them) toward their children. When this state determines behavior, an individual is authoritative, solicitous, condescending, and bound by rules that give him or her a fixed, inflexible outlook. Examples of this state are "Stop smoking; you'll ruin your health"; "You'll either live within the budget, or I'll divorce you"; and "One thing that I demand of my employees is punctuality." The *Child State*, which is a carry-over into adulthood of childish attitudes and behaviors, is characterized by dependence, irresponsibility, inconsistency, and creativeness. Statements that might occur when this state is in control include "Let's go get a beer and study in the morning"; "Yes, sir, you can count on me to be on time"; and "You're always putting me down, and I hate you." Finally, the *Adult State*, which everyone should hope to develop and which ideally controls behavior, is characterized by objectivity, emotional control, and responses based on calm thinking and attention to the facts. Examples of adult statements are "Your report seems accurate and well thought out" and "Let's look at our budget and see what adjustments we need to make."

Those who wish to improve in human relations, obviously, should cultivate the Adult State and should try both as senders and receivers for thoughtful, unemotional outlooks. Adding to the significance of this point is the fact that communication is process. As an exchange of messages continues, the state manifest in each comment and nonverbal sign exerts influence on the behavior of all other participants. The most serious problems arise, according to Berne, when transactions are *crossed* rather than *complementary*. In the former situation Mr. A predicts that Ms. B will respond to him from a particular state, but she reacts unexpectedly; in the latter, the predicted and the actual types of response coincide.

The value of Berne's approach is that it provides a tool for understanding what happens when a conversational exchange goes awry. The following are examples of crossed transactions in which the response causes disappointment and/or tension:

STIMULUS: "Too much studying is bad for the eyesight; let's go get a beer" (the Child State; the expectation is that the second person will reply from his or her own Child State).
RESPONSE: "I have to study; the test is tomorrow" (Adult State).

STIMULUS: "The traffic must have been heavy on the freeway this morning" (the Adult State; the expectation is that the receiver will respond from his or her own Adult State).
RESPONSE: "You're always getting on me for being late" (Child State).

The seriousness of the crossed transaction varies from temporary surprise and frustration to the start of an argument and confrontation. By recognizing what the speaker expects, the receiver can use transactional analysis to avoid inappropriate, tension-producing remarks; by analyzing the crossing as the reason for the rebuff or the fit of temper, the speaker can attain the understanding needed for beginning to restore equanimity.

The preceding examples, however, are oversimplifications that imply a linear relation in which a stimulus evokes a response. In reality, as other parts of this book point out, reactions are outcomes of multiple, interacting forces.

DEFENSIVE AND SUPPORTIVE COMMUNICATION

Good feeling or rapport between interactants depends also on the extent to which behavior is defensive or supportive. Jack R. Gibb, in the classic article on this topic, begins with the following explanation of defensiveness and its consequences:

Defensive behavior is defined as that behavior which occurs when an individual perceives threat or anticipates threat in the group. The person who behaves defensively, even though he also gives some attention to the common task, devotes an appreciable portion of his energy to defending himself. Besides talking about the topic, he thinks about how he appears to others, how he may be seen more favorably, how he may win, dominate, impress, or escape punishment, and/or how he may avoid or mitigate a perceived or an anticipated attack.

Such inner feelings and outward acts tend to create similarly defensive postures in others; and, if unchecked, the ensuing circular response becomes increasingly destructive.[5]

In subsequent pages Gibb discusses the kinds of messages that *as perceived* elicit defensiveness: (1) content or manner that seems to be evaluating or judging; (2) attempts by the sender to control or to manipulate the listener; (3) messages that seem to be stratagems with ambiguous and multiple motivations; (4) an apparent lack of sympathy or concern; (5) open or subtle indications that the speaker considers himself or herself superior to the listener; and (6) dogmatic statements and a lack of tolerance for "wrong" views.[6] The absence of these qualities or the presence of their opposites, in contrast, produces a supportive atmosphere.

---

[5] Jack R. Gibb, "Defensive Communication," *Journal of Communication*, 11 (September 1961), 141.
[6] *Ibid.*, pp. 142–148.

In the years since the publication of Gibbs' article, scholars have recognized increasingly the significance of defensiveness/supportiveness as a factor in communication. Relevant research includes the study by Wheeless showing that the number of receivers who are highly apprehensive is "substantial."[7] Perhaps the principal value of this line of research and theorizing is that it provides the communicator with an approach that helps him or her to understand the dynamics of interpersonal communication, to appreciate the reasons when stress develops, and ideally to initiate corrective measures.

SUMMARY

Interpersonal conversation is more art than science, more a matter for guidelines and judicious applications than one for directives and foolproof rules. Listing specific attitudes and behaviors that arise from the principles developed in the preceding pages, nevertheless, should help the student to function effectively as interactant.

1. Through grooming and behavior, make the first impression interest-catching and favorable.

2. Respond to each conversational item so that the other person will find it easy to keep the exchange going.

3. Be considerate of the other person's interests.

4. In speech and in manner, be lively, wholehearted, and fully attentive.

5. Through reading and other activities, build up your stock of facts and experiences, and draw on these to provide interesting substance for any prolonged conversation.

6. Look for opportunities to proffer deserved praise.

7. Search for interests and qualities that you share with the other interactant.

8. Develop an other-orientation; feel and express concern.

9. Insofar as circumstances permit, be cheerful, good-humored, friendly, and optimistic; avoid snideness, sarcasm, viciousness, and pessimism.

10. Use self-disclosure to bring about a close relationship, if desired.

11. Use touch to emphasize expressions of friendliness, grief, and other emotions.

12. Use your knowledge of transactional states to analyze problems, if they arise.

13. Avoid content and manner that cause defensiveness.

[7] Lawrence R. Wheeless, "An Investigation of Receiver Apprehension and Social Context Dimensions of Communication Apprehension," *Speech Teacher,* 24 (September 1975), 261–268.

THE ROLE OF SPEAKER

The intention is not to divide the communicator, like Caesar's Gaul, into three parts, but clear exposition requires a separate focusing on each of the three roles. Of these, the most active is that of sender; and although a conversation may consist of alternate contributions, one of the participants often initiates the topic and remains the dominant power in determining the course that the series of exchanges takes. In the lengthy example of Barney and Lucy, even though the latter talked every other time, the more concerned individual was the former.

ADAPTATION TO THREE TYPES OF CUES

First, the communicator needs to understand the implications that the earlier section on the many kinds of cues (pp. 95–103) have for him or her. The most important of these implications is the generalization that the overt message rarely is the sole stimulus determining a listener's response. Some speakers prepare their messages carefully, even painstakingly, give no thought to the many other cues that may be operative, and then wonder what went wrong.

Of these other cues, some are subject to manipulation. Among these are many specific instances that fall within the classes of stimuli explained in Chapter 5: the covert message; cognitive context; affective or emotional factors; noise; situational influences; the presence of a third party; perceptions of credibility; and secondary cues in response to feedback. The easiest to handle are the observable stimuli. Knowing the probable effects on others of such obvious signs as a firm step, a scowl, or a slammed door, the communicator can control these aspects of the message. Similarly, one should be alert to signs provided by receivers and should adapt to them. If a communicatee, for example, has made strong remarks about a campus politician, the starting point for interpreting any new message about the student leader is clear. In general, knowing which cues are likely to affect decoding can suggest effective adjustments in handling materials, in the choice of plan, in language, and in the use of nonverbal elements.

A second class of cues affecting the respondent are those that the communicator may be able to guess. For example, unless the receiver has spoken out on the particular issue, the sender can only conjecture about his or her outlook on conventional marriage as a prerequisite for living together, on the use of marijuana, on having an abortion, on equal rights for women, on hiring someone to write a term paper, on the socialist platform, on the suggested impeachment of the student president, on the editorial policy of the campus newspaper, or on whatever else the topic may be. Strategic adaptations by the communicator, nevertheless, are possible much of the time, for attitudes and beliefs tend to cluster. In other words, since the prospective receiver normally has a high level of internal consistency, knowing some of his or her views permits the sender to predict stands on related topics. The individual known to support the socialist platform, thus, probably will join a demonstration for jailed party agitators or cooperate in a boycott for migrant grape pickers.

Guesses, although less serviceable than certainties, are better than nothing when the communicator is deciding on which arguments and amplifying materials to use and on which strategic approaches to employ. This truism is even more important in a platform address than it is in a conversation or a discussion. As the number of receivers increases, the likelihood of having accurate knowledge about their attitudes and beliefs declines.

Third, some cues affecting the respondents may be unknown. Perhaps the other person mentions a headache or exhibits other outward signs, but often inner tensions, pains, worries, and ideas are both unmentioned and unobservable. How large this area is depends on how well sender and receiver already know each other and on the communicator's perceptiveness. Adaptation to stimuli of this third type obviously is impossible—at least in the beginning; but sometimes either directly or indirectly these at first unknown influences come to the surface. The receiver may mention a sister who died from cancer or an uncle who fought in Vietnam, or through some sign he or she may reveal an emotional factor that is influential. Such information, coming during the communication event, makes adaptation difficult but still important. Preparation for any type of dyadic or small-group situation should include possible adjustments to any likely developments, and during a meeting the speaker needs to remain observant and flexible.

From the complexities of the communication transaction, therefore, come several important guidelines for speakers. Cues affecting decoding are of many types—observable, guessable, and unknown. Not only should senders utilize those that they originate, but also they should appreciate and adjust to the forces affecting the receivers.

RESPONSIVENESS TO FEEDBACK

Parts of the preceding section, although the word does not appear, are on feedback. Its effects on the sender, according to experimental research, are varied and pronounced. Williams and Alexander conclude that the oral "interpreter does more than differentiate positive and negative audience response. The interpreter perceives the responses multidimensionally."[8] James C. Gardiner reports that the nature of response—positive or negative—affected the ratings the speaker gave the audience, the speaker's own

---

[8] David A. Williams and Dennis C. Alexander, "Effects of Audience Responses on the Performance of Oral Interpreters," *Western Speech*, 37 (Fall 1973), 280.

Feedback during a public address poses dangers as well as potential advantages. By the speaker's expression how responsive do you think he is to the unseen person who has made a comment? (Jeff Albertson/Stock Boston)

self-attitude, the likelihood that he or she would maintain a belief-discrepant position, the speaking rate, and fluency.[9] "Positive feedback," he concludes, "improves attitudes, feelings, and efficiency, while negative feedback produces a deteriorating effect."[10] Still others state that positive feedback had a favorable effect on self-esteem[11] and that negative feedback adversely affected delivery, especially fluency.[12]

But does feedback improve the quality of communication? Yes, according to Leavitt and Mueller, whose measure was the accuracy of the sender-receiver circuit.[13] An affirmative answer comes also from Pryer and Bass, who found that feeding back information to discussion groups resulted in

[9] James C. Gardiner, "A Synthesis of Experimental Studies of Speech Communication Feedback," *Journal of Communication*, 21 (March 1971), 17–35.
[10] *Ibid.*, p. 28.
[11] Churchill Roberts, "The Effects of Self-Confrontation, Role Playing, and Response Feedback on the Level of Self-Esteem," *Speech Teacher*, 21 (January 1972), 22–38.
[12] Among these studies are Philip P. Amato and Terry H. Ostermeier, "The Effect of Audience Feedback on the Beginning Public Speaker," *Speech Teacher*, 16 (January 1967), 56–60; and Jon A. Blubaugh, "Effects of Positive and Negative Audience Feedback on Selected Variables of Speech Behavior," *Speech Monographs*, 36 (June 1969), 131–137.
[13] Harold J. Leavitt and Ronald A. H. Mueller, "Some Effects of Feedback on Communication," *Human Relations*, 4 (November 1951), 401–410.

better decisions.[14] Even more interesting is a study comparing an experimental condition including feedback and a comparable condition in which it was absent. Although Haney comments that feedback is time consuming and probably unnecessary for routinized messages, he found in the experimental setting less frustration, higher accuracy, more confidence in the accuracy of information, a greater willingness by receivers to decide and act, and a lesser morale problem.[15]

The significance of feedback, therefore, is well established, but what do the preceding findings mean to the communicator in the role of speaker? Briefly, the knowledge that feedback can improve the quality of a discussion or a speech should motivate the sender to understand the process fully, to be sensitive to the cues that are available, and to adapt constructively to them. He or she should learn to give an example to remove perplexity, to dramatize or personalize the point to relieve boredom, to shorten the message when listeners are tired or already convinced, and to adjust the argument when it is ineffective. The following example is from history:

During the graft trials in San Francisco, Hiram Johnson, together with two other prominent lawyers, J. J. Dyer and Matt I. Sullivan, had taken over the prosecution. . . . By mutual consent, Johnson took the lead. . . . Upon one occasion, Johnson was setting forth a cogent line of argument for the jury, when, all of a sudden, he stopped, pondered a moment or two, and then began to speak again. He had changed completely his line of argument. He continued the new theme to the end of his address. When he sat down Sullivan and Dyer asked him why he had stopped in the middle of the strong argument he was pursuing. Johnson answered immediately that it was not going over with the jury.[16]

THE DEVELOPMENT OF IDENTIFICATION

A third topic relevant to the role of speaker is identification. The most important authority on this process is Kenneth Burke, for whom identification is the key to persuasion. Burke notes the desirable effects of focusing attention on common or shared aspirations, needs, experiences, and/or values; and he also writes about the strategy of manipulating the message so that receivers feel that they and the sender are in collaboration. The form

---

[14] Margaret W. Pryer and B. M. Bass, "Some Effects of Feedback on Behavior in Groups," *Sociometry*, 22 (March 1959), 56–63. Another study showing the value of feedback for small groups engaged in problem solving is that of Ewart E. Smith and Stanford S. Kight, "Effects of Feedback on Insight and Problem Solving Efficiency in Training Groups," *Journal of Applied Psychology*, 43 (June 1959), 209–211.

[15] William V. Haney, "A Comparative Study of Unilateral and Bilateral Communication," *Academy of Management Journal*, 7 (June 1964), 128–136.

[16] E. R. Nichols, Jr., "Hiram Johnson, the Man Whom the People Believed," *Speech Activities*, 5 (Winter 1949), 163.

into which the message is cast also can lead to identification. Antithesis and *gradatio* (climax) are especially effective devices, Burke says. A repeated pattern, he continues, can condition hearers to anticipate words and to call them out silently, if not publicly.[17]

Closely related to Burke's identification, which is an emotional binding of sender and receiver(s), is polarization, which occurs when the members of an audience become unified into a highly suggestible, unreasoning entity. The speaker who can achieve this condition, be it a demagogue like Hitler or a religious cultist, finds that numerous listeners have become pliable. Banners, flags, music, and spotlighting facilitate polarization, but more important are devices calling for chants, songs, prayers, and actions in unison.

A contemporary speaker who has used identification is the Reverend Arthur Blessitt, who in his ministry to hippies and dropouts sometimes calls out, "Give me a 'J,' " and then after the response, "Give me an 'E.' " The audience in unison spells out "Jesus." Blessitt also seeks identification through carefully chosen language, references to approved persons, the espousal of prevailing values, and dress. "His hair," Dorothy M. Mansfield writes, "was trimmed well below his ears; his vestments were a brightly printed, full-sleeved shirt, leather vest, bell-bottom hip-hugger trousers, and boots."[18]

A second article that provides an instructive analysis of the use of identification is on Lincoln's speech at Cooper Union. The authors report three devices: First, by pointing out Stephen A. Douglas's implicit attack upon basic Republican Party principles, Lincoln bound "speaker and audience together in opposition to a common enemy."[19] Second, Lincoln "associated himself and his audience with the spirit, the principles and the actions of the founding fathers, and in doing so, he [took] the first steps toward ingratiation."[20] And third, he created a mock debate in which as spokesman for the party he assumed a role that strengthened "the identification between himself and the available audience."[21]

THE UTILIZATION OF CREDIBILITY

The focus of this chapter, however, is on interpersonal communication, and here, as well as in platform speaking, the sender should follow a commonsense course in respect to *ethos*. Since, as pointed out in both Chapters 1 and 5, listeners tend to believe those that they like and respect, the speaker

---

[17] Kenneth Burke, *A Rhetoric of Motives* (Englewood Cliffs, N.J.: Prentice-Hall, 1950), esp. pp. 55–59.
[18] Dorothy M. Mansfield, "A Blessitt Event: Reverend Arthur Blessitt Invites Youth to 'Tune In, Turn On, Drop Out,' " *Southern Speech Communication Journal*, 37 (Winter 1971), 165.
[19] Michael C. Leff and Gerald P. Mohrmann, "Lincoln at Cooper Union: A Rhetorical Analysis of the Text," *Quarterly Journal of Speech*, 60 (October 1974), 349.
[20] *Ibid.*, p. 352.
[21] *Ibid.*, p. 353.

should try to manifest specific aspects of competence, trustworthiness, good character, and dynamism.[22]

Fortunately, research studies suggest a number of specific ways the sender can induce favorable perceptions of himself or herself. At least one experiment supports each of the following suggestions for increasing credibility:

Use a conversational style to increase perceptions of trustworthiness.[23]

Maintain eye contact with the receiver.[24]

Use speech that suggests that you are a person of high status.[25]

Employ visual aids when giving speeches.[26]

Through good grooming and other means, make yourself physically attractive.[27]

Include personal observations and experiences that are related to the topic.[28]

Subtly and skillfully indicate your credentials on the topic.[29]

If lacking in credibility, include evidence for your statements; if highly credible, use evidence if other speakers have done so.[30] (Substantive proof never is harmful, but it seems to be of significant value only in special circumstances.)

Use an interesting verbal style.[31] Listenability, human interest, vocabulary diversity, and realism are qualities that arouse interest.[32]

---

[22] Aristotle listed good sense, good character, and good will as the three constituents of *ethos* (*Rhetoric* ii.1.1378^{a}10–14). Modern quantitative studies add dynamism and change the labels for the constituents, but otherwise confirm the Athenian's analysis.

[23] W. Barnett Pearce and Forrest Conklin, "Nonverbal Vocalic Communication and Perceptions of a Speaker," *Speech Monographs*, 38 (August 1971), 235–241.

[24] Steven A. Beebe, "Eye Contact: A Nonverbal Determinant of Speaker Credibility," *Speech Teacher*, 23 (January 1974), 21–25.

[25] James D. Moe, "Listener Judgments of Status Cues in Speech: A Replication and Extension," *Speech Monographs*, 39 (June 1972), 144–147.

[26] William J. Seiler, "The Conjunctive Influence of Source Credibility and the Use of Visual Materials on Communicative Effectiveness," *Southern Speech Communication Journal*, 37 (Winter 1971), 174–185; William J. Seiler, "The Effects of Visual Materials on Attitudes, Credibility, and Retention," *Speech Monographs*, 38 (November 1971), 331–334.

[27] Robin N. Widgery, "Sex of Receiver and Physical Attractiveness of Source as Determinants of Initial Credibility Perception," *Western Speech*, 38 (Winter 1974), 13–17.

[28] Terry H. Ostermeier, "Effects of Type and Frequency of Reference upon Perceived Source Credibility and Attitude Change," *Speech Monographs*, 34 (June 1967), 137–144.

[29] John D. Gibb, "An Experimental Study of the Effects of a Subthreshold Prestige Symbol in Informative and Persuasive Communication," Ph.D. diss., Wayne State University, 1966; Lawrence R. Wheeless, "Effects of Explicit Credibility Statements by More Credible and Less Credible Sources," *Southern Speech Communication Journal*, 39 (Fall 1973), 33–39.

[30] James C. McCroskey, "The Effects of Evidence as an Inhibitor of Counter-Persuasion," *Speech Monographs*, 37 (August 1970), 188–194.

[31] Charles R. Gruner, "The Effect of Humor in Dull and Interesting Informative Speeches," *Central States Speech Journal*, 21 (Fall 1970), 160–166.

[32] Tamara Carbone, "Stylistic Variables as Related to Source Credibility: A Content Analysis Approach," *Speech Monographs*, 42 (June 1975), 99–106.

Be discriminating in your opinions, neither accepting all proposals nor rejecting all; be consistent in your statements about an issue; show that your view is generally consistent with that of others.[33]

If the speech is fear arousing, add elements that are reassuring; do not create tension without providing a solution for the problem.[34]

Speak frequently, but not excessively; ideally, a little more than your proportionate share of the time.[35]

How, then, does one utilize credibility in communication? Briefly, "one puts one's best foot forward." Within the limits of intellectual honesty, one finds a meeting place between his or her views and those of the auditors, one creates the impression of being on the side of the listeners, one shows that he or she is competent, and one manifests dynamism. The recognition of the importance of credibility is as old as the works of the early Greek philosophers and rhetoricians. Timely even today is this statement by Isocrates:

Furthermore . . . the man who wishes to persuade people will not be negligent as to the matter of character; no, on the contrary, he will apply himself above all to establish a most honourable name among his fellow-citizens; for who does not know that words carry greater conviction when spoken by men of good repute than when spoken by men who live under a cloud, and that the argument which is made by a man's life is of more weight than that which is furnished by words.[36]

THE UTILIZATION OF SIMILARITY

Although often a factor in credibility and identification, similarity is a complex communication variable that has led to its own body of theory and research. Some kinds of likeness, to point to one complication, are more meaningful than others. To have impact the similarity must be relevant to the particular message and situation, and it must appear to the receiver to be significant. If the student candidate, for example, establishes that he and his listeners are alike in believing that the foreign language requirement is a needless barrier to graduation, the prospective persuadees can readily believe that the similarity may produce a mutually beneficial message.

---

[33] Stuart J. Kaplan, "Attribution Processes in the Evaluation of Message Sources," *Western Speech Communication*, 40 (Summer 1976), 189–195.

[34] Frances Cope and Don Richardson, "The Effects of Reassuring Recommendations in a Fear-arousing Speech," *Speech Monographs*, 39 (June 1972), 148–150.

[35] John A. Daley, James C. McCroskey, and Virginia P. Richmond, "Judgments of Quality, Listening, and Understanding Based Upon Vocal Activity," *Southern Speech Communication Journal*, 41 (Winter 1976), 189–197.

[36] Isocrates *Antidosis* 278.

Complicating similarity as a variable is the fact that it has subtypes, which the communicator needs to distinguish and appraise. An early work in this area was by Jones and Gerard,[37] who generalized that like values, such as basic views on personal behavior, increase persuasiveness. On the other hand, they said, on beliefs and factual matters, similarities reduce effectiveness. No one would want the pilot of a plane, for example, to know as little about flying as one knows oneself; and on such topics as international trade or cancer research, one prefers a speaker whose expertness exceeds one's own.

A second useful distinction among kinds of likeness is one between the so-called objective and subjective types. In one experiment when the points of similarity were age, occupation, income, and educational level, the speaker that the receiver perceived as dissimilar was the more influential; but when the points in common were attitudes toward the Vietnam War, the vote for eighteen-year-olds, the draft, racial integration, and the pass/fail option, the sender whom the listener viewed as similar produced the greater attitude change.[38]

In practice many communicators try to project both likenesses and dissimilarities. By referring to their research studies and positions of responsibility, they try to impress listeners with their authoritativeness; but at the same time through ideas and manner, they try to show similarities in objectives, values, beliefs, hobbies, affiliations, worries, problems, and opponents. As Fishbein and Ajzen summarize, "A positive relationship between attraction and similarity of beliefs, values, attitudes, personality, characteristics, interests, etc. has been found consistently. In the period covered by our survey more than 35 publications have again demonstrated that this relationship holds."[39]

SUMMARY

In the role of speaker, the communicator has several areas of opportunity for self-improvement: (1) adaptation to three types of cues; (2) responsiveness to feedback; (3) the development of identification; (4) the utilization of credibility; and (5) the utilization of similarity. Through work in these areas the communicator can increase personal effectiveness in conversations, discussions, and public speeches.

---

[37] Edward E. Jones and Harold B. Gerard, *Foundations of Social Psychology* (New York: John Wiley & Sons, 1967).
[38] Stephen W. King and Kenneth K. Sereno, "Attitude Change as a Function of Degree and Type of Interpersonal Similarity and Message Type," *Western Speech*, 37 (Fall 1973), 218–232.
[39] Martin Fishbein and Icek Ajzen, "Attitudes and Opinions," *Annual Review of Psychology*, 23 (1972), 511–512. This survey covers material published between June 1, 1968, and December 31, 1970. For a similar conclusion see Charles R. Berger, "Task Performance and Attributional Communication as Determinants of Interpersonal Attraction," *Speech Monographs*, 40 (November 1973), 281.

THE ROLE OF LISTENER

The old riddle "If a tree fell in the forest when no one was there, would it make any noise?" emphasizes the fact that without listeners the speaker's message is pointless. Human beings spend more time listening than speaking; obtaining information is as important to one's welfare as giving it; receiving and evaluating persuasive messages determine one's future as often does the sending of such appeals. In group and audience situations the number listening is greater—sometimes much greater—than the number speaking, and in dyadic communication the individual alternates in the roles of sender and receiver.

Less emphasized in many textbooks and classrooms than it should be, listening is an important factor in determining the quality of the communication event. By words and nonverbal cues listeners give encouragement and support; by feedback they guide the sender in the development of additional messages; by understanding and reacting they carry forward the give-and-take in which two minds interact. Improvement in these and related skills is possible, as the following sections on constructive feedback, increased comprehension, and critical listening will elaborate.

CONSTRUCTIVE FEEDBACK

Harry's reactions to Millie illustrate one function of feedback. Why he enjoyed talking to her was unclear to him, but a perceptive observer could have supplied the explanation. Through word, look, tone of voice, and manner, no matter what the topic, she said to him, "You are an important person to me; what you are saying is interesting and worthy of my attention."

In contrast to Millie, who encourages her fellow conversationalist, is the person who "puts down" the speaker. Some individuals by their eye movements appear to be more interested in passers-by than in their companions, and they may even interrupt the sender by shouting to a third party; others by their lethargic behavior feed back the uncomplimentary message, "I'll tolerate your conversation, but you're not worth my full attention." Equally negative are the cues that occur when a person is using a situation to bolster self-image. While someone else is talking, this individual is deciding what to say next. If the initial speaker tells a funny story, the insecure listener tries to think of one that is even more entertaining; and if the first person cites an amazing statistic, the second surpasses him or her by reporting facts even more astounding. This upstaging of one's colleague, needless to say, leaves the speaker frustrated and the listener with few friends.

One list of favorable and unfavorable cues appears in Blubaugh's description of an experiment that showed the adverse effects of discouraging stimuli on delivery. The subjects responded in the following ways:

The positive behaviors were: (1) constant eye-contact, (2) smiling, (3) positive head nods, (4) comfortable, but erect posture, (5) note-taking, and (6) little or no movement of the body or limbs. The negative behaviors were: (1) no eye-contact, (2) "slouched" posture, (3) manipulating or "playing with" objects, (4) manipulating, examining, or touching parts of the body, (5) looking around the room or at others, (6) frequent shifting of body position, and (7) "doodling."[40]

Still other stimuli, both hostile and supportive, occur, but the important point is that to some degree in all situations the listener and the initial sender interact, the one with the other, so that the outcome is a joint product and a joint responsibility. Clear, efficient communication occurs only when participants are "on the same wave length" or "in tune" with one another—sensitive not only to overt meanings but also to purposes, feelings, and moods. Misunderstandings occur, for example, if the encoding includes a dry sense of humor and the decoding does not go beyond the literal meanings. Some of the funniest scenes in the theater are those in which two characters talk past one another with the spoken words having different meanings. One example of this occurs in the play *The Country Wife*, in which the roguish central character has deceived the husbands into thinking that he is a safe and reliable protector of their wives. When the rogue talks about his china, he and the wives understand the meaning; but the husbands believe that the conversation is about table settings.

INCREASED COMPREHENSION IN AN AUDIENCE

Prior to feedback there must be understanding. Comprehension affects grades on examinations, it determines success in following directions, and it is essential to sound decision making in a variety of practical circumstances. The buyer who does not understand what the sales representative is saying, for example, is likely to make a bad decision.

The extensive research on listening, when analyzed, indicates that the degree of comprehension depends on only two major factors: natural ability and a combination of motivation and set.[41] Since the first of these is relatively fixed, trying harder—to use plain language—is the best way to improve. In addition, a few common sense suggestions may be helpful:

Motivate yourself. Experiments show that classes learn more if told that a test will follow the lecture or that those performing well will receive a reward. Think of the lecture as important. See its relation to your own

---

[40] Blubaugh, p. 133.
[41] Wayne N. Thompson, *Quantitative Research in Public Address and Communication* (New York: Random House, 1967), pp. 133–136, 140–141.

needs and interests. Decide at the beginning that you are going to be fully attentive.

Prepare yourself intellectually. Unfamiliar material is hard to grasp. Find out in advance the topic of the lecture. Read in your textbook or elsewhere on the topic so that you know the meanings of technical terms and so that you have a background for the speaker's ideas. If the lecture is in a series, review your notes from the preceding presentation.

Stay away from those who whisper to you or to others; do not sit near open doorways; and do not sit where an air-conditioning vent or a glare will make it hard to concentrate.

Prepare in advance for note taking. Arrive early enough to put unneeded books away and to get out your writing materials. Avoid any necessity for fumbling through handbags or briefcases during the lecture. Doing two things at once requires a shifting of attention, and some losses in comprehension are probable.

Strike a balance between too much and too little note taking. Some individuals miss parts of lectures because they write too much, but limited note taking can increase attentiveness besides providing a summary of the principal ideas. Abbreviations and sentence fragments save time, but shortly after a lecture you should expand notes that later on will become puzzling.

Utilize any signposts that the speaker provides. Try to grasp the purpose and the structure of the address. As the lecturer moves to a new idea, observe how it relates to the preceding point and to the talk as a whole. Use the speaker's summaries as a time for reviewing and checking your notes for accuracy.

Restore attention quickly when it strays. Since the mind of even the most conscientious student wanders during a class period, one difference between the good and the poor listener is the length of time that he or she permits the diversion to last. Self-awareness, determination, self-discipline, and eventually good habits are critical.

Give the speaker a chance, even though you find the views or the personality objectionable. Don't let anger, prejudice, or any other form of emotion or irrationality distract you from following the remaining parts of the presentation. Respond to the speaker's ideas and not to prejudgments based on stereotypes of age, sex, race, or position. First impressions of an argument can be inaccurate; don't reject an idea until you are sure that you understand it.

Review the lecture, usually by going over your notes, soon after its completion. If practical, discuss the material with a classmate.

If the circumstances permit, check the accuracy of your listening. Compare your notes with those of another student; and if feasible, summarize the message in your own words and ask the communicator whether you are correct.

INCREASED COMPREHENSION DURING GROUP PARTICIPATION

Much of the preceding advice is helpful when the individual is a participant in a conversation, a discussion, or a conference, but small-group situations pose special problems. The most important of these is the increased likelihood of distractions when circumstances are informal and when the roles of speaker and listener change rapidly. Sometimes subgroups form, each with its own conversation, and whispered comments also occur. Under these circumstances "trying harder" becomes essential to both good listening and effective participation. Discussants must bring their minds back quickly to the major train of thought when distractions occur and must refuse to involve themselves in subgroups.

Still another difficulty is the need for frequent changes in role from receiver to sender. If one can listen carefully and comment spontaneously, the problem is minimal; but some discussants think so intently about what they are going to say and how they are going to say it that they miss the points that someone else is expressing. During the time that one is listening, attention must be kept primarily on the ideas that others are stating; and if it is necessary during these periods to formulate one's own ideas, then attention must be switched back to the person speaking often enough to keep up with the train of thought. Particularly destructive is the practice of looking through clippings, file boxes, or books for facts or quotations to use as a speaker; and even if one can shift attention back and forth from listening to searching, shuffling papers is a distraction to others. The discussant or conferee should prepare for the meeting so that reference materials are so well organized that finding a needed fact takes but a moment.

The listener in a group situation, to conclude, has both the problems of the person in an audience and hazards peculiar to informal, give-and-take discourse. Attentive, supportive listening is a significant factor in producing and maintaining a constructive, workmanlike atmosphere, for it brings out the best in other participants and helps to provide a solid base for the further exploration of ideas.

CRITICAL, RESPONSIBLE LISTENING

In both audience and group situations, understanding the ideas that one hears may be only a beginning, for one's welfare depends on the ability to distinguish true claims from false ones and sound arguments from those that are illogical and/or unfounded. Otherwise, one purchases a CB radio or a stereo that is overpriced or buys a car or power boat that does not fit one's needs. Equally significant is the role of critical listening in a democratic society, whose decisions reflect the thoughtfulness of voters as they appraise the appeals in behalf of candidates, the special issues on the ballot, or the positions of vested interest groups on public questions. All that stands between the demagogue and the success of his or her self-serving schemes is the good sense of the people; and ultimately the course of history, for better or for worse, depends on the judgments of receivers of messages and on the officials whom they elect and support.

How does one go about listening critically? The first general answer is that a person should check the claims of a speaker or discussant against any other information that is available. Multiple sources favoring a proposal do not guarantee its worth, for a series of speakers may come from the same party or may for some other reason reflect the same biases; but as a general proposition, repeated endorsements suggest that ideas deserve respect. Likewise, a new approach is not necessarily wrong; it only requires careful scrutiny. One must look at any new proposal thoughtfully, and in many instances one should suspend judgment until one has made a personal investigation. The claim by the political candidate that he or she is a friend of consumers, for example, deserves skepticism until the listener has checked the voting record and the entire party platform.

The qualifications of the source are a second consideration in responsible listening. What position does the speaker or the conferee hold? Is he or she an authority on this topic? May there be a selfish reason for supporting a particular viewpoint? Information on these questions often is hard to secure, for unscrupulous groups deliberately conceal the true affiliations of those who speak for them. As a minimum, nevertheless, the listener should examine the information that is available and should discount the testimony of anyone whose bias is obvious or whose competence is questionable.

Finally, how much sense does the message make, and to what extent does the speaker offer proof for his or her statements? Is the speech or article internally consistent? Does the thought progress logically without disturbing leaps or gaps? Do statistics and other forms of evidence come from reliable and clearly identified sources? Does the speaker substitute strong language or sarcasm for proof? Are the responses to questions forthright? Are the alleged facts verifiable? In conversation standards of documentation by custom are less stringent than in platform speaking, but even in dyads and small groups the general thrust of the message on any serious topic should be thoughtful, reasonable, and unbiased.

CONCLUSION

To improve in dyadic and small-group communication, the student needs to think of himself or herself as interactant, as speaker, and as listener. As interactant, one needs to give favorable first impressions, to develop the skills of social conversation, to use touch with discrimination, to apply knowledge of transactional levels, and to use supportive rather than defensive communication. As sender, one needs to adapt to the different types of cues, to be responsive to feedback, to develop identification, and to utilize credibility and similarity. As receiver, one should provide constructive feedback, increase skills of comprehension, and be a critical, responsible listener.

Transactional forces are particularly obvious and influential in two-person and small-group situations, but they also operate to a degree in platform address. Even during preparation the fact that an audience will be present affects plans, and the anticipated characteristics of that group and their expected reactions may alter considerably the communicator's first inclinations. During delivery a constant interchange occurs, with frowns, sighs, yawns, squirming about, laughter, and applause having their effects on other members of the audience and on the sender. Throughout the period of delivery, the message is in process with the fluid and changing forces that surround the words.

PROBLEMS AND EXERCISES

1. Write down five strengths and five weaknesses that you feel that you have as a sender in dyadic and/or small-group communication.

2. Along with your classmates, prepare a slip of paper containing an easy conversational topic such as "My Hardest Subject" or "My Favorite Television Program." Three students should form a group, draw a slip, and converse for ten minutes. The remaining members of the class should be divided into thirds, each of which should observe the contributions of an assigned participant and discuss with him or her the strong and weak points observed. Repeat the exercise with a second trio as conversationalists.

3. Using a familiar but controversial topic—perhaps one on a current campus, moral, or social issue—form a group of five or six. As an exercise in listening, follow the rule that no one can speak until he or she has restated the preceding point in a way that its author certifies as accurate.

4. Observe conversations for half a day for examples of statements that come from the Parental State, the Child State, and the Adult State. Be selective; record only the most interesting statements that you hear. Try to remember the exact words. Write down the examples as soon as you can do so without being conspicuous.

5. Attend a meeting of a group such as the student senate, a dormitory council, or the executive committee of an organization. Look for instances of defensive and supportive communication. Write down examples. Report informally to the class on these examples and on the effects of defensive and supportive statements on the atmosphere of the meeting.

6. Observe a conversation in which one person is trying to persuade a second to go surfing, to clean up the apartment, to raise an allowance, or to perform some other action. Did the attempt succeed? Why or why not?

7. Recall some former friend or associate who was an unusually interesting conversationalist. Prepare a brief but informal analysis for presentation to your class. Explain the reasons for your favorable evaluation.

8. Join with five or six classmates for a detailed discussion on a topic appropriate to the chapter. Use the entries under "References" and other sources for information. Some possibilities are the following:

> What are the qualities of a good conversationalist?
> Feedback in interpersonal communication
> Touch and interpersonal communication
> Transactional analysis
> Supportive and defensive communication
> Why are some persons more credible than others?
> My personal problems as a listener
> The art of critical listening

9. Attend a speech on a controversial topic, and write a paper on the extent to which the listener should accept what he or she hears. If attending a speech is impossible, analyze for believability a speech published in a recent issue of *The Vital Speeches of the Day*.

10. Take notes on a classroom lecture, and compare these with those taken by another student. If you find discrepancies, check the notes of still another student or, if possible, have the lecturer criticize your work for accuracy and selectivity.

REFERENCES

Barker, Larry L. *Listening Behavior.* Englewood Cliffs, N.J.: Prentice-Hall, 1971.

Berne, Eric. *Games People Play.* New York: Grove Press, 1964.

Byker, Donald, and Loren J. Anderson. *Communication as Identification.* New York: Harper & Row, 1975.

Duker, Sam, comp. *Listening: Readings.* Metuchen, N.J.: Scarecrow Press, vol. I, 1966; vol. II, 1971.

Gardiner, James C. "A Synthesis of Experimental Studies of Speech Communication Feedback," *Journal of Communication,* 21 (March 1971), 17–35.

Goldhaber, Gerald M., and Marylynn B. Goldhaber, comps. *Transactional Analysis: Principles and Applications.* Boston: Allyn & Bacon, 1976.

Harris, Thomas. *I'm O.K., You're O.K.* New York: Harper & Row, 1967.

Johnson, David W. "Communication and the Inducement of Cooperative Behavior in Conflicts: A Critical Review," *Speech Monographs,* 41 (March 1974), 64–78.

King, Stephen W., and Kenneth K. Sereno. "Attitude Change as a Function of Degree and Type of Interpersonal Similarity and Message Type," *Western Speech,* 37 (Fall 1973), 218–232.

Lewis, Thomas, and Ralph Nichols. *Speaking and Listening.* Dubuque, Iowa: William C. Brown Co., 1965.

Pearce, W. Barnett. "The Effect of Vocal Cues on Credibility and Attitude Change," *Western Speech,* 35 (Summer 1971), 176–184.

Petrie, Charles R., Jr., and Susan D. Carrel. "The Relationship of Motivation, Listening Capability, Initial Information, and Verbal Organizational Ability to Lecture Comprehension and Retention," *Communication Monographs,* 43 (August 1976), 187–194.

Powell, James L., and James T. Kitchens. "Elements of Participant Satisfaction in Dyads," *Southern Speech Communication Journal,* 41 (Fall 1975), 59–68.

Schlenker, Barry R., and James T. Tedeschi. "Interpersonal Attraction and the Exercise of Coercive and Reward Power," *Human Relations,* 25 (November 1972), 427–440.

Siegel, Elliot R., Gerald R. Miller, and C. Edward Wotring. "Source Credibility and Credibility Proneness," *Speech Monographs,* 36 (June 1969), 118–125.

Simons, Herbert W., Nancy N. Berkowitz, and R. John Moyer. "Similarity, Credibility, and Attitude Change: A Review and a Theory," *Psychological Bulletin,* 73 (January 1970), 1–16.

Stroebe, Wolfgang, *et al.* "Effects of Physical Attractiveness, Attitude Similarity, and Sex on Various Aspects of Interpersonal Attraction," *Journal of Personality and Social Psychology,* 18 (April 1971), 79–91.

Weaver, Carl H. *Human Listening.* Indianapolis: The Bobbs-Merrill Co., 1972.

Wheeless, Lawrence R. "Relationship of Four Elements to Immediate Recall and Student-Instructor Interaction," *Western Speech Communication,* 39 (Spring 1975), 131–140.

Whitehead, Jack L., Jr. "Factors of Source Credibility," *Quarterly Journal of Speech,* 54 (February 1968), 59–63.

Widgery, Robin N. "Sex of Receiver and Physical Attractiveness of Source as Determinants of Initial Credibility Perception," *Western Speech,* 38 (Winter 1974), 13–17.

8
COMMON INTERPERSONAL AND SMALL-GROUP SITUATIONS

After studying this chapter the reader should be able to do the following:

Create a list of key questions for an information-seeking interview if given information about a hypothetical situation

Prepare a neat, orderly résumé that includes all relevant information on his or her qualifications for employment

Contribute to a thirty-minute information-sharing discussion at least (a) two specific statistics, facts, examples, or quotations, and (b) two comments that build on preceding statements by other participants

Contribute to a thirty-minute problem-solving conference at least three of the following: an example or a fact showing the nature of the problem or its seriousness; a cause of the problem; a criterion; a description of a possible solution; an argument for or against a proposed solution

A major news story in the 1970s was the shuttle diplomacy of Henry Kissinger; on one day he was in Cairo or Alexandria meeting with the head of the Egyptian government, and a day or two later he was in Tel Aviv. At this same time President Ford called George Meany to the White House to discuss the unwillingness of the longshoremen to load grain on ships bound for Russia, and the head of the Federal Mediation and Conciliation Service was seated at a table with management and labor trying to settle a strike. Although these men sometimes gave speeches, the activities just described were interpersonal or small group.

So it is, also, with the student and with the adult whose role is something less than that of a cabinet member. Although platform addresses often are critical factors in professional advancement and in furthering worthy causes, less formal transactions, which are more numerous, also bear heavily on both business and personal success. These communication situations vary among themselves in the degree to which they are organized; but the interview, the discussion, and the conference, which are the topics for this chapter, require planning and attention to content as well as to processes, dynamic factors, and roles.

INTRODUCTION: OBJECTIVES AND MATERIALS

The informality and apparent simplicity of interpersonal and small-group situations constitute a pitfall for the unwary student or adult. Whereas the prospect of addressing one hundred persons dramatizes to the communicator the need for preparation, visualizing oneself as seated in a group leaves room for excusing negligence in planning and research. "Some one else will do it;" "The chairman will plan the meeting;" and "No one will ask me that question" are verbalizations of common attitudes. The person presiding, true enough, does have special obligations; but the advantages of group thought depend on bringing together individuals whose supply of information is ample and whose viewpoints are well reasoned. Intelligent decisions never come from a pooling of ignorance.

Especially important in small-group discourse, as in every form of communication, is the preparation of both general and specific objectives. Building principal Helena Hackberry, for example, realizes that the general purpose "to secure information on the applicant's qualifications" is inadequate for planning a particular interview. Since the new teacher will be assigned to the remedial English sections, patience, understanding, and skill in discipline will be of special importance. These requirements lead Helena to the formulation of two specific objectives: (1) to form a judgment of the job seeker's probable performance as a patient, understanding guide to children who are slow learners; and (2) to make an estimate of the applicant's ability to maintain discipline in a remedial classroom.

Most situations, like Helena's, call for exact planning. The following are additional illustrations of the sharper focus that results from phrasing specific objectives:

GENERAL OBJECTIVE: To exchange ideas on how the operation of the motel can be made more profitable
SPECIFIC OBJECTIVE: To consider how other departments can help the restaurant and the bar to be more profitable

GENERAL OBJECTIVE: To consider possible improvements in the course in speech communication
SPECIFIC OBJECTIVE: To develop ideas on how the criticism of speeches can be made more useful to the students

GENERAL OBJECTIVE: To find out whether the job is one that I should accept
SPECIFIC OBJECTIVE: To ascertain whether the job offers good opportunities for advancement

Also important to every type of communication is the assembling of materials. Statistics, examples, expert opinions, reasoned analyses, and possible solutions form the substance of the group meeting. Sometimes the chairman assigns responsibilities for certain kinds of research; at other times the position that a participant holds dictates the kinds of knowledge that he or she should be ready to supply; and at still other times each person has the obligation to collect as much information as possible on all aspects of the topic.

The value of the individual's contribution—and the degree of prestige that he or she is likely to gain through participation—depends largely on the number of relevant facts that the individual has in hand and on the ability to present them clearly and at the proper time. The useful participant, in other words, must do homework. The sales manager must be ready to cite facts and figures for his or her department, and the director of publicity must be prepared to cite the unit costs for television commercials, radio spots, newspaper half-pages, and other possible forms of advertising. Truth and sound argument, according to data collected on 878 discussions, are basically persuasive. In this experiment students talked in groups of five or six about a problem with five possible answers, one of which, according to experts, was right. Those offering correct choices, no matter whether they were in the majority or in the minority, were able to change attitudes.[1]

The preceding statements, with appropriate adaptations, are applicable to the information-seeking interview, the job interview, the information-sharing discussion, and the problem-solving conference—the four communication situations that are the topics for the remainder of the chapter. The statements also are applicable to other types of small-group discourse, such as the persuasive, the counseling, the appraisal, and the dismissal interviews.

---

[1] William E. Utterback, "Majority Influence and Cogency of Argument in Discussion," *Quarterly Journal of Speech*, 48 (December 1962), 412–414.

INFORMATION-SEEKING INTERVIEWS

When Barney Borwinkel goes to the Financial Aid Office, he is seeking information on the grant, loan, and scholarship programs that are available, on the requirements for qualifying, and on the conditions for repayment. When his father, Barney Senior, goes to an account executive in a brokerage office, he likewise desires financial information. Lucy Miller, not concerned at the moment with money, goes to a professor's office to find out what is expected on a term paper; and later she assembles research material by interviewing the mayor, the head of a local welfare agency, and/or a union official.

Planning is critical to the success of the information-seeking interview. Barney, Barney Senior, and Lucy should take some time out of their busy lives to sit down and think through the upcoming meeting and to prepare notes. *Completeness, priorities,* and *approaches* are key words. Lucy needs to include on her list all the aspects of the paper that are in doubt; the question that occurs to her when on her way home is too late. Priorities are important, because the interviewee may terminate the meeting before the visitor has time to cover everything on the list. Approaches become significant if the topic is one on which the interviewee is reluctant. Investigative reporters become highly skilled at phrasing questions that elicit information on delicate or semiconfidential topics. The persistent, bullying tactics of the reporters that a person sometimes sees on television, however, are not recommended for the student who is interviewing someone whose status is higher than his or her own.

Tact and courtesy are qualities that are conducive to a friendly, cooperative atmosphere. In contrast, "That term paper you assigned really is a blockbuster" is likely to produce defensiveness; and "We hear a lot about corruption in City Hall" is not the best way to begin an interview with the mayor or an administrative assistant. Some questions are too personal, and thoughtless wordings can seem to imply criticism. The best way to avoid offensiveness is forethought. Any reasonably intelligent person would know better than to begin interviews in the ways exemplified above; yet, blunders occur when the details of the interview are handled impromptu.

A check list is the best way to insure that one uses common sense in planning and carrying through an information-seeking interview. With modifications the following recommendations should be serviceable in almost any situation.

A CHECK LIST FOR THE INTERVIEWER

1. Make an appointment convenient to the interviewee; don't put pressure on him or her to conform to your schedule.

2. Prepare a list of questions covering the information that you need.

Begin the list several days in advance so that you can add further items as they occur to you.

3. Arrange the questions strategically. Some logically go before others, and some should be last because of lesser importance. On sensitive topics, general or innocuous questions should precede inquiries that are relatively specific, personal, and/or embarrassing.

4. Groom yourself according to the preferences and the expectations of the interviewee. A middle-aged business executive does not expect a college girl to dress like a grandmother, but apparel that seems attractive and in good taste to him or her may differ from the student's preferences.

5. Plan so that being late for the appointment is impossible. If you arrive in the vicinity of the interviewee's office too early, buy a cup of coffee, walk around the block, or sit on a bench. Present yourself to the receptionist a few minutes before the scheduled time, but not too early—three to five minutes is about right.

6. If appropriate, ask for permission to record the interview. Memory and notes are sufficient for most meetings; but in some instances it is better to give full attention to the conversation and to take notes later from the recording.

7. If you plan to quote the interviewee, ask for permission. A customary courtesy is to submit the manuscript, or the relevant part of it, to the authority so that he or she can check the accuracy of the citation and see the context in which it is to appear. If you submit the entire paper, mark conspicuously the section containing the quotation or reference.

8. Use follow-up questions when an answer is unclear. Sometimes approaching a topic from a new direction is the only way to obtain a plain answer. One possibility is to submit a hypothetical case, and to request a judgment about it. If necessary, read the point as you have it in your notes, and ask whether your wording is correct.

9. Respect the time allotted, and be sensitive to the interviewee's apparent wishes.

10. Thank the other person for the time and help. If you plan any follow-up, such as submitting a manuscript for approval, state your expectations.

JOB INTERVIEWS

Many items on the preceding check list also apply when Barney or Lucy hunts for a job and changes from interviewer to interviewee. As a job applicant, one should be on time, courteous, and appropriately groomed.

The woman on the left is interviewing the man on the right. What good and poor qualities do you see? (Anna Kaufman Moon)

Dissimilarities between the two situations, however, are significant. As an applicant, one is on exhibit, and the outcome depends on the impressions that one makes. Is one qualified for the job? Does one seem reliable? Would one grow with experience? Is one flexible enough to take orders, but independent enough to be resourceful and innovative? Salary expectations that are too high cause rejection, but too small a figure suggests that a person has a low self-evaluation. Dogmatic positions on working hours, vacations, and other fringe benefits suggest inflexibility, but one also can seem apathetic and spineless. Some statements sound unpleasantly ambitious, but others suggest that the applicant would be a drone whose value to the company never would increase. Some job seekers act as if "they know it all" and would adapt unwillingly to the company's routines, whereas others seem to know too little. Some persons are shy and reserved, but others put themselves on the same level as that of the prospective employer and seem brash and disrespectful. Most important of all in job hunting, according to a study of sixty-four employers, was the projection of oneself as being intelligent-competent; next as determiners of employability were self-assurance and being agreeable.[2]

[2] Robert Hopper and Frederick Williams, "Speech Characteristics and Employability," *Speech Monographs,* 40 (November 1973), 296–302.

PREPARATION AND CONDUCT

Whether one creates these favorable impressions depends both on the content of one's remarks and on a number of specific nonverbal and verbal behaviors. One source includes the following points:

1. Sit up straight.

2. Keep your feet on or near the floor.

3. Look at the interviewer much of the time, but not with a fixed, constant stare.

4. Keep your hands still, and avoid other movements that make you appear nervous or restless.

5. Speak firmly and with enough volume to be heard easily.

6. Respond to open-ended questions with answers that require ten to sixty seconds.

7. Show that you have at least minimal information about the job for which you are applying.

8. Comment on prior jobs positively or neutrally.

9. Follow the interviewer's lead when he changes topics.

10. Ask at least three questions about salary, work hours, or other particulars.

11. Let the interviewer initiate comments on when a decision will be made and on when you will be notified.[3]

How easy is it to carry out these eleven desirable behaviors? "Not at all" must be the answer, but preparation, as Lucy illustrates, can be helpful. Thinking about the specific job, the company, and her own preferences, she jots down a series of questions: "How much does the job pay?" "What are the chances for promotion?" "Does the company offer in-service training classes for its employees?" "What are the provisions for parking?" "Is there a plan for group health insurance?" Then, Lucy turns her attention to her best selling points, such as the honors she won in school, a hobby that fits in with some aspects of the job, and an award received in a former position. Although Lucy realizes that she should let the employing official control the agenda, she is watchful during the interview for opportunities to present her strongest features. Finally, to facilitate crisp, straightforward answers, Lucy anticipates questions that might otherwise be puzzling or embarrassing, and she visualizes the situation as a means of

---

[3] Adapted from a list in Richard R. Lee, "Linguistics, Communication, and Behavioral Objectives," *Speech Teacher*, 20 (January 1971), 7.

reducing tension. In this last phase of preparation she is observing advice that General Electric offers its prospective interviewees:

Know the routine of an interview. Students who don't have any idea what's going to happen in the interview won't be relaxed, and won't present their natural personality. So we tell them to discuss it with their counselor. Or find a friend who's had a few interviews and ask what they were like. We even suggest a role-playing exercise. With the friend as interviewer. And the student as himself.[4]

THE RÉSUMÉ

General Electric is equally plain spoken in advising the job applicant on paperwork:

Some students don't think filling out the paperwork is very important. They give incomplete answers. Or don't take the time to be neat. But they're only hurting themselves. Because they keep the interviewer from learning everything possible about their past achievements and interests. We tell them to take time to fill out a company's information form completely. If one isn't available at the placement office, we suggest bringing a résumé along to save time.[5]

The example in Figure 8.1 includes the sections that appear on most résumés—name, address, and telephone number; job desired; education; experience; personal information; and references. Regardless of whether an advance copy has been mailed, the applicant should carry one for presentation at the start of the interview.

CONCLUSION

Most of the specifics of successful interviewing are matters of common sense, but a surprisingly large number of college students injure their chances of employment through ignorance and/or carelessness. The dean of one business college issued a list of "do's" and "don't's" when he observed that graduating seniors were going to on-campus interviews with dirty fingernails and a generally unkempt, unwashed appearance. The handout that follows, prepared by an employment agency, is worth serious consideration.

[4] "What Students Should Know about Interviewing," n.d. and n.p.
[5] *Ibid.*

Résumé

Name: Sally Beth Sharp

Address: 4141 Forty-first Avenue
Houston, TX 77001

Telephone: 622-6262

Job desired: Receptionist

Education:
Graduate of Lee High School with two years of typing and one year of shorthand
In third year of the Business Technology program at the University of Houston
Experience:
Clerk-typist, American Amalgamated Insurance Co., Summer, 1976

Cashier, Longjohn Cafeteria, Saturdays and Sundays, Sept., 1976–

Personal information:
Age: 22

Marital status: single

Present salary: $3.00 per hour

Salary desired: $600 per month

Reason for leaving present job: Because of financial pressures, I must quit school to work full time. I hope to complete my degree by going to school nights.

References:
Ms. Sheila Gordon, Office Supervisor, American Amalgamated Insurance Co., 2222 Allen Parkway, Houston, TX 77005 (Tel.: 224-2424 x 2001)

Mr. Billy Bob Murphy, Manager, Longjohn Cafeteria, 3333 West Felipe, Houston, TX 77010 (Tel.: 781-7818)

Prof. Leroy Ditto, Department of Business Technology, University of Houston, Houston, TX 77004 (Tel.: 749-7494)

Figure 8.1 A sample résumé.

---

34 WAYS APPLICANTS STRIKE OUT ON INTERVIEWS

Based on reports from 153 firms

1. Poor personal appearance—Need haircut, suit unpressed, fingernails dirty, shoes not shined, white socks, mismatched clothes.

2. Lack of interest & enthusiasm—Passive & indifferent attitude.

3. Over emphasis on money—interested only in best dollar offer.

4. Condemnation of past employers—Bad boss, unfair treatment, etc.

5. Failure to look at interviewer when he is talking & when you are.

6. A limp, weak, fishy handshake—It should be firm and friendly.

7. Unwilling to go to work at location where needed.

8. Arrive late for interview—If you are running late, let him know.

9. Failure to express thanks for interviewer's time.

10. Ask few or no questions about the job—Indicates either lack of interest in the job or stupidity and both are fatal.

11. Indefinite response to questions—Sounds evasive and is bad.

12. Overbearing, over aggressive, conceited with a superiority or "know-it-all" attitude.

13. Inability to express yourself clearly—Poor diction, bad grammar, slang, mumbling, speaking too low, etc.

14. Lack of planning for a career—No purpose, no goals set forth.

15. Lack of confidence and poise—Nervous, ill at ease, tense.

16. Failure to participate in the interview—Pay no attention when he is talking, let your eyes wander around the room, etc.

17. Unwilling to start at the bottom—expects too much too soon.

18. Makes excuses, evasive—Hedges on unfavorable factors in record.

19. Lack of tact—Discussion of personal matters not related to job.

20. Lack of courtesy—Ill mannered, crude language, etc.

21. Lack of maturity—Child-like opinions and attitudes.

22. Lack of vitality—Slouchy walk, lounge in the chair, etc.

23. Indecision—Weak, vacillating answers to questions.

24. Sloppy application blank—Be neat.

25. Merely shopping around—No particular interest in his job.

26. Wants job only for short time—Just stop-gap employment.

27. No particular interest in the company or in the industry—Fatal.

28. A cynical attitude—This implies a contempt and distrust that's a k.o.

29. Low moral standards—Self explanatory.

30. Intolerant—Bigoted strong prejudices.

31. Narrow range of interests—Is usually associated with a dull mind.

32. Inability to take criticism—Not a mature response.

33. Lazy—Interested only in the easy, unchallenging job aspects.

34. The high pressure type—Domineering manner, "vise-like" handshake, etc.

Provided By
M. DAVID LOWE PERSONNEL SERVICES, INC.
Maury J. Biggs (713) 621 9050[6]

[6] Reprinted by permission of the M. David Lowe Personnel Services, Inc.

INFORMATION-SHARING DISCUSSION

"Student Leaders Go to State Meet" and "Retreat for Cabinets of Church Groups" at times are headlines in campus papers, and similar events play a prominent part in adult religious, civic, and business organizations. The assumption behind such gatherings is that assembling informed citizens is a pleasant, effective way to exchange ideas for the betterment of all. As a rule, these meetings provide the participants with new ideas and heightened enthusiasm; but useful, rewarding results require both good leadership and intelligent participation. "How does one organize a discussion?" "How does one lead a discussion?" and "How should one participate in a discussion?" are all practical questions.

ORGANIZATION OF A DISCUSSION

The number of chiefs is smaller than the number of braves, but some person or committee must make the necessary arrangements. Some of these, such as setting a time, issuing invitations, and reserving a room, are obvious; but others, equally important, do not occur to inexperienced leaders. The well-trained planner provides pencils and note pads in front of each chair, selects a room that will be quiet and comfortable, and forestalls possible interruptions and distractions. As a minimum, he or she makes sure that a chalkboard or a pad of blank newsprint on an easel will be available; and in many instances he or she arranges for projectors and screens. If the meeting is to be in a suite of offices, the host should arrange for a secretary to hold all telephone calls and to protect against other interruptions.

Also important to the success of a discussion is the selection of participants. Sometimes the organizer has no choice—if the meeting is for the officers of the fraternities and the sororities, one must invite everyone who holds these positions; and if the meeting is for the department heads of a corporation, the list likewise is predetermined. Even in a less tightly structured situation, the positions that individuals hold should be a major consideration. If a university president, for example, wishes to hold a discussion on "How does today's student look at graduation requirements?" he or she is likely to include the president of the student senate and the editor of the campus newspaper. Not only is the support of these individuals valuable if the group produces recommendations but also those who hold responsible positions usually are intelligent, articulate, and respected.

Sometimes diversity among participants is desirable. Two examples follow:

TOPIC: How well are minority students doing on this campus?
INVITED DISCUSSANTS: The registrar, the director of student financial aid, the head of the black studies program, and the president of the black student union.

TOPIC: How serious is the problem of discipline in our public schools?
INVITED PARTICIPANTS: A member of the school board, a building principal, a classroom teacher, a counselor, a parent, and the president of the senior class.

Whoever the participants, they are likely to be more productive if the organizer provides them with advance materials—still another of the duties. The leader of the discussion on school discipline, for example, could mail out a list of questions for possible consideration and copies of a magazine article on the topic. Under other circumstances those responsible might send out suggested agendas and/or bibliographies.

The responsibilities of the person organizing a discussion for a business, professional, religious, community, or campus group, thus, are varied and significant. By comparison the resources for holding an educational discussion in class are slender, and the almost daily contacts of the participants eliminate some problems that arise elsewhere. The basic requirements, nevertheless, are the same. The student in charge should have the chairs arranged in advance, should do everything possible to stimulate preparation, and should make all possible plans to facilitate the exchange of ideas. If the planner anticipates, for example, that two persons are likely to monopolize the session, he or she should consider the means of controlling the situation. One possibility, according to research, is to seat the two overly talkative members side by side; for in general, "the greater the seating distance between two people, the greater the chance that they will follow one another verbally."[7] Properly managed, an information-sharing discussion can be of value to the participants as a means of exchanging information, as a vehicle for learning the skills of group communication, and as a training device for developing open-mindedness.[8]

LEADERSHIP

Whether a group should have a formally designated leader is a topic for scholarly argument; the recommendation here is that the organizer remain in charge or appoint a leader who will have time to prepare for assuming this important role. The next best procedure is for the group to select one of its members as its first action after assembling; the obvious democracy of this method can improve morale. Regardless of whether a formal designation occurs, functional leaders emerge as a discussion proceeds. As Knutson and Holdridge point out, research shows the emergence of two types of

---

[7] Bernard Steinzor, "The Spatial Factor in Face to Face Discussion Groups," *Journal of Abnormal and Social Psychology*, 45 (July 1950), 554.
[8] Franklyn S. Haiman, "Effects of Training in Group Processes on Open-Mindedness," *Journal of Communication*, 13 (December 1963), 236–245.

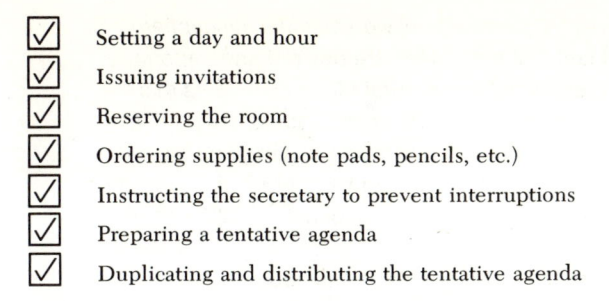

- ☑ Setting a day and hour
- ☑ Issuing invitations
- ☑ Reserving the room
- ☑ Ordering supplies (note pads, pencils, etc.)
- ☑ Instructing the secretary to prevent interruptions
- ☑ Preparing a tentative agenda
- ☑ Duplicating and distributing the tentative agenda

Figure 8.2 A check list for a person organizing a discussion.

leaders: "a *task* and a *socio-emotional* leader."[9] The former "participates more than other group members and offers more problem-solving contributions,"[10] whereas the latter is liked best and contributes to a congenial atmosphere.

When the leader is designated, he or she ordinarily fulfills the following purposes:

To check on physical arrangements just before the meeting, and to make whatever changes are necessary.

To bring the group to order, and to make a brief opening statement about the topic and the purposes of the meeting. If the participants are not acquainted, the leader should introduce each one. After that, he or she can tell a story relevant to the subject, give a real or a hypothetical example, offer a case study, present startling facts or statistics, relate the topic to a contemporary event or situation, read a quotation, summarize the arguments on both sides, ask a series of provocative questions, or outline the probable sequence of subpoints. As with the introduction to a platform speech, the leader has a number of single options and possible combinations of them. Which is the best choice depends on such considerations as the complexity of the material, how familiar the participants are with the topic, the purpose of the meeting, and the presence or absence of an audience. In many instances a short, simple statement is best.

To ask a question that will get the discussion under way. This initial inquiry may be directed to an individual or to the entire group. "John, will you begin our discussion by talking about some of the causes for this situation?"

---

[9] Thomas J. Knutson and William E. Holdridge, "Orientation Behavior, Leadership, and Consensus," *Speech Monographs*, 42 (June 1975), 109.
[10] *Ibid.*

To maintain a permissive, cooperative, but workmanlike atmosphere. So that all participants will feel that their ideas are desired and important, the leader should listen respectfully and refrain from comments that reduce the significance of contributions. He or she should resist the temptation to "top" a speaker by displaying superior knowledge on the same point. Although to a degree the leader should be tolerant of digressions that reduce tension or simply rest the group, he or she should also sense when to bring the members back together and on course. Discussions, true enough, move forward by fits and starts; but the advice that follows from one experimental conclusion is clear: "Furthermore, when group members discussed one issue at a time, instead of simultaneously treating two or three, groups were more likely to reach consensus."[11]

To maintain a reasonably equal distribution of contributions. Especially when the discussion is a learning device, as in the classroom, the leader should try to draw out reticent members. Doing this requires care, however, for to ask a retiring person a question that he or she cannot answer increases shyness.

To utilize the strong points of those who have special knowledge. Usually the expert speaks up willingly, but not always. In some instances, questions directed to the shy person will benefit both the individual and the group.

To regulate the rapidity of movement. Some leaders, overly eager to make the discussion conform to a preset pattern, shut off lines of development just as they begin to arouse enthusiasm; others, overly polite or insensitive to shades of significance, permit the consideration of a subtopic to become tiresome. Judgment and tact are requirements for effective leadership.

To handle special problems, such as bitter arguments or a garrulous member. Vigorous controversy is an indispensable tool for testing many ideas, but the leader should intervene if arguers become angry or engage in personal attack. He or she should call on someone else for a contribution, interject a moderately lengthy comment, summarize, suggest a brief recess, change the topic, or create a digression. If such measures, along with warmth and friendliness, are insufficient to control disruptiveness, then stronger and blunter words are necessary. "Let's give everyone a chance" and "Let's hear from someone besides Ronnie" are possible wordings.

To keep the sequence of ideas clear, and to summarize. The final summary corrects possible misconceptions, sometimes specifies follow-up actions, and often boosts morale by conveying the impression that the group has said much that was worthwhile. Internal summaries may be

---

[11] Leonard C. Hawes and David H. Smith, "A Critique of Assumptions Underlying the Study of Communication in Conflict," *Quarterly Journal of Speech*, 59 (December 1973), 433.

unnecessary, but are sometimes useful when confusion arises over what the group has accomplished. In these circumstances a summary clarifies the status of the discussion and enables the group to start anew, everyone together.

To assume responsibility for follow-up reports and actions. Delegating duties is permissible and often desirable, but the ultimate responsibility for what happens after the meeting is the leader's. In some instances nothing more is necessary, but at times distributing a written summary builds good will and facilitates group solidarity in the future. With some topics the group may decide on a letter to a public official, the circulation of a petition, the sponsoring of a sandwich sale, or the preparation of campus posters. Unless someone follows through on these decisions, plans fade, enthusiasm dwindles, and discussants think back on their experience as meaningless and frustrating.

To summarize, the discussion leader serves as facilitator, regulator, summarizer, inspirer, conciliator, and resource person. He or she should be intelligent, well informed, friendly, sensitive, self-confident, emotionally stable, and firm but tactful. Ideally, he or she talks neither too much nor too little and leads without dominating. Sensitive to dynamic factors, the leader maintains a working, cooperative atmosphere; astute in perceiving thought relationships, he or she does whatever may be necessary to combine the pieces—the individual contributions—into a cogent, incisive whole.

PARTICIPATION

Without informed participants, the leader can accomplish but little. For every chairman there are numerous discussants; and for every time the average student will be a leader, he or she will be a participant a dozen times or so.

What qualities does a good participant have, and what does he or she do both before and during a discussion? The example of Lucy Miller supplies answers to both questions. Upon receiving notice that she is to be one of six participants in a public discussion at the University Center on the topic "How do students feel about the way the money from the student activity fee is being spent?" she begins with a mental inventory of her own knowledge and feelings. To her surprise, she discovers that she knows very little. The amount involved must be large, but she recalls no precise figure. Last year the school paper contained a number of editorials and letters to the editor when the marching band missed one out-of-town game for lack of money. Thinking further, she remembers that student activity money goes for rock concerts, lectures, and free movies. "Obviously," Lucy says to herself, "I have some work to do if I am to be a useful, informed discussant."

Lucy begins her research by going to the office of the Student Activity Fee Committee and, with permission, making a photocopy of the current budget. She now knows to a degree how the money is being spent, but in many instances line items are unclear. The committee itself receives twelve thousand dollars for "office operating expenses and incidentals," and the Department of Ethnic Affairs is getting seventy-five hundred dollars. What do these sums really go for? Lucy does not have time to investigate all of the questionable appropriations, but she does go to some offices for information. It would have been a good idea, she thinks, if the person planning the discussion had assigned each participant a certain group of items to check out.

Then Lucy commences a second kind of preparation. She talks to friends and classmates about their ideas on the best ways to use student fees. Should the band have had a supplemental appropriation last year? If so, where should the governing board have made corresponding budgetary cuts? Should the fee be reduced and activities curtailed? Are officers of the Student Association overpaid? Should money go for highbrow events that few students attend? These conversations do not measure opinion as a scientifically conducted poll does, but as rough indications of student thought they enrich Lucy's resources.

On this topic Lucy decides not to go to the library, even though information on how other universities handle money from student fees would be valuable. Sometimes books, magazines, and pamphlets are the best sources when one is preparing for a discussion, but in this instance Lucy was sensible in concentrating on the local situation.

The time for the discussion is at hand. As a final step in preparation, Lucy assembles her notes for ready reference. She still has her photocopy of the budget, and on separate file cards, each with its own headline, she has put her notes on "Ethnic Affairs," "Salaries of Officers," "Drama Club," and similar items. She does not know which subtopics will emerge when the group assembles, but she has her ideas and notes well organized.

During the meeting Lucy tries to be useful. She listens carefully to others, and she relates her comments to the preceding points. She provides factual information when it is relevant, and she asks questions when contributions are unclear or sketchy. She tries to work with others in a friendly, mutually encouraging atmosphere, and on issues that arouse strong opinions she tries to apply the advice implicit in the following description of useful and harmful argument:

The person who is antagonistic to the others in his manner of speaking, who refuses to accept the procedure others desire, who treats majority opinion and its holders with sarcasm or contempt, who pursues his solitary way precisely because the others have chosen a different path, will injure any discussion. The person, however, who sees the issue differently, who introduces a view held by no one else in the group, who can

Free interaction among participants is important to the effectiveness of a discussion or a conference. At times one person may be the center of attention, but other members should be active participants at other times. (Jim Scherer)

support it with data when it has been challenged, who examines the hasty generalization made and accepted by the majority, who raises the overlooked question to impede the rush toward specious agreement, will generally contribute most to the thinking of the group. Cooperation, harmony, and group centeredness are necessary for the procedure of discussion, but independent thought and judgment are essential to the handling of its ideas.[12]

Not all participants are as conscientious and unselfish as Lucy or fit the descriptions in the preceding quotation. The following catalogue of the undesirable characters in discussions suggests faults to avoid.

The Twelve Cardinal Sinners

Mr. Ignorant. His negative value is compounded if he also does not know that he does not know and if he cannot distinguish opinion from fact and vague generalities from precise information.

Ms. Nonlistener. So busy thinking what next to say, she misses what is being said. Inevitably, her comment won't be relevant to the preceding one.

Mr. One-Track-Mind. His one prejudice on the topic erupts over and over, whether appropriate or not to the chain of thought.

---

[12] Stanley F. Paulson, "Pressures Toward Conformity in Group Discussion," *Quarterly Journal of Speech,* 44 (February 1958), 54.

Mr. Topper. He never lets anyone else have the last word on a topic. He knows something more than the prior contributor, and he has a compulsion to surpass others.

Mr. Show-Off. A less subtle cousin of Mr. Topper, this character seeks the center of the stage with a series of jokes and stories that distract the group from its agenda.

Ms. Sarcasm. Another cousin. She seeks attention through attempts at cleverness. She reassures herself of her own importance by degrading others.

Ms. Pedant. Having read a book on discussion, she insists on rigid procedures and sometimes stifles promising lines of development.

Mr. Nicely. A cousin of Ms. Pedant, he has misread part of a book on discussion. Misinterpreting the meaning of *cooperativeness,* he attempts to nip arguments at their beginnings and to maintain a perpetual smiling sweetness.

Ms. Garrulous. A compulsive talker, her words are more numerous than her ideas.

Ms. Silent. Sometimes the wisest and best-informed member of the group, she contributes little.

Mr. Skeptic. Trusting no one and doubting whatever evidence his colleagues contribute, he creates a sense of uneasiness that makes constructive group thought ever more difficult.

Ms. Naive. Trusting and believing everything, she is an easy prey for the manipulator who wishes to subvert the discussion to serve selfish ends.

Besides avoiding poor practices, discussants can take positive steps to improve their performances and to increase the ratings that others give them. A number of research studies are enlightening. The member who exercises the greatest influence[13] and who receives the highest ratings[14] is the one who contributes the most frequently. Hawes and Smith modify this finding when they conclude that ". . . the most influential member in a group decision making process is the person who communicates most frequently in a directive fashion."[15] Johnson includes in his summary of research the generalization that especially effective discussants include those who are responsive to the messages of others and those who clearly

---

[13] Don Willard and Fred L. Strodtbeck, "Latency of Verbal Response and Participation in Small Groups," *Sociometry,* 35 (March 1972), 161–175; Donald P. Hayes and Leo Meltzer, "Interpersonal Judgments Based on Talkativeness," *Sociometry,* 35 (December 1972), 538–561; John A. Daly, James C. McCroskey, and Virginia P. Richmond, "Judgements of Quality, Listening, and Understanding Based Upon Vocal Activity," *Southern Speech Communication Journal,* 41 (Winter 1976), 189–197.

[14] Robert N. Bostrom, "Patterns of Communicative Interaction in Small Groups," *Speech Monographs,* 37 (November 1970), 257–263. See also Knutson and Holdridge, p. 113.

[15] Hawes and Smith, p. 434.

state their intention to be cooperative.[16] Gouran found that the perception that others were strong contributors resulted in a feeling of satisfaction at the close of a discussion.[17] Finally, Valentine and Fisher, among others, conclude that social conflict and deviant behavior are innovative and constructive.[18]

CONCLUSION

The information-sharing discussion, whether it occurs inside or outside the classroom, is generally a pleasant and effective way to exchange facts and ideas. As compared with reading articles or reports, which in a given period of time might provide as much information as a discussion, the face-to-face meeting enables members to ask questions and to build on one another's comments.

Most research studies conclude that discussion is a tool for learning as well as for problem solving. One interesting investigation in speech communication is an experiment on the quality of debate decisions. In one part of the project, the judges proceeded in the customary way, each working independently; in the second part they conferred. Although the wins and losses were almost the same in the two instances, judges who consulted were more confident of their decisions and the analysis of the debate was more "vigorous and reflective."[19]

PROBLEM-SOLVING CONFERENCES

Research on groups engaged in problem solving has been much more extensive than has research on the sharing of information; and although scholars raise some objections to the studies, the preponderance of evidence substantiates the conclusion that the group ordinarily does better than the individual working alone.[20] Three other generalizations that research supports are (1) that improved reasoning and other educational values for the discussants result from participation, (2) that high scores on measures of reflective thinking correlate somewhat with good performance,

---

[16] David W. Johnson, "Communication and the Inducement of Cooperative Behavior in Conflicts: A Critical Review," *Speech Monographs*, 41 (March 1974), 72–73.
[17] Dennis Gouran, "Correlates of Member Satisfaction in Group Decision-Making Discussions," *Central States Speech Journal*, 24 (Summer 1973), 93.
[18] Kristin B. Valentine and B. Aubrey Fisher, "An Interaction Analysis of Innovative Deviance in Small Groups," *Speech Monographs*, 41 (November 1974), 413–420.
[19] J. Robert Cox and Julia T. Wood, "The Effects of Consultation on Judges' Decisions," *Speech Teacher*, 24 (March 1975), 118–126.
[20] For a summary of early research see Wayne N. Thompson, *Quantitative Research in Public Address and Communication* (New York: Random House, 1967), pp. 104–105. More recent studies, in general, are in agreement.

and (3) that the position of the majority is likely to influence others in the group.[21] Both the values and the pitfalls of discussion, Harry Hazel, Jr., claims, are illustrated in history. The discussions by President Kennedy and his advisors at the time of the Cuban missile crisis, he argues, "[point] up the necessity of an organized agenda, the advantages of having participants prepare research in advance, the need to disagree on the idea level while avoiding interpersonal clashes, the advantages of careful listening and the impact of effective leadership. By contrast, the committee discussions surrounding the Bay of Pigs fiasco and Watergate emphasize the lack of these same qualities."[22]

However, even if no research findings existed, valid reasons for studying and practicing problem solving would be apparent. In education, in business and industry, in civic organizations, and in campus groups, problems arise that call for solutions. Such questions as these are real: "How can we reduce thievery in the dormitory?" "How can we make our parking lots safer?" "How can we curtail the mutilation of library books and magazines?" "How can we protect our subdivision against declining property values?" "How can we improve the quality of our public schools?" "How can we make our fund-raising campaign more effective?" "How can we decrease absenteeism in the plant?" "How can we increase our sales?" and "How can we get out the vote?"

TECHNIQUES

Much of the preceding information on leadership and participation is as applicable to problem solving as it is to information sharing. Two major differences, however, exist, the first pertaining to organization and content and the second dealing with the motivations of participants.

Organization and Content

First, the purposes and the topics common to a problem-solving session call for an outline that varies significantly from that for information sharing. Whereas the exchange of ideas is likely to follow some topical pattern (e.g., "operational expenses," "athletic groups," "campus special interest groups," "concerts and lectures," and "publications"), the sequence of subtopics for a problem-solving gathering ordinarily is an adaptation of the following:

The statement of the problem

The nature and the seriousness of the problem

---

[21] *Ibid.*, pp. 99–104.
[22] Harry Hazel, Jr., "Group Problem Solving and the Historical Example," *Communication Education*, 25 (January 1976), 81. Hazel based his article on Irving Janis, *Victims of Groupthink* (Boston: Houghton Mifflin Co., 1972).

Causes

Criteria for testing solutions

Suggested solutions

The evaluation of the suggested solutions against the criteria

Conclusions

The leader, sometimes in collaboration with the group, makes a preliminary decision on what adaptation of the preceding outline will best serve the immediate situation. Sometimes he or she distributes an agenda and then begins the meeting by agreeing on it as submitted or as amended. As sessions progress, leaders often record key contributions on a chalkboard or on a large sheet of blank newsprint.

Attempting to follow the agenda slavishly, however, is likely to stifle participation. Although keeping the outline prominent is a necessary protection against aimlessness, research studies indicate that discussions usually do not conform rigidly to any one pattern. Placing the criteria after the introduction of solutions, according to Larson, can be beneficial;[23] and Fisher found that discussants often proceed through four phases: orientation, conflict, emergence, and reinforcement. By his analysis, after a tentative conclusion emerges, controversy continues but gradually lessens and contributions that reinforce the choice become more frequent.[24] In another article Fisher describes decision making as a process that moves in leaps and jerks: "Group members introduced a particular decision proposal, discussed it for some length of time, dropped it in favor of another decision proposal, and then re-introduced it."[25] Often a consensus did not occur, he continues, until after several rounds of consideration, in each of which the proposal had somewhat different forms.[26] From these research studies comes an important guideline for both leader and participant: Prepare an agenda and use it as a guide, but do not be distressed when the group observes it only loosely.

An analysis of certain parts of the agenda, nevertheless, should be instructive. The least-understood part probably is the *criteria,* which a person or a group finds by answering the question, "What are the qualities that any acceptable solution must have?" Two examples follow.

TOPIC: How can we curtail the mutilation of library books and magazines?

---

[23] Carl E. Larson, "Speech Communication Research on Small Groups," *Speech Teacher,* 20 (March 1971), 93–94.

[24] B. Aubrey Fisher, "Decision Emergence: Phases in Group Decision-Making," *Speech Monographs,* 37 (March 1970), 60–65.

[25] B. Aubrey Fisher, "The Process of Decision Modification in Small Discussion Groups," *Journal of Communication,* 20 (March 1970), 56.

[26] *Ibid.*

CRITERIA:
- The cost of an acceptable solution must be minimal.
- Books and magazines must remain available for circulation.

TOPIC: How could the university improve the parking facilities for students?

CRITERIA:
- The plan should be financially feasible.
- The plan should be operational within a year.
- The plan should meet the parking needs for the next ten years.
- The plan should be fair to every group within the student body.
- The plan should provide for the safety of all students.
- The plan should protect the natural beauty of the campus.

Once phrased, criteria can serve the practical purpose of providing the bases for testing proposed solutions. Sometimes this testing occurs when a proposal is made, but in other instances the group chooses to list all of the suggestions and to test them later as a separate step. Some evidence exists for the belief that separate steps increase productivity (see the section on brainstorming in Chapter 3). No matter when evaluation occurs, however, it involves much judging, arguing, and shaping. In many instances a significant part of this process is an ordering of priorities among criteria. Is it more important to have convenient parking or to preserve the natural beauty of the campus? If the two are in conflict, what is the best possible compromise? Difficult problems rarely have simple solutions, but the collective judgment of those in a problem-solving conference is as good a means as any of making rational decisions.

Not always, however, does a conference end with a decision; but even if no decision is reached, the conclusion should be definite and positive. Especially if a meeting is one in a series, the group may not reach a solution; in such a case, circulating a summary is valuable because it gives the group a solid basis for beginning the next session without wasting time. An oral summary at the close of a meeting also is desirable, because it can improve morale by giving a sense of accomplishment. In addition, these final minutes may further the long-range goals by setting specific tasks for individual participants and by stimulating thought on the subtopics for the next session.

On the other hand, if the meeting is the only one to be held or is the final one in a series, the conclusion, if at all possible, should be an announcement of a chosen solution. Preferably this final statement is unanimous or at least a consensus that all are willing to support. Talking until the group reaches consensus is preferable to voting to impose the wishes of the majority, but sometimes circumstances compel the discussion leader to report a conclusion that still is controversial. Often accompanying such a statement is an accurate, unbiased report of the minority view(s). Whatever the complications may be, the leader should try to obtain a definite conclusion that he or she can report orally and perhaps in writing. Sending a written draft to each participant is a courtesy, and the conclusions may be of interest to other members of the organization and to selected outsiders.

Motivations of Participants

A second significant difference between a discussion and a conference is that the participants in the latter may have competing, irreconcilable interests. Whereas in an information-sharing session the assumption is that every member expects to profit from a cooperative pooling of facts and ideas, in a problem-solving gathering competitiveness, either open or concealed, may be stronger than mutuality. In a meeting on a future budget, for example, each department head must try to further the interests of those whom he or she represents; likewise, the choice of one site for a new public library will benefit some persons but injure others.

When special interests are obvious, the discussion leader's main responsibilities are to insure fairness and to avoid controversy that is ill-tempered and disruptive. Unrevealed selfish motivations, however, are a more serious problem, for a clever individual may succeed in blocking the proceedings or in manipulating the meeting so that the outcome serves selfish ends. Inquiries prior to the conference may reveal previously unsuspected connections between a participant and a special-interest group, and certain lines of comments during a session may arouse suspicion. Only by recognizing the presence of self-seekers can the leader discharge the obligation to conduct a conference that is fair to everyone and that results in a solution that will serve the public interest.

PRACTICE SESSIONS

Classroom practice sessions are the best possible way for students to sharpen their skills in group deliberation. One procedure is to choose problems that call for participants to present their personal views on a campus, a community, or a national issue. A second possibility is a simulated situation in which each participant plays an assigned role. On the topic of mutilated books and magazines, for example, students can respectively portray the roles of head librarian, chief of campus security, a professor, a graduate student, and an undergraduate. In studying the topic each conferee should try to gain the kinds of knowledge and the special viewpoints that the character that he or she is playing would have.

In conducting a conference for practice, the members of a class should follow these steps:

1. Form groups of four to seven.

2. Select a general topic, and phrase a question that specifies the problem to be discussed and perhaps solved.

3. Choose a leader. If the conference is to involve role playing, decide the special responsibilities of each member.

4. Prepare a tentative agenda.

5. Do research.

6. Make the physical arrangements for the meeting.

7. Hold the conference.

8. Draft a report summarizing the meeting and/or stating the recommendations for dealing with the problem.

9. If the group agrees on follow-up activities, carry them out.

CONCLUSION

"For when you assemble a number of men to have the advantage of their joint wisdom," Benjamin Franklin observed, "you inevitably assemble with those men, all their prejudices, their passions, their errors of opinion, their local interests, and their selfish views."[27] Today the world is no better than it was in the Colonial Period, and the men and the women in it have the same frailties. The information-seeking interview, the job interview, the information-sharing discussion, and the problem-solving conference, because they involve transactions between and among human beings, are complex, often unpredictable, and frequently fruitful. To do well in them is a means both of self-advancement and of furthering the best interests of groups as diverse as churches and corporations. Because of the complexities, the individual needs to know as much as possible about each of these four interpersonal and small-group situations. The purpose of the chapter, with its analyses of the special features of each of the four and its advice to participants, is to help the reader today as a student communicator, tomorrow as a participant in business and professional life, and always as a citizen in a democratic society.

PROBLEMS AND EXERCISES

1. Prepare a list of questions for a possible interview with the mayor of your city on a topic that you might be using for a term paper. Meet with four or five classmates to discuss the lists.

2. Choose a partner from the class for a practice job interview. Tell the partner the name of the company that he or she represents, the position he or she holds, and the

---

[27] As cited in Max Farrand, ed., *The Records of the Federal Convention of 1787* (New Haven, Conn.: Yale University Press, 1911), 2:642.

type of vacancy for which you are applying. If you wish, supply your partner with a list of questions that an interviewer would be likely to ask. Prepare a résumé, think through your objectives, and prepare your own questions. Hold the interview before the class, and ask for criticisms.

3. Meet with four or five classmates for a problem-solving conference on the question, "Which topic should we choose for an information-sharing discussion?" Follow an orderly process, including the setting up of criteria and the evaluating of suggested solutions. Conclude by selecting a topic.

4. Engage in a discussion before the class on the topic chosen in Problem 3.

5. Write a research paper of about seven hundred and fifty words; include footnotes and a bibliography. Use one of the following topics or something similar:
Reflective Thought in Small-Group Communication
Interviewing
Different Theories of Discussion Leadership
Encounter Groups
Discussion as Psychotherapy
The Qualities of the Useful Participant
Group Decisions Versus Those of Individuals
Research Findings on the Values of Training in Discussion

REFERENCES

Applbaum, Ronald, et al. *The Process of Group Communication.* Chicago: Science Research Associates, 1974.

Argyle, Michael, ed. *Social Encounters: Readings in Social Interaction.* Chicago: Aldine Publishing Co., 1973.

Baird, John E., and Jerome C. Diebolt. "Role Congruence, Communication, Superior-Subordinate Relations, and Employer Satisfaction in Organizational Hierarchies," *Western Speech Communication,* 40 (Fall 1976), 260–267.

Cathcart, Robert S., and Larry A. Samovar, eds. *Small Group Communication: A Reader.* Dubuque, Iowa: Wm. C. Brown Co., 1970.

Cheatham, T. Richard, and Margaret L. McLaughlin. "A Comparison of Co-Participant Perceptions of Self and Others in Placement Center Interviews," *Communication Quarterly,* 24 (Summer 1976), 9–13.

Cox, J. Robert, and Julia T. Wood. "The Effects of Consultation on Judges' Decisions," *Speech Teacher,* 24 (March 1975), 118–126.

Daly, John A., James C. McCroskey, and Virginia P. Richmond. "Judgements of Quality, Listening, and Understanding Based Upon Vocal Activity," *Southern Speech Communication Journal,* 41 (Winter 1976), 189–197.

Davis, James H. *Group Performance.* Reading, Mass.: Addison-Wesley Publishing Co., 1969.

Fisher, B. Aubrey. "Decision Emergence: Phases in Group Decison-Making," *Speech Monographs,* 37 (March 1970), 53–66.

Fisher, B. Aubrey. "The Process of Decision Modification in Small Discussion Groups," *Journal of Communication,* 20 (March 1970), 51-64.

Gouran, Dennis S. "Correlates of Member Satisfaction in Group Decision-Making Discussions," *Central States Speech Journal,* 24 (Summer 1973), 91-96.

Hawes, Leonard C., and Joseph M. Foley. "A Markov Analysis of Interview Communication," *Speech Monographs,* 40 (August 1973), 208-219.

Hayes, Donald P., and Leo Meltzer. "Interpersonal Judgments Based on Talkativeness," *Sociometry,* 35 (December 1972), 538-561.

Henderson, George, ed. *Human Relations.* Norman: University of Oklahoma Press, 1974.

Hinton, Bernard L., and H. Joseph Reitz, eds. *Groups and Organizations.* Belmont, Cal.: Wadsworth Publishing Co., 1971.

Hopper, Robert, and Frederick Williams. "Speech Characteristics and Employability," *Speech Monographs,* 40 (November 1973), 296-302.

Knutson, Thomas J., and William E. Holdridge. "Orientation Behavior, Leadership, and Consensus," *Speech Monographs,* 42 (June 1975), 107-114.

Larson, Carl E. "Speech Communication Research on Small Groups," *Speech Teacher,* 20 (March 1971), 89-107.

Larson, Charles U. "The Verbal Response of Groups to the Absence or Presence of Leadership," *Speech Monographs,* 38 (August 1971), 177-181.

Mabry, Edward A., and Charles M. Rossiter, Jr. "Laboratory Training and Problem-Solving Groups: Distinctions and Relationships," *Western Speech Communication,* 39 (Spring 1975), 102-111.

McGrath, Joseph E., and Irwin Altman. *Small Group Research: A Synthesis and Critique of the Field.* New York: Holt, Rinehart and Winston, 1966.

Rosenfeld, Lawrence B. *Human Interaction in the Small Group Setting.* Columbus, Ohio: Charles E. Merrill Publishing Co., 1973.

Stewart, Charles J., and William B. Cash. *Interviewing.* Dubuque, Iowa: Wm. C. Brown Publishing Co., 1974.

Sussmann, Lyle. "Communication Training for Ad-Hocracy," *Speech Teacher,* 24 (November 1975), 335-342.

Willard, Don, and Fred L. Strodtbeck. "Latency of Verbal Response and Participation in Small Groups," *Sociometry,* 35 (March 1972), 161-175.

Yerby, Janet. "Attitude, Task, and Sex Composition as Variables Affecting Female Leadership in Small Problem-Solving Groups," *Speech Monographs,* 42 (June 1975), 160-168.

III
RHETORICAL FACTORS: CHOICES FOR GREATER CLARITY AND EFFECTIVENESS

To become a meaningful, responsible communicator requires the utilization of techniques that support the content and that contribute to establishing and maintaining a favorable transactional climate. These techniques are in the areas of arrangement, the oral and the visual elements of delivery, verbal language, and nonverbal stimuli. By making sound choices in these four areas, the communicator enhances both clarity and effectiveness.

With Part III, *Responsible and Effective Communication* becomes complete:

The communicator must say something that is worthwhile.

He or she must say it under favorable transactional circumstances.

He or she must employ rhetorical resources to express and transmit the message with maximum clarity and effectiveness.

9
ARRANGEMENT: ORGANIZING, BEGINNING, AND CONCLUDING

After studying this chapter the reader should be able to do the following:

Deliver a satisfactory two-minute speech introduction when given a topic, a hypothetical situation, and thirty minutes to prepare

Deliver a satisfactory two-minute conclusion when given a topic, a hypothetical speech situation, and thirty minutes to prepare

Explain in one or two sentences the essential difference between an outline and a rhetorical plan

Name no fewer than five rhetorical plans for persuasion, and explain each briefly

Name no fewer than four rhetorical plans for exposition, and explain each briefly

This story is true. The scene was a small lecture hall at the University of Denver; the speaker, the outstanding scholar in his field of specialization;

the audience, professors and graduate students who were deeply interested in the topic. Despite these favorable circumstances, long before the end of the lecture more than half those present were obviously asleep. This story also is true. At an evening lecture at the University of Texas, the Ball Room of the University Center was almost full. The speaker was a novelist, the author of a best seller that was alive with vitality and color. Before he had droned through his manuscript, more than half the auditors had walked out.

The two points made by both stories are the same:

Although knowledge and worthwhile ideas are essential to meaningful, responsible discourse, they do not guarantee that communication will be clear and effective.

Although the initial sender-receiver relationship may be favorable, the skillful use of rhetorical techniques is essential to a continuing effective transaction.

These means for enhancing clarity and effectiveness cluster into several groups, the first of which is arrangement or the handling of the problems of organizing, beginning, and concluding. No two speaking situations ever are alike, and the outcome of a communicative effort depends partly on the astuteness of the sender in making rhetorical choices. Having in mind the topic, the purpose, and an assessment of the values and the motivations of the audience, the speaker decides on one rhetorical plan in preference to all others and selects from the available introductions and conclusions those that are best adapted to the circumstances.

The purposes of this chapter are twofold: (1) to catalogue the possibilities from which the communicator can choose; and (2) to discuss some of the circumstances that make a particular rhetorical plan, introduction, or conclusion a prudent choice. Although some of these guidelines are more applicable to one type of communication than another, collectively they are of value to all types—to conversation, interviewing, discussion, conference, and public address.

THE BASES FOR CHOICES

" 'Choices' is the name of the game," a student commented to some classmates as they were relaxing after their most recent session of Speech 101. "That's what our prof really was talking about. When you express yourself, you select one word rather than another and one gesture or no gesture at all instead of a second. And when you plan a speech or an interview, you decide how to begin and end and to arrange the order of your ideas one way instead of another."

"You know, I think you're right," said Mr. B. "If you make the right choices, you speak well; and if you don't, you confuse others and don't get your message across."

"But," asked Miss C., always the analytical member of the little group, "on what bases do you make these decisions?"

The preceding conversation, invented to be sure, is insightful. In preparing for any communication event, the Barneys, the Lucys, and the Barney Seniors choose materials, styles of delivery, media of expression, and—the concern of this chapter—introductions, conclusions, and rhetorical plans. These choices, called rhetorical choices because they bear so heavily on the clarity and the persuasiveness of the message, are limited by certain constraints. The first of these is best understood by distinguishing between *substantive* and *strategic* elements. The substantive materials are those ideas and arguments that are essential to the intended message—that is, the communicator cannot omit certain thoughts and contentions without altering the substance of what he or she wishes to say. Strategic elements, on the other hand, are not the critical content and are modifiable according to their anticipated effects; they are examples, comparisons, language choices, and approaches, whose alteration or deletion leaves the basic thought unchanged but whose inclusion may increase clarity and effectiveness.

Limitations of a second sort stem from meager research and inexperience in communication. If one knows nothing of the residue plan, one lacks an important resource for organizing material strategically; and if one is unfamiliar with the visualization of the future as a type of conclusion, one is so much the poorer in the available options. Likewise, one cannot begin with a funny story if one does not know an appropriate anecdote, and one cannot cite a pertinent example or an impressive statistic if research so far has produced none. This second type of limitation, of course, is remediable. Speech textbooks and classes exist so that students may increase their knowledge of rhetorical choices and thus become increasingly resourceful when preparing for either the platform or the conference room.

Ideally, the communicator is an artist who freely and consciously makes those choices that will give the message maximum clarity and impact. "What is my exact purpose?" "How much do my listeners know about my topic?" "How does the attitude of my hearers compare with the attitude that I would like for them to have?" "How well do the members of the audience know me, and how much do they like me?" "What are the possible bonds between my listeners and me?" These questions and others like them—most of them discussed earlier in this text—are the means of using self-appraisal and audience analysis as the bases for strategic choices.

Additional guidelines are inherent in the nature of the forms of discourse, the most common of which are exposition and persuasion. The two following subsections are statements of broad principles that the communicator should have in mind when he or she makes decisions on the rhetorical plan, the introduction, the conclusion, and still other rhetorical elements.

CHOICES FOR EXPOSITION

Exposition is discourse whose purpose is to inform or to explain and whose ultimate test is clarity. Lucy Miller engages in exposition when at a breakfast meeting she explains to the executive council of her campus religious group the procedure of the national board in evaluating local projects for funding. Later in the day in her political science class she answers a question by explaining the main principles of parliamentary government, and still later she demonstrates to a troop of Girl Scouts how to use a loom. Before retiring she explains to a friend how to take care of the potted plants during her absence on a skiing trip. Giving directions, explaining processes and concepts, answering most questions, reporting on experiences, and summarizing information from a printed source are all types of exposition.

Since *explanation* and *clarity* are the key concepts, the principal guidelines for the communicator are obvious. In making selections among possible introductions, one asks oneself:

How much does the audience already know?

What preliminary or background information must I supply?

Which terms or concepts require definition?

How rapidly can I proceed without causing confusion?

How necessary is it for me to arouse interest in the topic before moving into the body of my address?

Similarly, in drafting the conclusion, the knowledgeable communicator raises questions related to clarity:

Is it necessary to repeat the main points?

Will a brief summary suffice, or do I need to go over subpoints as well?

Is a final example or analogy needed to make the main points specific?

Is there a need to visualize what would happen in a single, real situation?

Whereas most types of introductions and conclusions can serve either expository or persuasive purposes, rhetorical plans tend to be more valuable for one form of discourse than for the other. In choosing a plan, the communicator should keep in mind four generalizations that collectively are the essence of exposition:

Exposition is a process of moving from the known to the unknown. Estimate accurately what your listeners already know, and proceed step by step from a solid foundation. Define any words that may be unfamiliar, and use examples freely.

The rapidity of exposition should be adjusted for topic and communicatee. Go slowly enough so that your listeners can follow you as you develop your topic, but don't bore them by dwelling unnecessarily on a point. Predict the best rate of development by considering the complexity of the topic, the educational level of the listeners, and the extent to which they already are familiar with the topic. During the presentation watch the faces for reactions that indicate how well your explanation is being received.

A presentation should cover only a limited number of points. Don't try to cover too much in one speech. Group ideas so that the number of main points is only three or four.

Exposition profits from devices that make main points easy to remember. Some speakers find ingenious ways to dramatize their principal ideas, but as a minimum devise a brief label for each. A short sentence is easier to remember than a long one, and a word or a brief phrase is even better than a short sentence. Preview the main points, summarize, and use repetition. Put diagrams and lists on the chalkboard, and prepare other types of visual aids that reinforce main ideas. Repetition in unison and performing actions together are still other devices that can increase comprehension.

CHOICES FOR PERSUASION

Acting and speaking in unison also can serve the ends of the communicator who wishes to alter an attitude or a belief or to bring about an action. Barney is trying to persuade when he argues in his political science class for a single six-year term for the president or when he tries to induce a friend to go with him for a weekend of surfing. As with exposition, persuasion as a genre suggests some broad questions to raise when planning a presentation.

How to begin? The following are strategic inquiries:

What information must I provide so that the audience will understand the issues?

How important is it that I arouse the interest of the listeners?

How credible am I to this group?

What opportunities are there for building common ground with the audience?

Broad strategic considerations, similarly, are helpful in making decisions about the conclusion:

If the persuasive attempt has relied on a set of logical arguments, the communicator should relist them.

If the body of the speech has failed to specify the desired action, the conclusion should make the objective explicit.

If the listeners lack the excitement to give more than verbal approval, the speaker should try to arouse them through challenges and appeals for action.

If the atmosphere is one of discouragement, the sender should offer a positive ending by visualizing a bright new day.

If the listeners think of the message as remote, the communicator should close by applying its substance to their daily lives.

In raising and responding to the preceding possibilities, as well as in choosing a rhetorical plan, the persuader should keep in mind seven principles that are vital to the process of influencing attitudes, beliefs, values, and actions:

1. Persuasion occurs, if at all, within the receiver. An analysis of the prospective persuadee and adaptation to him or her is essential. Entreaties must be to his or her values, not the speaker's; motivational appeals must be to his or her needs and desires, not to anyone else's or to humanity's in general. The basis for choices of examples, arguments, sources of evidence, and even words must be the preferences of the receiver, not those of the sender. The effective utilization of these analyses of the audience includes the shrewd selection of the rhetorical plan.

2. Some receivers are more strategic targets than are others. An especially good example of the usefulness of selecting a part of the total audience as a target is the 1972 campaign of Richard Nixon. Prior to the election his advisors concluded that 85 percent of the voters had made their decisions and that a strategic campaign would concentrate on the concerns of subgroups within the remaining 15 percent. The next problem was to ascertain which individuals had which worries, and the method was to use market-research workers, who questioned citizens door to door. A father of teen-agers, for example, might say that he was worried about drugs. If so, he received a letter a few weeks before the election telling him that Nixon was supporting a program of neighborhood drug councils.[1]

Other situations also make targeting strategic. The student in the speech class receives his or her grade from the professor, not from the other students; and the trial attorney knows that the verdict comes from the jury and not from the spectators. The recruiter for the debate team need not appeal to all listeners in a freshman orientation group; the target is that small number whose intellectual inclinations and professional objectives make them potential debaters. Although neither student recruiter nor political

---

[1] Richard Reeves, "Nixon's Secret Strategy," *Harper's*, 243 (December 1971), 97.

candidate intends to antagonize those who are beyond persuasion, the primary appeal often should be tailored for a limited group.

3. *The credibility of the communicator and identification between sender and receiver largely determine impact.* The person of high status is more persuasive than the one of low, and the audience that moves step by step with the speaker is more responsive than the one that sees itself as separate from him or her.

4. *Only small shifts in attitude are likely to occur in a single communication event.* The sender must estimate accurately the present attitude of listeners and build a message that calls for an obtainable amount of change. The highly credible person can ask successfully for a larger shift than can the one of low *ethos,* and audiences are more flexible on issues of limited personal involvement than they are when they feel strongly. A considerable body of research supports these generalizations, but the scholars who first studied the relation of persuasion to the size of attitude discrepancy were the Sherifs.[2]

5. *Persuasion often occurs through a forced choice.* Which item to cut from the budget, which dress to leave on the rack, which movie to attend, and which policy to choose on an international issue often are choices among the least of the evils. In many situations people must do something, or at least the persuader can make them think so. Action is less pleasant than inaction, but act one must. This feature of persuasion, like the first three, often is decisive in determining one's choices of introduction, rhetorical plan, and conclusion.

6. *Producing a change in attitudes often results in no corresponding modifications of behavior.* Voting, almost all agree, is a citizen's responsibility; but in one election in Texas 96 percent of the registered voters did not cast ballots. A new soap may sound superior, but shoppers buy the old brand through habit. Millions regard smoking as harmful but continue the practice. This discrepancy between attitude and performance is so commonplace that no speaker whose objective is behavioral change can afford to ignore the tendency to inaction when making rhetorical decisions.

7. *Attention is a prerequisite to persuasion.* More important, flickering attention is likely to mean limited effectiveness, and a high level of interest often portends substantial success. Requirements for gaining and holding interest vary according to topic, audience, and situation; the speaker's estimate of the seriousness of this problem is an important factor in deciding on materials and on types of introduction, conclusion, and rhetorical plan.

---

[2] See, for example, Carolyn Sherif and Muzafer Sherif, *Attitude, Ego-Involvement, and Change* (New York: John Wiley & Sons, 1967).

How does one apply the preceding features of persuasion when making the choices basic to composing the message? As obvious examples, if the situation calls for choosing among disagreeable possibilities, one selects the residue plan (see pp. 208–209); and if one wishes to carry one's audience along through the thought process, one uses the problem-solution. The descriptions later of the other plans will suggest still other correlations between situational features and the best choices.

OUTLINES AND RHETORICAL PLANS

Careful preparation often entails the drafting of both an outline and a rhetorical plan. The outline is a set of points and subpoints that covers the topic in an orderly fashion. A logical document, it helps the communicators to inventory their knowledge and materials and to understand their topics more clearly. Fulfilling these purposes does not necessitate audience analysis and adaptation; in theory, if one gave a speech on a single topic to half a dozen audiences, one could use the same outline each time. The rhetorical plan, on the other hand, is likely to be different for each audience. A psychological and strategic document, its function is to arrange points and subpoints for maximum clarity and effectiveness. The logical outline, the analysis of the audience and the speech situation, and the speaker's objective(s) are the major considerations in choosing the best possible plan.

THE OUTLINE

Barney, who is an assistant professional at an indoor tennis center, has decided to give his next classroom speech on his favorite sport. Having rejected "Some Pointers on Tennis" as too broad and "Mechanics of Serving" as overly technical, he is going to speak on "The Serve: Winning Through Strategy." "What shall my central idea or purpose be?" he asks himself. After some deliberation, he phrases this answer:

Purpose

I. To discuss the serve from both the server's and the receiver's viewpoints.

"What shall be my main points?" Barney next inquires. The answer is twofold:

I. Strategies in serving.
II. Strategies in returning service.

"What are the principal subpoints that I would like to take up under each of these headings?" Barney then wonders. Various options occur to him, but the allotted time is brief, and the eventual choices for the first main point are these:

I. Strategies in serving.
   A. Getting in a high percentage of first serves keeps your opponent from taking the offensive on the service return.
   B. The basic strategy is to use your most effective serve most of the time.
      1. Different players have different placements and types of serve that they do unusually well.
      2. Each opponent has his or her own strengths and weaknesses.
      3. The serve that works best in most situations is the moderately hard ball hit to the opponent's backhand.
   C. Variety in speed, spin, and placement often is strategic.
      1. A varied serve may surprise an opponent into making an error.
      2. Variety prevents an opponent from getting set and grooving his or her return.
      3. For a right-hander, a sliced serve to the extreme forehand in the receiver's right-hand court can pull him or her out of position.
      4. Scores of thirty-love, forty-love, and advantage-in are especially good times to risk a surprise serve to an opponent's strength.

Having worked out the first part of the body of his speech as far as the second-order subpoints, Barney is ready to proceed to his exposition of returning service. Finally, he asks himself two more questions: "How shall I begin?" and "How shall I close?" He responds to each with brief paragraphs that give the final outline this skeletal form:

THE SERVE: WINNING THROUGH STRATEGY

Introduction

I. Everyone would like to be a champion, and you are probably no exception. I can't honestly say that I win every time, but as an assistant pro at the Fifteen-Thirty Tennis Center, I have picked up some ideas on serving and receiving serve that may help you to play a better game. Your first shot on every point is either a serve or a service return, and there's a lot more to winning tennis than simply pulling the racket back and whamming the ball.

Purpose

I. To discuss the serve from both the server's and the receiver's viewpoints.

Body

I. Strategies in serving
   (Subpoints)
II. Strategies in returning service
   (Subpoints)

Conclusion

I. The next time you go out to play tennis, be a champion, not a chump. Don't bash the ball about brainlessly; use your head. Play the winning percentages, but use the surprise element, too. And regardless of whether you do or don't play tennis yourself, get more fun out of the next tennis match you watch on TV. Match wits with Chrissie Evert or Jimmie Connors or whoever is playing. Try to guess where they are going to serve or return; and if they cross you up, try to figure out why they did what you didn't expect. Watching is more fun this way, and you may learn something that will make you a better player.

The preceding example follows the mental processes of outline preparation and affords an illustration of an acceptable form. The following is a summary of rules for outlining:

1. The top line is the title for the speech. The title should be centered. Usually no quotation marks are necessary.

2. The four headings—Introduction, Central Idea or Purpose, Body, and Conclusion—should be centered, and each should be on a line by itself.

3. The Introduction and the Conclusion may be brief paragraphs, or they may be sets of points and subpoints.

4. The Body consists of a series of points, designated by Roman numerals, and one or more orders of subpoints. The first order of subpoints is identified by capital letters, and the second by Arabic numerals. The sequence of symbols through five levels of points and subpoints is I, A, 1, a, (1).

5. A period should follow each symbol. Prior to the fifth level, no other mark of punctuation is correct.

6. In general, the words following a symbol should be a complete sentence, but exceptions may be sensible.

7. In the Body of the outline, no more than a sentence should follow a symbol. "For each symbol, a single sentence; for each sentence, a single symbol."

8. When a statement requires two or more lines, the indentation at the left-hand side should be even. The purpose of this rule is to make the symbols stand out.

RHETORICAL PLANS FOR PERSUASION

An outline that covers a topic logically may or may not be the most successful approach when addressing a particular audience with its own special motivations and prejudices. Adaptation, although the focus of the following materials is on platform address, is also significant for the conferee, interviewer, and purposeful conversationalist. A person seeking an increase in salary, greater freedom from office routine, more liberal rules at home, or approval of a new idea increases his or her chances for success by studying the listener(s), appraising the situation, and ordering the series of ideas strategically. Plunging straight ahead toward one's objective may be the best procedure, but the communicator should consider other possibilities.

Topical

One basis for organizing persuasive appeals, as well as items of information, is the topical. Some common systems of arrangement are the following:

Past, present, and future: history of the topic, status today, and prospects for the years to come

Economic, social, and political

Arguments for and arguments against

Place designations: effects on New England, the Midwest, the Far West, and the South

Time divisions: developments in the 1950s, the 1960s, and the 1970s

More specialized systems of organization are suitable for particular speech subjects. Thus, one may argue for a new research bureau by picturing its services to (1) the university and (2) the community; or one may show the disadvantages of eliminating compulsory physical education by talking about the effects of the change on (1) the students, (2) the faculty, and (3) the university as a whole.

Problem-Solution

Especially common and frequently useful, the problem-solution plan is adaptable to almost any time limitation and to almost any topic. The name is an accurate description: The first part of the address is a description of the problem and an explanation of its seriousness; the second part is a presentation of a solution with or without supporting contentions.

The advantages of this rhetorical plan, besides its simplicity, are several. The first section offers opportunities for presenting examples, for using vivid, colorful materials, for stimulating interest, and for showing the present or potential consequences for each individual in the audience. Moreover, since the discussion of the problem rarely evokes controversy, this section enables the communicator to appear as a likeable, credible person who shares with listeners a common problem.

An interesting experiment related to this plan was a study of the materials a speaker used with audiences whose attitudes toward his thesis were very opposed, moderately opposed, moderately in favor, and "no opposition." The results were that "The greater the opposition of the audience, the fewer solution arguments and the more problem arguments were used."[3] A second interesting study was a comparison of the effectiveness of a speech following the problem-solution order with that of a speech beginning with a solution. The outcome, as predicted, was that starting with the problem was the more persuasive.[4]

Criteria-Solution

Another possible pattern, useful when the nature of the problem is too obvious to require discussion, is to begin by specifying the tests that a solution should meet. The second and usually longer section then begins with a statement of the speaker's proposal, continues by showing how this plan meets each of the tests forming the criteria, and possibly concludes with an appeal for action or support.

A famous example of a speech following this plan is the 1956 address by John F. Kennedy nominating Adlai Stevenson for the presidency. After describing the kind of man that the country needed, Kennedy showed how Stevenson fulfilled each of the requirements. In 1976 John Connally at the Republican national convention organized one section of his address by stating criteria and then assessing how well they had been met.

Deductive

"What are the reasons that I should support that candidate, bill, or proposal?" is a reasonable question, and sometimes the best rhetorical plan is one whose answers are plain and direct. The speaker in the introduction makes the thesis clear and then begins the body of the address by stating and proving the first contention supporting the thesis. After this he or she states and substantiates in turn each of the remaining major arguments. "There are three reasons that we should support the legalization of parimutuel betting in Texas," began one speaker. "First, legalization would provide the state treasury with a large amount of money annually. Second . . ." Deductive speeches often include a list of the arguments in the

---

[3] Michael D. Hazen and Sara B. Kiesler, "Communication Strategies Affected by Audience Opposition, Feedback, and Persuasibility," *Speech Monographs*, 42 (March 1975), 59.
[4] Arthur R. Cohen, "Need for Cognition and Order of Communications as Determinants of Opinion Change," in Carl I. Hovland, ed., *The Order of Presentation in Persuasion* (New Haven, Conn.: Yale University Press, 1957), pp. 102–120.

introduction, numbers before each contention in the body, and a restatement of the points in the conclusion.

A combination of the deductive plan with some other pattern often is effective. Even though the communicator may choose a different approach as the grand strategy, he or she may decide to develop some part of the presentation by the straightforward pattern of "state your argument; then prove it."

This direct presentation of contentions and their support is orderly, concise, clear, and businesslike; it works well with audiences that are objective, intelligent, and motivated to listen. This approach, however, does little to arouse interest or to conciliate those who are hostile toward the thesis.

Inductive (Examples . . . Final Appeal)

Also useful as the pattern for either a part of a speech or for an entire presentation is the inductive plan, which may be especially strategic when listeners are opposed to the speaker's position. Since this opposition usually is to the plan itself, starting with examples gives the speaker time to win respect and to build common ground. In a campus address opposing the reelection of the president of the student body, one speaker began by saying that she had a few remarks to make about the coming election. Without revealing the eventual position, she gave an example of misconduct by the president and followed this with an instance showing poor judgment. Two more unfavorable illustrations preceded a direct statement of the conclusion, "A vote against _____ is a vote for the best interests of all of us."

Residue

Also highly suitable for a special circumstance is the residue plan, which works well when all possible solutions are disagreeable. Unfortunately many modern problems fit this description. What is the best way for the state to increase its income from taxes? What is the least painful way to reduce gasoline consumption? What is the best plan for providing welfare?

The procedure is to list all viable suggestions and then to expose the difficulties attached to each one of these excepting the one that the speaker favors. "Only four courses are possible. Number one should be rejected because . . . number two because . . . number three because. . . ." "Proposal number four," the speaker may concede, "also has its weaknesses, but under the circumstances we must do something, and it is the best that we can do." A section minimizing the weaknesses and/or offering constructive arguments completes the speech. Success with the plan depends, first, on firm and reasonable support for the arguments and, second, on a seemingly accurate and complete listing of all possibilities. A brief development of a residue appears in a speech by Martin Luther King, Jr.:

> Now there are three ways that oppressed people have generally dealt with their oppression. One way is the method of acquiescence, the method of surrender; that is, the individuals will somehow adjust themselves to oppression, they adjust themselves to discrimination or to segregation or colonialism or what have you. The other method that has been used in history is that of rising up against the oppressor with corroding hatred and physical violence. . . .
>
> But there is another way, namely the way of nonviolent resistance.[5]

Reversal of Apparent Position

Still another means of dealing with hostility toward one's position is a plan that begins with the case against one's proposal and concludes with favoring arguments. "These have been good contentions," the speaker says either expressly or by implication at the pivotal point, "but to be fair we must now look at the other side to see how much merit it has."

Extensive research comparing the "both-sides" and the "one-side-only" speeches suggests some tentative guidelines for when to use each:

1. The two-sided speech is more effective when the listeners have completed at least a high-school education, and the one-sided speech is more effective with persons of limited backgrounds.

2. The two-sided speech is especially effective if the evidence clearly supports the thesis.

3. The two-sided presentation is more effective when listeners oppose the speaker's position, and the one-sided is more persuasive when receivers already support the thesis.[6]

A fairly recent study includes an examination of the relationship of the climax-anticlimax variable with one-sidedness and two-sidedness. Anthony J. Clark found that with one-sided messages, the climax order (the weakest argument first and the strongest last) was superior to the anticlimax and that with two-sided messages the most effective arrangement was to use the climax order for the first half and the anticlimax for the second.[7]

---

[5] Martin Luther King, Jr., "Love, Law, and Civil Disobedience," a speech delivered on November 16, 1961, as reprinted in Marcus H. Boulware, ed., *The Oratory of Negro Leaders: 1900–1968* (Westport, Conn.: Negro Universities Press, 1969), p. 260.
[6] Research supporting these generalizations has been extensive. The original study was by Carl I. Hovland, Arthur Lumsdaine, and Fred Sheffield, *Experiments on Mass Communication:* Vol. III of *Studies in Social Psychology in World War II* (Princeton, N.J.: Princeton University Press, 1949), pp. 213–214.
[7] Anthony J. Clark, "An Exploratory Study of Order Effect in Persuasive Communication," *Southern Speech Communication Journal*, 39 (Summer 1974), 331.

Clark reports, in other words, that in a two-sided speech the first argument for the speaker's actual position should be the strongest.

Alternate Illustration and Argument

In this pattern the speaker begins pleasantly with a story designed to build attention and to establish rapport. Unobtrusively he or she moves to a statement of the lesson that the story illustrates. Not tarrying on the generalization, he or she proceeds easily to a second story, which in its turn is followed by a comment on its meaning. Similar to the inductive pattern, the alternate illustration and argument plan is the basis for a great many sermons and also for a number of nonfiction best sellers on self-improvement or on other aspects of popular psychology. Dale Carnegie's *How to Win Friends and Influence People* is an excellent example. The problem for the speaker, of course, is finding stories that illustrate the thesis.

Extended Analogy

An even greater test for the communicator's inventiveness is devising an appropriate analogy and carrying its applications throughout an address. The result, however, can be highly effective.

The most common but not the most imaginative analogies are those based on history. By examining the past and drawing parallels, one can argue that the time is near for the second coming of Christ, that a terrible depression threatens, or that the United States is doomed to the fate of some past empire. More inventive speeches utilize analogies in which the two parts are from different fields. One student attacked the pending agricultural bill by describing the classroom building as a storage depot for textbooks that the publisher kept producing, although unneeded, because of a government subsidy. Another speaker, whose point was that life is like a great work of art, took the qualities of a great painting one by one and applied each to the problems of human life in a technological society.

Conclusion

How does one use the preceding information on rhetorical plans? Assuming that one has evolved a specific purpose, has collected most of the needed material, and has organized the essential ideas into a logical outline, one is ready to find the answer to the question, "How can I make my ideas the most effective?" To answer this question, one must know the audience—their motives, their beliefs, their values, and especially their attitudes toward the topic. With this information in mind, the speaker can select the rhetorical plan or the combination of plans that seems the most likely to produce the desired results.

RHETORICAL PLANS FOR EXPOSITION

Not all speaking, even on serious issues, is persuasive. The purpose sometimes is to explain the nature of a problem, the provisions of a bill, the process by which a regulatory agency functions, or how a solution would work. Ultimately such explanations may serve persuasive functions, and even frankly persuasive speeches may include sections of exposition that are long enough to require an organizational pattern. The available choices, as with persuasion, are numerous; each plan has its own attributes, advantages, disadvantages, and special uses.

Analytical Plan

With many topics the problem is that of dividing the whole into parts small enough to be manageable. Almost any system of division that is appropriate to the topic can be satisfactory if the subheadings do not overlap and if collectively they encompass the whole. Examples of systems of division are the following: offense and defense; land, sea, and air; forehand, backhand, and serve; primary and secondary; facts and theories; immediate and ultimate effects; economic, social, and political results; comedy, tragedy, and farce; intrinsic and extrinsic *ethos;* kinesics, proxemics, and paralinguistics; upward, downward, and horizontal communication; deliberative, demonstrative, and forensic types of oratory; and competence, trustworthiness, and dynamism as aspects of credibility.

Place Arrangement

A second means of dividing the whole into workable units is the rhetorical plan of place arrangement. The requirements are the same as for the analytical pattern—the parts must not overlap and collectively they must cover the topic. One speaker in talking about the probable effects of a new treaty discussed successively the predicted impact on Western Europe, the Soviet bloc, and the United States. Another communicator analyzed a new bill on the sources of energy by discussing the changes that it would bring to New England, to the Southeast, to the Midwest, to the Southwest, and to the Far West. Thus, geographic divisions are serviceable in discussing major public issues, even though one more commonly associates them with simpler tasks of exposition and description. Among the other useful schemes of place arrangement are these: foreground and background; left to right; around the circle or semicircle; exterior and interior; top to bottom; bow, cabin, and stern; north to south; and ceiling, walls, and floor. Combining two of these often is necessary. In a description of a painting, for example, the main points were foreground and background, but the subpoints followed an order from left to right.

Chronological Order

Frank Ikard, president of the American Petroleum Institute, analyzed the energy crisis into three periods and gave a descriptive heading to each: In the first, the public claimed that the crisis did not exist; in the second, the scapegoat stage, people looked for someone to blame; the third, one hopes, will be characterized by realistic recognition and resolution.[8] Other possible uses of time order include the following: prewar, wartime, postwar; the administrations of Johnson, Nixon, Ford, and Carter; the early days of television, the years of growth and development, the modern era; and past, present, and future. Any unit of time that is meaningful to a topic is possible—by centuries, by decades, by years, or by seasons.

Step-by-Step Progression

Applied to a process, time order becomes step-by-step analysis. "How does a bill become a law?"—the best expository method probably is step by step. The plan also works well in describing how to bake a cake, how to program a computer, and how to conduct an experiment in chemistry.

The reason for proceeding step by step is that data otherwise become unmanageable. The tennis professional cannot talk about all aspects of the forehand drive at the same time; but it is possible to explain successively the backswing, the step and swing, and the follow-through. Similarly, how a proposal moves through the General Assembly of the United Nations is unclear unless one isolates each of the stages. So abundant are the examples of this plan that this generalization is secure: When the task is to explain a process, the communicator should consider the advisability of choosing this rhetorical plan and begin looking for dividing points in the continuous sequence.

Simple-to-Complex

Simple-to-complex and known-to-unknown are fundamental patterns for the exposition of a difficult topic. Many curricula are thus founded. Instruction in a foreign language or a new field of mathematics starts with simple principles and builds day by day on the prior foundations. Less obviously, in teaching bridge or chess or any other intellectual game, one starts with fundamentals and reserves until later the complex strategies.

Determining what is simple is not easy, but both the difficulty of the idea and the listener's familiarity with it are factors. The key concepts of a philosophic system, for example, are easier for someone who knows similar philosophies than for someone unfamiliar with the general area. Similarly,

---

[8] Nick Thimmesch, "Okay, Frank, One More Time—," *Signature*, 10 (May 1975), 43.

a person with a broad knowledge of electronics finds it easier to grasp an explanation of a new device than does someone without a comparable background. Deciding what is simple depends, therefore, on an analysis of the audience as well as on an appraisal of the ideas themselves.

"What does the listener already know?" The speaker begins at this point and proceeds with the explanation by degrees, each of which should be made clear before advancing. The utilization of feedback, a process discussed elsewhere, can be helpful.

Extended Analogy

An analogy often is the best means of explaining the unknown in terms of the known. Thus, a speaker can talk about the rotary engine by comparing it with a motor of the piston type, about rugby as compared with football, about an Oriental religion in relation to Christianity or Judaism, about wedding customs in an aboriginal society as being like and unlike those of the Western world, about the operation of the World Bank in relation to borrowing money from a neighborhood lending institution, about a new penal code as compared to the old one, and about transportation ten years hence as compared to what it is today. The process of explanation by analogy is relatively simple: The communicator thinks of something that listeners already understand and then shows how an unfamiliar game, custom, law, or process is like or unlike what is known.

An analogy sometimes can provide the organizational basis for the entire speech. The calendar, with its seven columns and five rows, was the basis in a radio lecture for an explanation of the periodic table of chemical elements. Such an extended comparison requires care and ingenuity, for an old block of knowledge rarely fits the new one point by point. When the extended analogy does work out, the effect, however, can be both clear and interesting. Inspirational speakers sometimes build their appeals for better living around comparisons with some object or natural phenomenon, such as the wheel or the rainbow. They draw points for their speeches from the brightness and variety of the colors, the fleetingness, the location high in the distant sky, and the symmetry.

Extended Example

One child is more appealing than a set of generalizations about a relief program; one athlete's training regimen is more interesting than an essay entitled "How to Keep in Condition." Likewise, the clearest and most effective way of explaining the process of court appeals may be to follow through a single case, either real or hypothetical. Other topics that lend themselves to the use of the extended example include the enactment of a bill into law, the computation of odds in pari-mutuel betting, the processing of a loan, and the operation of the local program for responding to a disaster. In all of these instances the use of the example facilitates the employment of vivid description, the maintenance of suspense, and the creation of human interest.

Conclusion

Whichever rhetorical plan or combination of plans the communicator selects, he or she still must devise engaging introductions and motivating conclusions—the topics for the next two sections of the chapter. Many of these are useful for both exposition and persuasion.

BEGINNING THE SPEECH

"The beginning is the most important part of the work," Plato wrote.[9] Almost any Lucy or Barney can confirm this observation by recalling personal experiences. "Turning off" listeners were Mr. Boorish, who seemed pompous and self-conscious; Mr. Hesitant, who appeared to be ill prepared and unsure of both himself and his material; Mr. Stale, who repeated a familiar joke and told it badly; and Ms. Dull, who read a manuscript without thought or expression, scarcely noting the presence of her audience. But some listeners have been fortunate. Happier memories are those of Ms. Sparkle, whose friendliness and vivacity engaged attention; of Mr. Business, who went straight to the point and thus suggested that his speech was well prepared; and of Mr. Similarity, who without obvious effort made his interests seem to coincide with those of his receivers. Some research scholars claim that listeners in the first thirty seconds make a judgment about the speaker that they rarely change.

In all types of communication an effective beginning is important. If the objective of a conversation is to obtain money from one's parents for a trip during Easter vacation, how should one begin? If a person is leader of a group, how much information do the participants need? If one is interviewing for a job, how can one make an initial impression that will be favorable? And in platform address, which purposes must the introduction fulfill in the specific situation, and which type(s) will work the best?

PURPOSES OF THE INTRODUCTION

"Why do I need an introduction?" is a reasonable question, and "Sometimes you don't" is part of the answer. Since every speaking situation is

[9] Plato *The Republic* ii.377B.

different, the best introduction may be either long or short, serious or humorous, formal or relaxed. For some topics the audience requires background information in order to understand the body of the speech, and for most subjects materials arousing interest and a preview of the main points are helpful. Still other important purposes are building credibility, establishing common ground and rapport, and developing self-confidence.

Providing Needed Background Information

An appreciation of this first purpose goes back at least to Aristotle, who regarded the *narratio* as one of the parts of the speech. He really had in mind courtroom oratory; and the *narratio,* which preceded argument, was a statement of the facts of the case. Today many situations call for background information. Listeners need to know what the World Bank does before they can judge arguments about its revision, and they require a description of the city's present facilities for waste disposal before they can view favorably a proposed bond issue. True enough, speakers often blend explanation and argument in the body of a speech; but this practice does not mean that opening explanations of problems, plans, processes, causes, and past history are not often advantageous and even essential.

"What needs explanation?" and "How much?" are the critical questions pertaining to this first purpose, and pat answers are impossible. Audience analysis is basic. "How much do these listeners already know? How much must they know before they can follow my line of argument in the body of the address?" Still other considerations are holding attention and keeping the speech proportional. Too long an introduction can tire an audience and leave too little time for the development of the main points.

Previewing the Structure and/or Listing
the Main Points

A second section of the oration, as described in classical rhetoric, was the partition, or the listing of the principal subtopics or arguments. The desirability of an opening preview is no less today.

Formal and informal partitions are both useful. The former, a brief listing of points, usually in the exact wordings to be employed later, saves time and suggests a brisk, businesslike presentation. The informal approach, on the other hand, is more likely to seem friendly, to arouse interest, and to build rapport. In this type the speaker, instead of numbering and listing points, weaves the main subtopics or contentions into an expository paragraph:

As we make an imaginary tour on our flying carpet, we see below several "hot spots"—real puzzlers for American diplomacy. Looking downward, we see South Africa, whose racial tensions may erupt at any time; and flying north over the long Italian boot, we see a country whose strong nationalist communism threatens NATO. And at the eastern end of the Mediterranean we see Lebanon, the Palestinians, and Israel.

Useful though it generally is, the preview poses one danger—destroying suspense by telling too much. The preceding example avoids this fault, as does the following:

As we look together at this major problem, we will study first its history and causes, we will look briefly at the solutions that are commonly proposed, and finally I will state my own plan and the reasons that I favor it.

Arousing Interest

Suspense, as the analysis in Chapter 4 pointed out, is only one factor in arousing interest—a function that every introduction should serve, no matter what the other emphases. Stories, examples, humor, and vivid descriptions—the ways of arousing interest are many—are all useful; but not to be neglected is personal relevance. Such questions as these are in every auditor's mind: "Why should I spend my time listening to this speech?" "What's in it for me?" "Why do I need to know this?" "How does this problem affect me?" Satisfactory answers to these questions insure at least initial interest.

Establishing Credibility

Showing an awareness of the listener's concerns and interests is also a means of building credibility, a purpose that needs attention in almost every speaking situation. The precise nature of the problem varies, as three brief case studies illustrate.

Joe Anonymous is essentially unknown to the audience. He comes from another city, or perhaps from another campus or a different church congregation. News stories and placards have identified him as state secretary of the Young Republicans; but as he sits on the platform, he is a stranger who must prove himself. To do this, Joe arranges for the chairman of the meeting to give him a favorable introduction, not too long and not effusive, but factual and substantial. Joe has supplied the chairman with information on his educational background, the offices he has held, the title of the book that he has written, and an exact statement of a special honor. Joe recognizes, however, that the primary burden for strengthening ethos is his own. He grooms himself with the values and the customs of his audience in mind; he keeps himself alert and composed before and during the chairman's introduction; and he uses words, ideas, and delivery during the opening moments to create favorable impressions. He combines friendliness with dignity and appears self-assured without being pompous. He begins smoothly and thoughtfully, as if well prepared, and he mentions facts bearing on his qualifications while avoiding unsupported claims.

Jo Clubwoman is well known to her fellow members, but not as an authority—the usual situation, also, when a student addresses classmates. Since Jo's peers have firm opinions about her already, the most that the introduction can do is to give information on her qualifications on the day's topic. If she has lived for a year in Hong Kong, she should say so near the beginning of a speech on the Far East. If she has spent summers as a park ranger, she should mention this in starting an address on the protection of wild life. If she has been a major in anthropology and recently has written a term paper on life in the Outback, she should provide this information as part of the introduction to a talk on Australia.

Joey Clown is of limited credibility. A student in a college speech class, he has given two humorous, trivial speeches and has acted the role of the comic at every opportunity. Now as he faces his classmates attempting to fulfill an assignment for a serious, responsible speech, a few people snicker, others giggle, and the merriment spreads contagiously before he even begins. To say that establishing credibility is a problem for Joey is an understatement.

More common problems than clownishness are those arising when one represents a minority or unpopular viewpoint or when one's reputation is damaged. Before a typical middle class audience the Socialist Workers candidate or the person convicted of fraud begins with a handicap. Poor choices of topic also can create problems for the speaker—for example, the school principal (a bachelor) who addressed the mothers of the PTA on rearing children; and the bright-eyed economics major who talked to mature business executives on improving collections and cash flow. In all of these situations, adjustments are possible if the communicator appraises the problems honestly and objectively. Sometimes, as in the case of the socialist, one can appeal to the American beliefs in fair play and freedom of speech and can identify values and goals that capitalism and socialism have in common. As with other situations, factual statements about one's qualifications, the avoidance of belligerency, moderation in language and delivery, and tact in ideas and materials are useful in allaying fears and promoting credibility.

Building Common Ground and Establishing
Rapport Between Speaker and Listener

Besides promoting credibility, common ground provides a basis for understanding new ideas and for receiving plausible arguments. It also creates a mental set that predisposes listeners to judge favorably both the speaker and the message.

The belief by listeners that their needs, objectives, and best interests coincide with those of the speaker probably generates greater confidence in the sincerity and truthfulness of the communicator than does any other type of common ground. "Jimmie Green sells Chevrolets for less not because he wants to but because he has to" is an attempt to apply this principle. Whereas prospective customers are incredulous of any claim that a dealer is giving bargains voluntarily, so Jimmie Green must have reasoned, they may believe that he will do so if he too will profit by lowering prices. The critical point in this particular radio commercial was the plausibility of the statement, "Jimmie Green has to."

Helping to Establish Self-Confidence

Finally, the introduction can help the speaker with one of the most common problems in communication. Stage fright is both frequent and worrisome among beginning speakers, and even many persons with extensive experience must deal with it. Since waiting one's turn is likely to build up nervous tension, getting through the opening sentences is crucial. For this reason, if for no other, a speaker should prepare the introduction with great care and should know exactly what the first sentence is going to be and what he or she is going to do following it. If preceding addresses or events suggest an appropriate revision, the wording of the new opening sentence again should be thought through carefully.

Except for persons who are unusually gifted, some groping for words in the body of a speech is inevitable; but preparation should be so thorough that fumbling never occurs in the opening thirty to sixty seconds. The smooth, firm beginning, in addition to suggesting competence to the audience, gives the speaker self-satisfaction. "I got through it, I'm on my way, and all is well."

The preceding six purposes are not mutually exclusive. Although the amount of time to be spent in achieving different purposes should vary with the situation, most introductions should accomplish a combination of objectives. Time limitations, however, necessitate selectivity.

TYPES OF INTRODUCTIONS

How to achieve the preceding purposes? The possibilities are numerous, and in many instances types of introductions should be combined. The important point for the student is not so much the details that follow as it is the realization that many types of introduction are possible and that the speaker has numerous options. Only an uninformed, unimaginative person starts every speech in the same way. A humorous story is a good device in

Types of introductions.

- Straightforward, businesslike beginning
- "Ladies and Gentlemen..."
- Partition
- Background information and analysis
- Immediate references
- Common ground
- Personal experiences and other narratives
- Humor
- Example; dramatic description
- Series of questions or startling facts
- Quotations; literary or historic allusions

some circumstances, but not in all; likewise, a formal partition, despite its many advantages, sometimes is ill advised.

1. Straightforward, businesslike beginning. "I am here today to talk about the problems of the housing industry." In today's rapidly moving, impatient world a statement of the topic, often followed by a partition, frequently is the best way to begin. Such abruptness may catch some listeners unready to give full attention, but it may heighten credibility by suggesting candor, decisiveness, and full preparation.

2. Partition. Efficiency also characterizes a simple partition or preview that is confined to a listing, usually numbered, of the main points. An address by Robert S. McNamara, president of the World Bank, illustrates this practice:

This morning, I would like to address two specific issues: the operations of the Bank, both for the past fiscal year and for the period covered by our Five-Year Program; and the relationship of the Bank to the rest of the U.N. system.[10]

---

[10] Robert S. McNamara, address before the U.N. Economic and Social Council, New York City, November 13, 1970, as published in *Vital Speeches of the Day*, 37 (December 15, 1970), 135.

Research showing the value of partition is not extensive, but one experimenter found "that inclusion of a preview or a review produced significantly more comprehension than did inclusion of no summaries whatsoever."[11] In this study the research worker administered two forms of a speech, one with summaries and the other without them, and then gave a twenty-five-item multiple-choice test to the respective audiences.

3. Background information and analysis. Experimental data on the value of background information do not exist, but experience indicates the importance of asking the questions "How much do my listeners already know?" and "How much must they know if they are to understand my speech and its arguments?" Senator Frank Church began an address opposing the renewal of foreign aid by summarizing the preceding ten years:

Looking back on the sixties, no one can deny that we were indeed "the greatest power in the world" and that we surely did "behave like it"—if throwing our might and money around is the correct measure of "behaving like it." Nonetheless, we not only failed to accomplish what we set out to accomplish ten years ago; we have been thrown for losses across the board: in the name of preserving peace, we have waged an endless war; in the guise of serving as sentinel for the "free world," we have stood watch while free governments gave way to military dictatorship in country after country, from one end of our vast hegemony to the other. Today, confidence in American leadership abroad is as gravely shaken as is confidence in the American dollar.[12]

4. Immediate references. Valuable both in building rapport and in arousing interest, this fourth type of introduction is moderately easy to prepare. One possibility for collecting information of immediate relevance is library research on the history of the city or organization, on local persons who are prominent, on parks and museums, and on facts pertaining to industrial and agricultural production. A second possibility is to arrive early enough to talk to local persons, to look over the auditorium, and to scan a campus or city newspaper for current interests and issues. Still a third approach is to draw on items that are immediate chronologically rather than geographically. References to current comic-strip characters, sports heroes, television personalities, movies, and song titles tend to catch attention and to establish a common bond. One successful speaker who believed in the value of this fourth type of introduction was Harry Truman. "My introduction," he said, "usually consists of some reference to the audience, to the circum-

---

[11] John E. Baird, Jr., "The Effects of Speech Summaries upon Audience Comprehension of Expository Speeches of Varying Quality and Complexity," *Central States Speech Journal*, 25 (Summer 1974), 127.
[12] Frank Church, address to the Senate, October 29, 1971, as published in *Vital Speeches of the Day*, 38 (November 15, 1971), 66.

stances surrounding the speech or to the locality in which it is to be delivered."[13]

An example of a reference to immediate interests is the following excerpt from a speech by a man who at the time was the Secretary of Labor for the United States. He began by mentioning the date on the calendar and proceeded with a questionable attempt at humor:

> I don't know whether it's by design or accident that I am appearing here on the first day of Lent. Perhaps it has occurred to some of you that a talk on labor-management relations might be an appropriate way to usher in a period of mourning.[14]

5. *Common ground.* A special form of the immediate reference is the identification of some quality or problem that the speaker and many of the listeners share. An example is this opening by the chairman of General Motors, who was addressing the Executive Club of Chicago:

> I was very pleased to receive Bill Clark's invitation to address the Executive Club of Chicago. It is always pleasant to return to where I have so many fond memories and pleasant associations. Your Club has a well-earned reputation. Your membership reflects a great diversity of interests and a fine record of accomplishments. The Club is known as an excellent forum for frank and thoughtful discussion. Here is a place to raise issues that should concern all of us who care about the well-being of our country and its economy.
>
> Today, then, let me call your attention to a serious, yet subtle, threat to our American system of free enterprise.[15]

6. *Personal experiences and other narratives.* Stories, whatever the source, are usually attention-getting, noncontroversial, and conducive to a relaxed, friendly atmosphere. The best ones in many instances are those that are personal and essentially true, though sometimes embellished. Being original, these accounts are new and fresh to the audience. Well-told and selected with discretion, they can increase authoritativeness and project warmth and humaneness.

Problems, nevertheless, arise. Stories that degrade the speaker, that are mean and sarcastic toward others, that make the sender sound boorish or conceited, or that an audience finds vulgar, tasteless, and offensive obviously do more harm than good. Moreover, recalling or inventing a narrative that is relevant to the topic and that meets at least minimum standards

---

[13] As cited in Eugene E. White and Clair R. Henderlider, "What Harry S. Truman Told Us about His Speaking," *Quarterly Journal of Speech*, 40 (February 1954), 40.

[14] J. D. Hodgson, address in Moline, Ill., on February 24, 1971, as published in *Vital Speeches of the Day*, 37 (April 1, 1971), 382.

[15] James M. Roche, address on March 25, 1971, as published in *Vital Speeches of the Day*, 37 (May 1, 1971), 445.

for conflict, suspense, human interest, and humor is difficult; and still another problem is the danger that the story will be too good—that it will set off such waves of laughter or emotional reminiscing that the audience will be inattentive to the body of the address.

If the purpose of a story is to prove an argument, ethics demands strict accuracy in the details; but usually an introductory narrative need not meet this standard. Indeed, the art of the speaker may have more to do with the quality of a story than does its intrinsic nature. By adding details, exaggerating some features, creating dialogue, and describing feelings as well as events, a clever speaker can transform a relatively routine experience into a tale that has suspense, charm, and humor. Sometimes the narrative quality is only a stylistic ploy. "When I was going through the letters of reference that students wrote for these teacher-of-the-year candidates, I came across some items that gave me fascinating insights into the teen-age mind" was the beginning of one speech. It sounded like a story, and the speaker preserved the chronological development; when analyzed, though, the content was an exposition of certain impressions.

7. *Humor.* Humorous attempts, whether stories or assorted witticisms, can brand a speaker as tasteless, dull, and unimaginative, or they can make a person seem lively, interesting, and clever. The following example illustrates both the good and the bad. The first paragraph is a strained, unfunny story that the speaker drags into the speech; the second and the third paragraphs, although improbable, are personalized and original:

Mr. Chairman, ladies and gentlemen: I am deeply grateful for the warm and overly generous introduction. I am reminded of the grandmother who had her grandchild out in a baby carriage in Central Park one day, and a friend came along and looked into the carriage and said, "That's a beautiful grandchild you have there," and the grandmother replied, "That's nothing. You should see his picture."

So I appreciate very much having Carroll Johnson tell you about my picture. I am also appreciative of my introduction because I have been introduced in so many different ways. Not long ago, a college president finished his introduction of me by saying, "And now we want to hear the latest dope from New York." And last year, before a physical education group my introducer characterized me as "a warm athletic supporter."

Carroll Johnson is a charming person. . . . I turned down his first invitation . . ., but he persuaded me to come by saying that it was uncharacteristic of me to deny any audience my views and that I was the only person he knew who could meet every issue with an open mouth.[16]

---

[16] Ewald Nyquist, Commissioner of Education for the State of New York, address at the Thirtieth Annual Superintendents' Work Conference, New York City, July 15, 1971, as published in *Vital Speeches of the Day*, 37 (August 15, 1971), 645.

8. *Example; dramatic description.* Humorous or nonhumorous, an example is any single instance that illustrates a point or supports a generalization. As an introduction, its principal advantages are that it usually arouses interest and that it seldom creates resentment or antagonism. The principal problems are (1) locating something that is typical, informative, and interesting and (2) working up the material to a suitable length and to the form that best fulfills the speaker's purposes.

How material is worded—a topic for detailed discussion in Chapter 11—affects the value of all types of introductions, examples included. The skillful speaker can describe a particular scene, such as the devastation following a hurricane, with such vividness that listeners can almost see the broken trees and the windowless, roofless homes. By a careful choice of details and words, other craftsmen can picture a scene so that it is hilariously funny or so that the tragic elements are moving.

A written passage that illustrates the potential strength of crisp, evocative language follows. This selection adds the attention-holding values of surprise and paradox:

> Electricity is paradoxical stuff: an invisible mover, power without substance. It responds silently to the flick of a switch; it is seemingly clean and cool, plentiful and cheap. But behind all the switches, at its source, electricity is none of these.
>
> Electric power is expensive. It is the most capital-intensive of all industries, requiring a four-dollar investment to generate one dollar in sales. . . . Electric power is dirty: generating it produces wastes that poison the nation's air and degrade its water. And it is scarce.[17]

9. *Series of questions or startling facts.* The rapid movement of ideas in a series of questions or facts tends to carry an audience along, to arouse interest, and to impress upon listeners the seriousness, the timeliness, or the relevance of the topic. The famous scholar Susanne K. Langer includes a series of questions in the introduction to a journal article:

> When, why and how did man begin to speak? What generations invented that great social instrument, language? What development of animal communication has eventuated in human communication? What pre-Adamite thought of assigning a particular little squeak to a particular object as the name of that object, by which you could refer to it, demand it, make other people think of it? How did the other pre-Adamites all agree to assign the same squeaks to the same things? What has led to the concatenation of those primitive words in syntactically structured sentences of interrelated meanings?[18]

---

[17] Anthony Wolff, "The Price of Power," *Harper's*, 244 (May 1972), 36.
[18] Susanne K. Langer, "The Origins of Speech and Its Communicative Function," *Quarterly Journal of Speech*, 46 (April 1960), 121.

10. Quotations; literary or historic allusions. Ralph McGill, illustrious Southern journalist, began an address with "It is written in Proverbs that a word fitly spoken is like apples of gold in pictures of silver."[19] Such a beginning adds a touch of class that suggests that the speaker is literate and cares enough about the audience to exert special effort in preparation. Other types of material offer similar but different advantages. Familiar sayings establish common ground and give audiences the pleasure of recognition, and some poetry impresses through its distinctive form and pleasing expression.

The following are brief examples of allusions and quotations: "When Washington and his men endured that terrible winter at Valley Forge . . ." "In *Dr. Zhivago* a scene that remains vivid in my mind is . . ." " 'Better be ignorant of a matter than half know it'[20] is a maxim credited to Publilius Syrus, who lived half a century before Christ. Nowhere is this maxim more applicable today than in the present controversy. . . ."

CONCLUSION

Fifteen centuries ago St. Augustine wrote, "Because a speech which begins immediately with the matter itself, without an introduction, is premature and wholly chopped off and without a head, we use introductions even in controversies which are in good repute with the listeners."[21] Today most persons agree, despite the advantages on some occasions of the businesslike beginning. Because of custom, listeners expect some opening materials, and they must adjust their mental set when the introduction is omitted. The first summarizing generalization is, therefore, that some kind of introduction is desirable. Other conclusions are these:

1. Every speaker should know that there are many possible types of introduction.

2. The preparation of the introduction should begin with an analysis of the situation and an informed decision on the purpose(s) to be fulfilled.

3. The speaker should have the opening sentences so well in mind that the chances of stumbling over them are slight.

4. Since audiences make judgments about speakers very quickly, a good beginning is imperative.

5. Since an introduction often should fulfill more than one purpose, in many instances it should consist of a combination of two or more types.

---

[19] As cited in Cal M. Logue, "Ralph McGill's Speech Education," *Southern Speech Journal*, 35 (Winter 1969), 139.
[20] Publilius Syrus Maxim 865.
[21] As cited in Otto A. L. Dieter and William C. Kurth, "The *De Rhetorica* of Aurelius Augustine," *Speech Monographs*, 35 (March 1968), 106–107.

6. In many interpersonal and group-communication situations, as well as in public addresses, introductory material to fulfill one or more of the six purposes is helpful.

CONCLUDING THE SPEECH

"Great is the art of beginning," Henry Wadsworth Longfellow wrote, "but greater the art is of ending."[22] The author was thinking about the composition of poetry, but the statement is also applicable to speech writing. If not more difficult than the introduction to prepare, the conclusion certainly is equal to it in both troublesomeness and importance.

The significance of the conclusion is inherent in its position. Constituting the last impression that the speaker makes, it may have special emphatic power besides serving as a final corrective. If listeners are puzzled, a summary or an application even yet may clarify; if they are unconvinced, a forceful and dramatic appeal still may bring success; if they believe but don't know what to do, a clear-cut directive can remove the doubt. No one should view the conclusion as an opportunity to offset a bad performance, but the high level of attention that it often commands does give it great potential for both clarifying and emphasizing. When a speaker says, "Now we come to the conclusion," listeners tend to turn their minds hopefully toward the following words. Those who have had trouble following the thought see the next sentences as a final chance to grasp the essential structure and content, whereas those who think they have understood are likely to welcome the opportunity to check their notes.

PURPOSES

As with the introduction, the conclusion may serve either one objective or a combination of several. The first two steps in its preparation always are to visualize the probable state of the audience at the close of the body of the address and then to choose the purpose(s) that are appropriate to both the anticipated situation and the objective of the total message.

Leaving the Audience Well Disposed Toward the Speaker

The first purpose in Aristotle's analysis of the objectives of the conclusion,[23] this goal seems even more important in today's context than it was

---

[22] Henry Wadsworth Longfellow, *Elegiac Verse*, stanza 14.
[23] Aristotle *Rhetoric* iii.19.1419^{b}19–20.

in classical times. The third quarter of the twentieth century has been a period in which image and credibility have been increasingly prominent in analyses of persuasive success. Decisions in some political campaigns, many observers argue, depend on the image of the candidates; and the role of the public relations agency in elections has come to surpass that of experts who study the statesmanlike course to follow on the issues. Nor has the importance of personality been confined to politics. Projecting oneself favorably is seen as a way to get ahead in business and the professions. Books and adult courses in personal improvement have flourished, and the effect has extended even to departments of speech communication, which have increased their emphasis on improving interpersonal relations.

High prestige serves at least three ends. First, it increases the persuasive power of the message, for the credibility of the speaker interacts with other factors in determining the total effect. Briefly, liking and respecting the speaker make the acceptance of the message more probable because the elements in the situation then are consistent. Second, enhancing prestige is advantageous if the individual speaks again to the same audience. Third, a final impression of high credibility may result in desirable outcomes, including promotions, contracts, and salary increases, that are unrelated to the immediate topic.

How does one close a speech so that one strengthens one's image as competent and trustworthy? The subject of *ethos* is treated in detail elsewhere in this book (especially see Chapter 7), but here is brief advice: Through content, language, and delivery, manifest those qualities that people generally admire. Among these are fairness, clarity of mind, good humor, decisiveness, optimism, practicality, and good intentions.

Summarizing

Like the preview (see pp. 215–216), the summary may be either formal or informal. The former, as illustrated below, is a brief, precise list of the main points, usually with no changes in wording.

My description of the Central Intelligence Agency has been divided into three sections: first, its overseas activities; second, its analysis of documents; and third, its liaison with the military high command and with the White House.

The informal summary, which uses less obvious organizational devices than the formal, makes the speaker seem less machinelike. As with the formal, it must cover all of the principal points, preferably without changing the order, but the exact wording used earlier in the address need not be repeated. Numbering seldom appears in the informal summary.

Some research on the value of a summary as measured by comprehension has been inconclusive, but one recent study found it valuable. John

E. Baird, Jr., whose subjects were the students in thirty-two sections of a beginning speech course, concluded "that inclusion of a preview or a review produced significantly more comprehension than did inclusion of no summaries whatsoever."[24]

Making the Desired Action or Belief Explicit

A common scene, especially in the classroom, is the following: The speaker has spoken eloquently of the shortage of blood in local hospitals or of the threat that many toys pose for children. "What do I do?" the listener wonders. "That's a big problem all right, but where do I go, how do I sign up, to whom do I write?" Such speeches obviously fall short of their potential. In many instances the remedy is easy: "Here is the phone number for the local blood bank, 222-2222. Here's a card for each of you with that number. Call immediately after the close of this class period. Volunteer. Make an appointment. It's the number of life or death."

"Donate generously as the ushers pass among you;" "Return the pledge card that I am passing out;" "Go to the student aid office at the end of this class to register your protest;" and "Be one of the first ten to dial this number and get a free prize" are still other examples of highly explicit appeals, the value of which at least one research study confirms.[25] Nor is the value of explicitness confined to the speech whose purpose is an overt action; the desired change in a belief or an attitude likewise should be plain.

Advertisers and professional speakers, such as fund raisers and evangelists, appreciate the value of specificity. Billy Graham closes a sermon by telling his listeners exactly what they are to do: They are to come down to the front and stand in front of the pulpit. The salesman for a new record album on television likewise leaves no doubt; he repeats the address for placing the order over and over and at the same time shows the information on the screen in large print.

Making the Desired Response Easy and Immediate

The preceding examples also illustrate this fourth purpose of conclusions. Billy Graham and other evangelists do not ask those in the congregation to go home and think over the message, nor do advertisers permit delays. "This offer is for today only;" "Only the first ten persons to call receive the discount;" and "This free lot is yours, but only if you and your spouse come to Weeping Willows no later than next Sunday."

Contrary to the preceding examples is the usually futile concluding plea

---

[24] Baird, "The Effects of Speech Summaries . . . ," p. 127.
[25] Stewart L. Tubbs, "Explicit Versus Implicit Conclusions and Audience Commitment," *Speech Monographs*, 35 (March 1968), 14–19.

for listeners to write letters to their congressional representatives—a response that is neither easy nor immediate. Composing a letter is more difficult than signing a pledge or walking down an aisle, and during the interval between the speech and the individual's arrival at home, the enthusiasm for the cause ordinarily diminishes. Inertia is so strong that on most fund-raising telethons the money pledged by phone calls is several times greater than the money donated by writing out and mailing in a check. In one instance when a cab company sent a driver promptly to the home of each person pledging, the rate of collection improved greatly.

Arousing Emotion

Also one of Aristotle's objectives for the conclusion, this fifth purpose is one requiring careful judgment. In some instances, as the research on fear appeals indicates, extreme emotional materials are counterproductive; in other situations the best place for strong appeals is in the body of the address; and in still others a nonemotional or low-key treatment is most suitable to the topic, the purpose, and the image the speaker desires.

Overcoming lethargy, nevertheless, may be the speaker's most difficult task. People believe, but they won't trouble themselves. In the late sixties and early seventies the campaign for protecting the environment won overwhelming approval but obtained meager results. The means for producing emotional appeal are no different in the conclusion than they are in other parts of the address. Human interest stories, vivid descriptions, applications to local situations, the connecting of the speech purpose with vital interests, striking language, and heightened delivery are all means of increasing impact.

Preparing the Audience for Silence, and
Terminating the Speech Gracefully

The transition from the active speaker-listener transaction to silence can be a shock to an audience and a problem for the speaker. The warning to hearers can be as simple as "In conclusion . . ." followed by enough verbiage to permit each person to adjust to the termination of sound. A clear sign, however, is necessary; the speaker should not simply quit.

A more common problem for the communicator, however, is not abruptness but rambling. Without a fully prepared ending, including a closing sentence that the speaker knows well, many persons find closing an address puzzling and difficult. Not knowing how to manage, they ramble and backtrack, thus creating an anticlimax, reducing credibility, and probably eroding any desirable results established up to that time. Such a hesitant, painful conclusion is especially unfortunate, because its prevention through specific preparation is so easy.

TYPES

How does one realize the foregoing purposes, singly or in combination? As with introductions, several possibilities exist, and communicators should realize that they have many choices. Summaries, for example, often are useful, but they are not always the best selection.

1. Formal and informal summaries. As discussed in the section on "Purposes," a summary may be either a plain list of points, usually with a number preceding each, or it may be a series of sentences repeating the main ideas but without obtrusive organizational devices. The following is an example of an informal summary:

This brings me to the completion of my last major idea. I have enjoyed being with you today, and I hope that you have found my remarks informative. In closing, let us review where we have been. I began, as I'm sure you recall, with a summary of the pending legislation for stricter controls over air pollution. Then we looked at the major opposing arguments for the purpose of seeing how much merit there was in them. We summarized the scientific evidence on the technological problems, we looked at the possible loss of employment, and we also analyzed the claim that the increased costs to consumers would be excessive. My conclusion, which I hope that you share, was that these objections have some validity but are exaggerated and that on balance this pending law deserves our support.

2. Appeals for action; challenge to the audience. These two overlapping conclusions are excellent means of heightening emotion and making the desired action or belief explicit. An interesting example from history of a closing emotional appeal is an address by a Southern orator speaking in Cincinnati. Observers reported that tremendous cheering was evidence of the favorable reception:

I am no prophet. I make no prophecy. It does not become me to indulge here in gasconade. But, my countrymen, you cannot carry out the policy of the Black Republican party. . . . But if you have power, exercise it like men. If you have intelligence, show it in the manner in which you administer this government. If you have justice, let justice prevail though the heavens fall. But do not, do not, my friends of the North— . . . merely because you feel you have the power, do not wreathe your arms around the pillars of our liberty and, like a blind Samson, pull down that great temple upon our heads as well as yours.[26]

---

[26] As cited in Merwyn A. Hayes, "William L. Yancey Presents the Southern Case to the North: 1860," *Southern Speech Journal*, 29 (Spring 1964), 205–206.

Formal and informal summaries

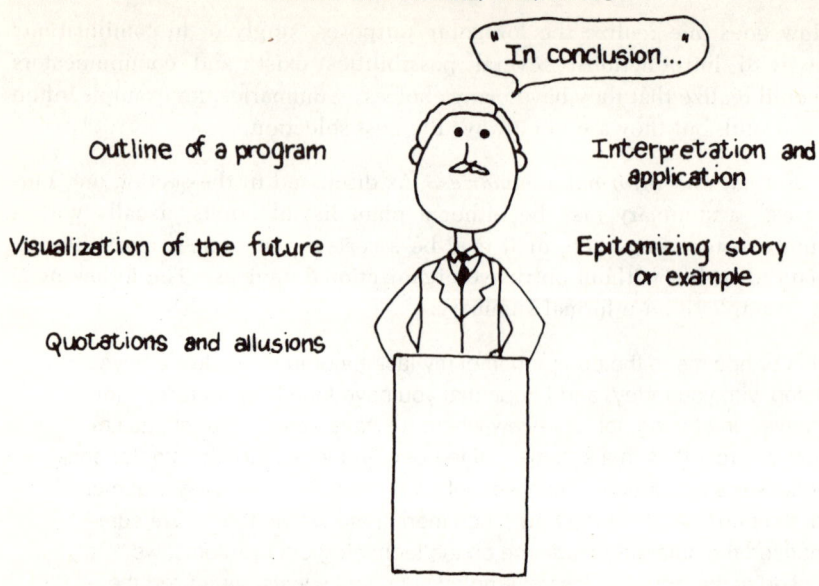

"In conclusion..."

Outline of a program

Interpretation and application

Visualization of the future

Epitomizing story or example

Quotations and allusions

Appeals for action; challenge to the audience

Types of conclusions.

Features of the preceding passage that the student can emulate are the use of short sentences, the variety in sentence length, the repetition of a pattern, the directness of address, the use of Biblical allusion, the appeals to generally held values (manliness; justice), and the use of words with strong emotional associations.

3. *Outline of a program.* Another, but less striking, way to conclude is by presenting in a one . . . two . . . three order the planks of a platform or the parts of a remedial program. A speech following the problem-solution rhetorical plan (see pp. 206–207), in particular, often should close with a positive, constructive proposal. Example:

To improve study conditions in the dormitories, I propose the following program:

1. The designation of certain floors as "study floors" with all residents pledged to the maintenance of quiet conditions at all times.

2. Permitting residents to transfer rooms so that those who desire to live on the "study floors" may do so.

3. The designation of the hours 7 P.M. to 9 P.M. as quiet hours throughout the dormitories except for lounges and game rooms.

230   RHETORICAL FACTORS: CHOICES FOR GREATER CLARITY AND EFFECTIVENESS

4. Authorizing monitors to ask anyone violating the quiet hour to leave the area of sleeping rooms for one of the lounges.

That is my program. I hope that you will support it and that you also will support my candidacy.

4. Visualization of the future. As a means of "selling," a glowing description of the future is subtle enough to reduce potential offensiveness but emotional enough to be emphatic. "That is my program," says Lucy Miller. "Let's look ahead five years and see what life would be like in Highroad City if we put it into operation." Lucy then proceeds to describe area by area the wonders that would follow. She states; she does not argue. Apparently without doubts or reservations, she describes confidently, as if no controversy is possible. At least momentarily, this positive approach lulls listeners. As an added advantage, a vivid, imaginative description of the future is likely to hold interest at a high level.

Only slightly different is the "Dawn of a New Day" conclusion, whose purpose is to inspire. Such endings often are appropriate for commencement and other ceremonial addresses, but they also are common in political speeches. By necessity politicians must spend much of their speaking time on issues that are troublesome, unpleasant, and controversial; ending on a negative note may create a generalized dissatisfaction that spreads from the listener's perception of the situation to his or her judgment of the speaker. A frequent solution is the inspirational ending. Attempting to sound statesmanlike rather than political, the speaker shows that, although aware of immediate problems, he or she is capable of larger visions. For the moment, also, the communicator speaks for all the people and is not a partisan. This type of ending, finally, gives the communicator a chance to espouse traditional and largely noncontroversial values and to express confidence that the great American heritage of freedom and self-reliance, with God's help, will bring the nation a secure and happy future. While president, Richard Nixon used this type of ending in many of his speeches, including his address before the twenty-fifth anniversary session of the General Assembly of the United Nations (December 7, 1970) and his speech announcing Phase II of wage and price controls (October 7, 1971).

Can the student or the young adult use these techniques? Yes, but with adaptations and modifications. A plea for a campus child-care center can close with a word picture of the new facility, and a request that the PTA donate money to buy some new learning equipment can end with a passage visualizing a child participating in the new program.

5. Interpretation and application. "What does all of this mean to me, to my family, or to my community?" may be the puzzled reaction of the listener when the speaker completes the body of an address on a complex topic. Interweaving practical applications with exposition in the body of the address may keep the preceding question from arising, but with some topics the natural order is a detailed exposition followed by closing interpretations.

In some situations, then, an interpretation or an application is an excellent way to close. Listeners find practical, personalized ideas easier to understand and more interesting than those that are national and global or those that are abstract and philosophic. Psychologically, this fifth type of ending, because of the heightened interest and sense of immediacy, brings the speech to a climax. Logically, it seems a reasonable way to conclude. Finally, as a means of persuasion the method is sound. Most individuals feel little concern for the value of the dollar in the international money market, but they become aroused over a problem that affects how much they must spend when traveling abroad or how much they must pay when purchasing imported goods.

6. *Epitomizing story or example.* Another persuasive conclusion is the story or the example that restates the essence of the speaker's message. An old, but still striking, illustration of this device is the story of the Chinese bandits. These marauders threatened to loot a house at the edge of a village; and since the prospective victim's neighbors thought only of themselves, the bandits succeeded. The next night the robbers returned, and the pleas of their new target to the neighbors again were unheeded. And so, the bandits proceeded house by house with their murdering and pillaging. The body of the speech had been on the need for the United States to participate in a defensive military alliance in the Far East.

Such a highly applicable story is not always available, but a resourceful speaker usually can find an illustration that with some revising will serve to epitomize. For example, in closing a talk on the need for donations to the Heart Fund, a speaker can say, "Now, for an example that epitomizes the nature and the seriousness of this problem." There follows the story of a Juan or a Josie who prior to surgery was a semi-invalid, unable to play with other children, and who after remedial measures became an active, normal child. "Research," the speaker concludes, "made this miracle possible; and your money contributed to the Heart Fund will support further research."

7. *Quotations and allusions.* Like the epitome, the quotation or the allusion adds distinctiveness. Listeners become accustomed to hearing summaries and appeals for action; such endings seemingly are within every speaker's repertoire. But the individual who does something different appears to have originality and to care enough about the audience to make the extra effort that creativeness requires.

The sources for quotations and allusions are endless. Most allusions pertain to history or to literature, but some are from folklore, which is a bit of each. Sources for quotations are of two general types. First, some quotations are from contemporary authorities, whose testimonies strengthen the probative force. Second, some quotations, which have no value as proof but which add interest and individuality, come from Shakespeare, the Bible, Pope, and scores of other literary sources. A few lines of poetry can be an especially pleasing ending.

CONCLUDING OBSERVATIONS

The final remarks on the conclusion are counterparts to those for the introduction. A conclusion is necessary, and every speaker should know that the number of possible types and combinations of types is large. The choice of type(s) should depend on an analysis of the probable state of the audience and on the speaker's purposes. Conclusions should be well prepared, because the final impression is influential.

Interpersonal and group situations, as well as platform addresses, require thoughtfully planned conclusions. Every conversation and conference comes to an end; but whether it is definite, graceful, and friendly depends on the skills of the participants.

A PRACTICE SESSION IN EXPOSITION

How does one increase the skills of exposition? One does so by understanding certain principles, by preparing carefully, by practicing, and by responding positively to criticism.

TOPIC AND PURPOSE

The first steps in preparation for any significant communication event are the choice of topic and the phrasing of the exact purpose. Much of Chapter 2 is on possible topics, and Chapter 1 includes advice on four criteria to consider in making a choice. The following suggestions include both topics drawing on personal experiences and those requiring library research:

Scuba-Diving	Surfing
Judging a Painting	Theatrical Make-up
Home Gardening	Grooming a Poodle
Making Wine	Tuning an Auto Engine
The World Bank	Exploration for Petroleum
Solar Energy	Celestial Navigation
The Dow-Jones Average	The State Court System
Voodooism	Marriage Customs in the East Indies

To limit the topic and to give the speech precise direction, a written, revised, and rewritten purpose is advisable. "To explain the properties of the new composite tennis rackets" or "to explain the duties of each player in doubles" is more helpful to the speaker than "to talk about tennis."

FURTHER STEPS IN PREPARATION AND PRESENTATION

After choosing the topic and phrasing the purpose (the first steps in preparation), the communicator should follow the orderly steps that appear in the closing part of Chapter 1:

2. Take an inventory of ideas and materials, and make a preliminary outline.

3. Engage in research and creative thought (see also Chapters 2 and 3).

4. Assess the transactional elements (see also Chapters 5–8).

5. Make strategic rhetorical choices (see also the first part of this chapter and Chapters 10–12).

6. Draft the speech, and rehearse it.

7. Present the speech or interpersonal message.

CRITICISM AND RESPONSE TO CRITICISM

Two speech professors were discussing their experiences at a convention.

"Half or more of my undergraduate students show significant improvement in speaking during a semester," one man said.

"I'd put the figure a little higher," responded the other, "but like you I find that some students go on from assignment to assignment and make the same mistakes at the end of the term as at the beginning."

Why is it that some students improve and that others do not? In some instances the quality of criticism differs: Some faculty members are more diligent and perceptive than others, and some are unusually skillful in making their suggestions for improvement clear and specific. More significant, however, is the student's character—his or her self-motivation, willingness to change, and courage. To free oneself from dependence on a manuscript, for example, requires a willingness to try. As the student proceeds through the semester, he or she should be determined to make each presentation better than its predecessor. To do this, the student must receive competent criticism from professor, classmates, and friends, must take the comments seriously, must set specific and attainable personal goals, and must spend enough time on preparation to give special attention to those goals as well as to the total demands of the entire speech.

A PRACTICE SESSION IN PERSUASION

As with exposition, preparing and presenting a persuasive speech is the best possible way to learn about choosing rhetorical plans and types of introductions and conclusions.

TOPIC AND PURPOSE

The topic for a practice session in persuasion ideally is an attitude or a cause about which the speaker feels strongly. Perhaps one believes that women should have equal rights, that the federal budget should be balanced, that the movement for female equality in intercollegiate athletics is unrealistic, or that the university should oppose the adoption of open admissions. The possible concerns are almost as numerous as the total enrollment in any given class, and they are likely to include such diverse areas as codes of behavior, university regulations, law enforcement, problems of the disadvantaged, protection of the environment, consumerism, labor relations, big government, political candidates and campaigns, and religion. "What do I care about?" and "What would I like others to believe or to do?" are key questions to raise in choosing the topic for a persuasive speech.

Besides deciding what the speech is to be about (the topic), the communicator needs to decide exactly what he or she wishes to accomplish (the purpose). Since movement is the essence of persuasive success, the framing of the purpose centers in thoughtful, astute answers to these two questions:

What is the present attitude of the audience toward the belief or the attitude that I am advocating?

What position can I reasonably hope that they will hold when I finish?

To expect a reversal or even a large movement is unrealistic; how much change can one hope for depends on the firmness of the original position, the credibility of the speaker, the dramatic power of the supporting materials, the strength of counter forces, the personality traits of the listeners, and various other factors. On the continuum below, which is applicable to any topic, movement of more than a single position would be unusual:

Attitude toward any concept

Highly opposed	Moderately opposed	Neutral	Favorable, but won't act	Will act, if easy	Will sacrifice

The following examples are sensible applications of the preceding advice:

TOPIC: The proposed increase in the student activity fee.
PRESENT POSITION OF THE AUDIENCE: Opposed to an increase, but too little discussion up to this time for the opposition to be firm or for it to be related to specific facts and issues.
DESIRED POST-SPEECH POSITION: A willingness to consider the proposal fully before making a decision.
SPEECH PURPOSE: To move my audience from a position of opposition to a position of neutrality on the proposed increase in the student activity fee.

TOPIC: Car pooling.
PRESENT POSITION OF THE AUDIENCE: Favorable to the idea as a broad principle, but scarcely any of them participate in a car pool.
DESIRED POST-SPEECH POSITION: To fill out an information card for submission to the computer.
SPEECH PURPOSE: To move my audience from a position of being favorable but not acting to a position of willingness to take the first step toward joining a car pool.

FURTHER STEPS

The further stages in preparation are the same as for the expository speech with thoughtful response to competent criticism being equally important for the two types of discourse. In following the additional steps from framing the purpose to final presentation, the mental set of the speaker, however, is much different for persuasion from what it is for exposition. Instead of asking "How much do my listeners know?" and "How can I best clarify each of my points?" the persuader inquires mentally, "What do my listeners feel and believe?" and "Which ideas, materials, and rhetorical devices will be the most influential?" In choosing an example, for instance, the expositor asks, "Will it clarify?"; but the persuader decides by judging, "Will it be believable and impressive?" Likewise, the viewpoints in choosing the rhetorical plan and in working out introductions and conclusions are quite different for the two types of discourse.

CONCLUSION

"Discourse is put together like a living creature—it has a kind of body of its own, and hence lacks neither head nor foot, but has both middle and extremities, all composed in such sort that they suit each other and the whole," Plato observed in the *Phaedrus* (262). The observation is as true today as it was 2,300 years ago. Every communication event must begin and end somehow—perhaps so abruptly and crudely that the effect is confusion and resentment, but one hopes so prudently that both opening and closing further the speaker's purpose. Likewise, some ordering, whether meandering, mangled, clear, or artful, is inevitable.

Rhetorical choices pertaining to speech arrangement have been the topic for this chapter. Like the decisions bearing on delivery, language, and nonverbal elements, these choices affect the clarity and the effectiveness of the substance of the message and they interact with other elements to produce the transactional atmosphere that largely determines the nature of decoding and feedback.

PROBLEMS AND EXERCISES

1. Examine the speeches in a recent issue of *Vital Speeches of the Day* for their introductions and conclusions. Classify each introduction and each conclusion according to the types discussed in this chapter; if one does not fit any classification, describe it. Also, consider the purposes that you believe that each introduction and conclusion was supposed to serve.

2. Using the material collected in the preceding exercise, meet with four or five of your classmates for an exchange of ideas. Also discuss which types of introduction and conclusion you consider the most effective.

3. Give an informal three-minute report on your plans for the introduction to your next major speech. Talk about purposes, types, and materials.

4. Repeat Exercise 3 for the conclusion to your next major speech.

5. Prepare notes on a speech that you have observed that used a rhetorical plan skillfully. Use the notes in a class discussion of plans. If you cannot recall a speech to use for this exercise, be ready to talk about the rhetorical plan that you will use in your next major presentation.

6. Prepare and deliver an expository speech on some topic with which you are thoroughly familiar, such as a hobby, a job you have held, or an experience during a vacation. Have previously appointed critics from the class criticize the speech. One should comment on the rhetorical plan, one on the introduction, and one on the conclusion.

7. Prepare and deliver a persuasive speech. Have one previously appointed member of the class criticize your rhetorical plan; one, your introduction; one, your conclusion; and one, your purpose.

8. Prepare careful notes, but communicate informally with the class on the topic "Rhetorical Problems for My Next Major Speech and My Solutions to Them."

REFERENCES

Baird, John E., Jr. "The Effects of Speech Summaries upon Audience Comprehension of Expository Speeches of Varying Quality and Complexity," *Central States Speech Journal*, 25 (Summer 1974), 119–127.

Burgoon, Michael, and Lawrence J. Chase. "The Effects of Differential Patterns in Messages Attempting to Induce Resistance to Persuasion," *Speech Monographs*, 40 (March 1973), 1–7.

Clark, Anthony J. "An Exploratory Study of Order Effect in Persuasive Communication," *Southern Speech Communication Journal*, 39 (Summer 1974), 322–332.

Hazen, Michael D., and Sara B. Kiesler. "Communication Strategies Affected by Audience Opposition, Feedback, and Persuasibility," *Speech Monographs*, 42 (March 1975), 56–68.

Johnson, Arlee. "A Preliminary Investigation of the Relationship Between Message Organization and Listener Comprehension," *Central States Speech Journal*, 21 (Summer 1970), 104–107.

Luchins, A. S., and E. H. Luchins. "The Effects of Order of Presentation of Information and Explanatory Models," *Journal of Social Psychology*, 80 (February 1970), 63–70.

McCroskey, James C., Thomas J. Young, and Michael D. Scott. "The Effects of Message Sidedness and Evidence on Inoculation Against Counterpersuasion in Small Group Communication," *Speech Monographs*, 39 (August 1972), 205–212.

Rosnow, Ralph L. "Whatever Happened to the 'Law of Primacy'?" *Journal of Communication*, 16 (March 1966), 10–31.

Spicer, Christopher, and Ronald E. Bassett. "The Effect of Organization on Learning from an Informative Message," *Southern Speech Communication Journal*, 41 (Spring 1976), 290–299.

Thompson, Ernest. "Some Effects of Message Structure on Listener Comprehension," *Speech Monographs*, 34 (March 1967), 51–57.

Tubbs, Stewart L. "Explicit Versus Implicit Conclusions and Audience Commitment," *Speech Monographs*, 35 (March 1968), 14–19.

Vickrey, James F., Jr. "An Experimental Investigation of the Effect of 'Previews' and 'Reviews' on Retention of Orally Presented Information," *Southern Speech Journal*, 36 (Spring 1971), 209–219.

10
DELIVERY: ORAL AND VISUAL ELEMENTS

After studying this chapter the reader should be able to do the following:

Walk to the speaking position, stop, look at the audience, and deliver two sentences with satisfactory degrees of poise, fluency, and directness when given five minutes to prepare on a familiar topic such as "My Hobby" or "My Future Job"

Give a two-minute speech on a topic of one's own choice with no more than four vocalized pauses, with no more than two instances of random hand movements, and with a rating of "satisfactory" by 75 percent or more of one's peers on posture and self-control

After giving a speech, answer three questions in a manner that the instructor rates as satisfactory for directness and fluency

Speak without a public address system so that classmates scattered about a small lecture hall can hear readily

Many years ago the writer had an interesting experience when he was coaching a high-school track team. Each time that his high jumper came down the runway, planted his left foot for the take-off, and kicked his right foot high into the air, the writer observed to his embarrassment that he was kicking his own right foot several inches off the ground. No words were spoken, but the jumper's actions in conjunction with the writer's emotional involvement created a communicative relationship in which the one man influenced the other.

The preceding example of empathy contains two important characteristics of a phenomenon that is important, either powerfully or marginally, to many transactions. First, empathy occurs only when the receiver is emotional; and second, the outcome is imitative. Because of empathy a jovial companion elicits smiles and chuckles, a tense individual makes others uncomfortable, and a lethargic speaker causes listeners to feel dull and sleepy. Enthusiasm, cheeriness, fearfulness, and suspicion are among the many qualities that are contagious.

Two additional illustrations of empathy that show the relation of delivery to transactional success are actual examples from a recent college class in freshman speech. The first of these, a success story, is about a young man who in his first talks twisted about, moved his hands constantly, and grinned self-consciously in those rare moments when he looked at his audience. Becoming increasingly nervous and uncomfortable as this student spoke, listeners attended to the message with difficulty. In the final presentation of the semester, however, he stood straight and kept his hands still. Although he relied on his detailed notes too much of the time, during two internal summaries and his conclusion he looked at his listeners and both voice and facial expression were earnest. The audience response mirrored his seriousness. The second example, a less happy one, is of a second young man during the same round of speeches. Although his topic was significant, he was insufficiently prepared both intellectually and emotionally. Several times, being unsure of himself, he giggled nervously. Because of the unsatisfactory interaction between speaker and audience, his talk was less successful than its content warranted. Both students exemplified, one positively and one negatively, the conclusion by Maslow, Yoselson, and London that manifestations of confidence increase persuasiveness. In their experiment an actor presented the same message in three ways—with confidence lacking, with confidence projected verbally, and with confidence shown through manner. Both the confident presentations were more effective than was the one in which the quality was missing.[1] Confirming this result is the experimental finding by McCroskey and Richmond that persons with low communication apprehension were rated more credible and more attractive than were those with high apprehension.[2]

---

[1] Catha Maslow, Kathryn Yoselson, and Harvey London, "Persuasiveness of Confidence Expressed via Language and Body Language," *British Journal of Social and Clinical Psychology*, 10 (September 1971), 234–240.
[2] James C. McCroskey and Virginia P. Richmond, "The Effects of Communication Apprehension on the Perception of Peers," *Western Speech Communication*, 40 (Winter 1976), 14–21.

One final introductory point is important. Any thoughtful communicator plans his or her presentation and manages delivery so that the likelihood of a favorable transactional relation will be high; the outcome, nevertheless, depends also on audience and situational factors that sometimes are beyond control. At a recent national convention of speech teachers a professional performer did a one-man show based on the songs and writings of Woody Guthrie. A warm, close bond between reader and audience characterized the first part of the program, a delightful experience for all; but after the intermission, all was changed. The small number who remained were scattered about a large ballroom, passers-by frequently opened and closed a side door, and hotel employees were setting up the back of the room for a social function.

METHODS OF DELIVERY

Just as the atmosphere most favorable to the attainment of one's purpose varies with the situation, so does the best method of delivery. For Ms. Herma Presenter, whose task is a brief eulogy to a retiring colleague or the recital of part of a lodge ritual, the proper form of presentation is memorization; and for the Honorable Josiah Diplomat, whose words may be twisted into an international insult, the safe method is a manuscript. For most men and women, however, the best form of delivery usually is the extempore. Having thought through the topic and organized carefully, they prepare a set of brief notes for use on the platform. Although they often virtually memorize opening, closing, and other critical sentences, in general they word their ideas as they speak, just as they do when conversing or discussing. This on-the-spot verbalizing tends to produce a direct, varied delivery that preserves many of the desirable qualities of conversation, such as naturalness and friendliness.

How many notes one should have depends on the complexity of the topic and on personal characteristics and preferences. One research study shows that notes in short speeches did not increase self-confidence as much as speakers thought that they would,[3] and the colorfully worded advice of Cotton Mather still is sound:

[Your notes ought to be no more than] a *Quiver,* on which you may cast your Eye now and then, to see what Arrow is to be next fetch'd from thence [so that] your Eye . . . may be on them whom you speak to.[4]

---

[3] K. Phillip Taylor, "The Effect of Speech Presentation Methods upon Speaker Self-Confidence and Effectiveness," *Speech Teacher,* 18 (January 1969), 84–85.
[4] Cotton Mather, *Manductio ad Ministerium,* pp. 105–106, as cited in Howard H. Martin, "Puritan Preachers on Preaching," *Quarterly Journal of Speech,* 50 (October 1964), 291.

The best platform delivery on most occasions, therefore, is the extempore, whose superiority observers in all ages and cultures have noted. Alcidamas in the fourth century B.C. wrote, "I believe too, that extemporaneous speakers exercise a greater sway over their hearers than those who deliver set speeches."[5] John Wesley, according to an anecdote, forgot his manuscript one Sunday morning in 1735, bravely spoke without it, and from then on preferred the extempore method because of its greater animation and directness.[6] In modern times Harry Truman and Eugene McCarthy have been among those for whom extemporizing was more effective than other forms of delivery.[7]

TALENTS AND OPTIONS

When speaking directly and earnestly, both Truman and McCarthy, as well as many other national leaders, were highly effective. From the examples that they offer, students reading this book can learn much that they can use. To begin, they can develop an awareness of differences in delivery and an appreciation of the role that good speaking plays in communication. In the last round of classroom speeches, was everyone equally talented and well prepared? Are all sports announcers alike in their styles and effectiveness? If one goes to several churches, will one find each minister alike in speaking skill, in speech manner, and in listenability? Aren't some doctors clearer and more reassuring than others, and don't sales representatives differ widely in their powers of speech? Whether one judges the importance of good delivery by his or her own experiences or by research reports,[8] the conclusion is the same: A positive relation exists between delivery and measures of comprehension and persuasiveness.

What should the student do to bring about self-improvement? The remainder of the chapter is the full answer to the question, but two viewpoints should guide the individual in dealing with specifics. *Make the most of your own talents* is another way of saying "To thine own self be true."[9] Personalities, temperaments, voice qualities, body builds, and normal speaking rates all vary, and the best style of delivery for one person is not the best for someone else. Franklin D. Roosevelt did not speak like

---

[5] Alcidamas, *On the Writers of Written Discourses*, as cited in Frederick H. Turner, Jr., "Alcidamas: An Early Rationale for Extemporaneous Interpersonal Communication," *Southern Speech Communication Journal*, 39 (Spring 1974), 225-226.
[6] James L. Golden, "John Wesley on Rhetoric and Belles Lettres," *Speech Monographs*, 28 (November 1961), 261-262.
[7] Cal M. Logue, "The Political Rhetoric of Ralph McGill," *Speech Monographs*, 35 (June 1968), 122-128; David Halberstam, "McCarthy and the Divided Left," *Harper's*, 236 (March 1968), 44.
[8] For a summary of early studies see Wayne N. Thompson, *Quantitative Research in Public Address and Communication* (New York: Random House, 1967), 83-85.
[9] William Shakespeare, *Hamlet*, act 1, scene 3, line 75.

Alben Barkley, or John F. Kennedy like Harry Truman; but each, making the most of his own gifts, was highly effective.

But whatever the basic style that is natural to the individual, improvement is possible. Charlton Heston, the respected actor, once told a small group that he had attended the movie *Hamlet* eleven times so that he could learn about acting through his observations of Laurence Olivier. Some recent American presidents have hired full-time advisers to help them with speech delivery, and others have used recordings of their addresses for self-analysis. The pages that follow describe in detail the principal qualities of effective delivery and suggest means of improvement.

This need for doing the best that one can in the manner that is natural to oneself affects the application of the second injunction: *Make sensible rhetorical choices.* As students gain in competence and versatility, they increase the number of options that they can exercise according to the probable effect on observers. Should I wear a business suit and tie or appear in blue jeans and a sweat shirt? Should I speak deliberately as if the matter is momentous, or should I talk rapidly as if I am a dynamic person who is eager to communicate? Should I stand without notes in front of the desk or the podium to create a close, friendly atmosphere, or should I stand behind the furniture to emphasize my role as speaker? Should I sit on the desk for informality, or should I stand for greater dignity? Should I use or not use visual aids; and if I use them, what purpose should they serve?

On most of these alternatives no research evidence exists, but studies do support the generalization that the conversational and the dynamic styles produce different effects. In one experiment, for example, the conclusion was that when a speaker was conversational, listeners perceived him as more attractive, better educated, more professional, more honest, and more person-oriented than when he spoke dynamically; but "When he used dynamic delivery, he was described as more toughminded, task-oriented, self-assured, and assertive."[10]

APPREHENSION

Appearing to be self-assured is an asset, but for many persons composure is far from easy. Indeed, worrying about a coming speech experience is a major source of discomfort that in extreme cases interferes with effective communication. Since the causes for the problem are complex, disappointment should not arise if improvement is slow.

Some progress, beginning with an understanding of the phenomenon,

---

[10] W. Barnett Pearce and Forrest Conklin, "Nonverbal Vocalic Communication and Perceptions of a Speaker," *Speech Monographs,* 38 (August 1971), 239–240.

however, is possible. Since stage fright is an almost universal experience,[11] a sense of uneasiness is neither unusual nor abnormal. One also should realize that he or she probably looks better than he or she feels, for only in extreme cases are the seemingly flushed cheeks or trembling hands conspicuous. Moreover, the positive view that the heightened awareness that one is experiencing may help by increasing animation and alertness can be beneficial. And, finally, the beginning speaker should be comforted by the knowledge that with experience stage fright almost always diminishes.[12]

Not all improvement, however, needs to be long range. All speakers, no matter how severe their apprehension, should be able to apply many of the following suggestions:

Prepare thoroughly. Give yourself reason for self-confidence.

Phrase the opening two or three sentences carefully, and have them firmly in mind. Be sure that you start well.

While awaiting your turn, think about your speech constructively, if at all. For example, making minor adaptations as you listen to other parts of the program can increase freshness and timeliness.

Plan to display visual aids, use the blackboard, or perform some other purposeful action.

Try to look like a poised public speaker. The success of a speech depends more on how you look than on how you feel. Build good habits through sound rehearsal practices and through the exercise of will power during the performance. Control telltale signs of nervousness, such as twisting buttons and playing with pencils or paper clips.

Some individuals find devices unique to themselves to be of value; "If something works for you," the advice is, "use it." Some speakers take a deep breath when walking to the platform or into a personnel manager's office, and others visualize themselves ten minutes later seated safely and the speech or interview over.

ORAL ELEMENTS

How can the student improve from assignment to assignment in the oral aspects of presentation? Understanding principles of delivery and creating

---

[11] According to a survey of 2,543 male and female adults, speaking before a group is the most common fear. Fear of height ranks second, and fear of insects and bugs, of financial problems, and of deep water are third, fourth, and fifth. "Fears," *Spectra*, 9 (December 1973), 4.

[12] Evidence is abundant that stage fright or speech apprehension lessens with experience. For a summary see Thompson, *Quantitative Research*, pp. 174–176. For reports of recent experiments

for oneself a mental picture of good speaking is the initial step. Reading textbooks such as this one and observing speakers are the major ways to build up a concept of good speech. If an address was pleasing and impressive, which specific qualities were responsible? Do I see some of my own faults in some other speaker? What did this communicator do that I can emulate? Appreciating the qualities of good delivery, however, does not guarantee improvement. Students need specific advice on how to meet their problems—the topic for the second part of the present section.

DESIRABLE ORAL QUALITIES

Although delivery is complex, the major points about it fall under four headings: (1) directness, communicativeness, and wholeheartedness; (2) fluency and rate; (3) variety and aliveness; and (4) clarity, projection, and pleasantness.

Directness, Communicativeness, and Wholeheartedness

By no accident, directness is first on the present list. Communicative speakers talk with hearers, not at them or over their heads. They do not bury their faces in their notes or stare into space while collecting their thoughts. During the presentation they change their gazes from time to time so that they see individuals in all parts of the room. Addressing men and women as living persons, they make contact with their auditors' eyes, not with the space that these listeners occupy. For the inexperienced speaker, often burdened by stage fright, the attainment of directness is difficult. Eye contact is a beginning, and any conscientious person with even a small amount of will power can learn rather quickly to look much of the time at where people are sitting. One must stop relying on detailed notes, and when on the platform one must exercise determination. With each assignment the task ordinarily becomes easier, and in time eye contact becomes habitual.

Much more significant than physical directness is communicativeness, which comes from a genuine desire to speak. Testimony to the important role of wholeheartedness appears in many times and cultures. Adolph Hitler said, ". . . only he who harbors passion in himself can arouse passion";[13] and William M. Kunstler, a contemporary trial lawyer, observed in

---

showing a decrease as college students gain speaking experience, see Anthony Mulac and A. Robert Sherman, "Behavioral Assessment of Speech Anxiety," *Quarterly Journal of Speech*, 60 (April 1974), 134–143; and W. Clifton Adams *et al.*, "Effects of Radio Announcing Experience on Self-Perceived Anxiety," *Western Speech Communication*, 39 (Spring 1975), 120–122.

[13] Adolph Hitler, *Mein Kampf*, trans. Helmut Ripperger (New York: Reynal & Hitchcock, 1939), p. 137.

an interview: "But if one is impassioned, if one feels what one is doing, I think almost anyone can speak well. I've listened to Daniel Ellsberg when he doesn't feel impassioned and he's a very bad speaker then, and I've listened to Dan when he feels impassioned."[14] Cicero, the first great rhetorician to write on the topic, said:

> Moreover it is impossible for the listener to feel indignation, hatred or ill-will, to be terrified of anything, or reduced to tears of compassion, unless all those emotions, which the advocate would inspire in the arbitrator, are visibly stamped or rather branded on the advocate himself.[15]

The great evangelist Dwight L. Moody, according to his son, believed, "If I can only get people to think that I am talking with them, and not preaching, it is so much easier to get their attention."[16] Franklin D. Roosevelt, according to one critic, "understood better than any politician of his day that even though a radio audience might include millions, the mode of address should be that of one person speaking to another."[17]

Are more examples needed of the importance of directness, communicativeness, and wholeheartedness? Surely not, but the student can learn by observing and comparing those who have these qualities, be they conversationalists, discussants, or public speakers, with those who do not.

Fluency and Rate

Observation can also help the student gain an appreciation of the importance of fluency and rate. Excessive rapidity may suggest nervousness and make listeners uncomfortable, but labored delivery creates inattentiveness and boredom. Since a pace that is "just right" depends on topic, circumstances, listener expectations, and the speaker's personal qualities, the communicator must rely on the advice of qualified critics for guidance.

More often a problem than rate, however, is fluency. Hesitations, especially when vocalized as "and-uhs," "the-uhs," and the like, are annoyances that suggest to listeners that the speaker is amateurish, short on self-confidence, and perhaps poorly prepared and unsure of his or her ideas. Fluency, according to several research studies, is one of the most significant of the specific factors bearing on effectiveness. An especially careful research project was that of McCroskey and Mehrley, who in a study of 352

---

[14] Beatrice K. Reynolds, "An Interview with William M. Kunstler," *Today's Speech*, 22 (Fall 1974), 45.
[15] Cicero *De Oratore* ii.44.185–186.
[16] W. R. Moody, *The Life of Dwight L. Moody* (New York: Fleming H. Revell Co., 1900), p. 459.
[17] Edgar E. Willis, "Radio and Presidential Campaigning," *Central States Speech Journal*, 20 (Fall 1969), 189.

respondents found that nonfluency had an adverse effect on both the amount of attitude change and the ratings of credibility given the speaker.[18]

The sources of nonfluency are complex, but the cause that yields the most readily to improvement is poor concentration. Part way through a sentence or a paragraph the speaker momentarily loses the train of thought and inserts a vocalized pause while recovering. Tighter self-discipline and a determination to resist intrusive vocalizations are the basic factors in reducing the severity of the problem.

Variety and Aliveness

Most professional sports announcers, disk jockeys, and newscasters hold their jobs in part because their voices are vibrant, alive, enthusiastic, and communicative. Similarly, most speakers at the recent national political conventions, whatever their other shortcomings, were vigorous, and the few who weren't produced restlessness. Aliveness, to a large extent, is a natural gift, but to a degree its cultivation is possible. Those in a class who possess the quality should be grateful; those who lack it should begin the long road of building habits that convey a greater sense of enthusiasm.

Variety, which is more within the individual's control than vibrancy, refers to the total impression that delivery makes when all factors—voice quality, pitch, loudness, rate, and pauses—are considered jointly. The average person in natural surroundings has little trouble with variety; for as ideas change, he or she adjusts delivery to emphasize key words, to group words through pauses, and to express such nuances as earnestness, self-doubt, lack of trust, and sarcasm. When individuals become self-conscious, however, they frequently suppress these natural variations. Speaking words, not word groups, they become unresponsive to ideas. The problems that result belong under four headings:

Overphrasing, or choppiness because of too frequent pauses. For example: Now / is the time / to come / to the aid / of the party.

Underphrasing, or using too few pauses and running words together. For example: Nowisthetimetocometotheaidoftheparty.

Monotony, or little variety in rate, rhythm, or inflections.

Recurrent melody, or the repeated use of a single speech pattern without regard to changes in thought. In this type of delivery the individual sentence may have variety, but each sentence sounds like the one that was just before it.

---

[18] James C. McCroskey and R. Samuel Mehrley, "The Effects of Disorganization and Nonfluency on Attitude Change and Source Credibility," *Speech Monographs,* 36 (March 1969), 13–21. See also Gerald R. Miller and Murray A. Hewgill, "The Effect of Variations in Nonfluency on Audience Ratings of Source Credibility," *Quarterly Journal of Speech,* 50 (February 1964), 36–44.

Recognizing that one is deficient in variety is a step toward improvement, but the student should realize that the four preceding items are manifestations, not causes. The sources of the problem are self-consciousness, anxiety, and inattentiveness to content.

Clarity, Pleasantness, and Projection

Finally, good delivery has the qualities of clarity, projection, and pleasantness. To be heard clearly and easily, indeed, is a minimum requirement for communication, and to have a pleasing voice is an asset. Of these elements, the hardest to change is quality, which results from a combination of inborn factors and well-established habits, but even here the student who recognizes the problem and tries to modify his or her usual manner can make small improvements.

Whether those in an audience can hear comfortably depends on several interacting factors, the most important of which are loudness, precision in articulation, and directness. Those individuals whose voices lack natural carrying power should try to compensate by strengthening their presentation in precision and directness.

Severe problems in clarity, such as those of some international students and individuals with speech defects, require the special attention that most universities provide through clinics and special courses. Lesser difficulties, such as those arising from insufficient lip and jaw movement, however, are remediable through limited instruction and conscientious effort.

Conclusion

If an ideal speaker existed, what would he or she sound like? What qualities should serve as objectives for the student who wishes to become increasingly clear and effective? To answer, skillful speakers look at their audiences and establish psychological contact with individuals. Through involvement in the topic, they address others earnestly and wholeheartedly. They talk at a moderate rate, and they speak each group of words fluently. They make their voices as alive as their natural abilities permit, and they group words and emphasize ideas by varying rate, rhythm, pauses, voice quality, pitch, and force. Finally, they articulate clearly, they project sufficiently for all listeners to hear comfortably, and they try to be pleasant.

SPECIFIC SUGGESTIONS FOR IMPROVEMENT

What works well for one student does not always benefit a second, and exceptions arise for every generalization. For most students, nevertheless, the following list of suggestions is likely to be beneficial:

1. Use few notes or none. Avoid visual aids that create a temptation for you to look at them instead of at the audience.

2. Do not begin until you are ready, poised, and looking at the listeners. Try to look at different persons during the speech.

3. Include phrases that call for contact. Examples are "You and I," "What does this mean to you?" "Friends," and "Please think about this with me."

4. Choose topics that deal with beliefs or experiences that you wish to share.

5. In a one- or two-minute presentation on a familiar subject, use no notes and try for eye contact 100 percent of the time. In the same or a different assignment, try to speak for one minute without any vocalized pauses.

6. To avoid misplaced hesitations, practice a "stop-go" technique. Bring each idea to a firm conclusion, maintain momentary silence, get the next words in mind, and then proceed.

7. Have the opening words firmly in mind, so that you can start smoothly and confidently. Prepare the entire address thoroughly, so that you are familiar with your material.

8. Use rehearsals if your habitual rate requires adjustment. If you talk too fast and your first rehearsal lasts five minutes, stretch the time in the next rehearsal to six.

9. Control your rate in the beginning so that you counteract either excessive rapidity or slowness.

10. On your notes mark three or four checkpoints as places for correcting any habitual fault. If you talk too fast, slow down as you come to each place that is marked; if you tend to be excessively loud, commence the marked sections with moderation.

11. Become sensitive to the sound of speech by observing professionals, such as radio and television announcers, newscasters, and disc jockeys. Develop the concept that speech consists not of words but of word groups.

12. When you are to speak in a large and unfamiliar auditorium, check the acoustics beforehand. Experiment to determine whether a friend who is in a distant part of the room can hear you comfortably, and make the necessary adjustments. If you will be using a public address system, check on the proper distance to stand from the microphone.

13. Especially if projection is a problem, articulate carefully and look at the audience so that your lip and jaw movements will be visible. Listeners, without realizing that they are doing so, supplement auditory signals with visual cues.

14. For practice, watch your lips and jaw in a mirror while speaking. If the movement is negligible, repeat the sentences with exaggerated action.

15. When speaking in a small group, look at your colleagues most of the time, be friendly and earnest, and talk with enough firmness and fluency so that you sound prepared and knowledgable.

VISUAL ELEMENTS

Some years ago when the writer took students to intercollegiate forensic tournaments, he noted that the contestants from one university won more than their share of trophies. Although they were excellent in other respects as well, their skill in the visual elements was especially noteworthy. They stood so that they looked like speakers, they moved easily but not often, they gestured naturally, and their bodies and faces reinforced the meanings that their words expressed. These young people were fulfilling their listeners' expectations in formal situations, but visual cues also contribute significantly in conversations, interviews, and discussions. The closeness of participants in small groups makes it easy to see signs that provide some information on the content of the message and that seem to say much about the sender's personal qualities, such as sincerity.

DESIRABLE VISUAL QUALITIES

What the communicatees will consider appropriate depends on the occasion and on the speaker's age, sex, and role. These factors affect decisions pertaining to first impressions, position and posture, self-possession and gesture, and facial expression.

First Impressions

The old saying that "first impressions are lasting" is applicable to the platform speaker or to the newcomer to a small gathering. On many occasions discussion groups and audiences see the speaker, often at length, before they hear the first words. The communicator enters the room, ascends the platform, or sometimes sits on the stage during an introductory speech or even a series of items on a program. During this period respondents form judgments that the sender is poised and well prepared, nervous and unsure, good-humored and responsive to others, or tense and self-centered.

To make the best possible first impression, speakers should sit erect but comfortably with hands quiet and without other conspicuous actions.

Then, if the situation is a public address, they should, when introduced, walk erect and somewhat briskly to the speaking position. Audience evaluations of behavior as either slovenly or excessively formal can be harmful to the sender's *ethos*.

Position and Posture

For a platform speech the best initial position for the speaker normally is one with about half the listeners to the left and half to the right. Many public address systems, of course, necessitate standing in front of a microphone, but otherwise one has the option of a position in front of the desk or lectern for greater closeness and friendliness or behind the furniture for formality and authoritativeness. Whatever the position, speakers should be unhurried in arranging notes and hand properties, if any. Before uttering the first words, they should stop walking, take a position with the weight on both feet, look at the audience, and pause momentarily. Whether walking, standing, or sitting, they should handle themselves so that they look their best. For most persons in most situations, this means head up, shoulders back, hands at sides unless gesturing, and weight on both feet.

During the speech the preceding advice on position and posture continues to be generally applicable, but some additional considerations become relevant. In short presentations movement may be unnecessary and even distracting, but long speeches call for changes in position, both to rest the speaker and to add variety to the stage picture. Just as a moving sign holds attention better than an unchanging one, so does a communicator tend to keep and restore interest by moving from behind the lectern to the side, by walking to and from the chalkboard, and possibly by leaving the speaker's stand and going close to the audience.

Standing, moreover, is not a requirement. The erect position commands attention and makes it easier for those in large groups to see and to hear, but a seated posture may suggest informality, increase directness, and engender a close speaker-audience relation. Leaning or sitting on the desk, especially in long presentations, also can add variety, improve attentiveness, and increase rapport. All changes in position, however, should be clean-cut, definite, and timed so that they coincide with transitions and reinforce points of emphasis. Whereas purposeful movement is an asset, nervous pacing or random shifting about distracts attention and may reduce confidence in the speaker.

Informality, or deviations from the standard speaker's position and posture, can go too far. A minister on network television often gives part of his sermon while sitting on one of the steps leading to the platform, and audiences seem to respond favorably. On one occasion, however, when he leaned to the side with his weight on one hand, the judgment was that his behavior no longer befit a preacher.

The speaker, Hubert Humphrey, illustrates excellent posture, earnestness, and apparent spontaneity. The gesture with the left hand is full and vital. (Richard Kalvar/Magnum)

Self-Possession and Gesture

The avoidance of mannerisms and of purposeless, awkward movements is important, therefore, to effective communication. The poised, self-controlled speaker avoids all repetitive, distracting mannerisms, such as twisting a lock of hair, rubbing the nose, playing with a paper clip, buttoning and unbuttoning a jacket, removing glasses and putting them back on, shuffling notes, stroking the lectern, waving the hands about, and standing on each foot alternately. Stiffness, also, is no virtue. Movement, gesturing, and expressiveness in the face and the eyes, all of which are normal in conversation, are useful in platform address. Appropriate gestures, according to one experiment, increased comprehension, whereas inappropriate actions reduced understanding.[19] Five types of gesture, natural to most people, are fairly easy to incorporate into a presentation:

Literal description. With one or both hands a communicator can add color and clarity to such sentences as these: "The midget was only this tall." "It cleared by no more than this." "I need a box about this long and this wide." "The plant was this much higher than my head."

---

[19] Gerald R. Popelka and Kenneth W. Berger, "Gestures and Visual Speech Reception," *American Annals of the Deaf,* 116 (August 1971), 434–436.

Suggestive description. Although an exact representation is impossible, a speaker can reinforce such ideas as size, smoothness, and irregularity: "The lifeboat was bouncing up and down." "O.J. went straight ahead and then cut to the left." "The land was flat as far as we could see." "The wind whooshed by us."

Pointing. Often in conversation, less frequently in public address, an extended arm and forefinger can clarify better than words: "At the corner, go to the left." "Monkey Island is that way." "Salad dressings are over there."

Emphasis. An extended finger held aloft adds force, but the clenched fist is a stronger gesture for reinforcing critical words, such as those in the following sentences: "We shall never, never surrender!' "This second half fight harder and harder and harder!" "Until those criminals are behind bars, we cannot rest!" Some speakers pound a clenched fist into the other hand or against the lectern or a table.

Enumeration. Especially easy for the beginning speaker who is afraid to gesture is the use of the fingers to number a series of points. One method is to hold up one finger when saying "one" or "first," two when saying "two" or "second," and so forth. A second possibility is to use both hands with the one "pulling" one or more fingers away from a lightly clenched fist.

Facial Expression and Other Visual Cues

As the following story of Wanda illustrates, facial expression, especially through the eyes, is a highly effective means of visual communication. To the boredom of her classmates, Wanda half an hour earlier had plodded through a five-minute speech on "Underwater Swimming." Although she spoke positively of the pleasures of the hobby and even described it as "exhilarating," her appearance belied her words. Like a manikin wired for sound, she showed no emotions. Her eyes were as lifeless when she said, "The brilliant colors are so beautiful that I tingled with excitement," as when she reported, "Equipment is not expensive." Throughout the drab performance, Wanda, normally a lively, attractive person, was about as appealing as a squeezed orange. Now, however, the situation was different as Wanda visited with friends in the vending-machine area. She smiled, her eyes sparkled, she looked alive. As the content of the conversation moved along, she changed in inner reactions and in outward expression.

Such problems as Wanda's are especially significant because of the influence of subtle cues on respondents. Both cues that observers know that they are receiving and perceivable but marginal stimuli are influential. In other words, although communicatees usually think primarily about the words that they are hearing, they simultaneously are noting such signs as tense muscles, furtive eyes, and restless hands. Through these secondary sources they judge the communicator to be confident, good-humored, selfish, or untrustworthy, and they combine these evaluations with all other stimuli in forming responses to both message and sender.

SPECIFIC SUGGESTIONS FOR IMPROVEMENT

How does the student improve in the visual aspects of delivery? Included in the preceding sections are numerous recommendations on appearance, position, posture, gesture, and facial expression; but the following suggestions are specific:

1. As a basic posture, stand on both feet with your hands at your sides. Stand up so that you make the best possible appearance.

2. For variety and for creating special impressions, deviate from the basic posture. The variations should be intentional and not the result of carelessness.

3. Movement from one position to another should be purposeful and definite. Stand still, move, and stand still again without random or needless action.

4. Keep the hands quiet except when moving them for a purpose.

5. Gesture with the full arm or arms. Do not gesture with the elbows against the body.

6. Avoid using the same gesture repeatedly. Use a variety, some with the left arm, some with the right, and some with both.

7. Mark two or three checkpoints on the outline, preferably at divisions of the speech. No matter what the problem, at each checkpoint monitor your performance and begin the new section properly.

8. Avoid temptations. Stand far enough from the furniture so that leaning is impossible. Do not take to the platform rubber bands, paper clips, pencils, or other objects that you are inclined to play with.

DELIVERY IN SMALL GROUPS

The preceding emphasis on platform speaking is a recognition that the problems in formal situations seem more difficult to most students than do those that occur in conversations, discussions, and conferences. In group situations, nevertheless, delivery affects both clarity and effectiveness. Some persons, as even a casual observer can note, speak better than others, and almost anyone can do better than he or she ordinarily does.

The principles previously discussed are important in all types of communication, but the degree of emphasis that the learner should place on each general rule varies with the situation. In interpersonal relations empathy is especially significant, for feelings of congeniality, similarlity, community of interests, and trust are highly important in determining outcomes. Communicativeness, fluency, appropriate rate, varied and interesting melodic patterns, and pleasantness are all conducive to producing a close, warm relation. Likewise, self-possession and good posture give favorable impressions, which in turn increase the likelihood of a satisfying exchange of ideas.

CONCLUSION

Delivery is a significant element that interacts with other factors to form the communication event. Informed, thoughtful content, as this book so often emphasizes, is the basis for responsible communication; but the transmission of advice and argument occurs through delivery, both oral and visual.

The specific skills of delivery, in the idealistic view, flow from belief in the message, confidence in oneself, concern for the listeners, and the desire to communicate. To strengthen oneself in these basic respects is a sound objective, and in time the student can look forward to greater ease on the platform and to better habits in the mechanics of presentation. Simultaneously, however, one should seek improvement by utilizing specific suggestions, such as those that appear in the chapter. To a certain extent the process is circular. To stand straight on both feet and to speak firmly increase the inner sense of authority, and the heightened confidence makes it easier to stand well and to speak without hesitation. "Delivery," the great Demosthenes supposedly said, "is the most important part of oratory." "And what is second in importance?" he was asked. "Delivery," he said again. "And the third?" Once more the answer was "Delivery."

The ancient anecdote may or may not be true, but other great rhetoricians and orators, both classical and modern, agree. ". . . it is of little consequence to discover what is *proper* to be said," Cicero wrote, "unless you are able to express it in a free and agreeable manner; and even that will be insufficient, if not recommended by the voice, the look, and the gesture."[20]

PROBLEMS AND EXERCISES

1. Observe two conversational groups, and write reports of about 150 words on each. Try to choose two groups that differ in the number of participants, in the atmosphere

---

[20] Cicero *Brutus* ch. 29.

(friendly or tense), and/or in setting and level of formality. Describe the general spirit of the meeting, note changes in atmosphere, if any, and discuss specific aspects of delivery that were influential.

2. Sit in a chair at the front of the classroom, and tell the other students about your next major speech or about a paper that you are writing for one of your classes. Talk about your subject, the subpoints you expect to cover, where you have found material, and problems that you are encountering. Look at one person or a small group as you begin, and keep eye contact with different listeners throughout. Maintain a sharing, friendly manner, encourage suggestions and questions, and respond conversationally.

3. Stand and deliver a two-minute speech on the topic "How I Would Like to Change This Campus." Include at least three phrases that identify listeners with yourself, such as "my friends," "my fellow members," "you and I," and "What can we do about it?" Be direct and conversational.

4. Give a five-minute speech on a topic requiring research and original thought. Afterwards answer questions on your analysis and your proposed solution. One possible class procedure is to prearrange for half the students to raise issues exposing weaknesses in your message and for the other half to ask questions giving you opportunities for reinforcing your position.

5. Give a two-minute speech on some familiar topic such as a hobby or a place that you visited while traveling. Say to yourself, "For a short two minutes I can be perfect in the essentials of delivery." Upon reaching the speaker's position, put your weight on both feet, look at the audience, and pause momentarily. For two minutes maintain eye contact, avoid vocalized pauses, and make no random movements. Close with a preplanned sentence, and walk to your seat.

6. Keep a one-day log of your comments on speech patterns that you hear. Include observations, both favorable and adverse, on fluency, rate, loudness, aliveness, variety, pleasantness, appropriateness, and clarity. Observe at least six persons, who may be friends, lecturers, radio or television performers, or strangers that you overhear. Decide whether the speech pattern is helpful or harmful, and then try to isolate the specific factors responsible for the overall effect. Share your findings with five or six classmates that you join as a discussion group.

7. Either alone or with the help of your professor decide on one aspect of delivery that you should try to improve. Prepare a short speech, and, while delivering it, concentrate on this one problem. Use any of the suggestions in the body of the chapter that seem likely to be helpful.

8. Attend a meeting that includes a public address of at least ten minutes. Take notes on the speaker's prespeech appearance, opening, and posture, movement, and gesture. Exchange your findings with five or six classmates in a discussion. Try to form generalizations about the visual elements in communication.

9. Present a three- to five-minute speech in which you include at least three gestures. Good topics include such hobbies or activities as "How to Make a Kite," "Correcting a Slice," "Assembling a Toy," and "Different Ways to Throw a Frisbee."

REFERENCES

Addington, David W. "The Effect of Vocal Variations on Ratings of Source Credibility," *Speech Monographs*, 38 (August 1971), 242-247.

Beebe, Steven A. "Eye Contact: A Nonverbal Determinant of Speaker Credibility," *Speech Teacher*, 23 (January 1974), 21-25.

Boyd, Stephen D. "Delivery in the Campaign Speaking of Frank Clement," *Southern Speech Communication Journal*, 39 (Spring 1974), 279-290.

Jensen, Keith. "Self-Reported Speech Anxiety and Selected Demographic Variables," *Central States Speech Journal*, 27 (Summer 1976), 102-108.

McCroskey, James C., and R. Samuel Mehrley. "The Effects of Disorganization and Nonfluency on Attitude Change and Source Credibility," *Speech Monographs*, 36 (March 1969), 13-21.

McCroskey, James C., and Virginia P. Richmond. "The Effects of Communication Apprehension on the Perception of Peers," *Western Speech Communication*, 40 (Winter 1976), 14-21.

Maslow, Catha, Kathryn Yoselson, and Harvey London. "Persuasiveness of Confidence Expressed via Language and Body Language," *British Journal of Social and Clinical Psychology*, 10 (September 1971), 234-240.

Mehrabian, Albert. "Significance of Posture and Position in the Communication of Attitude and Status Relationships," *Psychological Bulletin*, 71 (May 1969), 359-372.

Pearce, W. Barnett. "The Effect of Vocal Cues on Credibility and Attitude Change," *Western Speech*, 35 (Summer 1971), 176-184.

Pearce, W. Barnett, and Bernard J. Brommel. "Vocalic Communication in Persuasion," *Quarterly Journal of Speech*, 58 (October 1972), 298-306.

Pearce, W. Barnett, and Forrest Conklin. "Nonverbal Vocalic Communication and Perceptions of a Speaker," *Speech Monographs*, 38 (August 1971), 235-241.

Rhodes, Steven C., and Kenneth D. Frandsen. "Some Effects in Feedback Utilization on the Fluency of College Students' Speech," *Speech Monographs*, 42 (March 1975), 83-89.

Schweitzer, Don A. "The Effect of Presentation on Source Evaluation," *Quarterly Journal of Speech*, 56 (February 1970), 33-39.

Turner, Frederick H., Jr. "Alcidamas: An Early Rationale for Extemporaneous Interpersonal Communication," *Southern Speech Communication Journal*, 39 (Spring 1974), 223-232.

Vickrey, James Frank, Jr. "The Lectures on 'Discoveries and Invention'—A Neglected Aspect of the Public Speaking Career of Abraham Lincoln," *Central States Speech Journal*, 21 (Fall 1970), 181-190.

Weaver, J. Clark, and Richard J. Anderson. "Voice and Personality Interrelationships," *Southern Speech Communication Journal*, 38 (Spring 1973), 262-278.

Weidhorn, Manfred. "Churchill as Orator: Wish and Fulfillment," *Southern Speech Communication Journal*, 40 (Spring 1975), 217-227.

11
THE MEDIUM: USING LANGUAGE

After studying this chapter the reader should be able to do the following:

Present five pairs of words in which one member of each pair is less abstract than the other

Present five pairs of words in which one member of each pair is stronger emotionally than the other

Present at least two examples of each of the following: god-terms, devil-terms, and opinionated sentences

Rewrite a passage that is jargon-ridden, drab, or affected so that at least 75 percent of the students in the class will identify the rewritten version as clearer, more natural, and in better taste than the original.

Provide at least one example of each of the following: metaphor, irony, antithesis, parallelism, alliteration, and any other three stylistic devices included in the chapter

The same three students who were talking about rhetorical choices at the beginning of Chapter 9 met once again at the close of another meeting of their beginning class in speech communication.

"Do you remember our saying that 'choices is the name of the game' when we were talking about arranging the speech?" asked Mr. A.

"I surely do," said Mr. B.

"And now that we are studying language as a factor in communication," added Miss C, still the analytical member of the group, "the number of possible choices becomes almost infinite."

"Right on," Mr. B continued, "and in thinking about choices in language we need to begin by considering the purposes."

"And after that," Miss C added, "we need to think about the resources that are available when the communicator makes the selections."

As in Chapter 9, the three students were exactly right in their views, and this time they also identified the two subtopics for the chapter.

LANGUAGE CHOICES: THEIR PURPOSES

Why does Mr. B or Miss C or any other serious communicator feel concern over the language that he or she uses—over the choice of a familiar word rather than one that is technical, of a simple sentence rather than one that is involved, of a direct oral style rather than one that is reserved and formal? Analyzed, the reasons for trying to use language skillfully are threefold: to attain clarity, to increase emotional power, and to enhance credibility and improve the sender-receiver transaction. All three of these are aspects of verbal language, which is the principal medium of transmission from sender to receiver. Through language the communicator encodes or expresses ideas, sometimes in a simple sentence and at other times in a long and complex explanation or argument; in turn, but almost simultaneously, the receiver re-creates in his or her mind the meanings that the words and sentences and paragraphs stimulate. Basic to this event is the clarity of the content, but also affecting the emotional impact and the receiver's perceptions of the sender are the choices in language.

ATTAINING CLARITY

"Where can I find poppyseed dressing?" asks the shopper. "It's on Aisle 7B just beyond the cross aisle," answers the employee. Assuming that *poppyseed dressing* and *cross aisle* have the same meanings for the two conversationalists, communication in this example is successful. Unfortunately, many verbal exchanges are not so satisfactory. The writer when in Italy, for example, received no positive response when he asked a waiter to bring "water in a pitcher," and a few weeks later a request in a cafeteria for "Waldorf salad" was equally baffling to an immigrant employee. At a cocktail party two guests disputed the artistic merits of *The Great Gatsby* for some time before discovering that one was praising the novel and the other was condemning the movie.

Factors Affecting Clarity

The preceding instances illustrate two major barriers to accurate communication—the use of a word unfamiliar to the receiver and the employment of a term whose context is ambiguous. Of these two, the latter is the more subtle. Words mean whatever thoughts or images, correct or erroneous, they evoke in the minds of individual listeners. Whether *grass* arouses thoughts of marijuana or of ground cover depends on whether the conversation has been on teen-age problems or on taking care of the lawn.

Words, as linguists point out, are symbols—abstractions without being or reality. No one can eat, drink, throw, or sit on a "word," but one can do so with the *referent*, which is the linguist's term for the object, image, place, or concept for which the word stands. This relation between symbol and referent, to use technical language, is the source of difficulty when the speaker is talking about a gala party but the listener is associating *ball* with a round object that bounces. Dissimilar backgrounds, a possibility that every sender should take into consideration, increases the likelihood that the intended idea will be misunderstood.[1] If *democracy* means imperialism to a Latin American who has listened to communist propaganda, the American diplomat who talks of the democracy of the United States will fail in the attempt to build respect. People who differ in race, nationality, culture, and socioeconomic class talk to one another successfully only if they are careful about word choice and contexts.

A different but likewise powerful factor affecting communication is the level of abstraction. At the lowest level is a word with only one possible referent, such as the name for a particular cat. Thus, when the members of a household speak of *Golden Boy* (the cat's name), each one creates in his or her mind essentially the same image. In that family, assuming that *Golden Boy* is the only pet, the words *the cat* would be almost equally clear, but the increasingly abstract terms *feline, animal,* and *living creature* would be ever more diverse in their possible referents. Unless Mr. A is careful to supply a context, a statement about *an animal* or *a living creature* can call up in the receivers almost as many different mental pictures as there are persons attending to the message.

Finally, long, involved sentences affect clarity adversely. "As we look about us at the interfaces of the several agencies and then think about the many possible sources of confusion, not to mention actual mistakes, we

---

[1] For a research study showing the value of similar past experiences to clear communication, see Charles F. Vick and Roy V. Wood, "Similarity of Past Experience and the Communication of Meaning," *Speech Monographs,* 36 (June 1969), 159–162.

```
┌─────────────────────────────────────────┐
│           Living creature               │
   ┌─────────────────────────────────────────┐
   │              Animal                     │
      ┌─────────────────────────────────────────┐
      │              Feline                     │
         ┌───────────────────────────────┐
         │             Cat               │
            ┌───────────────────────────────┐
            │          Golden Boy           │
            └───────────────────────────────┘
```

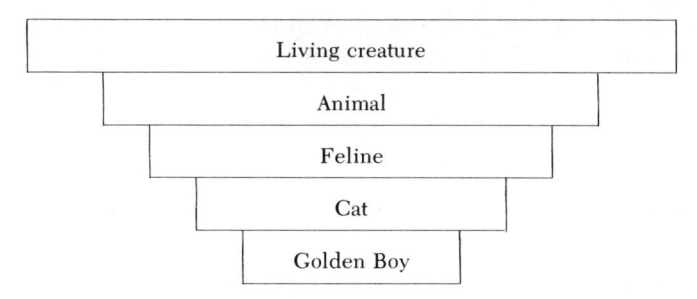

Figure 11.1 Levels of abstraction. The word that is the least abstract in a series is the most specific and includes the smallest number of objects or living beings in the real world.

begin to see that negative deceleration, or to put it another way, the absence of a lack of growth, may have more to do with the outcome than the critics, of whom there are many, may think" is a puzzle to the reader and almost incomprehensible to the listener. Varied structures add interest, and several basic patterns are acceptable, but in general the short sentence is easier to grasp than the long one. In many instances communicators improve their use of language when they replace a lengthy, rambling sentence with two or three short ones.

Clarity in language, therefore, depends on the familiarity of words, the context, similarity in background, the level of abstraction, and the firmness of sentence structure. How does the communicator apply this information to reduce the likelihood of misunderstanding? Most of the following specific suggestions are applicable during initial preparation, during revision, and during an extempore presentation.

Suggestions for Attaining Clarity

The preceding brief analysis leads to ten recommendations for the better use of language.

1. Use simple words and short sentences. In time listeners may apprehend *modicum, pedagogue,* and *bifurcated,* but they may miss part of the next sentence. *Limited amount, teacher,* and *divided* convey the same meanings, but more quickly and easily. Technical language is justified when common words are either unavailable or misleadingly imprecise, but so-called scholars offend when they unnecessarily substitute *valued others* and *cognitively complex subjects* for suitable everyday expressions.

Several research projects on sentence structure are significant. In separate quantitative studies John P. Parker and Alan Nichols found that both short sentences and simple words increased comprehension,[2] and in still another experiment Baird confirmed that simply worded speeches were the ones the most easily comprehended.[3]

2. Use near-synonyms with discretion. Many words are so similar in meaning that careless usage is common and causes needless confusion. Examples of near-synonyms are these: *misdemeanor-felony; burglary-robbery; printer-publisher; director-producer; instructor-professor; to rescind-to reconsider; editor-compiler; barrister-solicitor.*

3. Use as low a level of abstraction as possible. Say "animals" if referring to the many creatures in a zoo, but use "bears" or "zebras" if referring to the single species. When the message pertains to such high level abstractions as *love, jealousy, envy, patriotism, democracy,* and *transcendentalism,* move to more specific terms whenever possible, define by describing what you have in mind, and give illustrations. When appropriate to the intended meaning, talk about what's best for another's happiness rather than of *love;* and if the meaning pertains to theft through dishonest bookkeeping, say so and don't prattle about *morality in business.* The following list gives further examples of levels of abstraction:

Less Abstract	More Abstract
Volvo sedan	Automobile
Tennis player	Athlete
Systems analyst	Employee
Golf	Form of recreation
Baptist	Protestant
Rape	Violent crime
Willingness to work overtime	Loyalty

Does the level of abstraction really matter? Yes, it does, according to a research study on the relation of abstractness to retention. Sixty-six juniors and seniors enrolled in an advanced speech course did better on sixty multiple choice questions when the language used for a message was low in abstractness.[4]

4. Define unusual words or familiar words used in new senses. The communicator's problem, of course, is foreseeing which words will be puzzling

[2] John P. Parker, "Some Organizational Variables and Their Effect upon Comprehension," *Journal of Communication,* 12 (March 1962), 27–32; Alan Nichols, "Effect of Three Aspects of Sentence Structure on Immediate Recall," *Speech Monographs,* 32 (June 1965), 164–168.
[3] John E. Baird, Jr., "The Effects of Speech Summaries upon Audience Comprehension of Expository Speeches of Varying Quality and Complexity," *Central States Speech Journal,* 25 (Summer 1974), 119–127.
[4] G. Wayne Shamo and John R. Bittner, "Recall as a Function of Language Style," *Southern Speech Communication Journal,* 38 (Winter 1972), 181–187.

to listeners. "How well educated are they?" "How much background do they have on this particular topic?" and "What seems to be their intellectual level?" are questions that can help the speaker adjust language during preparation and revision. Equally important are changes during the presentation itself when restlessness and puzzled glances can suggest the need for definition or explanation. "In other words" or "Let's look at an example" then become valuable transitions.

Especially tricky are familiar words that the communicator is using in a special or technical sense, for in these circumstances listeners are likely to think that they understand what they are hearing when they really do not. The word *suggestion,* for example, has a common meaning, as in the sentence "That is a good suggestion"; but as a term in persuasion its scope is restricted to appeals that are in the marginal fields of attention. Similarly, the words *science, demonstration,* and *necessary* in a scholarly lecture on Aristotle have precise meanings that few listeners, unless assisted, will recreate.

5. *Use indexing, dating, and other qualifiers.* "Cow_1 is not cow_2," and "the Civil Rights $Movement_{1976}$ is not the Civil Rights $Movement_{1963}$," say the general semanticists, who use subscripts for indexing and dating. Less showy than subscripts but serving the same purpose are verbal qualifiers that specify the period in the orator's career that is being described or the type of commercial that is objectionable. Some types of qualifiers that increase precision are the following:

GENRE: She is a great lyric poet (not necessarily outstanding in other types).
PLACE: The candidate is strong in Alabama and Georgia (not everywhere).
PERSON: This critical analysis is not about all filmmakers but is about Fellini.
VIEWPOINT: The judgment, if one uses dramatic principles, is unflattering.

6. *Adjust your language so that it will fit the receiver's backgrounds and expectations.* Dime means "ten cents" to most persons, but it designates a large sum of money among gamblers. To a child the word *story* calls up memories of animals that talk and go on delightful adventures; to a long-suffering spouse the word is a synonym for "lie." To a middle-class white a policeman is someone who protects the law-abiding; to those in the ghetto an officer is a "pig" who evicts the poor and beats up the innocent. Since the message that the receiver re-creates is a product of the experiences and the associations that the words evoke, the sender can convey what is intended only if he or she appreciates differences in backgrounds and expectations.

7. *Supply a context.* Avoid plunging into the middle of an account. Make sure that you and your listeners start together, and then proceed step by step. This ordering of items is important, whether the message is complex or simple. In a telephone inquiry or complaint, for example, forethought about the arrangement of sentences can save time and avoid confusion.

8. *Make language suitably redundant.* How much repetition should a passage contain? If you cite a person's name, how soon should you say it again? How often should you summarize? Redundancy, a concept brought from engineering to communication, occurs when a word conveys no new information—when a listener could make a correct prediction of the word if a blank replaced it. Theory and actuality, however, often are discrepant, for a word is redundant only if the listener has been attentive to the preceding material and has comprehended it. Also missing from the theory of redundancy is the possiblity that repetition will add emphasis or serve some stylistic purpose.

Some redundancy, therefore, is necessary, but how much? The answer lies in the truism that communication is more an art than a science, that the right amount is a matter of "feel" and not of formula. One must follow a course that avoids both extremes. Too much redundancy is tiresome, inefficient, and even an insult to the intelligence of listeners; too little causes a loss of comprehension. Whereas one baseball announcer is boring because of frequent repetition, another annoys by talking for an entire inning about "the pitcher" without giving the name.

9. *Use nonverbal factors that clarify and reinforce.* "The one person whom I hate to see" has one meaning when the speaker is smiling, and a different one when he or she looks serious. "Put the book over here" and similar expressions derive much of their meaning from the accompanying actions and inflections. Tone of voice, gestures, facial expression, and other nonverbal indicators normally reinforce spoken messages without conscious effort, but self-examination or experimentation is worthwhile if problems arise. The writer some years ago was not entirely successful in pleas requesting students not to mark up their examination booklets. Different wordings did not solve the problem, but one day he held the booklet aloft and waved it from side to side when making the announcement. Compliance thereafter was almost universal.

10. *Anticipate sources of confusion.* One speaker confused and irritated an audience by talking about Abraham Lincoln's failures as a speaker without explaining that the precise topic was Lincoln's brief career as a public lecturer. The communicator should have anticipated that the great respect that most persons have for the Civil War president would make them uncomfortable, disbelieving, and even angry when they heard a seemingly sweeping and unwarranted criticism.

The shortcoming in the preceding example is the omission of qualifiers, but several of the nine other recommendations relate to this tenth point. What background does the listener bring to the situation? In what context will the communicatee see the word or the idea? Which words will be unfamiliar, or which ones will be used in a special and unexpected way? Which parts of the message, because of difficulty or unfamiliarity, will require extra time for full comprehension? Speakers should be especially on guard whenever they and their respondents differ markedly in nationality, in socioeconomic background, or in age.

Numerous means, therefore, exist for increasing the accuracy with which one communicates. Clarity, or precision in designation, is the objective in most situations—the boss telling the secretary how to perform a task, the customer explaining what is wrong with the family television set, the orientation officer distributing information to new students, the lecturer telling a class the meaning of *proxemics* or *feedback*, or the advertiser describing a product.

Clarity, it is interesting to note, is not always a speaker's objective. Diplomats by talking of "taking appropriate action" leave all options open. Politicians, who like to please all and to offend no one, also may be deliberately vague. They favor tax reform, safer working conditions, and better schools without taking a stand on specific proposals for taxes, safety, and education. Parents, supervisors, and others in authority likewise may find vagueness strategic. The threat of punishment, if unexplained, leaves them all possible choices if the offense occurs, and to promise "a reward" permits a later decision on form and value.

Listeners should be on guard against intentional vagueness. If possible, they should ask questions; if not, they should suspend judgment.

INCREASING EMOTIONAL POWER

"God-terms" and "devil-terms" are coinages of Richard Weaver, who noted that some words evoke favorable ideas and pleasant associations whereas the effects of others are the opposite. The principal god-term in 1953, he said, was *progress*. Others that he listed were *fact, science, modern, efficient,* and *American. Prejudice, reactionary,* and *aggressor* were among his examples of devil-terms.[5] A quarter of a century later all of these words, so it seems, still belong on the two lists, and adding others is not difficult. Political candidates try to label themselves *liberal* rather than *conservative* or *radical* and to associate themselves with *innovation, freedom,* and *equal opportunity* rather than with *bureaucracy* and *bigotry.*

Further examples of god- and devil-terms, based on an analysis of the

---

[5] Richard Weaver, *The Ethics of Rhetoric* (Chicago: Henry Regnery Co., 1953), 211–232.

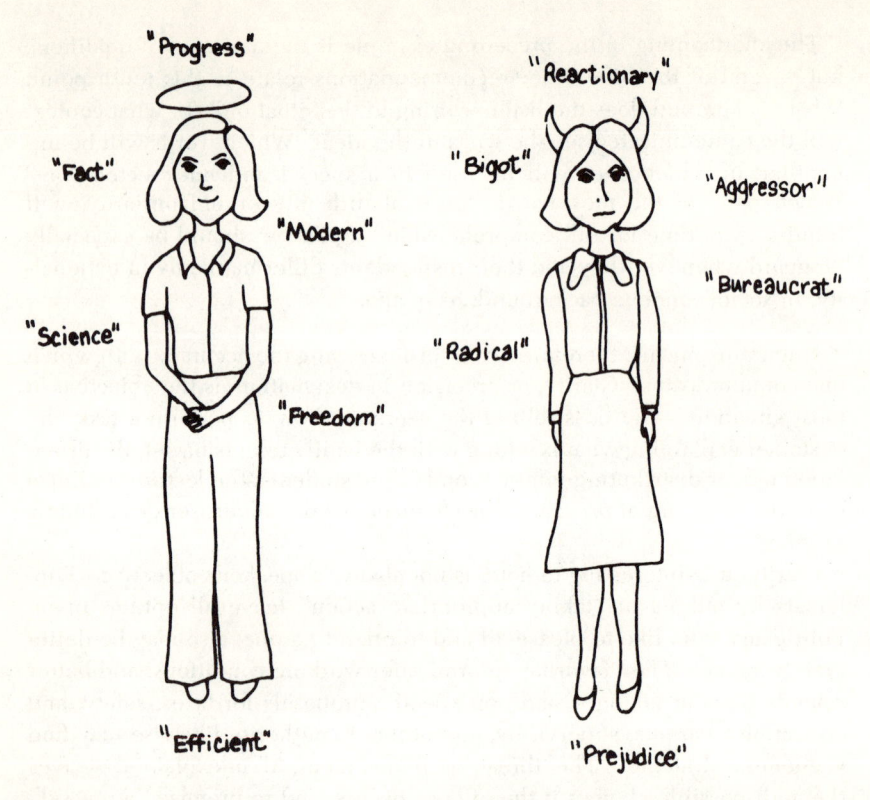

God-terms and devil-terms add emotional power to messages.

speeches of a prominent political figure, appear in the following passage on George Wallace:

> The key god-term was, of course "law and order," but Wallace also referred frequently to "law-abiding citizens." A multitude of devil-terms characterized those blamed for the increase in crime: "rabbles," "militants and activists and revolutionaries," and "Communists." Most often heard, however, was the word "anarchist." In Toledo, for example, the term was used no less than five times within a two minute span. . . . In 1972 . . . again god- and devil-terms occupied a paramount position in Wallace's rhetoric. "Quality education," said to be on "a non-discriminatory basis, regardless of your color," was the chief god-term. Devil-terms were used both to describe busing itself—"asinine," "callous and cruel," "subordinate to the power of the state," and "totalitarian" and to describe those who advocated busing—"limousine liberals" and "social schemers."[6]

[6] Richard D. Raum and James S. Measell, "Wallace and His Ways: A Study of the Rhetorical Genre of Polarization," *Central States Speech Journal*, 25 (Spring 1974), 30.

That the speaker can use language to control the emotional impact of the message is apparent to any thoughtful observer. *Home* and *mother* are stronger words than *house* and *woman*, and they differ qualitatively from *dump*, *hovel*, *broad*, and *biddy*. To say "the market plummeted" rather than "the market dropped" adds force without giving offense, but to describe one's boss as "a goon" or "a satanic monster" is likely to offend listeners unless one's credibility with them is unusually strong or unless they share the attitude. An unusually impressive study on the power of words pertained to judgments by subjects playing the role of jurors. After showing a film on a traffic accident, the experimenter asked each panel a form of the question "About how fast were the cars going when they (hit, smashed, collided, bumped, or contacted) each other?" The average estimate of speed when the question contained the word *smashed* was 40.8 m.p.h. (the highest figure), whereas it was only 31.8 when the word was *contacted*. A week later the subjects were tested to see whether they thought they had seen any broken glass. There had been none in the film, but twice as many subjects reported seeing glass when the word *smashed* was in the question as when the verb was *hit*.[7]

The practical questions for the communicator, in conclusion, are "How strong should I make my language?" and "In what ways should I seek strength?" In answering these questions the sensitivities of the listeners are critical, and the dividing line between the acceptable and the offensive depends on the situation. Words that embarrass, that seem vulgar or tasteless, that seem exaggerated, or that sound mean and sarcastic are likely to damage the speaker more than they do the one accused.

Research on Intensity

Since the response to intensity or language strength depends on its interaction with *ethos*, prior attitudes, and still other factors, research has been inconclusive. Whereas Bowers found the low-intensity form of a speech to be the more effective for two of four topics,[8] McEwen and Greenberg obtained higher ratings for messages and their authors when intensity was high.[9] To add to this diversity of results, Burgoon and Chase found language of moderate intensity to be superior.[10] Obviously, these findings provide no guidance other than demonstrating the importance of being attentive to intensity as a factor in communication. As Greenberg says in

---

[7] Elizabeth Loftus, "Reconstructing Memory: The Incredible Eyewitness," *Psychology Today*, 8 (December 1974), 119.
[8] John W. Bowers, "Language Intensity, Social Introversion, and Attitude Change," *Speech Monographs*, 30 (November 1963), 345–352.
[9] William J. McEwen and Bradley S. Greenberg, "The Effects of Message Intensity on Receiver Evaluations of Source, Message and Topic," *Journal of Communication*, 20 (December 1970), 340–350.
[10] Michael Burgoon and Lawrence J. Chase, "The Effects of Differential Patterns in Messages Attempting to Induce Resistance to Persuasion," *Speech Monographs*, 40 (March 1973), 1–7.

summarizing both his own findings and prior research: "This work adds to the research evidence that manipulation of language intensity can evoke differential responses to message content and message sources."[11]

Research on Opinionation

Findings are more helpful on opinionation, which is a usage in which the sender adds a label characterizing the person or the group to which the message is directed. The two following pairs of examples contrast straightforward and opinionated statements:

NONOPINIONATED: I am very much in favor of school busing.
OPINIONATED: Anyone who opposes school busing is a bigot. (The speaker labels those who disagree.)
NONOPINIONATED: All of us should oppose this proposal.
OPINIONATED: Only a communist sympathizer could support this proposal.

Except for certain special situations, opinionated language, according to most research, is harmful to the speaker. Miller and Lobe found nonopinionation to be more effective for both open- and closed-minded receivers;[12] and Hill found that obviously opinionated group leaders were perceived as less competent and less objective than those moderately opinionated or unopinionated and that opinionation interfered with consensus.[13] Infante, although his results included some inconsistencies, found nonopinionation to be superior both as a means of counter-persuasion and as a source of high ethos.[14] "The 'pro' speaker," he summarizes, "was derogated with respect to character and authoritativeness when he used opinionated as compared with non-opinionated language."[15]

Four exceptions to the preceding general rule, however, have at least some research support. Under the following circumstances opinionated language was advantageous:

When the communicator was highly trusted[16]

---

[11] Bradley S. Greenberg, "The Effects of Language Intensity Modification on Perceived Verbal Aggressiveness," *Communication Monographs*, 43 (June 1976), 138.
[12] Gerald R. Miller and Jon Lobe, "Opinionated Language, Open- and Closed-Mindedness and Response to Persuasive Communications," *Journal of Communication*, 17 (December 1967), 333–341.
[13] Timothy A. Hill, "An Experimental Study of the Relationship Between Opinionated Leadership and Small Group Consensus," *Communication Monographs*, 43 (August 1976), 246–257.
[14] Dominic A. Infante, "Effects of Opinionated Language on Communicator Image and in Conferring Resistance to Persuasion," *Western Speech*, 39 (Spring 1975), 112–119.
[15] *Ibid.*, p. 119.
[16] Gerald R. Miller and John Baseheart, "Source Trustworthiness, Opinionated Statements, and Response to Persuasive Communication," *Speech Monographs*, 36 (March 1969), 1–7.

When the receivers had a high need for social approval[17]

When the receivers were neutral toward the topic[18]

When a following speaker on the opposite side was low in authoritativeness[19]

Conclusion

Opinionation is a subvariety of "loaded" language, a term that encompasses all types of strong word choice that are attempts to substitute name calling or labeling for evidence and reasoned proof. How a particular listener responds to a particular usage depends on past associations, attitudes toward the speaker, and the immediate situation. Partisans at pep rallies and political conventions, for example, expect speakers to lambast the opposition. Whatever these variables, however, the conclusion is certain that the affective or emotional power of words is an important aspect of all communication situations—public address, conversation, interview, and discussion. As one part of preparation, the communicator should consider the probable effects of words on the anticipated listener or group. When concepts are noncontroversial or when respondents agree with the sender, strong words, with some limitations imposed by good taste, add emphasis without antagonizing, but in many situations moderate language is more effective.

ENHANCING CREDIBILITY AND IMPROVING
THE SENDER-RECEIVER RELATIONSHIP

The levels of credibility and of sender-receiver rapport, as must be obvious, depend substantially on the skill of the communicator in making ideas clear and in controlling language for emotional impact. Larger considerations, however, are also important. The total quality of the communicator's style is likely to exert an influence beyond that of the individual word or phrase. Abraham Lincoln spoke as a statesman; Adlai Stevenson and John F. Kennedy conveyed impressions of wit and urbanity; Winston Churchill personified strength; Harry Truman projected his incisiveness and common-man quality; Franklin D. Roosevelt managed to elevate himself above his opponents; Everett Dirksen suggested intentional pomposity with an underlying folk wisdom; Will Rogers preserved the stereotype that true wisdom lies with the common folk; Lyndon Johnson

[17] John Baseheart, "Message Opinionation and Approval-Dependence as Determinants of Receiver Attitude Change and Recall," *Speech Monographs*, 38 (November 1971), 302–310.
[18] R. Samuel Mehrley and James C. McCroskey, "Opinionated Statements and Attitude Intensity as Predictors of Attitude Change and Source Credibility," *Speech Monographs*, 37 (March 1970), 47–52.
[19] Dominic A. Infante, "Forewarnings in Persuasion: Effects of Opinionated Language and Forewarner and Speaker Authoritativeness," *Western Speech*, 37 (Summer 1973), 185–195.

always sounded patronizing and raised questions of credibility; and Richard Nixon never escaped from an image of stuffiness, shiftiness, and self-centeredness. Others—both historic figures and commoners—employ language, intentionally or accidentally, for their own special purposes. The agitators of the late sixties, such as Abbie Hoffman, Jerry Rubin, and Mark Rudd, deliberately used words for their power to shock most hearers. Stokely Carmichael has been especially skillful in strengthening his leadership through language tailored to the particular audience.

All persons, not just the great and the famous, create impressions through their stylistic qualities. Those who are untutored hurt themselves by exposing their lack of education and thus seeming crude and ignorant.[20] A few help themselves by using language (inevitably interacting with ideas) that connotes fair-mindedness, good humor, graciousness, vivacity, concern, or some other admired quality. Still others lack distinctiveness, either positive or negative. Grammatically correct but without life or sparkle, they rarely coin a phrase that rises above the commonplace. Even prominent persons may appear to be without style, but this "no-style" is itself a language quality in the sense that its author seems ordinary and uninspired. Gerald Ford's speeches as president, at least to many, were undistinguished. The ideas flowed one after the other with correctness, clarity, and labored attempts at emphasis, but the listener felt that a properly programmed computer could have written a speech of equal quality.

Every person reading this book, in summary, creates broad impressions, and to some extent he or she has the power to alter the effects. "To some extent" is an appropriate limitation, for style is a product of personality, natural talent, and habit as well as an outcome of conscious effort and intelligent revision.

What can one do to lay the foundation for sound stylistic practices? Taste and judgment are essential, and a major step in developing these is that of gaining an appreciation of the major types of style, both good and poor. What are their characteristics? Under what circumstances should they be used?

The Scholarly, Technical, and Dignified Style

Encompassing a cluster of styles, this first heading is unified in that it pertains to discourse in which a well-qualified speaker wishes to convey important information. The tone is serious, the content is factual, and the manner is confident and informed. Sentences are complete and grammatical, and the speaker does not hesitate to use scientific and technical words

---

[20] For a study of the poor ratings given speakers who were deficient in word choice and sentence structure, see James J. Bradac, Catherine W. Konsky, and Robert A. Davies, "Two Studies of the Effects of Linguistic Diversity Upon Judgments of Communicator Attributes and Message Effectiveness," *Communication Monographs*, 43 (March 1976), 70–79.

when standard English lacks accurate terminology. The communicator uses humor sparingly and avoids slang and vulgarity. The choice is "the heart," not "the old ticker," and "the police," not "men in blue" or "pigs."

When should one use a style that is scholarly, technical, and dignified? The following conditions, singly or in combination, call for seriousness:

When the time and the place, such as a convention of a learned society or professional group, call for dignity

When the position and the reputation of the speaker lead the audience to expect a formal presentation

When young or little-known persons wish to increase their credibility and when other situational factors make a high level suitable

When the topic makes a colloquial presentation inappropriate

For the student in a speech communication class the topic is usually the most important factor determining the best stylistic level. A serious subject, significant to the class and carefully researched, deserves a presentation that uses accurate language and that maintains an atmosphere calling for thoughtful listening.

The Pretentious, Pedantic, and Jargon-ridden Style

"Speaker confidence is a negatively accelerated monotonic growth function of experience in speaking," a quotation from a speech journal, is a pretentious way of saying, "A speaker grows in confidence with experience in speaking." Similar exercises in pedantry obscure meanings in almost every issue of the learned magazines. Research workers deal with "homophily" rather than "similarity," and to some authors superior individuals are now "cognitively complex" rather than "intelligent."

For the listener such atrocities pose even greater problems than for the reader, who in time may puzzle out meanings. The boundary between the scholarly and the pretentious is fuzzy, but whether the unusual word is necessary is the most important criterion. *Kinesics, paralinguistics,* and *proxemics* (see Chapter 12) are mouth-filling terms, but satisfactory substitutes for them do not exist. *Transcendence* and *differentiation,* likewise, are unavoidable if one is to speak informatively on the means for reducing dissonance. *Dissonance* itself is worth using, even though *incongruity* and *imbalance* are roughly synonymous.

How can speakers know that they are slipping beyond the bounds of good taste, beyond the scholarly to the pretentious? In word choice, as the preceding paragraph illustrates, they should question their selections if speech drafts contain unusual expressions when simple words are satisfactory; but pedantry is more than word choice. Manifesting itself also in excessively long, involved sentences, it is a frame of mind. The individual is less interested in conveying information than in bolstering self-image. Realizing that either depth or muddiness may keep the observer from seeing the bottom of the river, the speaker is hopeful that the receiver will mistake obscurity for profundity. "What I don't understand must be deep" is a listener's reaction, and the pedant hopes to turn that mindless attitude to advantage.

Examples of pretense, pedantry, and jargon are easy to find. On December 21, 1973, the United States House of Representatives, according to Taylor Branch, amended an energy bill by striking out the word *rationing* and inserting the words *end use allocation.* Branch goes on to offer these two further examples of jargon, which he ascribes to Dr. James H. Boren:

> The older departments always do well, too, because they have learned to blend any crisis into the harmonics of their programmatic functions by fuzzifying the viable options.
>
> We have received tentative reports from nearly forty ad hoc study committees showing that the energy crisis has more obital interfaces with government program parameters than any crisis since the Depression.[21]

This kind of language, Babcock states, has been labeled *Desperanto* by Jacques Barzun, *Polysyllabic monstrosititis* by James Thurber, and *insipidology* by Scott Corbett.[22] As a further example, Babcock cites this notice posted near a sidewalk: "This ground is temporarily closed for the grass to be reestablished after reinstatement."[23]

The Colloquial and Familiar Style

At some point the scholarly, dignified style melds into the colloquial and familiar. The one flows from a state of mind that is intent on the topic and to some degree detached and reserved; the other, from a mental state that, although serious about content and occasion, is friendly, relaxed, and communicative.

Specific characteristics also are identifiable. Colloquial and familiar sentences are those natural to speech—varied and fairly short. Speakers, if they would do so in serious conversation, use questions, direct address, personal pronouns, and even sentence fragments. Whenever possible, words are those familiar to most listeners. At times the speaker may use slang or a currently popular phrase, but substandard usages are infrequent and always by choice rather than through ignorance. Repetition, unlike in written composition, is considered natural and is retained.

How does one attain a colloquial, familiar style? In practice, it is harder

---

[21] Taylor Branch, "The Sunny Side of the Energy Crisis," *Harper's*, 248 (March 1974), 18, 22.
[22] C. Merton Babcock, "The Lingua Frankenstein of the Fabulous Fifties," *Journal of Communication,* 10 (March 1960), 41–43.
[23] *Ibid.,* p. 43.

to develop than the description in the preceding paragraph suggests. The colloquial and familiar slips readily into the drab and vulgar (see the next section); and the interesting, effective presentation is lively, distinctive, and personal as well as clear, correct, and free of pretense. A speech, in other words, should bear the imprint of the individual's own unique set of qualities, and it should owe its stylistic characteristics to the audience and the occasion as well.

The first step in developing a friendly, direct message is to prepare a draft that is natural—without any self-conscious attempt to conform to "rules" or to attain special effects. Second, in revision the speaker should preserve as much as possible of these natural qualities, but should smooth out rough spots and give special attention to language in the introduction, the conclusion, and points of emphasis in the body. Adding incisiveness, improving connective material, and heightening clarity need not—and should not—destroy the basic qualities of straightforwardness and directness.

One speaker who, although president of the United States, was comfortable with simple, natural, and personalized speech, no matter what the occasion, was Franklin Delano Roosevelt. A close associate gives this account of a transformation from the dignified style to the familiar and colloquial:

> The Treasury Department prepared a scholarly, comprehensive draft of the speech. The President saw that it would be meaningless to most people, tossed it aside without any attempt at rewriting, and proceeded to write his own instead. He dictated it in simple, ordinary language—he looked for words that he would use in an informal conversation with one or two of his friends. He found the kind of language that everyone could understand. And everyone did understand. Confidence was restored.[24]

Who should use the colloquial, familiar style, and under what circumstances? The brief answers are "most speakers," and "much of the time." Although everyone should be unassuming and friendly, individual differences make the dignified style easier for some and the familiar more natural for others. A Will Rogers, for example, no matter what the topic or the occasion, would be out of character if he became scholarly and technical, whereas it is hard to imagine a Henry Kissinger speaking as a common man. Students, similarly, differ in the styles with which they are the most comfortable.

The Drab and Vulgar Style

Misused, the colloquial, familiar style becomes the drab and/or vulgar. For most communicators the unrevised or unedited message is commonplace;

---

[24] Samuel I. Rosenman, *Working with Roosevelt* (New York: Harper & Row, 1952), pp. 92–93.

an effective "natural" style, paradoxically, requires revision. The first of the following illustrations of four styles is no exaggeration:

DRAB, VULGAR: If the government gives away money to the poor, one result that might happen is more spending.
COLLOQUIAL, FAMILIAR: A government subsidy to persons of low income would speed up the economy.
TECHNICAL, DIGNIFIED: A negative income tax would stimulate the economy.
PRETENTIOUS, PEDANTIC, JARGON-RIDDEN: An application of positive financial reinforcement to monetarily deprived human units will have an accelerating effect on critically influential segments of our system of production and distribution.

Subvarieties of the drab, vulgar style are several. At best, it is colorless and flabby; a bit worse, it is clumsy and grammatically unsure; still worse, it is error-ridden and suggests low status. One interesting research study on substandard speech compared recordings of an upper middle class male with those of a man from the ghetto. Both speakers covered the same ideas, but used the grammar and the word choice of their respective groups. Ninety-six listeners, coming from high, middle, and low social classes, evaluated the recordings with this outcome: "Subjects responded very positively to the grammar of the high-status syntactical patterns, which involved standard English. Conversely, subjects responded negatively to the syntactical patterns of the low-status dialect, which involved nonstandard English."[25] These differing reactions were especially strong for middle-class listeners. Other research studies, although they usually show substandard speech to be satisfactory for conveying ideas, regularly indicate that poor English affects ratings of credibility adversely.

At this point the reader may be thinking, "If substandard, vulgar speech is generally harmful to credibility, why does it seem to work so well for agitators and members of subcultures?" True enough, some individuals, although they antagonize most citizens, increase their identification with those whose slang and coinages are like their own and strengthen their hold on radical followers through obscenity and vulgarity. These practices, however, are not usually due to ignorance or carelessness but are calculated strategies for special circumstances. Some students find it advantageous to develop two spoken styles, using the first when with persons of their own backgrounds and the second with teachers, prospective employers, and others who are part of the mainstream of society. A research study in which a black student spoke to a predominantly black audience shows that he was rated as a more honest and reliable source when he used

---

[25] Brenda Bochner and Arthur Bochner, "The Effects of Social Status and Social Dialect on Listener Responses," *Central States Speech Journal*, 24 (Summer 1973), 81.

"jive" language than when he employed "straight" language; on the other hand, "straightness" produced the higher ratings for intelligence and status.[26]

The Elegant and Expressive Style

Rarely used, the elegant, expressive style is worth brief consideration because of the significance of the occasions that call for it. Exemplified by Lincoln at Gettysburg and in his second inaugural address, this style is appropriate for a memoriam to the dead or a eulogy to the living. At times a student ceremony calls for praise for someone receiving a special honor, and not uncommonly a corporation banquet includes an address praising a man or a woman who is retiring.

Such occasions demand the right touch. Speeches for the living usually are a mixture of good-natured humor, pathos, and praise that rings true and sincere. Not every section of such a speech requires stylistic elevation, but some parts do. In those moments the colloquial and familiar is inadequate, and the dignified style is too stiff and formal. Language should be elevated, and sentence structure graceful. Many of the figures and stylistic devices discussed later in the chapter, including metaphors, rhythmic phrases, balanced sentences, and antitheses, add sublimity.

The Ornate and Affected Style

When taste is deficient, the elegant, expressive style becomes ornate and affected. Although a critic can identify specific verbal excesses, the true sources of this deviate form are insincerity, misjudgment of the occasion, and immaturity. Praise that goes beyond the truth, statements that the speaker does not mean, and indiscriminate use of clichés are all misdirected efforts.

A second problem is a failure to respond with good taste to the situation. Truly momentous circumstances justify elevated language, but the same words on lesser occasions seem out of place. An attempt to glorify an event beyond its actual significance leads to inappropriate language that at its worst is ridiculous.

The following examples, the first from a United States senator and the others from students, illustrate the affectation that results when one tries too hard to impress:

Let us make it manifest that this must stop forthwith.

As time passed and the Soviet attitude became more and more bellicose, the embryo plans gradually matured.

---

[26] E. Hope Bock and James H. Pitts, "The Effect of Three Levels of Black Dialect on Perceived Speaker Image," *Speech Teacher*, 24 (September 1975), 218–225.

The oarsmen bent their backs to the task of piloting the raft of democracy through the perilous waters away as far as possible from the forbidding coasts of political Babylon.

Has catabolistic negativism ever resulted in amelioration for anybody?

SUMMARY

". . . style is expressive of the individual, . . . conscious style is the result of reflective thought, and . . . matter and manner are inseparable"[27] is a summary of the views on style of Thomas De Quincey, one of the great masters of language. The content of the preceding pages should help the student to use language clearly, effectively, and tastefully. Habits that the individual builds over a period of many years largely determine the quality of language, but careful observation of the usages of others and an effort at self-improvement can produce long-range gains, and intelligent revision of first drafts can lead to immediate benefits.

STYLISTIC DEVICES

Competent revision requires thought, effort, taste, and judgment. Although to a large extent it is an art, it also is a craft, whose successful practice depends on knowledge of the possible ways of handling language. The three subsections that follow—on figurative language, special kinds of sentences, and other devices—provide a large body of information on the tools that one may use in shaping style and in adding strength to those points that one wishes to emphasize. Although the total effect is more important than the single impressive word or phrase, individual items are the materials for determining overall tone.

FIGURATIVE LANGUAGE

"The pitcher threw nothing but aspirin tablets" contains a figure, because the communicator has transferred a word (*aspirin*) from its literal, usual meaning to a new context. Vigorous, fresh, and picturesque, this particular figure is almost as clear as the literal "The pitcher threw the ball so hard that it looked very small to the batters," and it is much more colorful and striking. This example is a metaphor, probably the most common figure, but other usages sometimes add interest and force. Rhetorics of the Renaissance listed as many as two hundred figures, but the following are the ones most used today.

[27] Paul M. Talley, "De Quincey on Persuasion, Invention, and Style," *Central States Speech Journal*, 16 (November 1965), 254.

Metaphor and Simile "Metaphor consists in giving the thing a name that belongs to something else," wrote Aristotle.[28] This definition still is accurate, as is his distinction between simile and metaphor: "The difference is but slight. When the poet says of Achilles that he 'Leapt on the foe as a lion,' this is a simile; when he says of him 'the lion leapt,' it is a metaphor."[29] The difference, to generalize, is that the simile contains a word such as *as* or *like*, whereas the metaphor does not. Examples:

METAPHOR: He is a cat.
SIMILE: He is as graceful as a cat.
METAPHOR: Barnhart blanketed the opposing forward.
SIMILE: Barnhart covered the opposing forward like a blanket.

Metaphors and similes, especially frequent and colorful in sports, also abound in conversation, and many usages become so common that the figurative quality ceases to catch attention. "The car shot ahead" and "He talked a blue streak" are examples of the thousands of expressions that at one time were new but that now are alternative ways of verbalizing ideas that add variety and richness to our language. New coinages, as compared with common usages, attract attention, as the two graceful similes by Birenda Bir Bikram Shah Dev at his coronation as king of Nepal illustrate: "I will be popular like the raindrop. I will be friendly like the sun."[30] Less delicate but equally striking is the metaphor of Felicia Lamport in her comparison of changes in lexicography: "The old rigid corset of correctness has given way to a flexible girdle of usage."[31]

Sometimes authors create vivid, forceful effects by sustaining a metaphor throughout a passage. Of special interest to students of speech communication are the two following examples, the first of which uses the human body as the base for the metaphor and the second of which employs fire as its foundation:

Style, like the human body, is then specially beautiful when, so to say, the veins are not prominent, and the bones cannot be counted, but when a healthy and sound blood fills the limbs, and shows itself in the muscles, and the very sinews become beautiful under a ruddy glow and graceful outline.[32]

Demosthenes' strength is usually in rugged sublimity, Cicero's in diffusion. Our countryman with his violence, yes, and his speed, his force,

---

[28] Aristotle *Poetics* 21.1457^{b}7–9.
[29] Aristotle *Rhetoric* iii.4.1406^{b}20–23.
[30] "Inter Alia," *Verbatim*, 2 (May 1975), 3.
[31] Felicia Lamport, "Dictionaries: Our Language Right or Wrong," *Harper's* 219 (September 1959), 49.
[32] Cornelius Tacitus, *The Dialogue on Oratory*, trans. Alfred Church and William Broadribb (London: Macmillan, 1911), p. 171.

his terrific power of rhetoric, burns, as it were, and scatters everything before him, and may therefore be compared to a flash of lightning or a thunderbolt. Cicero seems to me like a widespread conflagration, rolling along and devouring all around it: his is a strong and steady fire, its flames duly distributed, now here, now there, and fed by relays of fuel.[33]

Hyperbole This device is one of exaggeration. "He hit the ball a mile." "He was so quick that he could turn out the light and get into bed before the room was dark."

The opposite of hyperbole is understatement, a device said to be characteristic of the British. "It was a bit of a rough go."

Personification In this figure the speaker gives human characteristics to an inanimate concept. Ascribed to William Gibbs McAdoo is this description of Warren G. Harding: "[His oratory] left the impression of an army of pompous phrases moving over the landscape in search of an idea."[34]

A lengthy example of personification, only a part of which appears below, is George Campbell's exposition of the differences between probability and plausibility:

These two qualities, therefore, PROBABILITY and PLAUSIBILITY, I shall call sister-graces, daughter of the same father *Experience*. . . . The principal companion and favourite of the first is *Truth,* but whether *Truth* or *Fiction* share most in the favour of the second it were often difficult to say. Both are naturally well-disposed, and even friendly to *Virtue,* but the elder is by much the more steady of the two; the younger, though perhaps not less capable of doing good, is more easily corrupted, and hath sometimes basely turned procuress to *Vice*. Though rivals, they have a sisterly affection to each other, and love to be together. The elder, sensible that there are but few who can for any time relish her society alone, is generally anxious that her sister be of the party; the younger, conscious of her own superior talents in this respect, can more easily dispense with the other's company.[35]

Apostrophe This figure is an addressing of the dead as if living or of the inanimate as if a person. Examples: "Oh, great Cicero, what wisdom can you give to us now?" "Marble lips, let us hear once more that same message that you gave our people in that other troubled time!"

Metonymy The use of a concrete object to represent an abstraction can add vigor to an address. "The bottle was his downfall" is a common illustration. Example: "The voice of humanity issues from the shades of the

---

[33] Longinus *On the Sublime* 12.4.
[34] John D. Hicks, *Republican Ascendancy, 1921–1933* (New York: Harper & Row, 1960), p. 25.
[35] George Campbell, *The Philosophy of Rhetoric* (London: William Tegg, 1850), p. 85.

wilderness. It exclaims that while one hand is held up to reject this Treaty, the other grasps a tomahawk."[36]

Synecdoche The use of the part for the whole, the whole for the part, the general for the special, and the special for the general are still other ways of adding variety. Example: "I long for a sail and to be on my way."

Irony Allan Karstetter describes eight kinds of irony,[37] but the most common variety is one in which the speaker uses a term whose literal and present meanings are the opposite. Mother, for example, is being ironic when she says to her small son on one of his bad days, "You are such a sweet boy."

In the following passage, attributed to Archie Bunker, it is the solution that is ironic: "If society is at fault that we got killers running around murdering innocent people, then it's simple. We turn the killer loose, give him a pension for life and shoot the rest of the city."[38]

SPECIAL KINDS OF SENTENCES

Besides figures, special kinds of sentences are resources for gaining greater clarity, emphasis, and interest. At times these special types come to mind spontaneously, but more often the communicator creates them during revision by deliberate effort.

Antithesis A favorite device of the Classical Greeks, antithesis adds emphasis both by stating the idea a second time and by strengthening attention through the balanced construction. John F. Kennedy's inaugural address, according to Carpenter and Seltzer, contains "some twenty-eight antitheses." Examples include the following: "Support any friend or oppose any foe"; "The many who are poor [and] the few who are rich"; "United, there is little we cannot do . . . Divided, there is little we can do"; and "Ask not what your country can do for you—ask what you can do for your country."[39]

Parallel Structure A technique that is very helpful in revision, parallelism consists of a series of three or more items, each of which begins with the same grammatic element. That is, the opening word or words of each item

---

[36] Fisher Ames, address to the United States House of Representatives, April 28, 1796, as cited in James C. Ching, "Fisher Ames' 'Tomahawk' Address," *Speech Monographs*, 30 (March 1963), 36.
[37] Allan Karstetter, "Toward a Theory of Rhetorical Irony," *Speech Monographs*, 31 (June 1964), 162–178.
[38] Norman Lear, *The Wit and Wisdom of Archie Bunker* (New York: Popular Library, 1972), p. 89.
[39] Ronald H. Carpenter and Robert V. Seltzer, "On Nixon's Kennedy Style," *Speaker and Gavel*, 7 (January 1970), 41.

may be an infinitive, a participle, a relative pronoun, or a preposition, but not a mixture of these. When a first draft contains a clumsy, confusing sentence, three remedial measures work more often than all others: omitting something, creating two or more sentences, and putting the ideas into parallel structure:

CLUMSY: Decoding depends on how one perceives the stimuli, and it is also a matter of values and beliefs along with the immediate frame of reference and whatever habits of thought a person has.
IMPROVED: Decoding depends on perceptions of the stimuli, on values and beliefs, on the immediate frame of reference, and on habits of thought.

The preceding example is a series of items beginning with the same preposition, *on*. Other illustrations of parallelism are the following:

(A series of infinitives) The major speech purposes since the days of Cicero have been to inform, to please, and to persuade.

(A series of participles) Working hard on his research, thinking through his ideas carefully, and adapting his presentation to the audience, Jonathan was well prepared.

(A series of noun elements) Successful infiltration required food for the peasants, whiskey for the soldiers, and bribes for the officials.

Periodic Sentence A natural construction is best for most sentences, but an occasional periodic sentence can add emphasis. In this usage the details are at the beginning and the words carrying the main thought are at the end:

LOOSE CONSTRUCTION: The businesslike introduction has become common because of the high cost of broadcast time, the rapid pace of the modern world, and the changing tastes in oratory.
PERIODIC: Because of the high cost of broadcast time, the rapid pace of the modern world, and the changing tastes in oratory, the businesslike introduction has become common.

Repetition of a Pattern Less famous than the "I have a dream" portion of the same speech, the passage that follows is further evidence of the fondness of Martin Luther King, Jr., for repetition:

We can never be satisfied as long as the Negro is the victim of the unspeakable horrors of police brutality. We can never be satisfied as long as our bodies, heavy with the fatigue of travel, cannot gain lodging in the motels of the highway and the hotels of the cities. We cannot be satisfied as long as the Negro's basic mobility is from a smaller ghetto to a larger one. We can never be satisfied as long as our children are stripped of their selfhood and robbed of their dignity by signs stating "For Whites Only."[40]

Alternation of Long and Short Sentences Example: "My campaign is going to be far different from the evasive, double-talk, 'motherhood-and-apple-pie' kind of speech that you are accustomed to hearing. I shall take a stand. I shall give straight answers."

Question Followed by an Answer Example:

Our foolishness shines in curious opposites when assessing our national characteristics. Generous? To a fault. Production genius? Anything from cranes to watch parts. Wasteful? In food, time and money! Destructive? Ouch! Look at our parks, our playgrounds, our roads! Friendly? To a fault. Complaining? Yes. Respectful? Not so you'd notice.[41]

Sentence Fragment The preceding passage illustrates the use of the sentence fragment as well as the sequence of question and answer. The following example is from a direct-mail advertisement for a magazine:

At this very moment, NEWSWEEK's lively, informative issues are bringing readers important news articles crammed with facts that can be of real help in these troubled times. Like how to make sure you avoid the high cost of credit. Or how to inflation-proof your income tax. Or how to choose the best-qualified doctor for your family.

OTHER STYLISTIC AND RHETORICAL DEVICES

Some devices, including those in this third group, are hard to classify. They are common, nevertheless, in the discourse of effective communicators.

Alliteration A self-conscious, contrived device, alliteration makes a sequence of words easy to remember. In this century the prominent American who used alliteration the most was Warren G. Harding. The following passage also illustrates antithesis:

---

[40] Martin Luther King, Jr., address delivered in Washington, D.C., on August 28, 1963, as published in Wil A. Linkugel, R. R. Allen, and Richard L. Johannesen, eds., *Contemporary American Speeches* (Belmont, Cal.: Wadsworth Publishing Co., 1972), p. 291.

[41] Louise Bushnell, address at a sectional meeting of the National Association of Manufacturers, Palm Beach, Fla., February 11, 1973, as published in *Vital Speeches of the Day*, 39 (April 1, 1973), 372.

America's present need is not heroics, but healing; not nostrums, but normalcy; not revolution, but restoration; not agitation, but adjustment; not surgery, but serenity; not the dramatic, but the dispassionate; not experiment, but equipoise; not submergence in internationality, but sustainment in triumphant nationality.[42]

A second example is the following excerpt from a speech by Lyndon B. Johnson on the Middle East: "This is a time not for malice, but for magnanimity; not for propaganda, but for patience; not for vituperation, but for vision."[43]

Rhyme and Rhythm Like alliteration, these devices make ideas easy to remember; they also can add a touch of eloquence that reflects favorably on the speaker and that is pleasing to listeners. The following example consists of two versions of the same thought:

EARLY VERSION: In charity to all mankind, bearing no malice or ill-will to any human being, and even compassionating those who hold in bondage their fellow-men, not knowing what they do.[44]
LATER VERSION: With malice toward none, with charity for all; with firmness in the right as God gives us to see the right.[45]

An example of effective rhythm from this century is the following passage from Winston Churchill, who drafted sentences of delicacy and beauty as well as ones of energy and power:

Good night, then: sleep to gather strength for the morning. For the morning will come. Brightly will it shine on the brave and true, kindly upon all who suffer for the cause, glorious upon the tombs of heroes. Thus will shine the dawn.[46]

The preceding lines also illustrate parallelism and the use of sentences of varied length.

Concreteness and Specificity The impressiveness of a description, whether it pertains to the effects of famine, the consequences of air pollution, or the beauty of a rainbow, depends primarily on the use of concrete

---

[42] Warren G. Harding, as cited in Edwin A. Roberts, Jr., *Elections 1964* (Silver Springs, Md.: The National Observer, 1964), p. 144.
[43] Lyndon B. Johnson, as cited in Harry McPherson, "Beyond Words," *Atlantic Monthly*, 229 (April 1972), 44.
[44] John Quincy Adams, letter to A. Bronson, July 30, 1838, as cited in John Bartlett, comp., *Familiar Quotations*, ed. Emily M. Beck (Boston: Little, Brown and Company, 1968), pp. 502–503.
[45] Abraham Lincoln, "Second Inaugural Address," as cited in John Bartlett, comp., *Familiar Quotations*, ed. Emily M. Beck (Boston: Little, Brown and Company, 1968), p. 640.
[46] Winston Churchill, "To the French People," an address delivered on October 21, 1940, as published in Winston Churchill, *Blood, Sweat, and Tears* (New York: G. P. Putnam's, 1941), p. 403.

words and specific details. The following is from a news story on the first outdoor atomic explosion:

> . . . a great ball of fire about a mile in diameter, changing colors as it kept shooting upward, from deep purple to orange, expanding, growing bigger, rising as it was expanding, an elemental force freed from its bonds after being chained for billions of years.[47]

Another use of specificity is to add emphasis. "From Maine to California" is more memorable than "everywhere," and Churchill's well known "from Stettin in the Baltic" was more forceful than "all across Europe." Instead of saying "every citizen," Huey Long once said, "the lawyer, doctor, accountant, architect, dentist, grocer, baker, and candlestickmaker, who cannot make a living . . . ."[48]

Besides greater emphasis, the specific word, according to one research study, also increases comprehension. The reason for this, the authors speculate, is that an abstract noun has more referents than one that is specific. Thus, it gives the decoder more opportunities to make wrong choices.[49]

Labels and Signposts A word or a brief, catchy phrase is easier to remember than a sentence. Example:

LABELS FOR THE THREE MAIN POINTS: My speech will set forth the advantages that this proposal will have to three groups: *the consumer, the taxpayer,* and *the local jobseeker.*
HARDER TO REMEMBER: This proposal is going to bring lower prices to those who purchase goods, and it will be a pleasant surprise to the taxpayer and a benefit to those who are out of work.

Signposts are helpful because they show the direction a speech is going. They identify the beginning of a coordinate point ("my second reason is"), they indicate relationships ("for example"; "the result will be"), and they forecast new sections ("now to conclude"). Other common signposts, or transitional expressions, include the following: "third"; "in further proof of"; "because of this"; "a similar instance"; "on the other hand"; "despite this"; "therefore" and "finally."

Associational Devices Some devices facilitate memory by providing one item to which each point in a series is related. A common example is the acronym, a coinage in which the first letters of a title spell a word. Thus,

---

[47] William L. Laurence, *New York Times,* September 26, 1945, p. 16.
[48] Huey Long, address delivered on January 19, 1935, as cited in Ernest G. Bormann, "A Rhetorical Analysis of the National Radio Broadcasts of Senator Huey Pierce Long," *Speech Monographs,* 24 (November 1957), 253.
[49] G. Wayne Shamo and John R. Bittner, "Recall as a Function of Language Style," *Southern Speech Communication Journal,* 38 (Winter 1972), 181–187.

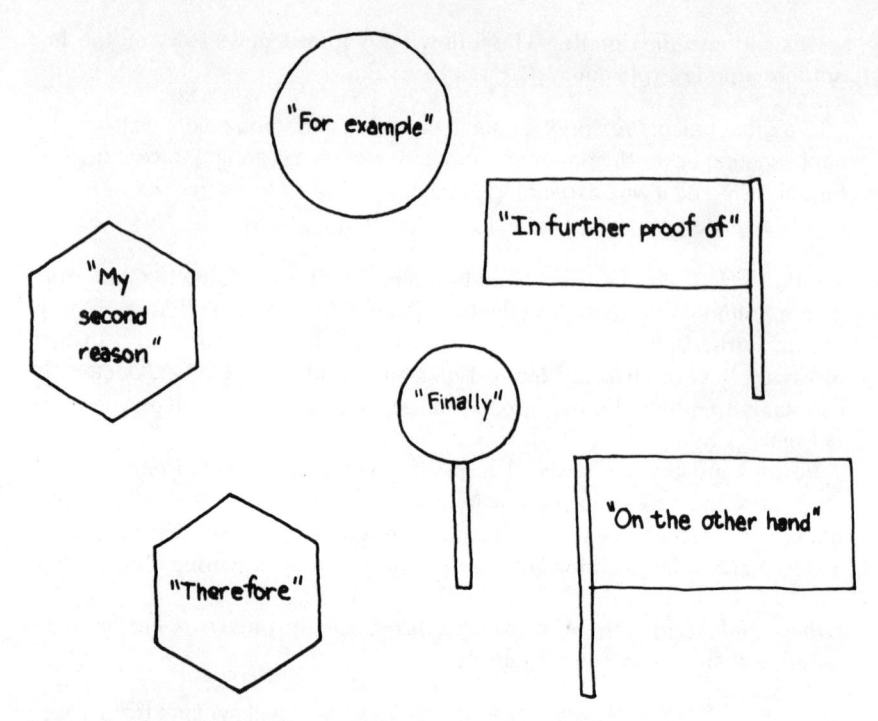

Skillful communicators help their listeners by using signposts that indicate the relation of the new point to the preceding one.

the acronym *NOW* makes it easy to remember that the name of the group is the "National Organization of Women."

Epigrams Terse, memorable statements have been an important part of rhetoric since the Classical period, when the memorization of *sententiae* was part of the schoolboy's education. The following examples come from the speeches of Eugene V. Debs, a major socialist leader in the early part of this century:

Character ought to count for more than cash.

Men who do nothing get all. Men who do all get nothing.

The rich get the passes . . . but the poor pay full fare or walk.

We must dethrone the dollar and enthrone the man.

The government is a repair shop for wrecked railroads.[50]

---

[50] Eugene V. Debs, as cited in Bernard J. Brommel, "Eugene V. Debs: The Agitator as Speaker," *Central States Speech Journal,* 20 (Fall 1969), 210.

Direct address Such expressions as "fellow students" and "ladies and gentlemen" may be preplanned, but many speakers insert them when they note that attention is waning. Example: "My friends, let us stop for a moment to see exactly what this proposed change would do to your own pocketbooks."

Emphatic position The word(s) stating the principal idea should be at either the beginning or the end.

CORRECT: A person perceived as trustworthy is likely to receive high credibility ratings.
IMPROVED: Trustworthiness contributes to high ratings on credibility.
CORRECT: If a person is going to have an effective style, he must revise his work.
IMPROVED: The source of an effective style is revision.
CORRECT: He was a speaker of great effectiveness in a number of respects.
IMPROVED: He was a speaker of great effectiveness.

Three techniques that are useful for putting the main idea in an emphatic position are these: (1) Recast so that the main idea is a noun rather than a verbal element (see the first two examples above); (2) delete unnecessary words (see the third example); and (3) alter the word order.

CONCLUSION

Why should the student who wishes to be a clear, effective communicator be concerned about language? What functions does language serve in the communication process? How can one increase verbal skills? Such questions as these have determined the content of this chapter. Seven statements summarize the basic ideas:

1. Responsible communication requires skillful language usage as well as worthwhile content and a good sender-receiver relation. The language choices of the speaker determine largely the clarity, the emotional power, and the pleasingness of the communication act.

2. Verbal language is the principal medium by which the sender encodes a message for transmission to the receiver, and it is largely this set of verbal stimuli that the latter decodes.

3. Clarity depends on the familiarity of words, the context, similarities in background between sender and receiver, the level of abstraction, and sentence structure.

4. Many words and phrases have emotional shadings that affect the impact on the listener and that contribute to perceptions of the speaker's credibility.

5. The total quality of the communicator's style is likely to exert an influence beyond that of the single word or phrase. Three desirable styles, each suitable for certain circumstances, are the scholarly, technical, and dignified; the colloquial and familiar; and the elegant and expressive. Each of these has subvarieties, and each has an undesirable counterpart.

6. In producing the desired effect, the speaker can use a great many stylistic devices.

7. In the long run the student can apply information and advice on language usage to advantage by gradually building better stylistic habits; at once he or she can revise first drafts of speeches with increased skill.

". . . it *does* matter how something is said," Donald C. Bryant wrote; ". . . that how a thing is said, in fact," he continued, "is an important part of what is said; that the selection and management of language—including the utterance of it—make the final meaning of the message; that they incarnate the thought and the intention; that they give form and ultimate significance to what is transmitted and received."[51] This statement does not recognize the importance of the transactional factor in communication, but otherwise it is a clear and eloquent statement of principles basic to this textbook.

Those who are serious about increasing their powers of communication, therefore, become students of verbal language. They try to improve their habits, and through revision they strive to increase the clarity and the effectiveness of each message. This emphasis on verbal language is applicable to all forms of communication—to conversation, conference, discussion, and public address.

PROBLEMS AND EXERCISES

1. Select a pair of groups which are likely to differ in the associations they make when they hear certain words. Among the possibilities are management-labor, teacher-student, parent-adolescent, and whites-blacks. Select five words that seem likely to elicit differences, and interview three representatives of each of the contrasting groups. Either tape-record the conversation or take detailed notes on the meanings that each interviewee holds. Prepare an oral report on your findings.

[51] Donald C. Bryant, "Critical Responsibilities of the Speech-English Program," *Speech Teacher*, 10 (November 1961), 277.

2. Divide the class into two teams for a contest on levels of abstraction. The leadoff speaker should call out a low-level noun that names a person or an object, and the first member of the opposing team should give a noun that is at the next higher level. The sides should alternate until a member of one team cannot continue, thus scoring one point against his or her group. A member of the losing side should continue the game by naming a different low-level noun.

3. Prepare an oral report on the information in a book on general semantics on dating, indexing, and other special devices for improving the use of language.

4. Write a paper of 150 to 250 words defining an abstract concept, such as *love, justice,* or *freedom.* Form a small group with others in the class, exchange papers, and through discussion try to arrive at a consensus on the meaning of each term.

5. Examine the language in a printed draft of a speech by someone who often is described as a demagogue or an agitator. This person may be a contemporary or a historic figure. Give special attention to god-terms, devil-terms, intensity, and opinionation. Record examples and make generalizations. In a discussion group of five or six members of your class, share your findings.

6. Compare the language in an article in a popular magazine, such as *Reader's Digest,* with that in a paper in a learned journal, such as *Communication Monographs.* Decide which stylistic level each uses, and select examples that justify your judgment. Analyze the two examples further in an effort to learn whether the general impressions result from word choice, sentence length, or some other factor.

7. Rewrite a common saying, such as "Speak softly and carry a big stick," in three of the six styles discussed in the chapter. Other possible sayings are "Little strokes fell great oaks"; "Time is money"; "God helps them that help themselves"; "A word to the wise is enough"; and "A rolling stone gathers no moss."

8. Comment on stylistic features in each of the following passages:

   a. There it is:
   Under God, a new birth of freedom;
   A new understanding of it;
   A new and deeper dedication to it.
   With such a rebirth within you and me, and within our beloved Party, we shall deserve to be entrusted by the people with the awful responsibilities of governing this great land. And they will turn to us and our country will be saved.
   And now let us get to work![52]

   b. Richard III is more *humanly terrible;* Iago more *devilishly perfect.* Richard *loves nothing* human; Iago hates *everything good.* . . . Richard is *fire;* Iago, *ice.* Richard III is more *objective;* Iago more *subjective.* . . . Richard III mounts the *throne of England* on a score of dead bodies; Iago wins the *throne of Hell* in three strides. The *conscience* of Richard wakes from its swoon; Iago has *no conscience.*[53]

---

[52] Walter Judd, as cited in Carl A. Pitt, "Judd's Keynote Speech," *Southern Speech Journal,* 33 (Summer 1968), 287.
[53] Robert M. LaFollette, an oration delivered at Beloit, Wis., on May 2, 1879, as cited in Ronald H. Carpenter, "The Rhetorical Genesis of Style in the 'Frontier Hypothesis' of Frederick Jackson Turner," *Southern Speech Communication Journal,* 37 (Spring 1972), 245.

c. . . . in short, they are, to use the emphatic language of Mr. Burke, a set of men whose ledger is their bible, whose counting-house is their church, and whose money is their God.[54]

d. It is currently proposed that necessary military action required to ascertain the point of maximum allowable hostile penetration at such predetermined delineation be initiated and maintained even if such action should necessitate the period required for its accomplishment extending through the conclusion of the first quarter of fiscal year 1865.[55]

e. An important factor in relation to safety precautions is first and foremost giving to workmen some kind of clear and definite instruction along the line of not coming into the radioactive area in connection with their work.[56]

f. You see a ladder—the social ladder—up which you wish to see that poor, depressed, and unfortunate . . . labourer ascend gradually. You would rejoice to see him getting up a few steps and becoming a farmer, even though it were in a small way, or becoming the owner of a piece of land. But you find that six or eight feet up, every stave in the ladder is broken out and from his low position he has no chance of ascending.[57]

REFERENCES

Benjamin, Robert L. *Semantics and Language Analysis.* Indianapolis: The Bobbs-Merrill Co., 1970.

Bock, E. Hope, and James H. Pitts. "The Effect of Three Levels of Black Dialect on Perceived Speaker Image," *Speech Teacher,* 24 (September 1975), 218–225.

Bradac, James J., Catherine W. Konsky, and Robert A. Davies. "Two Studies of the Effects of Linguistic Diversity Upon Judgments of Communicator Attributes and Message Effectiveness," *Communication Monographs,* 43 (March 1976), 70–79.

Gibson, James W., *et al.* "A Quantitative Examination of Differences and Similarities in Written and Spoken Messages," *Speech Monographs,* 33 (November 1966), 444–451.

Greenberg, Bradley S. "The Effects of Language Intensity Modification on Perceived Verbal Aggressiveness," *Communication Monographs,* 43 (June 1976), 130–139.

Hill, Timothy A. "An Experimental Study of the Relationship Between Opinionated Leadership and Small Group Consensus," *Communication Monographs,* 43 (August 1976), 246–257.

---

[54] Mr. Ferrand, M.P., *Hansard,* Third Series, 60:420.
[55] John B. Haney, "Colonel Blunderbuss' Battle Cry," *Journal of Communication,* 7 (Spring 1957), 25.
[56] Herman M. Weisman, "Problems in Technical Style, Diction, and Exposition," in *Proceedings of the 1959 Institute in Technical and Industrial Communications,* eds. Herman M. Weisman and Roy C. Nelson (Fort Collins, Colo.: Institute in Technical and Industrial Communications, 1960), p. 32.
[57] John Bright, as cited in Loren Reid, "John Bright: The Orator as Teacher," *Southern Speech Communication Journal,* 41 (Fall 1975), 53.

Infante, Dominic A. "Effects of Opinionated Language on Communicator Image and in Conferring Resistance to Persuasion," *Western Speech*, 39 (Spring 1975), 112–119.

Infante, Dominic A. "Forewarnings in Persuasion: Effects of Opinionated Language and Forewarner and Speaker Authoritativeness," *Western Speech*, 37 (Summer 1973), 185–195.

Jefferson, Pat. " 'Stokely's Cool': Style," *Today's Speech*, 16 (September 1968), 19–24.

Jordan, William J., Lyndia L. Flanagan, and Ronald W. Wineinger. "Novelty and Recall Effects of Animate and Inanimate Metaphorical Discourse," *Central States Speech Journal*, 26 (Spring 1975), 29–33.

Loftus, Elizabeth. "Reconstructing Memory: The Incredible Eyewitness," *Psychology Today*, 8 (December 1974), 116–119.

McEwen, William J., and Bradley S. Greenberg. "The Effects of Message Intensity on Receiver Evaluations of Source, Message and Topic," *Journal of Communication*, 20 (December 1970), 340–350.

Mehrley, R. Samuel, and James C. McCroskey. "Opinionated Statements and Attitude Intensity as Predictors of Attitude Change and Source Credibility," *Speech Monographs*, 37 (March 1970), 47–52.

Miller, Gerald R., and John Baseheart. "Source Trustworthiness, Opinionated Statements, and Response to Persuasive Communication," *Speech Monographs*, 36 (March 1969), 1–7.

Miller, Gerald R., and Jon Lobe. "Opinionated Language, Open- and Closed-Mindedness and Response to Persuasive Communications," *Journal of Communication*, 17 (December 1967), 333–341.

Mulac, Anthony. "Effects of Obscene Language Upon Three Dimensions of Listener Attitude," *Communication Monographs*, 43 (November 1976), 300–307.

Shamo, G. Wayne, and John R. Bittner. "Recall as a Function of Language Style," *Southern Speech Communication Journal*, 38 (Winter 1972), 181–187.

12
THE MEDIUM: COMMUNICATING NONVERBALLY

After studying this chapter the reader should be able to do the following:

Convey nonverbally such an assigned message as "showing approval" or "indicating deep conviction" so that 75 percent of the students in the class make the right interpretation

Perceive as a receiver at least three of the four thoughts or feelings that a communicator sends nonverbally

Produce a prospectus for the visual aids to be used in a ten-minute speech to a campus or community group

Create a set of visuals that will be easy to see and whose content will be clear

A sex goddess in a play popular on the dinner-theater circuits asserted confidently that she could break down the resistance of a "proper" husband by appealing to all his senses. The stage and the screen, as well as the world generally, provide many examples of hand gestures, raised eyebrows, and conspicuous vocal inflections that others in a group have no trouble understanding. "Meet me outside," "be quiet," and "move over" are messages that require no words, and sports spectators interpret readily numerous signals of basketball and football officials. Somewhat different are the finger signs of baseball catchers and the elaborate gyrations of third-base coaches, for their intention is to communicate meanings to team members but to no one else.

Besides the nonverbal cues that communicators create with their voices and bodies, there are a great many visual aids that speakers use to clarify and emphasize their verbal symbols. The first part of this chapter is on nonverbal cues: research findings, principles, and practices; the second is on the presentation that combines words and visuals. The outcome of any communication event, whether a speech, an interview, a discussion, or a conversation, depends in part on the soundness of the sender's choices among the available nonverbal resources and on the skill with which he or she follows up on these choices.

NONVERBAL CUES: RESEARCH FINDINGS, PRINCIPLES, AND PRACTICES

The origin of much modern thought and research on nonverbal communication has been the observation that most individual cues are classifiable under the headings *kinesics, paralinguistics,* and *proxemics.* All three terms pertain to stimuli that every communicator creates, unknowingly or intentionally, and that he or she can manage within certain limitations imposed by habits and abilities.

KINESICS AND PARALINGUISTICS

Usually defined as the study of body motion and facial expression as media of communication, *kinesics* encompasses a wide range of meaningful stimuli. Body tensions, scowls, raised eyebrows, flickering gaze, a curled-down lower lip, nods, clenched fists, a pointed finger, thumbs down, an upheld "O" or "V," a firm handshake, a wave, and an upheld fist are examples of actions or poses that communicate approval, friendliness, fear, hatred, passionate desire, loneliness, defiance, timidity, and a variety of commands and bits of information.

Paralinguistics refers to pitch changes, hesitations, sighs, breaks in vocalization, breathiness, staccato rhythm, rapidity, subdued volume, and all other voiced noises that the speaker produces and that the listener can hear. By paralinguistic cues the young woman or man knows whether "I love you" expresses devotion, casual admiration, or flattery. Through both vocal and kinesic signs, customers sense whether a sales representative is trustworthy and poker players estimate whether a fellow gambler has a strong hand or is bluffing. In varied situations speakers add emphasis, create humor, or simulate folksiness; and listeners make judgments about such traits as competence, self-assurance, and sincerity.

A common type of research on paralinguistics has been the experiment in which listeners record their impressions of speakers who are reciting the alphabet, a sequence of numbers, or nonsense syllables. Representative of these studies is one in which eight speakers expressed ten different feelings by repeating the alphabet. Thirty persons tried to identify the emotions in each of the ten instances, and they were correct significantly more often than would happen by chance.[1] A great many other experiments have confirmed the conclusion that paralinguistic cues convey meanings.

PROXEMICS

By one definition *proxemics* "is the study of how man communicates through structuring microspace—the distance that man consciously or unconsciously maintains between himself and another person while relating physically to others with whom he is interacting."[2] Research studies in this area have produced a number of interesting results:

1. People from Latin American countries stood closer together than did North Americans.[3]

2. ". . . the male-female groups interacted most proximally, the female-female groups were intermediate, and the male-male groups were most distant."[4] According to a second study, two males established greater distance in an interview than did any pair including at least one woman.[5]

3. Friends placed themselves closer together than strangers.[6]

4. Two to four feet was the normal distance for the subjects to stand apart. A lesser distance had a marked effect on heart rate and on verbal responses by the participants.[7]

---

[1] Joel Davitz and Lois Jean Davitz, "The Communication of Feelings by Content-free Speech," *Journal of Communication*, 9 (March 1959), 6–13.
[2] Robert F. Forston and Charles U. Larson, "The Dynamics of Space," *Journal of Communication*, 18 (June 1968), 109.
[3] Edward T. Hall, "The Language of Space," *Landscape*, 10 (Autumn 1960), 41–44; J. C. Baxter, "Interpersonal Spacing in Natural Settings," *Sociometry*, 33 (December 1970), 444–456.
[4] Baxter, pp. 444–456.
[5] Teresa J. Rosegrant and James C. McCroskey, "The Effects of Race and Sex on Proxemic Behavior in an Interview Setting," *Southern Speech Communication Journal*, 40 (Summer 1975), 408–419.
[6] Kenneth B. Little, "Personal Space," *Journal of Experimental Social Psychology*, 1 (August 1960), 237–247.
[7] Steven J. Finando, "The Effects of Distance Norm Violation on Heart Rate and Length of Verbal Response," Ph.D. diss., Florida State, 1973.

Speakers, even though well intentioned, can create discomfort in others by standing too close. (Mark Godfrey/Magnum)

5. Reactions to the invasion of personal space included moving away from the experimenter, shifting positions, and moving purses and coats so that they would serve as barriers.[8]

6. Placing two persons closer together than normal resulted in shorter glances and a lesser total amount of eye contact. These results were the most pronounced when the two participants were of the opposite sexes.[9]

7. Seating two persons side by side was harmful to social interaction.[10] According to another study, more conversation occurred when persons sat around the corner from one another than when they sat opposite or side by side.[11]

HABITS AND CHOICES

Why is it of practical value for the student to know research findings and scholarly theories of nonverbal communication? As Cicero wrote, ". . . it

---

[8] Nancy Jo Felipe and Robert Sommer, "Invasions of Personal Space," *Social Problems,* 14 (Fall 1966), 206–214.
[9] Michael Argyle and Janet Dean, "Eye-Contact, Distance and Affiliation," *Sociometry,* 28 (September 1965), 289–304.
[10] Albert Mehrabian and Shirley G. Diamond, "Effects of Furniture Arrangement, Props, and Personality on Social Interaction," *Journal of Personality and Social Psychology,* 20 (October 1971), 18–30.
[11] Robert Sommer, "Studies in Personal Space," *Sociometry,* 22 (September 1959), 247–260.

is possible by mere force of nature to say many striking things; yet, as they will after all be nothing more than so many lucky hits, we shall not be able to repeat them at our pleasure."[12] So it is with nonverbal cues; the untrained speaker, producing the nonverbal cues that are habitual, *at times* will use kinesic, paralinguistic, and proxemic signs that reinforce the words, whereas the informed communicator *with some regularity* can make strategic choices.

The following are examples of applications of research: (1) Knowing that hesitancy reduces ratings for competence, one can try to eliminate noticeable breaks from delivery. (2) Since the position at a table affects interaction, one can strengthen the likelihood of being influential by sitting around the corner from the probable conference leader. (3) Knowing that a lack of eye contact suggests timidity and even shiftiness to an Anglo personnel director, the black or the Latin or the Indian can try to overcome this habit of avoiding the gaze of others. (4) Conversely, understanding the nonverbal habits of an ethnic group, the interviewer can try to be tolerant in interpreting the behavior of a minority applicant.

As with the verbal medium, communication through gestures, spacing, inflectional patterns, and other signs is clear and effective only when sender and receiver make the same interpretations. For this reason problems are most likely to occur in cross-cultural situations. When the Latin stands close, the Anglo is uncomfortable and resents the seeming familiarity and pushiness; but when the Anglo backs away, the Latin interprets the action as coldness and even rejection. In some cultures it is conventional for men to kiss each other on the cheeks, but in other societies the same action seems strange and offensive. Whereas bowing is a common means of showing respect in the Orient, it is likely in the United States to seem mocking and ironic. Thus, communicators not only must control the cues that they produce but also must understand how the receiver is likely to interpret them.

NONVERBAL CUES AS SUGGESTION

The listener's perceptions, as stated previously, are critical to communicative success, and often they are hard to explain. Most students have had the experience of feeling distrust or dislike, confidence or attraction, without knowing the reason. The explanation often is that a person responds during the same time period to two sets of cues, whose messages are inconsistent. "How delighted I am to see you," says the hostess; but the expression in her eyes and the nuances in her voice are saying, "I'm surprised that you dropped in, and I wish that you had not come." The process of communicating ideas and impressions through cues that are outside the center of the receiver's attention is *suggestion*.

[12] Cicero *Brutus* ch. 29.

To generalize, at the same time that a communicatee's attention is primarily on the ideas that someone is verbalizing, he or she also is receiving and storing kinesic, paralinguistic, and proxemic cues. Thus, at the end of a conversation or a speech the respondent senses that the other person is tired, troubled, deceitful, well informed, trustworthy, or sincere. These "feelings," whose sources are identifiable only through deliberate analysis, are best understood by thinking about the three possible levels in the sender-receiver relation.

The first level, the center of attention, usually is the sequence of ideas that the communicator is verbalizing. Listeners know that they are hearing these words; and if asked what stimuli they have been receiving, they usually summarize this content.

The second level, the marginal fields of attention, consists of stimuli that are loud enough or visible enough for the respondent to perceive them, provided that he or she chooses to do so; when primary attention is on other stimuli, however, there is little awareness of these marginal cues, which are the sources of suggestion.

At the third level are stimuli so fast or so faint that the human senses cannot receive them. Some postal carriers, for example, carry a whistle whose sound is too high a pitch for human beings to hear but that dogs find very irritating. Although the mass media sometimes carry sensational stories on the successful use of subliminal stimuli to sell soft drinks or to control behavior in some other way, the research of reputable psychologists indicates that signals below the level of perception have no impact.

The appreciation of nonverbal stimuli as suggestion helps to explain the importance of these cues to the communication of meanings, feelings, and attributes of the speaker. They are not, however, the only sources of marginal effects, for the communicator's words also may carry messages through indirection. "I am a tolerant person" is a direct claim, but the sender can produce the same judgment through the suggestive process of telling a personal story that shows broad-mindedness. Such indirection, whether verbal or nonverbal, is strategic in some situations, for at times a direct approach evokes antagonism or sounds conceited. Similarly, saying that one is an authority may be less tactful than presenting a series of facts that leads others to a favorable conclusion.

Countersuggestion, which is the unintentional production of bad impressions, is a danger that one should guard against. A political candidate on television must ignore an itchy scalp lest a scratching motion be construed as uncertainty, and no matter how uncomfortable it is under the studio lights he or she must remain calm and collected. Beginning speakers often betray their inexperience by awkward and shifting posture, by random hand movements, and by a nervousness in fussing with notes and file cards. They sometimes suggest a lack of competence by unwise attempts at modesty or at attaining common ground. "I'm like you in that I'd rather not be here this evening, and like you I'm no great expert on what's going on in

Africa. But I've got to give a speech, so here I am." Probable reaction: "If you're no expert, why should I listen?"

Happier examples also are to be found; and improved skills in communication through suggestion, both verbal and nonverbal, are possible. Although written long ago, the so-called "Laws of Suggestion" of H. L. Hollingworth remain practical:

1. Be natural, spontaneous, and "artless." Lead the listener to think that the conclusion or the plan is his own.

2. Be forceful and vivid, especially when the suggested act is in harmony with the receiver's habits and tendencies.

3. Be positive. Tell the listener what he should do rather than what he should not.

4. Capitalize on whatever prestige you have, and try to enhance it.

5. Avoid anything that will arouse resistance. Do not make appeals that are counter to lifelong habits, firmly fixed moral feelings, or sacred relationships.

6. Repeat the request or the proposal several times.

7. Try to keep rival ideas from coming to mind, and minimize the number of choices.[13]

IMPROVEMENTS IN THE USE OF NONVERBAL CUES

How does one improve in the use of kinesic, paralinguistic, and proxemic stimuli, in habits and choices, and in the harnessing of suggestion? Individuals, of course, differ in their nonverbal communicative skills, and one research experiment found that females are better than males in expressing their attitudes so that observers can make accurate judgments.[14]

Both men and women, however, can improve over a time period such as a quarter or a semester. To do so requires self-analysis, goal setting, specific efforts, and an intellectual grasp of the nature of nonverbal stimuli. The following are six guidelines for improvement.

1. Both be and appear to be sincere. Ethics as well as practical reasons dictate that speakers should say what they believe, that they should speak the truth as their own powers and limitations permit them to know it. Earnestness and intellectual honesty are partial safeguards against the unintended production of paralinguistic and kinesic cues that belie the verbal message.

---

[13] Adapted from H. L. Hollingworth, *The Psychology of the Audience* (New York: American Book Co., 1935), pp. 142–144. Used by permission of the American Book Company.

[14] Joe Ayres, "Observers' Judgements of Audience Members' Attitudes," *Western Speech*, 39 (Winter 1975), 40–50.

Being sincere, according to several research studies,[15] is not enough. Respondents react primarily to whether the behavior that they observe conforms to their preexisting stereotypes for sincerity. A steady gaze, thus, may have more to do with judgments of trustworthiness than does the consistency of verbalized views with actual beliefs.

So, be sincere, but also know how to manage yourself.

2. *Have a good mental attitude during the speech, discussion, or interview.* "How do I do that?" argues the beginner. "I'm scared to death, and you tell me to have a good mental attitude. As if all I had to do was wave a wand! It isn't that easy!" The preceding statement is the truth, but not the whole truth. Managing stage fright, as Chapter 10 indicates, is possible; and although many persons never feel entirely comfortable when called on to speak, they can reduce the fear and, more importantly, they can control themselves.

Realistically, then, what can beginning speakers hope to achieve? They can gain a feeling of being ready. By giving attention to grooming, position, and posture, they can think of themselves as looking like speakers. By planning and rehearsing opening lines, they can go to the lectern with the knowledge that they know how they will begin. By careful preparation of the entire address, they can start with confidence in the worth of what they are going to say. "Here is an opportunity, and I'm ready for it" should be the attitude. Such positiveness can lead to better muscle tone, a firmer step, a higher level of eye contact, and other signs that elicit favorable impressions.

The preceding comments apply to all types of communication situations. No one should drift into an interview or a conference without advance preparation. Each participant should study the topic, consider the positions to take, and decide on the roles to play.

3. *Appreciate the special opportunities that nonverbal stimuli afford.* "In consciously seeking to relate to the poor," Allen H. Merriam writes, "Gandhi intuitively recognized the persuasive function of costume. The *dhoti* reflected Gandhi's humility and lack of official governmental position."[16] "Spinning, like wearing a loin-cloth," Merriam continues, "formed a means of nonverbal identification."[17]

Students, too, through astute choices in grooming, gestures, and body movements can use nonverbal cues for heightened clarity and power. A tender touch on the shoulder can express sympathy better than a fine speech, and a firm handshake with a look straight in the eye can show

---

[15] For a summary of these see Wayne N. Thompson, *The Process of Persuasion* (New York: Harper & Row, 1975), pp. 72–73.
[16] Allen H. Merriam, "Symbolic Action in India: Gandhi's Nonverbal Persuasion," *Quarterly Journal of Speech*, 61 (October 1975), 302.
[17] *Ibid.*, p. 304.

dependability better than words. The taciturn, true-blue character in the movie of the Old West is not necessarily an exaggeration: actions can do more than words to characterize.

One interesting and unusual example of a speaker's choice of a nonverbal strategy rather than verbal is Mrs. Madalyn Murray O'Hair's use of laughter:

> Perhaps most interesting was Mrs. O'Hair's use of directed laughter, neither casual nor accidental. She maintains that she stumbled across the real effectiveness of directed laughter three years ago when she was "debating" with a Catholic priest and wanted most of all to establish that she put absolutely no stock in his argument for Christianity and redemption. At the highest point of confrontation and seriousness she looked straight at the priest and laughed. The effect was substantial; seriousness was destroyed, the opponent was upset, and Mrs. O'Hair had "said" with a nonverbal gesture, that there are people who do not take these ideas to be meaningful or true. She employed the same tactic regularly in the exchange with McIntire, and gained flustered responses from him.[18]

Turning one's back, walking out the door, slamming a book shut, and upsetting an enemy's drink in a saloon are additional examples of actions whose emphatic power exceeds that of words.

4. *Conform to the expectations of the audience.* What the audience expects depends on their own backgrounds, on the occasion, and on the communicator's status. One major presidential candidate lost votes when he used crude language before factory workers; "he did not sound like a president."

Similarly, audiences expect preachers to look and sound like members of the clergy, doctors to look and sound like doctors, college deans to look and sound like educators, and students to look and sound youthful. The degree of leeway within these constraints is large, and within limits violations of the stereotypes can be helpful. Humor, according to one experiment, is of the greatest value when the speaker has been perceived as "aloof."[19] This principle, applied to the student, means that one can seem neat, informed, thoughtful, and responsible without dressing and acting like a grandparent.

5. *Observe Aristotle's "golden mean" in the use of nonverbal symbols.* Not too casual in grooming, but not too formal; not too sloppy in posture, but not too rigid; not constant gesturing, but not complete inactivity; not an

---

[18] Lee Hudson, "Belting the Bible: Madalyn Murray O'Hair vs. Fundamentalism," *Western Speech*, 36 (Fall 1972), 236.
[19] David R. Mettee, Edward S. Hrelec, and Paul C. Wilkens, "Humor as an Interpersonal Asset and Liability," *Journal of Social Psychology*, 85 (October 1971), 51–64.

incessant smile, but not impassivity—all of these directives, and others like them, are both "cop-outs" and profound truths; they sound easy but are hard to apply. "Just how much is right for the specific circumstance?" and "How does one achieve the desired point between the extremes?" are the practical questions. The preceding pages provide information relevant to both inquiries, but answers depend on the specifics of individual situations. As a philosophic viewpoint, as an all-inclusive guideline, the golden mean is the best doctrine available; but its application requires sensitivity, self-discipline, and judgment.

CONCLUSION

In 1956 Starkweather found in an experiment that those exposed to both verbal and vocal cues relied more heavily on the latter in judging the personality of a speaker,[20] and in another publication Birdwhistell, perhaps the foremost authority on kinesics, estimates that in a two-person conversation the verbal elements carry less than 35 percent of the social meaning.[21]

Although the preceding conclusions and estimates fall short of scientific proof, the judgment that the nonverbal medium is important to communication is sound. Many persons, nevertheless, do not have good habits and do not make astute choices. Suggestion, in particular, offers opportunities that they neglect. Kinesic, paralinguistic, proxemic, and other types of cues afford the individual a wide range of resources both for conveying messages without words and for adding clarity and effectiveness to verbal transmissions.

MULTIMEDIA PRESENTATIONS

In addition to the advantageous management of actions, facial signs, positions, and vocal nuances, how can a speaker strengthen a presentation? The answer is in the story told in the following radio commercial: Two salesmen, each trying to obtain a contract for a product, went to a meeting. The first gave a well-prepared verbal address, but the second had a slide presentation that showed the production of the appliance, pictures of it in operation, and the ways it could meet the needs of the prospective buyer. "Which salesman do you think received the contract?" the announcer asked. "The one with the hard-hitting pictorial presentation," he answered. Although the radio listener may have noted that the sponsor of the commercial, a photographic studio, was biased, he or she still probably

---

[20] John A. Starkweather, "Content-Free Speech as a Source of Information about the Speaker," *Journal of Abnormal and Social Psychology*, 52 (May 1956), 394–402.
[21] Ray L. Birdwhistell, *Kinesics and Context: Essays on Body Motion Communication* (Philadelphia: University of Pennsylvania Press, 1970), pp. 157–158.

found the story believable. And so one should. Both theorists and business executives speak out in support of multimedia presentations. Universities and school systems maintain audio-visual centers; many individual schools have replaced libraries with "learning centers"; and corporations employ full-time experts to make films, slides, and other types of visual aids.

SIMPLE MEDIA OF TRANSMISSION

Elaborate resources are not available to most student speakers, but numerous types of visuals are within their means. The following paragraphs enumerate these and include common-sense advice on how to use them.

Chalkboard illustrations cost nothing, and almost all rooms have boards available. The prudent person checks in advance to be sure that a board, chalk, and an eraser will be at hand. The board is useful for many kinds of aids, including drawings, graphs, statistics, and key words. Whether to write or draw the material before the speech begins or while speaking depends on the circumstances and on individual talents and preferences. If a visual is time consuming, advance preparation is a necessity; and most persons produce neater work when they are not hurried. However, unless one finds some means of covering advance drawings, viewers see the material before hearing the related part of the speech and the potential for holding attention through an unfolding presentation is lost. Whether prepared ahead of time or during the speech, illustrations should be large enough and made with a heavy enough line for everyone in the room to see the relevant details easily.

Newsprint mounted on an easel serves almost the same purposes as a chalkboard. It is superior to a board in that the speaker can easily conceal materials until needed and by using successive pages can unfold a continuing story that renews attention as each item appears.

Posters or *placards* are a means of conveying information similar to sheets of newsprint, but the higher quality of the material, usually a slick white cardboard, permits more attractive drawings. For some presentations, such as sketches by an interior decorator or a landscape gardener, this advantage is significant. The speaker must plan beforehand for displaying these materials, which should be large enough for everyone to see easily. An easel serves well, and sometimes one can set placards in the trough at the bottom of the chalkboard or can suspend them by large fasteners from a wire across the front of the room.

Demonstrations, with or without objects or models, cost nothing, and the activity may help the speaker hold attention and feel at ease. In planning, one must think carefully about sight lines between all parts of the room and the place where the demonstration will occur. In most rooms the action must be at least waist high; and unless one plans well, the hands conceal the action that the audience is supposed to observe. Small movements, as

The materials in the oval add clarity, interest, and force, but the printed information is too detailed and too hard to see to be of use if more than two or three observers are present. The plates of food should make certain points clearer than they would be otherwise, but whether the value gained offsets the time, trouble, and expense of preparation and transportation is questionable.

in tying a knot, and rapid movements are especially hard to see. To overcome some of these problems, a speaker may use *stop action* or *slow motion*. Combining the demonstration with blackboard drawings or illustrations on placards is another possibility.

PROJECTORS

Although less available to students than the visual aids just described, the various kinds of projectors are worth learning about. Properly used, they provide rich resources for adding interest, impressiveness, and clarity to a presentation. The practical problems are (1) locating a machine, (2) finding or making materials to project, and (3) transporting, setting up, and operating the equipment. Many families own at least one kind of projector, and on some campuses a student can borrow from the audio-visual department. Almost all classrooms have shades or drapes for darkening the room and outlets that carry the right type of current and voltage, but one should make sure of these facilities early in the process of preparation. The following are the principal types of projectors:

Movie projectors are familiar to most students, but they are of limited value for most speeches. Unless one chooses a topic to fit a film, finding substantial footage that is relevant is difficult. With sufficient time and money one can produce a film that conveys the desired message, but such an undertaking requires the resources of a corporation, a government bureau, an advertising agency, a television station, or a film class or research unit within a university. An 8 mm. homemade movie is a possibility, but even this requires time, planning, and expense.

Filmstrip projectors are more likely than movie projectors to serve the needs of Mr. Average Speaker, for the available materials are flexible. Since each short strip is a self-contained unit, the communicator can make choices that are appropriate to different parts of the presentation and arrange these strips to suit the message.

Slide projectors, common in the home, also afford flexibility. Sometimes the communicator can choose satisfactorily from the slides already on hand, but for many topics one must either make or purchase additional pictures to illustrate and reinforce the different parts of the talk.

Overhead projectors are versatile instruments that the speaker operates from the front of the room. This feature gives complete control over timing the displays, and it also facilitates a close sender-audience relation and response to feedback. Still other advantages are the inexpensiveness of the acetate transparencies used in the machines and the opportunity afforded speakers to write or draw as they talk and to have these words or figures instantly projected. The machine throws the image behind the speaker and in front of the receivers.

Opaque projectors have many of the advantages of the overhead, but they present opaque objects, such as a map, a document, or a page from a book. Pictures too small for direct display are readily visible when enlarged through opaque projection. A great advantage is that projecting materials in their original state eliminates the time and the expense required for preparing film, slides, or acetate transparencies.

MATERIALS

A second way to look at visual aids is to answer the question "In what form should the communicator cast facts and ideas?" Since most forms, such as the pie graph, are suitable for transmission through several media, such as a chalkboard, newsprint, or a projector, the variety of resources for the multimedia presentation is large.

Words and *numbers*, although the least imaginative type of presentation, are easy to manage. A series of words can clarify organization and heighten attention. Recording a statistic, similarly, helps to impress the figure on the memories of listeners, and leaving the statistic on display facilitates comparisons with data presented later. Sometimes speakers add

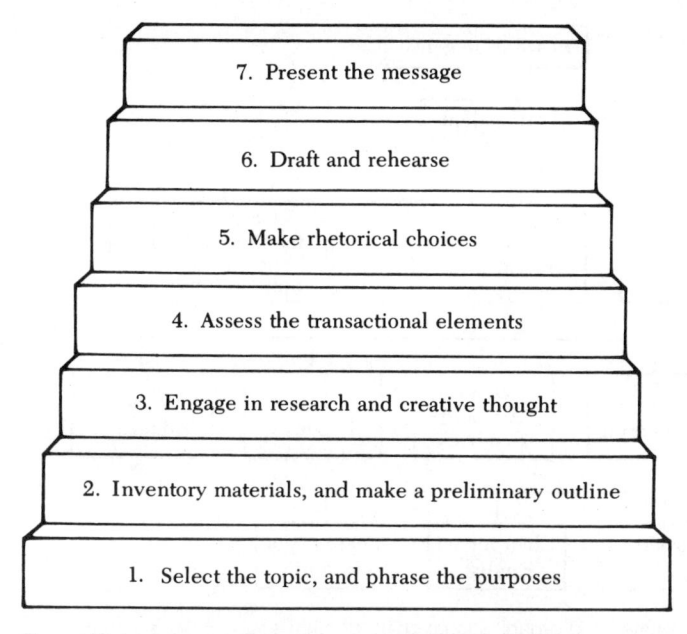

```
        ┌─────────────────────────────┐
        │   7. Present the message    │
      ┌─┴─────────────────────────────┴─┐
      │      6. Draft and rehearse      │
    ┌─┴─────────────────────────────────┴─┐
    │     5. Make rhetorical choices      │
  ┌─┴─────────────────────────────────────┴─┐
  │    4. Assess the transactional elements │
┌─┴───────────────────────────────────────────┴─┐
│   3. Engage in research and creative thought  │
└───────────────────────────────────────────────┘
```

Figure 12.1 Steps in speech preparation and presentation. An example of a visual presentation of the words stating the basic points in an informative message.

force to these simple presentations by using visual intensifiers, such as underscoring, exclamation points, all capitals, and more than one color. Special methods of display, such as pyramids, stairsteps, or triangular or circular arrangements, also can increase effectiveness.

Objects add interest to many speeches, and on many topics speakers already have such illustrative materials and can use them without cost. Sometimes a person chooses a topic because he or she has the objects available to make a speech informative and attention-holding. One problem with objects is size. Large ones are difficult to transport and awkward to handle, and small ones may be hard for the members of an audience to see.

Scale models are not likely to be in the home, but borrowing them may be possible. As compared with objects, they can be either enlarged or stepped down so that the size will be suitable. *Stripped-down models* are simplified structures that omit details which are irrelevant to the points under consideration.

Maps and charts, also, must be borrowed in most instances, but speakers sometimes make their own. Size and visibility again are important, and the speaker must plan ahead for the method of display. Sometimes one can arrange for a colleague to help hold the map; otherwise thumb tacks, scotch tape, or an easel are necessary. *Simplified maps,* such as those used by

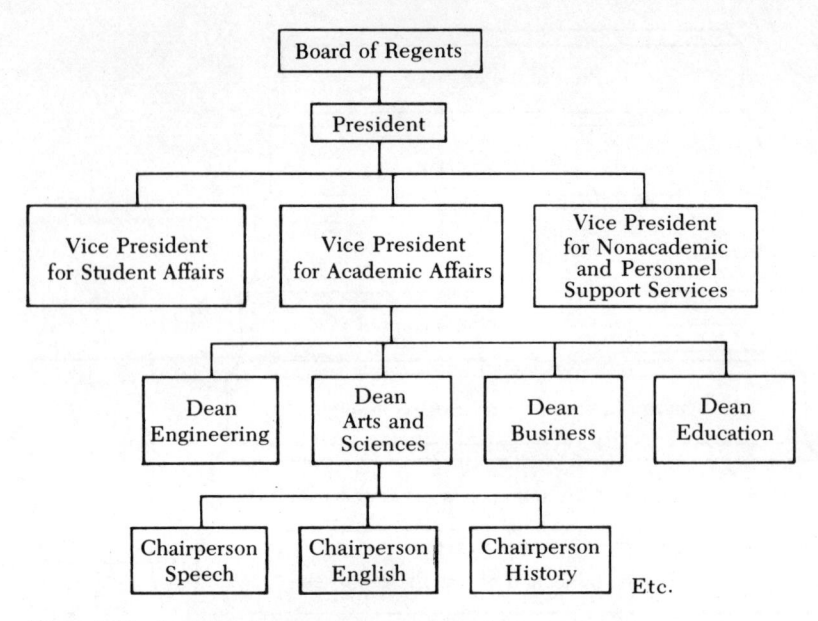

Figure 12.2 An abbreviated organizational chart for a university.

weather broadcasters on television, heighten clarity by eliminating all features except those pertinent to the topic.

Pictures often require special preparation that is beyond the resources of the average person. Without doubt, pictures of a product in use, or of the places the tourist would visit, or of the piteous cases that the charitable contribution would relieve are potent persuasive tools, but the readily available materials usually are too small to be satisfactory. To clip pictures from a magazine, for example, will work only with very small groups of listeners. Passing materials through the audience during a speech is inadvisable, because doing so distracts attention from the verbal part of the address.

Organizational charts, dear to the bureaucratic mind, consist of labeled boxes and a set of horizontal and vertical connecting lines. Other visual devices, such as arrows and broken lines may add further information. A solid line, for example, may indicate a formal relationship, and a broken line one that is informal. These charts commonly accompany speeches that explain the structure of corporate management, the channels within a given segment of government bureaucracy, or the administrative organization of a university or a school district. Labels for each of the boxes, as "president" or "vice president for sales," are necessary.

Tables organize statistical information. A simple table consists of one column or row, but most tables have two or more columns and two or more

	1976	1977
Armed robbery	21	27
Burglary	319	336
Automobile theft	195	178
Rape	37	41
Murder	8	5

Figure 12.3 A table showing statistical data on major crime in Alpha City.

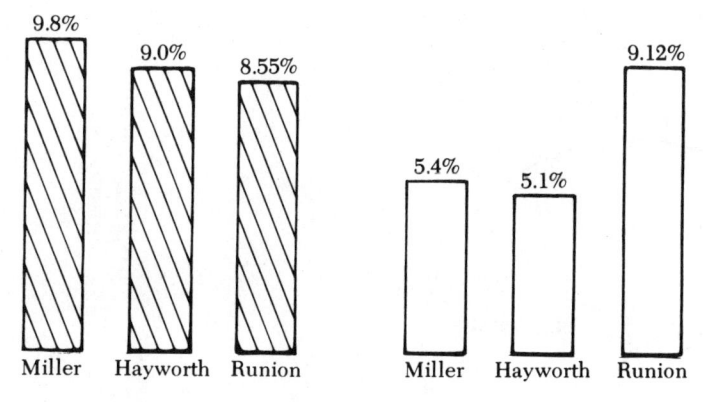

Figure 12.4 Percentages of total speaking time reported in three studies for introductions (striped bars) and conclusions (clear bars). (Donald Hayworth, "An Analysis of Speeches in Presidential Campaigns from 1884–1920," *Quarterly Journal of Speech,* 16 [February 1930], 35–42; Howard L. Runion, "An Objective Study of the Speech Style of Woodrow Wilson," *Speech Monographs,* 3 [1936], 75–94; Edd Miller, "Speech Introductions and Conclusions," *Quarterly Journal of Speech,* 32 [April 1946]: 181–183.)

rows with labels for each and with numbers in each of the squares. The accompanying example shows that a table is less complicated than it sounds in a verbal description.

Bar graphs are a relatively simple device for transforming numerical information into a visual form. The bars constituting the graph may run either vertically, as in the example, or horizontally. Simple to make and easy to interpret, bar graphs are useful aids to communication. Distortions

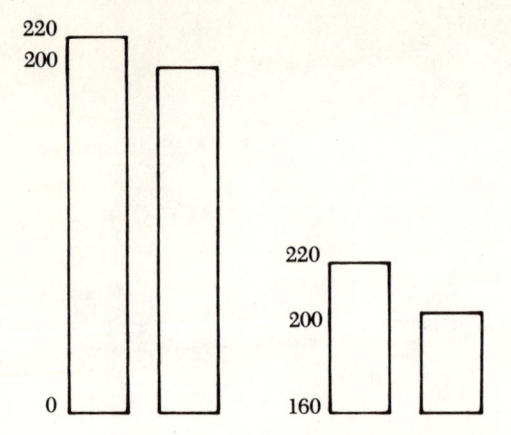

Figure 12.5 Pairs of bar graphs showing the figures 220 and 200 truly and with distortion.

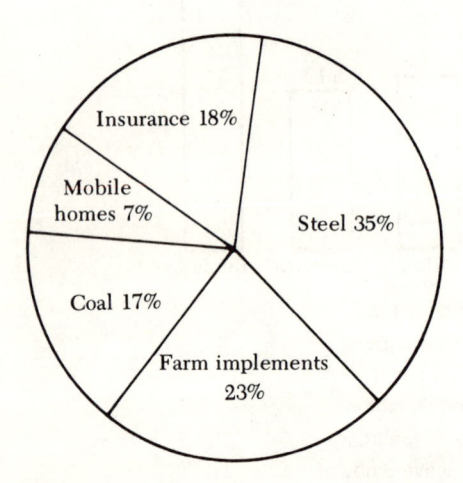

Figure 12.6 A piegraph showing the sources of income of the Alpha City Conglomerate Corporation.

occur unless the base of the graph is zero. The number 220 is 10 percent more than 200, and it will so appear if the respective bars are 220 and 200 units long. If the speaker, however, conserves space by using 160 as the base, then the bar for 220 is sixty units long and looks to be one-and-a-half times as large as the forty-unit bar representing 200.

Piegraphs are especially useful in showing graphically the relative sizes of the different parts of a whole. They are used frequently, for example, to show the sources of income for a college, a corporation, or a unit of government, and they work equally well to show the distribution of expenditures.

Pictographs, often eye catching, use stylized figures or objects to convey statistical information. Rectangles with wheels represent box cars or perhaps automobiles, and figures of men or women, according to their garb, represent farmers, miners, soldiers, or some other group. Each box or figure stands for a specified number of instances, and the longer the line the larger the statistic that it represents. A second type of pictograph, which shows numbers by adjusting the height, often gives an exaggerated impression of differences. The reason is that the artist alters the other dimensions as well as changing the height; therefore, the areas that two or more pictographs cover are no longer true representations of reality.

Finally, *cartoons* and *line drawings* are excellent for attracting attention, for illuminating a topic, and even for providing entertainment. The principal limitation is that most speakers are not cartoonists and must hire professional talent.

FACTORS DETERMINING CHOICES

"Should I use visual aids?" and "If so, which ones?" are practical questions. A human being can receive stimuli on only one channel at a time, say the psychologists, and switching from one channel to another causes a loss in reception. This loss, however, is slight, and in many speech situations the gains resulting from the intensity of the visual stimulus outweigh the small deficit.

Multimedia presentations, in general, are advantageous, but the communicator must consider specific circumstances. One positive factor is that such a presentation, if well done, gives an address a polished, professional touch. "Here's a person who is modern and alert and who knows how to use the latest technology," may be the unspoken audience reaction; "moreover, this speaker considers the occasion and ourselves important enough 'to go all out' in preparation." Some audiences expect a sophisticated, multimedia presentation; and others are likely to be impressed merely because the speaker is using visual resources.

The topic, too, is a factor. "The Pleasures of Hawaii" mandates pictures, whereas "The Sinking American Dollar" may or may not need visuals. Descriptive speeches or passages usually profit from the inclusion of pictorial materials, and the effectiveness of some persuasive messages, such as an appeal for support in the war against hunger, depends on how well the listener can visualize the human beings whom the problem touches. Still other topics, such as "The Backhand in Tennis," end ultimately in imitative actions; for these topics pictures, demonstrations, and other kinds of visuals are almost necessary.

Even for subjects that are not inherently pictorial, a multimedia presentation often adds interest, clarity, and force. "How can I enliven my speech?" the student sometimes asks as self-criticism. "Incorporate visual aids" may be the best answer. "What can I do to clarify this complex message?" in another instance may be the key question. Again, "Use visuals" may be the most helpful response. The value of diagrams and maps is obvious, but listing key words and leaving them on the board or on a sheet of newsprint also can assist the listener, for seeing them may make the overall structure of the message unmistakable. Still another use of visuals is to facilitate a comparison of one part of a speech with another. One speaker, for example, wrote a statistic on the chalkboard, left it there, and then returned to it while recording a second figure just under the first.

But in contrast to the many times that visual aids are of value, there are a few instances when they are harmful and numerous situations when they are not worth the time and the expense. A simple straightforward presentation sometimes is best, and a lack of clutter can be a source of strength. If visuals distract from the message, as they sometimes do, they are detrimental. If they are too flashy or sensational, one may have trouble in getting one's mind on what one's ears are receiving. If they are badly timed or displayed too soon, they may send one message while the words are expressing something else. Bad management also can create distractions. The audience that wonders whether the map will fall is only partially attentive to the verbal message.

Which type of visual aid? Should one show a picture or project it? Should one write key words on the chalkboard, on newsprint on an easel, or on a transparency for overhead projection? Should the communicator create visuals while speaking or prepare them beforehand? Should data be in a table, a bar graph, a piegraph, or a pictograph? Does the nature of the subject matter or audience expectations require visual materials of a particular type and degree of professional competence? To all of these questions the general answer is that the best course is the one that is the easiest, the most economical, and the most likely to be effective.

Finally, a combination of types of visuals may be best. During a slide presentation, for example, the speaker may increase clarity and emphasis by writing key words on the board; and in most "how-to-do-it" speeches, combining demonstration with chalkboard diagrams and pictures is advisable.

Speakers generally, in conclusion, do not use as many visual aids as they should. Some objects and devices, however, are not worth the effort and the expense, and a few are distracting. Considering the purpose, the topic, audience expectations, and the available resources, the communicator must evaluate each situation individually.

PRACTICAL HINTS

"Use your common sense" would encompass every item on the following list, but without some reminders even the most prudent person does not foresee all the potential problems.

1. Be sure that your visual aids are readily visible to every person in the audience. Perform demonstrations slowly enough so that everyone can see, and don't hide the action with your hands. Write with heavy lines, and make labels and diagrams large. Seeing a part of the aid, as well as the whole, can be critical to understanding.

2. Place materials high enough for easy viewing, and perform actions at least at waist height.

3. Conceal aids until they are relevant to the message. Turn the backs of posters to the audience, keep materials face down, or conceal them in a bag or a box. When a visual is no longer of value, put it out of sight.

4. Coordinate the display of material with the word or the sentence that it reinforces.

5. Either prepare material beforehand, or practice your drawing or demonstrating.

6. Check out the facilities in the room where you are to speak. Assume that anything that could go wrong probably will. Are there electric outlets; and if so, are they live and do they carry the right kind of current? Are there facilities for darkening the room? Do you know the location of the light switch and the outlets? Does the room have the items that you will need, such as chalkboard, table, lectern, easel, chalk, erasers, Scotch tape, thumbtacks, and pointer?

7. Check out machines, such as projectors, and working models. If you are going to use a model car, will it run?

8. Maintain eye contact with the audience. Don't let the presence of a visual aid serve as an excuse for losing contact. Point out whatever is pertinent, and then look at the audience. Be brief when writing or drawing on a chalkboard. If possible, stand behind or at the side of visual aids rather than in front. Avoid reaching across the body to write, draw, or point: if you are to the left of your material, point with the left hand so that you will not turn your back to the audience.

9. Maintain a good posture and position. If your aid is large and cumbersome, do not try to hold it while speaking. If using a large map, attach it to the wall or an easel or arrange for one or two classmates to hold it.

10. Simplify aids as much as possible. Use models that show only the parts relevant to the message, and use maps that eliminate all features except those that you are discussing.

11. Only in rare instances should you pass out materials during the speech. If the total cultural experience is more important than the specific points in the message, then perhaps the communicatees are as well off looking at pictures as they are listening to you. In most instances, however, the achievement of your purpose depends on maintaining attention to your words, and passing out materials is destructive to the holding of interest. Distributing items at the end of the speech does no harm, but you are responsible for collecting them before the next speaker begins.

CONCLUSION

In every book one chapter must be last. In no text, including this one, does this position indicate that the topic for the chapter is unimportant. Nonverbal cues occur almost unceasingly in every oral communication situation in which the receiver can see or hear the sender, and multimedia presentations, already significant in business and professional settings, provide many opportunities for almost every communicator to strengthen discourse.

Nonverbal cues are an important medium for the transmission of ideas from sender to receiver and for feedback from receiver to sender. Without these carriers of the message, communication would be impossible. In many instances the production of cues, for better or worse, is through habit; but as individuals become increasingly knowledgeable about the process of communication, they learn to make nonverbal and verbal choices with a view to increasing clarity and effectiveness.

Still other choices, the topics for Chapters 9 and 10, are in the areas of arrangement and delivery. The four areas—arrangement, delivery, verbal language, and nonverbal stimuli—comprise the third section of this textbook. Students need to understand these areas and to become skillful in applying their knowledge so that they can make their messages clear and effective and so that they can develop and maintain a favorable transactional relation with their fellow communicators. No matter whether the situation is a conversation, an interview, a discussion, a conference, or a public address, informed and thoughtful content is the basis of responsible, meaningful communication; but a favorable transactional relation and sound rhetorical choices are essential to a purposeful outcome.

PROBLEMS AND EXERCISES

1. During a round of classroom speeches divide into two groups—the one as observers of kinesic cues and the other as observers of paralinguistic cues. Keep a running record on paper of each cue, and tabulate at least the types occurring the most frequently, such as vocalized pauses and particular mannerisms. Compare your observations with those of others, and discuss the results with the speakers.

2. Along with the other members of the class turn in a slip of paper containing a description of a situation that is fairly easy to imagine and imitate—for example, "a pitcher having a bad inning," "a spectator at a tennis match," or "a bartender on a busy night." Draw a slip, and through gestures and other kinesic cues try to portray the person in the situation so that the other members of the class can tell who you are and what you are doing. Classmates may ask questions, but your replies must be through gestures. Continue until a guess is correct or for five minutes, whichever comes first.

3. By reciting the letters of the alphabet, convey a common emotional state such as hatred, anger, happiness, or affection. Members of the class should write down the emotion that they think you are expressing. Discuss the results.

4. Deliver a one-minute speech on any topic. Stand up on both feet, keep your hands still unless gesturing for a purpose, and permit no vocalized pauses. Tell yourself, "For one minute I can be perfect."

5. Observe someone that you do not know, possibly a salesclerk or a conversationalist that you can see on the far side of a lounge. What kind of person do you think that he or she is? What are the bases for these judgments?

6. Join with four or five of your classmates in a discussion group. Talk about the possibilities for using visual aids in your next major speech. Try to make constructive suggestions to each other.

7. Using books and articles listed at the end of the chapter as well as other materials, write an essay of five hundred words on one of these topics:

Body Language
Proxemics as a Factor in Interpersonal Relations
Suggestion
Strengths and Weaknesses in the Multimedia Presentation

REFERENCES

Albert, Stuart, and James M. Dabbs, Jr. "Physical Distance and Persuasion," *Journal of Personality and Psychology*, 15 (July 1970), 265–270.

Baxter, James C. "Interpersonal Spacing in Natural Settings," *Sociometry*, 33 (December 1970), 444–456.

Birdwhistell, Ray L. *Kinesics and Context: Essays on Body Motion Communication.* Philadelphia: University of Pennsylvania Press, 1970.

Bosmajian, Haig A. *The Rhetoric of Nonverbal Communication.* Glenview, Ill.: Scott, Foresman and Co., 1971.

Connolly, Patrick R. "The Perception of Personal Space Among Black and White Americans," *Central States Speech Journal*, 26 (Spring 1975), 21–28.

Davitz, Joel R., ed. *The Communication of Emotional Meaning.* New York: McGraw-Hill, 1964.

Duncan, Starkey, Jr. "Nonverbal Communication," *Psychological Bulletin*, 72 (August 1969), 118–137.

Eisenberg, Abne, and Ralph Smith, Jr. *Nonverbal Communication.* Indianapolis: The Bobbs-Merrill Co., 1971.

Ekman, Paul, and Wallace V. Friesen. "Hand Movements," *Journal of Communication,* 22 (December 1972), 353–374.

Fast, Julian. *Body Language.* Philadelphia: J. B. Lippincott Co., 1970.

Goffman, Erving. *Behavior in Public Places.* New York: The Free Press, 1963.

Haber, Ralph N., ed. *Information-Processing Approaches to Visual Perception.* New York: Holt, Rinehart and Winston, 1969.

Hall, Edward T. *The Hidden Dimension.* Garden City, N.Y.: Doubleday & Co., 1969.

Hinde, Robert A., ed. *Non-verbal Communication.* New York: Cambridge University Press, 1972.

Knapp, Mark L. *Nonverbal Communication in Human Interaction.* New York: Holt, Rinehart and Winston, 1972.

Leathers, Dale. *Nonverbal Communication Systems.* Boston: Allyn & Bacon, 1976.

Mehrabian, Albert. *Nonverbal Communication.* Chicago: Aldine Atherton, 1972.

Mehrabian, Albert. *Silent Messages.* Belmont, Cal.: Wadsworth Publishing Co., 1971.

Mehrabian, Albert, and Shirley G. Diamond. "Effects of Furniture Arrangement, Props, and Personality on Social Interaction," *Journal of Personality and Social Psychology,* 20 (October 1971), 18–30.

Merriam, Allen H. "Symbolic Action in India: Gandhi's Nonverbal Persuasion," *Quarterly Journal of Speech,* 61 (October 1975), 290–306.

Rosegrant, Teresa J., and James C. McCroskey. "The Effects of Race and Sex on Proxemic Behavior in an Interview Setting," *Southern Speech Communication Journal,* 40 (Summer 1975), 408–419.

Ruesch, Jurgen, and Weldon Kees. *Nonverbal Communication.* Berkeley: University of California Press, 1956.

Scheflen, Albert E., and Alice Scheflen. *Body Language and the Social Order.* Englewood Cliffs, N.J.: Prentice-Hall, 1972.

Weitz, Shirley, ed. *Nonverbal Communication.* New York: Oxford University Press, 1974.

Appendix A

DEVELOPING COMMUNICATION SKILLS THROUGH MODELS: TWO EXAMPLES OF STUDENT SPEECHES

One way to supplement the instruction in a textbook is through the study of sample speeches. The two texts that follow are final speeches delivered in November, 1975, in a section of the class in Beginning Public Speaking at the University of Houston. A brief critique follows each text. The publication of the texts is by permission of the two student authors.

HELP THE HANDICAPPED!

by Ardsley Fischer

The following is from a letter that appeared in "Viewpoints" in the *Houston Chronicle* in October of this year. It was from an appalled staff member of the U.S. Department of Health, Education and Welfare who had been in Houston for a conference:

I recently attended a meeting at the Astrohall, one planned by educators involved in Head Start for the Handicapped Child, and attended by 2,000-plus people.

Nice city, nice people, phenomenal weather on the heels of a norther [sort of like today, I guess],[1] nice facilities at Astrohall, except . . .

There is no restroom in the facility that a person in a wheelchair can use. Assuming I had not looked hard enough, I asked a person at the reference desk, who called, and sure enough, no restroom.

Incredible![2]

---

[1] Comment inserted by the speaker.
[2] William J. Bean, Ph.D., HEW, Washington, D.C., "No Restroom for the Handicapped," a letter to "Viewpoint," the Houston *Chronicle*, October 10, 1975, sec. 8, p. 5.

This, unfortunately, is the situation in many public buildings in Houston. Often, however, the handicapped person in a wheelchair cannot even get into the building, let alone the bathrooms, because it is inaccessible due to physical barriers such as a stairway up to the entrance.

In my talk this afternoon, I would like to accomplish three things: first, I want to give you a feeling for what a person confined to a wheelchair is up against in the way of architectural barriers when he tries to lead a normal life in Houston. Second, I want to show you that laws seem to have proved to be the only effective means of getting these architectural barriers minimized for the handicapped and that therefore Houston needs such laws. Third, I want to convince you that we, residents of the Houston area, should take the initiative to write the men at City Hall giving our support to the ordinance soon to be voted upon by City Council that would eliminate many of the unnecessary barriers which the handicapped individual is up against when he leaves his home for the day.

Much of the background information gathered for this speech came from interviews I had with three individuals deeply involved in eliminating these barriers: Mr. Joe Villareal, President of the Coalition for Barrier Free Living, a Houston organization whose purpose is to minimize the architectural barriers for the handicapped; Ms. Mary Ann Board, Coordinator of Handicapped Student Services here at the University of Houston (both of these individuals are in wheelchairs themselves); Mr. Mort Levy, President of the Houston Chapter of the American Institute of Architects and Chairman of the sub-committee of the Construction Industries Council which drew up the revisions to Houston's Building Code that are being considered in the ordinance.

Have you ever thought much about what you would be up against if your only means of mobility were a wheelchair? There would be parking spaces you couldn't use because of the width of your chair, buildings you couldn't enter, at least without help, because of stairs, telephones and water fountains you couldn't use because they were too high, etc., etc.

Let me give you some real examples of what you would face in Houston:

You couldn't stay at the Shamrock Hilton—you couldn't get into the bathroom.

How would you like to be stuck for a month in the orthopedic ward at Methodist Hospital, again unable to use your bathroom?

You need to go to the Administration Building of the Houston Independent School District? You could enter with help through the back kitchen door.

How about a concert at Jones Hall? You could get in all right and they would have spaces for you and your chair—but you'd have to pay for the highest priced seats in the house and sit way over to the left of stage.

Once someone lifts you up the steps to the Alley Theater, though, you can get around and they do have seats for you—but not much room for your feet.

But what about Hofheinz Pavillion? There would be a lot of room for you—behind all the other seats way at the top.

If you had a job, you might be in trouble like Mr. Villareal was when he worked at the County Treasurer's Office downtown. He couldn't use the bathrooms because the doors were too narrow for his wheelchair and consequently, he developed medical complications and had to be treated for two weeks in the hospital.

I could go on and on with similar examples, but there just isn't time. I hope these have given you a picture of what barriers the handicapped have to face day after day.

How can this picture be changed for the handicapped? My research has shown that laws requiring buildings to be accessible to and usable by the physically disabled are mandatory if changes are to take place.

Let's take our own campus as a case in point. Does a day go by that you don't personally see at least a dozen or so students going to class in wheelchairs? According to Ms. Board, the University of Houston has about 120 physically handicapped students, .39% of the total enrollment. But this has not always been so. Mr. Villareal attended the U. of H. ten years ago. Then there were only two others in wheelchairs, .02% of the total enrollment. The percentage of handicapped students has increased 1550%.[3]

What has made the difference? In the meantime Federal and State laws were passed (in 1968 and 1969, respectively) requiring all buildings and facilities constructed in Texas by the use of any federal, state, county or municipal funds to be made accessible to and usable by the physically disabled. Exact specifications were laid down which had to be followed. The University of Houston, being a publically funded institution, must abide by these laws. Yearly the campus is inspected by the State Building Commission and deficiencies are then to be corrected. From the late sixties on, the U. of H. has been energetically trying to abide by the laws, and the administration has shown great commitment to accommodating the needs of its handicapped students.

But all facilities used by the public are not constructed with public funds. There are theaters, restaurants, hotels, office buildings, shopping centers, for instance, which are required by no law to be barrier-free. Many cities already have barrier-free paragraphs in their municipal building codes, but Houston doesn't yet, and it desperately needs to.

How can we, caring Houston area residents, exercise our responsibility as human beings to help our handicapped brothers and sisters to be able to exercise their "unalienable right" of the "pursuit of happiness?" This right is certainly infringed upon when access to theaters, office buildings, etc., is limited for them by unnecessary barriers.

[3] These statistics were calculated by the speaker from estimates of the number of handicapped students at the University of Houston in the Fall, 1965, and the Fall, 1975, by J. Villareal and M. A. Board, respectively, and from the official University of Houston figures on total enrollment for these semesters as given the speaker by Mr. M. Lucchesi of the Registrar's Office.

What can we do? The Houston City Council will soon be voting on an ordinance which would revise Houston's building code, requiring accessibility to publicly used buildings, and we must show them that we, the public, strongly support such an ordinance.

Similar to the State and Federal requirements, the City's specifications include:

convenient seating accommodations in facilities like theaters, auditoriums, churches;

easy accessibility to hotels, restaurants, office buildings, etc.;

accessible building entrances on the same levels as the elevators;

a determined number of bathroom facilities, water fountains, telephones, installed according to barrier-free specifications;

a certain number of 12-foot-wide parking spaces which are accessible to the adjacent buildings.

Details of the specifications I have here if anyone is interested after class.

Are these things too much to ask? Certainly not—and we must tell that to City Council.

To make action easier, I have written and duplicated a letter to the men at City Hall strongly requesting support of the barrier-free ordinance. I have attached addressed and stamped accompanying envelopes. You may get them from me at the end of the hour.

I urge you all, help Mr. Reedy, who used to be in this class. Help the other handicapped fellow Houstonians. Sign a letter and mail it to City Hall today.

I would like to end this afternoon with a poem which has been circulating in wheelchair circles for some time. It emphasizes poignantly but with humor the plight of the handicapped in regard to barriers.

Dear John

Most architectural barriers I've learned to take in stride,
Those steps, those curbs, those revolving doors that make me stay outside.

I can live with water fountains that are level with my ears;
And I have never used a phone booth in all my many years.

But when it comes to restrooms, it really is a blow—
It's knowing that when I've gotta, I ain't gonna get to go.

I burn the rubber of my wheels; I can hardly wait.
But my chair is thirty inches wide, the John door twenty-eight.

If I stop down at the corner for a round of brew or two,
I may not only fill my bladder; I may also fill my shoe.

Some plead for civil justice when they are set upon;
I ask for only one freedom—the right to use the John.

But when I get to heaven and sit before the gate,
Will St. Peter say, "You're thirty inches wide; our John door twenty-eight"?[4]

CRITIQUE

Perhaps the most impressive quality of the speech by Ms. Fischer is that it shows that a soundly researched address can be rich in human appeal and hence highly interesting. Like any responsible speaker, Ms. Fischer knew what she was talking about. She had interviewed both university and community officials who were authorities, she had searched for materials that would work well as introduction and conclusion, and she had secured specific items of information, such as enrollment figures, when she found during preparation that she needed them.

The variety in material is an outcome of strong research that adds strength and interest. Ms. Fischer includes direct quotations, numerous specific examples, statistics, historic background, references to the law, and a humorous poem. Although she does not identify the source of each item, perhaps because doing so would become tedious, she does indicate her principal references and their qualifications early in the address.

Besides the strong content, the speech is commendable for maintaining a good speaker-audience relation. Early in the address Ms. Fischer establishes her credibility by showing that she is knowledgable, well prepared, warm-hearted, and compassionate. The efficient beginning, the opening quotation, the list of points to be covered, and the citation of sources are modest, inoffensive means of showing competence through suggestion. Largely because the topic arouses sympathy and is close to students, this good speaker-audience relation continues throughout. In a number of places the speaker uses wordings that continue and heighten listener involvement: "How would *you* like to be stuck for a month in the orthopedic ward . . . unable to use *your* bathroom?" "Have *you* ever thought about what *you* would be up against . . . ?" "*You* need to go

---

[4]Carl F. Ordner, Coordinator of Special Services, Mehlenberg Medical Center, "Dear John," as it appeared in a letter from Jim Berry, Department of Facilities Planning and Construction, University of Houston, to Connie Wallace, Assistant Dean of Students, University of Houston, February 8, 1973.

. . ." "Once someone lifts *you* up the steps . . ." "Let's take *our* own campus as a case in point." "How can *we*, caring Houston area residents . . ." "What can *we* do?" "I urge *you* all . . ." The speech abounds in sentences that remind listeners that the message is *for them* and about a problem close *to them*.

Sentences such as the preceding not only maintain a close speaker-audience relation but also illustrate the skill of Ms. Fischer in making rhetorical choices. She could have used more impersonal wordings for her ideas, and she could have chosen examples and statistics for the nation instead of those for the university and the city. For some topics it is persuasive to show that the scope of a problem is nationwide, but in this instance the decision to concentrate on familiar places and situations probably was sound.

Still other choices deserve comment. The material for the introduction consists of a lively quotation to arouse interest, a preview of the main points, and a paragraph identifying the principal sources—an interesting and effective combination. The conclusion begins with a simple, easy course of remedial action and continues with a poem. A critic could argue that this closing poem is superfluous, but this writer believes that any possible loss of emphasis on the requested action is offset by transactional gains. The poem is further evidence that the speaker prepared carefully and is sensitive to others. Showing that she has a sense of humor also adds another dimension to credibility.

The ethos of the speaker, however, is high throughout, for Ms. Fischer combines creative thought with sound research. Although much of the material comes from outside sources, Ms. Fischer has thought about the items that she has found, she has placed them in the speech according to her own pattern, and she has worded them in her own way. The organization of ideas is clear without using cumbersome, obtrusive devices. The points flow smoothly, one after another.

This excellent student speech, in conclusion, illustrates the three essentials of communication that are the framework for this text: The speaker has content that is worth presenting; she maintains a good speaker-audience relation; and she makes rhetorical choices for organization and style that enhance clarity and effectiveness.

TELEVISION VIOLENCE AND CHILDREN: HOW
WE SHOULD REGULATE BOTH

by Larry Bozka

On July 9, 1959, the New York *Journal-American* reported that four young boys, desiring a human skull for their club activities, broke into a Jersey City mausoleum, pried open a coffin, and took one. They brought the skull to their clubroom, where they desecrated it by sticking a lighted candle in it. Astonished police said the club members—seven boys, whose ages ranged from 11 to 14—got the idea from a TV horror show.

In Brooklyn, New York, a six-year-old son of a policeman asked his father for real bullets because his little sister "doesn't die for real when I shoot her like they do when Hopalong Cassidy kills 'em."

In Los Angeles, a housemaid caught a seven-year-old boy in the act of sprinkling ground glass into the family's lamb stew. There was no malice behind the act. It was purely experimental, having been inspired by curiosity to learn whether it would really work as well as it did on television.

"Interesting," you say. Yes, interesting, but also very serious. The effects of television violence upon children is an issue that is facing more and more people every day. There is a rather common opinion that the use of audiovisual equipment is a highly effective means of educating children. However, the same proponents of this idea tend to claim television violence to be of little influence upon children. Just where can we draw the line?

So you see there *is* a problem. But how do we go about approaching it?

First, I intend to convince you that television violence is a matter that needs to be taken seriously.

Second, I feel it will be necessary to give you the solutions offered by others.

And finally, I intend to give you arguments for these solutions, and my own solution.

Here is an excerpt from a statement by the National Commission on the Causes and Prevention of Violence, issued on September 23, 1969, and printed in the *U.S. News,* October 6, 1969: "Television enters powerfully into the learning process of children and teaches them a set of moral and social values which are inconsistent with the standards of a civilized society."

"How can television shows contain *that* much violence?" you ask.

The following is a quotation from an article by Leo Singer entitled "Join the Crusade Against Brutality" and printed in *Parents' Magazine,* October, 1974: "In 1968 the average child between ages 5 and 15 watched the violent destruction of more than 13,400 persons on TV." He added, "Since 1968, the percentage of violence on TV has remained virtually unchanged, but the violence today is more detailed, more graphic than ever before. . . . Half of all the people seen on TV today commit some violence. Six percent kill someone, and three percent are killed."

In a 1973 study cited by Mr. Singer, "The average TV viewer saw violence in eight out of ten programs and nine out of every ten cartoons."

Now maybe you can better realize the intensity and seriousness of this matter. A few standard statistics on the problem, and one soon understands how extensive and prevalent violence is in television programming today.

"What can we do about it?" you ask. "What is being done about it?"

Robert M. Siebert and John M. Neale in their book *The Early Window: Effects of Television on Children and Youth* state: "In many ways, the most obvious, and perhaps most feasible way of changing today's programming involves direct pressures on commercial broadcasting. The existing commercial system, with its enormous resources and potential, would thus be preserved. Two apparent means for accomplishing this goal are sanctions from the public and regulations by the federal government."

There are two means of private sanction.

First, you can refuse to purchase the products endorsed or sold by these violence vendors. In other words, if you see something you don't approve of, notify those responsible and boycott the product being endorsed.

Second, and perhaps even more effective, refuse to buy stock in their firms. "You have to be kidding," you say. "I'm just a smalltimer. If I didn't buy their stock for the rest of my life, they would never know the difference."

How many of you belong to churches, universities, or unions with pension plans? Here is your outlet to influence. Write someone a letter and they throw it away, but hurt them financially and they listen to what you have to say. Organizations like those just mentioned have tremendous financial power, power that can be very effective in aiding a cause.

The next means of changing today's programming is government regulation. According to the first amendment, broadcasters are immune from federal control, *except* if the materials presented are intrinsically injurious. Television violence *is* intrinsically injurious to children.

The task of government regulation falls upon the FCC. At this time the FCC does not seem to be taking its broadcast licensing job seriously. If they were taking it seriously, maybe there wouldn't be the amount of violence that is prevalent in the television programming. This government commission needs to be pressured by those who feel that they are not meeting their responsibilities.

Another thing we can do is contact the actual constituents of the television industry—local stations, networks, etc. Here's what to tell them:

Tell them to stop broadcasting children's cartoons containing serious, noncomic violence.

Tell them to reduce the time devoted to broadcasting violent crime, Western and adventure programs, and reruns of certain movies. Tell them to restrict showing these programs to late evening hours.

Tell them to try harder to write scripts in which problems are solved without violence. Now violence is "the routine method" of problem-solving on TV.

Tell them to do more research on the effects of TV violence. Tell them to pay more attention in setting broadcasting standards to the evidence already available from such research as the U.S. Surgeon General's study of TV violence.

Those suggestions were presented to the television industry by the Violence Commission, and I wholeheartedly agree with them.

Some years ago, a group of parents in Massachusetts formed ACT, Action for Children's TV. ACT has received foundation grants and will help you in the fight for television viewing reform. The address of this organization is 46 Austin Street, Newtonville, Mass., 02160. They have a lot of free information and will be more than willing to help you with whatever you have in mind.

Just in case you're still not convinced of the magnitude of the TV violence problem, I have another quotation from Leo Singer's article, "Join the Crusade Against Brutality": "By the time the average child graduates from high school, he or she has spent nearly 15,000 hours watching TV, compared with 12,000 hours in school."

Which does a child learn more from, be it good or bad?

To this point I have given you (1) examples of the seriousness of the TV violence issue and (2) other people's solutions and arguments for them.

I now give you my own solution. You, as parents or future parents, should watch what your children are watching. Too many parents turn their kids loose in the TV room and leave them prey to whatever programs are scheduled for that night. Become involved with your children and their TV viewing, and, most important of all, discuss the contents of TV shows with your children. Point out the "rights and wrongs" of the shows to them. Make television a teaching accessory, not a hindrance.

Finally, I also think you should encourage more research on television and children. Give constructive criticism to stations when necessary, and emphasize to them the importance of the material they broadcast.

So you see, the responsibility, as usual, inevitably falls on the shoulders of the parent or guardian. Live up to this responsibility, and you'll make this world a better place to live in.

In closing, I would like to relate to you a personal experience which made me more aware of the impact of television on children than any example or statistic I have yet to see. A good friend of mine's son was watching "Hawaii 5-0" one night. After a dramatic breakin into an alleged criminal's headquarters, Chief McGarrett ordered the place to be bugged and wiretapped. My friend immediately informed his son that this action was questionable, immoral, and illegal. His son looked at him incredulously and said, "But, Dad, if Chief McGarrett does it, it *must* be o.k."

Whom do you want your children to believe—you or the Chief?

CRITIQUE

In contrast to the heavy reliance by Ms. Fischer on interviews as a source of material, Mr. Bozka depends mainly on printed sources. His materials are commendable for a judicious blending of specific instances and statistics, the former having human-interest appeal and dramatic impact and the latter increasing significance because the large figures give a comprehensive picture. In the conclusion Mr. Bozka uses an example from his own experience to add pointedness to the presentation and to personalize the message for his listeners.

Also demonstrating thoughtful rhetorical choices are the introduction and the plan for the speech. The beginning consists of a series of three interest-arousing examples and a preview that lists the three main parts of the address. The announced pattern, a modification of the problem-solution plan, is appropriate for the topic. A weakness is the fourth paragraph, which contributes little to the achievement of the major purposes.

Cumulation is a device that the speaker uses skillfully in several places. The first three paragraphs, as already noted, are three dramatic examples with each one strengthening the effect of its predecessors. Another impressive section is the series of sentences in which each one begins with "Tell them . . ." The name for this device is repetition of a pattern.

Throughout the speech Mr. Bozka maintains a good speaker-audience relation. The topic is helpful in this respect, because it is familiar. This familiarity, however, is a potential problem, because of the possibility that listeners would think "More of the same old thing" and tune out the speaker. Mr. Bozka deals with this problem at the beginning when he gives three actual instances that probably were new to everyone. Because of sound research, he is able to continue to offer new facts, figures, and ideas.

Language also helps to keep the speaker and his message close to the listeners. "So *you* see," "*I* intend to give *you*," "Now maybe *you* can better realize," "What can *we* do about it?" "Another thing *we* can do," and similar expressions maintain an atmosphere of communication. Especially effective are two thoughts near the close. "*You*, as parents or future parents," the speaker says as he begins his final main point. Later, at the very end, after the story about McGarrett, one of the best known characters on television, he asks the question, "Whom do *you* want *your* children to believe—*you* or the Chief?"

This maintenance of a good speaker-audience relation and intelligent rhetorical decisions on the introduction, the conclusion, the organization, and the use of language make this speech effective. Even more significant, however, is the quality of thought and materials. By finding and using new examples, quotations, statistics, and narratives, Mr. Bozka creates a fresh, interesting, and informative speech on a familiar topic.

Appendix B

DEVELOPING COMMUNICATION SKILLS THROUGH PRACTICE: SPEECHES FOR SPECIAL OCCASIONS

A second way to increase communication skills is through practice sessions. The text includes several sections setting forth public address and interpersonal assignments, but still further experiences can be beneficial. Many instructors will wish to design their own projects, but the speech for a special occasion is an interesting possibility. Not only does the ceremonial speech make a good classroom assignment, but it also provides experiences of practical value. Such addresses as the introduction, the presentation, and the tribute are commonplace at meetings of campus, civic, church, labor, and business organizations.

In all of the following forms of the speech for a special occasion, as in all other types of communication, three factors are basic: sound, creatively invented content; a close, warm transactional relation; and effective use of rhetorical techniques.

SPEECHES OF INTRODUCTION AND WELCOME

Differences exist between the introduction and the welcome, but the similarities are so marked that most of the advice for one is applicable to the other. The speech of introduction occurs almost every time that an organization meets and has a guest speaker. Someone, often the president or the chairman, must give a short address that informs the audience of the speaker's qualifications and that in general helps the speaker to begin under favorable circumstances. The address of welcome, usually delivered by the person presiding at the meeting, acknowledges the presence of a distinguished guest, tells something of the guest's position and/or accomplishments, and calls for the group to welcome him or her through applause. The welcomer usually has the honored guest rise either at the beginning of the address or at its conclusion.

The principal point to consider in developing the content of these speeches is to use factual material rather than generalized praise:

HELPFUL: Professor _____ has forty patents on file, and his invention of the reverse accumulator, according to the *Wall Street Journal,* is the foundation of a $500,000,000 industry.

DOUBTFUL TASTE AND SOMEWHAT EMBARRASSING: Professor _____ is the greatest inventor of the last twenty-five years and is the most distinguished person that has honored our club with his presence.

Types of objective information usable in introductions and welcomes include present and past positions; publications; research findings; research grants; memberships in honorary societies; listings in biographical reference works; special awards; and personal investigations and travels. Quotations giving praise, especially if from prestigious sources, are still another type of material, and certain information seems to gain in impressiveness through quantification—for example, "forty patents," "author of seven books," and "winner of three most valuable player awards."

The best source for information is the visiting speaker or honored guest. If the honoree is unexpected, a quick interview with notebook in hand may be the only recourse for the presiding officer; but ordinarily arrangements for speakers are made well in advance. If so, the person who is to give the introduction should phone or write for a résumé including lists of positions, publications, and special honors. Still another possibility is the use of biographical reference works, some of which are listed and described in Chapter 2.

Building the prestige of the visiting speaker or honored guest usually is the most important purpose of the speech of introduction or welcome, but other objectives may be significant. On some topics the introducer can help the speaker by including background information that otherwise the latter would need to provide. This function is important if background material is personal and if statements by the speaker might seem exaggerated or immodest. Still another purpose is the arousal of interest in the topic. The introducer should avoid wearying the audience or giving away too much of the main speech, but he or she can help the speaker by challenging the audience and/or arousing curiosity.

Finally, speeches of introduction or welcome may serve the occasion by creating a warm, friendly, relaxed atmosphere. Certain kinds of humor may be helpful, and well-chosen personal details about the visiting speaker or honoree can relax the audience and humanize the guest. Besides being a distinguished nuclear physicist, the visitor may be the state senior squash champion or a licensed basketball referee. The guest lecturer may be a

Pulitzer Prize Winner, but have the same problems with lost airline luggage as those in the audience.

Research to find the needed materials and good judgment and taste in selecting and organizing them are the major considerations in preparing the speech of introduction or welcome. Delivery should be direct and fluent. Materials, often chosen with the help of the visitor, should be factual, but tactful humor and the humanizing touch can be helpful. The best length varies with the situation, but two to four minutes is likely to be about right. The address must be long enough for the audience to settle down and to focus attention on the platform, but not so long as to be tiresome.

SPEECHES OF DEDICATION AND PRESENTATION

A class or any other learning group can simulate situations calling for dedications and presentations, just as it can invent a condition requiring a speech of introduction or welcome. Students should have little trouble in imagining that they are the Briarcroft Garden Club or the Carpenters' Union Local and that the speaker is going to present a gift to the retiring president.

As with introductions and welcomes, speeches of dedication and presentation, although different in certain respects, use similar materials and approaches. Of the two, the presentation is the more common, for at least once a year almost every organization makes one or more presentations to retiring officers, winners of the top sales-representative or best-teacher award, or recipients of perfect attendance pins. Less common and almost always formal and highly dignified are dedications of bridges, branch libraries, buildings, statues, and commemorative plaques.

Possible materials for the speech of presentation or dedication are of three types. First, the nature and the history of the award may include such items as the criteria for judging possible recipients, the names of former winners, the reasons that some person or organization originated the award, and interesting facts about the donor. Second, the qualifications of the recipient may include both general accomplishments and achievements specifically related to the award. Content of this second type is similar to that in a speech of introduction. Third, the physical qualities of the award sometimes are of interest. What is its value? What materials are in it? Is it the work of a distinguished artisan? The person making the presentation, in summary, answers for the audience the questions "What is the award?" "Who won it?" and "Why did he or she win it?" On some occasions the speaker may also discuss the purposes of the organization and the worthiness of the cause with which the award is connected.

The length of the speech of presentation or dedication may vary from two or three minutes to thirty or forty. In most instances the presenter needs to speak only long enough to show respect for the recipient and to make the award seem significant. "Stanley Smith, you have the highest sales record in the district; here's your watch" is so abrupt that the award seems half-hearted; on the other hand, presentations of this type rarely need to be lengthy, and they can combine good-natured humor with serious ideas. On the other hand, the banquet closing a fund-raising campaign may combine the presentation of awards with a detailed report on the outcome of the drive, on accomplishments of the organization in the past twelve months, and on prospective future achievements. The purposes of such an address are to inform and to inspire the rank-and-file members and to lay the foundation for greater efforts in the future.

Speakers making dedications use many of the materials and techniques just described. They also are likely to be brief, but the customs of the sponsoring group may call for a full-length address of information and inspiration. A light touch is unlikely in a dedication; but if a speaker does include humor, it should be secondary. As in the speech of presentation, levity can be in good taste; but the closing effect should be one of respect to recipient, donor, and occasion.

SPEECH OF ACCEPTANCE

Audiences almost always expect those receiving awards to make speeches of acceptance. If the honor is a surprise, a brief expression of appreciation is sufficient. Recipients frequently thank the person or organization giving the award and express gratitude to coworkers, supervisors, coaches, teammates, present or former teachers, and parents and spouses. What the recipient says often is less important than the underlying manner. He or she should project qualities of appreciation, pride, humility, and a determination to live up to the high standards that the award signifies.

When the recipient knows of the award in advance, audiences may expect more than a few stammered phrases. Paradoxically, the task is more difficult when preparation is possible than when it is not. The reason is that spontaneous expressions of gratefulness and modesty almost always sound sincere, whereas studied phrases and controlled delivery may not. Certainly, the prepared speaker should avoid reading a manuscript or giving an oration. Style should be oral, and delivery should be friendly and direct. The one advantage of preparation is that it protects against the unintentional omission of the name of a helpful person when listing those deserving credit.

SPEECHES OF TRIBUTE AND FAREWELL

Addresses of tribute and farewell are so much like presentations that much of the advice on that type of speech is applicable and need not be repeated. Not all tributes, of course, are farewells, but the outlines and materials for the two are similar.

The typical speech of farewell occurs at a banquet when a colleague or an employee is retiring or moving from one city to another or from the present company to a new one. The usual outline is to begin by praising the individual for personal qualities and specific achievements. The speaker then is likely to express in behalf of the corporation or the group an appreciation for the helpfulness of the person retiring or transferring and a sense of loss at the departure. Finally, the speaker wishes the honored guest success on the new job and happiness in the new way of life.

The success of speeches of tribute and farewell, like all other speeches for special occasions, depends less on the content than on the atmosphere that the speaker creates—the total spirit or emotional effect. The personality of the honoree, the nature of the occasion, and the customs and expectations of both honoree and listeners may make a certain amount of "ribbing" appropriate; indeed, one way of expressing affection as well as respect is to include humorous reminiscences and engaging trivialities. True stories may also be excellent vehicles for making serious points and for bringing the audience back from a period of "kidding" or "roasting" to the overriding purpose of paying respect and wishing well.

AFTER-DINNER SPEECHES

Banquets include addresses of every possible type and length. The secretary of state may give a forty-minute address outlining a new policy toward the Middle East, or the president of a community club may report on the financial status of the organization and on plans for the coming year. The term *after-dinner speech*, nevertheless, by convention refers to a short to moderately long address whose primary prupose is to entertain. The individual performer has an excellent opportunity to become more favorably known with the group. He or she is center stage, is part of a situation that listeners are likely to remember pleasantly, and is blessed with an occasion permitting a display of wit and humor that others did not expect. Capitalizing on the opportunity to use humor, according to one experimental study, is especially likely to enhance ratings of competence when the speaker is thought to be humorless and aloof.[1]

---

[1] David R. Mettee, Edward S. Hrelec, and Paul C. Wilkens, "Humor as an Interpersonal Asset and Liability," *Journal of Social Psychology*, 85 (October 1971), 51–64.

The best way to begin a humorous speech depends on the situation and on the speaker's special talents—even among professional entertainers styles are diverse. One way to begin is with a series of staccato observations, each serving as a punch line and each building laughter upon the preceding one. "A funny thing happened to me on the way to the White House," Adlai Stevenson joked in beginning a speech soon after losing the election for the Presidency.

A second means of starting is to use a narrative, essentially true but with certain embellishing. Stories may pertain to a person's troubles with the travel agency that arranged the trip or with the problems of explaining to a son or daughter the nature of the organization that the speaker is going to address. If obviously good humored, a funny story about the program chairman or someone else well known to the audience may be well received; but the safer course is to talk about one's own mishaps and foibles. One officer of an association entertained listeners by talking about his feelings of inferiority at conventions because no one ever put a note on the bulletin board with his name on it or had him paged in the lobby.

Still other materials, helpful and harmful, are as follows:

USUALLY VALUABLE

Witty comments based on the remarks of preceding speakers or on earlier parts of the program, such as a song title or the words on a banner.

Spontaneous quips in response to unexpected happenings, such as a malfunctioning public address system or a noise in the hall. "Aristotle never had a problem like this," one lecturer commented when a technician interrupted to change microphones.

Humorous observations on world events, national personalities, local happenings, current television programs, or contemporary cultural characteristics. Professional humorists from Will Rogers to Bob Hope and Johnny Carson have built comedy routines on comments about news stories that were familiar to most listeners.

In-house jokes provided that the audience is restricted to those who are familiar with the personalities and events.

USUALLY POOR MATERIALS

Sarcastic remarks that hurt someone's feelings and that others regard as unfair and in poor taste.

Crudities and vulgarities that go beyond the standards of good taste held by the particular audience.

Remarks that degrade the speaker. Poking fun at minor faults is often a good technique, but a story on oneself should not reflect on basic intelligence or character.

Puns, stories, and witticisms gleaned from joke books, which seldom fit a new situation precisely. These materials suggest a lack of originality, and listeners may have heard them before.

Fresh, good-humored, original materials are basic to after-dinner speaking—just as good content is basic to all forms of communication—but the speaker-audience atmosphere and the skillful use of rhetorical techniques also affect success. Tactful, entertaining material is conducive to a relaxed, friendly spirit; but delivery and language also are influential. The presentation should be animated and direct; pleasantness begets geniality, and enthusiasm engenders aliveness.

Rhetorical skills in after-dinner speaking include vivid, pointed wordings, heightening a sense of conflict and drama in stories, maintaining interest, and devising a suitable framework for holding the separate ideas together. One speaker, developing his address as an imaginary trip through heaven, described what he found his present colleagues doing as he came upon them one by one. Another speaker linked humorous remarks to a developing picture of how the adult world looks to the child. Such unusual devices, although helpful, are not necessary for a good speech, but some pattern is essential to a sense of progress and development.

Closing the after-dinner speech requires forethought. Some speakers turn from humor to serious thoughts or sentiments, sincerely felt and briefly presented. Others try to end with a punch line. If nothing else comes to mind, one can prepare the audience for silence by predicting its arrival: "In closing, let me tell you how much a radio program once meant to me when I was on a lonely road near Banff."

CONCLUSION

Speeches for special occasions make excellent assignments for developing communication skills through practice. Outside the classroom, occasions arise that call for introductions, welcomes, presentations, dedications, acceptances, tributes, farewells, and after-dinner talks. Within the classroom the professor or a student group can devise situations that provide interesting opportunities for practice sessions.

INDEX

Abstraction, levels of, 260–262
Acceptance, speech of, 326
Acronyms, 283–284
Adaptation to listeners
   examples, 9, 156, 201, 298
   as factor in selecting material, 76–80, 215, 263
   methods of, 73, 78–80, 153–156, 236
   nature of, 5
   value of, 134–135, 206
A fortiori, 56–57
After-dinner speech, 327–329
Agenda
   for a conference, 188–190
   hidden, 113, 191
Alliteration, 281
Allusions, 224, 232–233
Amplification, 74, 75–76
Analogies
   extended, 210, 213
   figurative, 70
   as means of creativity, 61
Antithesis, 279
Apostrophe, 278
Applications as means of creativity, 60
Apprehension, 9, 218, 240, 243–244, 297
Aristotle, 3, 5, 17, 24, 56, 57, 132, 145, 215, 298

Arrangement, 7–8. *See also* Agenda; Organization, Outlines; Plans
Attention, 80–87
   conclusions about, 87
   importance of, 80, 202
   involvement related to, 115–116
   marginal fields, 295
   myths about, 80–82
   nature of, 80–82, 163
   in speech introduction, 216
   visual aids as factors in, 307
Attitudes, 127–128, 130–131, 134
   relation to behavior, 202
Attractiveness, *see* Credibility
Audience. *See also* Adaptation to listeners
   analysis of, 5, 134
   target, 201–202
Authoritarianism, 122
Authoritativeness of material, 74–75

Barnlund, Dean, 97
Beliefs, 127–129
   persuasion through, 132–134
Berne, Eric, 149–151
Bibliographic Index, 38
Birdwhistell, Ray, 299

331

Blessitt, Arthur, 157
Bozka, Larry, 318–321
Brainstorming, 49–50
Bryant, Donald C., 286
Bunker, Archie, 279
Burke, Kenneth, 156–157
Business Periodicals Index, 38

Campbell, George, 278
Campus and community, problems of, 25–27
Card catalog, 38
Carmichael, Stokely, 9, 108, 270
Causation
 in speech preparation, 53–54, 58
 tests of, 53
 types of, 51–53
Charts, organizational, 304
Choices, rhetorical, 14, 197–203, 243, 293–294
 for exposition, 199–200
 for multimedia presentations, 307–308
 for persuasion, 206–210
 in sample speeches, 318, 322
Churchill, Winston, 13, 269, 282, 283
Cicero, 3, 23, 246, 255, 293–294
Circularity, 107, 108. See also Feedback
Clarity
 avoidance of, 265
 in delivery, 248
 in language, 75, 259–265
Climax order, 125–126
Closed-mindedness, 49, 113, 122, 268
Commitment, 102, 119, 130–131
 external, 131, 135
Common ground, 145–146, 217–218, 221
Communication
 ethics, 10
 importance, 34
 model, 92–93
 principles, 2–10
 purposes, 2
 transactional nature, 93
Communicativeness, 245–246
Comparisons, 70
Conclusion, the, 190–191, 225–233
 purposes, 225–228
 in sample speech, 318
 types, 229–233
 value, 225
Concreteness, 282–283
Conference, problem-solving, 187–192
 conclusion, 190–191
 criteria for solutions, 189–190
 leadership, 189–191
 motivations during, 191
 organization and content, 188–191
 practice sessions, 191–192
 value of, 187–188

Consistency theory, 126–127, 129
Contemporary Authors, 40
Content. See also Materials
 in conversation, 144–145
 importance, 2–3, 23–24, 64–65, 93
 of note card, 25
Context
 affective, 97
 cognitive, 96–97
Conversation, 141–148
 common qualities and interests, 145–146
 content for, 144–145
 good humor and friendliness, 147
 guidelines for, 152
 other-orientation, 143–144, 146–147
 praise and rewards, 145
 "returning the ball," 143, 145
 self-disclosure, 147–148
 wholeheartedness, 144
Correlations as means of creativity, 60–61
Countersuggestion, 295–296
Creativity, *see* Inventiveness
Credibility
 attractiveness, 100
 effects of, 118, 125, 202
 enhancement of, 6–7, 73, 269–270, 317, 318
 examples, 216–217
 factors affecting, 8, 157–159, 268, 274
 importance, 99–100, 225–226, 240
 similarities, 7, 100, 159–160
Criteria for solutions, 189–190, 207
Criticism, response to, 234
Cues
 circular, 103
 covert messages, 96
 external, 95–98
 internal, 98–101
 marginal, 253–254
 nonverbal, 176–180. See also Medium, nonverbal
 overt messages, 95
 private affective, 99
 private cognitive, 98–99
 third-party, 102
Current Biography, 40

Dating, 263
Debs, Eugene V., 284
Decoding, 94–103
 circular cues, 103
 defined, 94
 external cues, 95–98
 internal cues, 98–101
 third-party cues, 102
Dedication, speech of, 325–326

Defensiveness, 151–152. *See also* Supportiveness
Delivery, 239–255. *See also* Apprehension
　clarity and projection, 248
　communicativeness, 245–246
　conversational and dynamic styles, 243
　facial expression, 253–254
　first impressions, 250–251
　fluency and rate, 246–247
　gesture, 252–253
　importance of, 242, 255
　methods of, 241–243
　oral elements, 244–245
　position and posture, 251
　in small groups, 254–255
　suggestions for improvement, 248–250, 254
　variety and aliveness, 247–248
　visual elements, 250–254
Demonstrations as visual aids, 300–301
Demosthenes, 255
DeQuincey, Thomas, 276
Description, dramatic, 223
Deutsch, Morton, 114
Devil-terms, 265–266
Dialogue, invented, 71
Dictionary of American Biography, 40
Dictionary of National Biography, 40
Dilemma, 57
Direct address, 285
Directory of American Scholars, 40
Discrepancy, tolerable degree of, 117–118, 202
Discussion, 179–187. *See also* Conference
　argument in, 184–185
　leadership, 180–183
　organization of a, 179–180
　participation in, 183–187
　research for, 183–184
　selection of participants, 179–180
　"Twelve Cardinal Sinners," 185–186
Dissonance, 126–127
Documents, 31–32, 38–39
Dogmatism, 122

Education Index, 38
Ego-involvement, *see* Involvement
Ego states, 150–151
Eisenhower, Dwight, 24, 130
Empathy, 239–240
Emphasis through position, 285
Encyclopedias, 39–40
Enthymeme, 5, 132–134
Epigrams, 284
Ethics of communication, 15–18
Ethos, *see* Credibility

Europa Year Book, 40
Examples, 66–67
　as the conclusion, 232
　contrary, 66
　extended, 213–214
　as the introduction, 223
　as proof, 66
　sources of, 66
Explicitness, 227
Exposition, 199–200
　practice session in, 233–234
　rhetorical plans for, 211–214
　topics for, 233
Extempore speaking, 14, 241–242

Facts, 58
Facts on File, 40
Farewell, speech of, 275, 327
Fear appeals, 125–126
Feedback, 103–108, 161–162
　adaptation to, 15, 154–156
　defined, 103
　effects of, 154–156
　importance of, 106, 108, 155–156
　in interpersonal and small-group situations, 106–108
　in platform address, 108
Fischer, Ardsley, 313–317
Fluency, 246–247
Ford, Gerald, 24, 170, 270
Franklin, Benjamin, 192

General Electric, 176
Germaneness, 75
Gesture, 252–253
Gibb, Jack R., 89
God-terms, 265–266
Good will speech, 36–37
Graphs, 305–307

Harding, Warren G., 278, 281–282
Hitler, Adolph, 245
Hollingworth, H. L., 86, 296
Humanities Index, 38
Humor
　as adaptation to listeners, 298
　in after-dinner speech, 327–329
　means of holding interest, 84–85
　as speech introduction, 222
Hyperbole, 279

Identification, 156–157, 274–275
Impressions, first, 140–141, 250–251
Indexes, periodical, 38
Indexing, 263
Induction, 57

Information Please Almanac, 40
Inquisitiveness, 50–51
Intensity in language, 267–268
Interactant, role of, 140–152. *See also* Conversation; Rapport; Supportiveness; Touch; Transaction
Interaction, defined, 5. *See also* Transaction
Interestingness, qualities that enhance, 82–87. *See also* Attention
Interviews, 172–178
　check list, 172–173
　information-seeking, 172–173
　job, 173–178
　planning for, 172–176
Introduction, speech of, 323–325
Introduction to a speech, 214–225
　need for, 224
　purposes, 214–218
　in sample speeches, 318, 322
　types, 218–224
Inventiveness, 4, 45–62
　bases of, 48–51
　brainstorming, 49–50
　the full mind, 48–49
　importance, 45–46
　inquisitiveness, 50–51
　levels of, 46–48
　open-mindedness, 49–50
　opportunities for, 51–56
　topoi, 56–62
Investigation as source of material, 37–38
Involvement, 115–119
　estimation of, 118–119
　relation to attention, 115–116
　relation to persuasibility, 116–117
Irony, 279
Isocrates, 2, 159

James, William, 86–87
Johnson, Lyndon, 130, 269–270, 282

Kennedy, John F., 13, 85, 99, 130, 134, 188, 207, 243, 269, 279
Kinesics, 291, 299
King, Martin Luther, Jr., 4, 209, 280–281
Kissinger, Henry, 169, 273

Langer, Susanne K., 56, 223
Language, verbal, 8–9, 258–286. *See also* Style
　clarity, 259–265
　emotional power, 265–269
　figurative, 276–279
　influence on credibility, 269–270
　intensity, 267–268

　levels of, 270–276
　"loaded," 269
　opinionation, 268–269
　oral style, 9
　redundancy, 264
　in sample speeches, 318, 322
　special devices, 279–285
Latitude of approval, 117
Leadership
　check list, 181
　of a conference, 189–191
　of a discussion, 180–183
Library, use of, 38–40
Lincoln, Abraham, 85, 134, 157, 264, 269, 275
Listeners, 161–165. *See also* Adaptation to listeners
　analysis and adaptation, 5, 76–80
　source of feedback, 161–162
Listening
　critical and responsible, 164–165
　effects of rewards, 162–163
　emotional control, 163
　in a group, 164
　importance, 161
　increased comprehension in an audience, 162–164
　note taking during, 163
　objectivity in, 93–94
　restoring attention, 163
　set, 162
　using signposts, 163
Lowe, M. David, 177–178

Maps, 303–304
Maslow, Abraham H., 123–124
Materials, 4–5, 64–88. *See also* Content; Research
　for business speaking, 34–35
　desirable qualities, 74–76
　documents, 31–32
　examples, 66–67
　general and specific, 40–41
　importance, 64–65
　kinds, 65–71, 302–307
　library, 38–40
　for multimedia presentations, 302–307
　personal investigations, 37–38
　purposes, 72–74
　quotations, 69–70
　radio and television programs, 37
　in sample speeches, 317, 322
　selection and uses, 71–87, 307–308
　in small-group communication, 171, 184
　sources, 34, 37–40
　for speeches of introduction and welcome, 324–325
　for speeches of presentation, 325–326

334　INDEX

statistics, 67–69
substantive and strategic, 198
visual aids, 302–307
Medium, nonverbal, 9–10, 250–254, 290–310. *See also* Suggestion; Visual Aids
   guidelines and choices, 10, 293–294
   importance, 9, 264
   improvements in using, 296–299
   kinesics, 291
   paralinguistics, 291–292
   proxemics, 292–293
Melody, recurrent, 247
Metaphor, 277–278
Metonymy, 278–279
Models as visual aids, 303
Monthly Catalog of United States Government Publications, 38
Moody, Dwight L., 246
Motivation, 122–127
   comparison of conferees and discussants, 113
   in conferences, 113
   desire for consistency, 126–127
   fear, 125–126
   hierarchical theory, 122–124
   program for using, 124–125
Multimedia presentations, 299–309. *See also* Materials; Visual Aids
   chalkboard illustrations, 300
   choice of materials, 307–308
   demonstrations, 300–301
   materials for, 302–307
   newsprint, 300
   posters or placards, 300
   projectors, 301–302

Narratio, 215
Narration, 221–222
Needs, *see* Motivation
News Dictionary, 40
Newspapers as sources, 39
New York Times Index, 39
Nixon, Richard, 99, 130, 201, 231, 270
Noise, 96
Norms, 102
Note taking
   content of note cards, 42
   effects on listening, 163
   example, 42
   techniques, 41–42

Objectives, *see* Purposes
O'Hair, Madalyn Murray, 298
One-source address, 47
Open-mindedness, 49–50, 268
Opinionation, 268–269
Opinions, 127–128, 130–131

Organization. *See also* Agenda; Arrangement; Outlines; Plans
   anticlimax or climax, 209–210
   one- or two-sidedness, 209–210
   in problem-solving conferences, 188–190
   value of, 8
Originality, *see* Inventiveness
Outlines
   example, 204–205
   preliminary, 12–13
   preparation of, 203–205
   relation to rhetorical plans, 203
   rules for, 205
Overphrasing, 247

Pamphlets, indexes to, 38
Pankhurst, Emmeline, 6
Paralinguistics, 291–292
Parallelism, 279–280
Participation in a group, 183–187, 189–192
   frequency of contributions, 186–187
   preparation, 183–184
   "Twelve Cardinal Sinners," 185–186
Partition, 219
Periodic sentence, 280
Personification, 278
Persuasion. *See also* Adaptation to Listeners; Attention; Credibility; Motivation; Rapport; Suggestion
   practice session in, 235–236
   rhetorical plans for, 200–203, 206–210
Place arrangement plan, 211
Plagiarism, 46–47
Plans, rhetorical
   considerations for choosing, 199–203
   defined, 203
   relation to outlines, 203
   types for exposition, 211–214
   types for persuasion, 206–210
Plato, 15, 214, 236–237
Polarization, 157
Position and posture, 251
Posters, 300
Posz, A. Conrad, 50
Preparation
   for a discussion, 170–171, 179–181, 183–184
   for an expository presentation, 233–234
   for an interview, 170–177
   methods of, 14, 241
   for a persuasive presentation, 235–236
   steps in, 10–14, 233–234, 236
Presentation. *See also* Delivery
   attitude during, 14–15
   type of business speech, 36
   type of occasional speech, 325–326

Problem-solution plan, 203, 206–207
Projectors, types of, 301–302
Proxemics, 292–293
Public Affairs Information Service, 38–39
Purpose as a factor in communication
 choice of, 235–236
 Cicero's analysis of, 3
 examples, 3–4, 12, 170–171, 234, 236
 general and specific, 170–171, 234
 importance, 3
 personal, 12, 112, 191

Qualifiers, 263
Quintilian, 17
Quotations
 introduction of, 70
 tests, 69
 type of conclusion, 232–233
 type of introduction, 224

Rapport, 73, 145–146, 148, 217–218, 269–270
Readers' Guide to Periodical Literature, 38
Receivers, *see* listeners
Redundancy, 264
Reference, frame of, 98–99
Referent, 260
Rehearsal for a speech, 14
Repetition of a pattern, 280–281
Research. *See also* Library, use of; Topics
 areas for, 24–37
 for a discussion, 183–184
 location of materials, 37–42
 note taking, 24–25
Residue plan, 57, 203, 208–209
Résumé, 176–177
Reversal of apparent position, 209–210
Rhetoric, defined, 7
Rhyme and rhythm, 282
Rogers, Will, 147–148, 269, 273
Rokeach, Milton, 49
Role
 of interactant, 140–152
 of listener, 161–165
 pressure for fulfillment, 102, 119
 of speaker, 153–160
Roosevelt, Franklin D., 13, 85, 242, 246, 269, 273

Salience, 119, 128
"Scissors-and-paste" speech, 47
Selected United States Government Publications, 38
Self-disclosure, 147–148

Self-esteem, 101, 113, 120–122, 125
Self-image, 119, 161
Self-references, 75
Semanticists, general, 263
Set, 162
Sherif, Carolyn W., 116, 117, 202
Sherif, Muzafer, 116, 117, 202
Signposts, 163, 283
Similarities as source of credibility, 7, 100–101, 159–160
Simile, 277
Simple-to-complex plan, 212–213
"Sinners, Twelve Cardinal," 185–186
Small-group situations, 169–192. *See also* Conference, problem-solving; Discussion
 delivery in, 254–255
 feedback in, 106–108
Social Sciences Index, 38
Speaker, role of, 153–160
Specificity, 282–283
Stage fright, *see* Apprehension
Statesman's Year-Book, 40
Statistical Abstract of the United States, 39, 67
Statistics, 67–69
 presentation, 68–69, 75
 sources, 39, 67
 tests, 67–68
Status, 119–120, 274
Step-by-step progression, 212
Stereotypes, 127–128, 131–132
Stevenson, Adlai, 207, 269
Stimuli, *see* Cues
Style
 colloquial and familiar, 272–273
 drab and vulgar, 273–275
 elegant and expressive, 275
 figurative language, 276–279
 oral, 9
 ornate and affected, 275–276
 pretentious, pedantic, and jargon-ridden, 271–272
 scholarly, technical, and dignified, 270–271
 special devices and sentence types, 279–285
Suggestion, 177–178, 253–254
 defined, 263
 "Laws of," 296
 role of nonverbal cues, 82, 294–296
Supportiveness, 151–152, 162, 164
Synechdoche, 279

Topics
 in business and the professions, 33–37
 campus and community problems, 25–27

economic problems, 30–32
international relations, 32–33
limitations on, 29–30, 33
selection of, 10–11, 23, 233, 235–236
social issues, 27–30
Topoi
ancient, 56–59
modern, 59–62
Touch, 148–149
Traits, personality, 113–122
authoritarianism, dogmatism, and closed-mindedness, 122
involvement, 115–119
role, status, and self-esteem, 119–122
trust, 113–115
Transaction, 5–7, 19, 149–151
complementary or crossed, 149–151
defined, 5
elements in, 13
importance, 5
levels, 149–151
Transitions, 8, 283
Tribute, speech of, 275, 327
Truman, Harry, 6, 130, 220, 241, 243, 269
Trust, 101, 113–115

Ulrich's International Periodicals Directory, 38
Underphrasing, 247

Understatement, 278
United Nations Documents Index, 39

Values, 127–128, 129–130
persuasion through, 132–134
Variety
in delivery, 247–248
example of, 317
value of, 76
Vertical File Index, 38
Visual aids, 9–10, 299–309
choices among, 307–308
disadvantages, 10, 308
hints for using, 308–309
means of transmission, 300–302
types of, 302–307

Wallace, George, 266
Weaver, Richard, 265
Webster's Biographical Dictionary, 40
Welcome, speech of, 323–325
Wesley, John, 241
Whately, Richard, 13
Whitaker's Almanack, 39, 67
Who's Who, 40
Who's Who in America, 40
Wiener, Norbert, 103
Wilson, Woodrow, 24
World Almanac, 39, 67

P
95
.T5

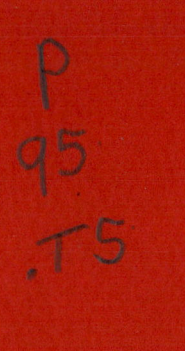

P
95
.T5